An Interdisciplinary Approach
to American History

VOLUME I

An Interdisciplinary

VOLUME I

PRENTICE-HALL, INC., ENGLEWOOD CLIFFS, N.J.

Approach
to American History

Edited by

ARI HOOGENBOOM
Brooklyn College

OLIVE HOOGENBOOM

Library of Congress Cataloging in Publication Data

HOOGENBOOM, ARI ARTHUR,   comp.
   An interdisciplinary approach to American history.

   Includes bibliographical references.
   1. United States—History—Addresses, essays,
lectures. I. Hoogenboom, Olive, joint comp. II. Title.
E178.1.H77   973   72-11764
ISBN   0-13-469213-6

AN INTERDISCIPLINARY APPROACH TO AMERICAN HISTORY, *Volume I*
by Ari Hoogenboom and Olive Hoogenboom

© 1973 by Prentice-Hall, Inc., Englewood Cliffs, New Jersey

Printed in the United States of America

10 9 8 7 6 5 4 3 2 1

PRENTICE-HALL INTERNATIONAL, INC., *London*
PRENTICE-HALL OF AUSTRALIA, PTY. LTD., *Sydney*
PRENTICE-HALL OF CANADA, LTD., *Toronto*
PRENTICE-HALL OF INDIA PRIVATE LIMITED, *New Delhi*
PRENTICE-HALL OF JAPAN, INC., *Tokyo*

For Albert W. Werline,
an outstanding teacher and friend

Contents

Preface, *xi*

1 *Sexual Roles, Child Behavior, and the Importance of Dreams in Iroquois Culture*

ANTHONY F. C. WALLACE

The Heyday of the Iroquois, *1*

2 *Modification of the "Historical" Colonial Family*

PHILIP J. GREVEN, JR.

Family Structure in Seventeenth-Century Andover, Massachusetts, *19*

3 *Cultural Patterns and Salem Witchcraft*

JOHN DEMOS

Underlying Themes in the Witchcraft of Seventeenth-Century New England, *37*

4   National Character and Farming Practices

James T. Lemon

The Agricultural Practices of National Groups in Eighteenth-
Century Southeastern Pennsylvania, 53

5   Origins and Success of the Great Awakening

Richard L. Bushman

Awakening, 77

6   A Study of Not-So-Democratic, Colonial Boston

James A. Henretta

Economic Development and Social Structure in Colonial Boston, 87

7   Symbols Reveal a Strong American Identity Before 1775

Richard L. Merritt

The Growth of American Community, 102

8   Unequal Representation Helped Ratify the Constitution

Charles W. Roll, Jr.

We, Some of the People: Apportionment in the Thirteen State
Conventions Ratifying the Constitution, 117

9   A Computer Tells When and Why Congressmen Drew Party Lines

Mary P. Ryan

Party Formation in the United States Congress, 1789 to 1796:
A Quantitative Analysis, 133

10 A Psychological Explanation for Jefferson's Racial Attitudes

Winthrop D. Jordan

Thomas Jefferson: Self and Society, 145

11 *Missionaries and the Fragmentation of Indian Culture*

ROBERT F. BERKHOFER, JR.

Christians Versus Pagans, *165*

12 *How Different Was the Second Party System, and Why Did it Fail?*

RICHARD P. McCORMICK

Political Development and the Second Party System, *176*

13 *Who Were the Jacksonians?*

LEE BENSON

Interpreting New York Voting, *192*

14 *The Rich Grew Richer in Jackson's Day*

EDWARD PESSEN

The Egalitarian Myth and the American Social Reality: Wealth, Mobility, and Equality in the "Era of the Common Man," *204*

15 *Early Beginnings of the Feminist Movement*

CARROLL SMITH-ROSENBERG

Beauty, the Beast and the Militant Woman: A Case Study in Sex Roles and Social Stress in Jacksonian America, *219*

16 *When Was the Critical Period in American Economic Growth?*

DOUGLASS C. NORTH

The Economy 1815 to 1860, *238*

17 *Even as Slaves, Blacks Were Articulate*

LAWRENCE W. LEVINE

Slave Songs and Slave Consciousness: An Exploration in Neglected Sources, *249*

18 Economically, Slavery Paid

ALFRED H. CONRAD AND JOHN R. MEYER

The Economics of Slavery in the Ante Bellum South, 272

19 Child-Rearing Practices and Intermale Aggression

MURRAY G. MURPHEY

An Approach to the Historical Study of National Character, 298

20 Section Versus Party

THOMAS B. ALEXANDER

Sectional Stress and Party Strength, 316

21 The Men Who Voted on Secession

RALPH A. WOOSTER

The Secession Conventions of the South, 321

22 The Lincoln Image

DAVID DONALD

The Folklore Lincoln, 332

23 Civil War Casualties Receive a Medical Examination

RICHARD H. SHRYOCK

A Medical Perspective on the Civil War, 343

24 Was Business also a Civil War Casualty?

STANLEY L. ENGERMAN

The Economic Impact of the Civil War, 355

Preface

Encompassing, as it does, all human experience, history more than any other field of scholarship depends on other disciplines. Other disciplines in turn need history (out of which many of them have developed) for a better understanding of their own specialties. In recent years awareness of this mutual dependence has become pronounced, with historians utilizing concepts and methodology originally designed for examining contemporary society and with nonhistorians testing their ideas and methods against records of the past. The results have produced profound changes in the study of American history.

American history is being written differently than it was a generation ago. There is more emphasis on analysis and less on narrative, more on concepts and less on institutions, more on statistics and less on manuscripts, more on the anonymous masses and less on the articulate elite. The drift away from political, military, and diplomatic history and toward economic, social, and cultural history has continued. Much political history has been rewritten with a heavy infusion of statistics and re-evaluated with the ideas of political scientists, sociologists, and social psychologists. By applying mathematical and theoretical models to available statistical data, econometricians have created the "new" as contrasted with the "old" qualitative economic history and have wrought a revolution in that area. Social history has particularly matured, with historians moving beyond emotional involvement with the pioneer, the laborer, and the immigrant to analyses of social mobility, social stratification, and the family. Formerly neglected groups, including blacks, Indians, women, and children, are receiving attention. Intellectual and cultural historians have broadened their interests. Influenced in particular by the American studies movement, they have found revealing insights in popular culture and music as well as in the folklore, images, symbols, and myths of the American people.

The best history is being written by those who incorporate these interdisciplinary approaches with traditional methods of research. Since much that is important cannot be counted, statistics are not a substitute for, but are to be used with, manuscripts and other conventional sources. Chronology—the sequence of events—remains the key to understanding the past, but insights from other disciplines help explain past events. The best narrative history is both interesting and analytical.

The following significant and challenging interdisciplinary readings are ideal for use in basic American history courses. The term *interdisciplinary* has been construed broadly. Selections have been chosen from or inspired by not only the social sciences—anthropology, sociology, political science, geography, economics, psychology, and psychoanalysis —but also medical science, American studies, folklore, and music.

Since this work is intended for students in college survey courses, we have eliminated most footnotes and all bibliographies. Students wishing to explore further the methodology utilized by the authors are urged to consult the original sources listed beneath each headnote. The brief headnotes do not summarize selections but suggest why they are important. The readings speak for themselves.

Our greatest debt is to the authors who have permitted us to present their work. We also wish to thank Howard Harris for help in making selections and Lynn Hoogenboom and Theodore Lauer for help in tracking down material.

A. H.
O. H.

An Interdisciplinary Approach to American History

VOLUME I

1

The Heyday of the Iroquois

ANTHONY F. C. WALLACE

Anthropologists have found American Indians the most diverse of races. In 1939 A. L. Kroeber divided North American Indians into seven major cultural areas and eighty-four subareas. In the Northeast the League of Iroquois tribes with its superior organization was dominant. These Indians, as well as the Indians encountered by settlers on the Atlantic seaboard, belonged to the Eastern Woodlands or Ultra-Mississippi Cultural Area.

Anthony F. C. Wallace, an anthropologist and a student of both Indians and religion, focuses on the destruction and demoralization of the great Iroquois nation that followed the arrival of Europeans and the ensuing cultural revival that took place around 1800 through the influence of the Seneca visionary Handsome Lake. Handsome Lake's religion, a mix of traditional Iroquois pagan beliefs and Quaker Christianity, restored the cultural health of his people.

The passages reprinted here examine the sources of Iroquois power and the roots of Iroquois behavior and discuss the culture of the Iroquois as it existed when the first European appeared.

THE IROQUOIS "MATRIARCHATE"

During the seventeenth and eighteenth centuries Iroquois men earned a reputation among the French and English colonists for being the most astute diplomatically and most dangerous militarily of all the Indians of the Northeast. Yet at the same time the Iroquois were famous for the

From Anthony F. C. Wallace, *The Death and Rebirth of the Seneca*, pp. 28–39, 44–50, 59–60, 74–75. © 1969 by Anthony F. C. Wallace. Reprinted by permission of Alfred A. Knopf, Inc.

"matriarchal" nature of their economic and social institutions. After the colonial era came to an end with the victory of the United States in the Revolutionary War, the traditional diplomatic and military role of the Iroquois men was sharply limited by the circumstances of reservation life. Simultaneously, the "matriarchal" character of certain of their economic, kinship, and political institutions was drastically diminished. These changes were codified by the prophet Handsome Lake. As we shall see later in more detail, the changes in kinship behavior that he recommended, and which to a considerable degree were carried out by his followers, amounted to a shift in dominance from the mother-daughter relationship to that of the husband-wife. Handsome Lake's reforms thus were a sentence of doom upon the traditional quasi-matriarchal system of the Iroquois.

The Iroquois were described as matriarchal because of the important role women played in the formal political organization. The men were responsible for hunting, for warfare, and for diplomacy, all of which kept them away from their households for long periods of time, and all of which were essential to the survival of Iroquois society. An expedition of any kind was apt to take months or even years, for the fifteen thousand or so Iroquois in the seventeenth and eighteenth centuries ranged over an area of about a million square miles. It is not an exaggeration to say that the full-time business of an Iroquois man was travel, in order to hunt, trade, fight, and talk in council. But the women stayed at home. Thus, an Iroquois village might be regarded as a collection of strings, hundreds of years old, of successive generations of women, always domiciled in their longhouses near their cornfields in a clearing while their sons and husbands traveled in the forest on supportive errands of hunting and trapping, of trade, of war, and of diplomacy.

The women exercised political power in three main circumstances. First, whenever one of the forty-nine chiefs of the great intertribal League of the Iroquois died, the senior women of his lineage nominated his successor. Second, when tribal or village decisions had to be made, both men and women attended a kind of town meeting, and while men were the chiefs and normally did the public speaking, the women caucused behind the scenes and lobbied with the spokesmen. Third, a woman was entitled to demand publicly that a murdered kinsman or kinswoman be replaced by a captive from a non-Iroquois tribe, and her male relatives, particularly lineage kinsmen, were morally obligated to go out in a war party to secure captives, whom the bereaved woman might either adopt or consign to torture and death. Adoption was so frequent during the bloody centuries of the beaver wars and the colonial wars that some Iroquois village were preponderantly composed of formally adopted war captives. In sum, Iroquois women were entitled formally to select chiefs, to participate in consensual politics, and to start wars.

Thus the Iroquois during the two centuries of the colonial period were a population divided, in effect, into two parts: sedentary females and nomadic males. The men were frequently absent in small or large groups for prolonged periods of time on hunting, trading, war, and diplomatic expeditions, simultaneously protecting the women from foreign attack and producing a cash crop of skins, furs, and scalps, which they exchanged for hardware and dry goods. These activities, peripheral in a geographical sense, were central to the economic and political welfare of the Six Nations. The preoccupation of Iroquois men with these tasks and the pride they took in their successful pursuit cannot be overestimated. But the system depended on a complementary role for women. They had to be economically self-sufficient through horticulture during the prolonged absences of men, and they maintained genealogical and political continuity in a matrilineal system in which the primary kin relationship (not necessarily the primary social relationship) was the one between mother and daughter.

Such a quasi-matriarchy, of course, had a certain validity in a situation where the division of labor between the sexes required that men be geographically peripheral to the households that they helped to support and did defend. Given the technological, economic, and military circumstances of the time, such an arrangement was a practical one. But it did have an incidental consequence: It made the relationship between husband and wife an extremely precarious one. Under these conditions it was convenient for the marital system to be based on virtually free sexual choice, the mutual satisfaction of spouses, and easy separation. Couples chose one another for personal reasons; free choice was limited, in effect, only by the prohibition of intraclan marriage. Marriages were apt to fray when a husband traveled too far, too frequently, for too long. On his return, drunken quarreling, spiteful gossip, parental irresponsibility, and flagrant infidelity might lead rapidly to the end of the relationship. The husband, away from the household for long periods of time, was apt in his travels to establish a liaison with a woman whose husband was also away. The wife, temporarily abandoned, might for the sake of comfort and economic convenience take up with a locally available man. Since such relationships were, in effect, in the interest of everyone in the longhouse, they readily tended to become recognized as marriages. The emotional complications introduced by these serial marriages were supposed to be resolved peacefully by the people concerned. The traveling husband who returned to find his wife living with someone else might try to recover her; if she preferred to remain with her new husband, however, he was not entitled to punish her or her new lover, but instead was encouraged to find another wife among the unmarried girls or wives with currently absent husbands.

THE IDEAL OF AUTONOMOUS RESPONSIBILITY

The basic ideal of manhood was that of "the good hunter." Such a man was self-disciplined, autonomous, responsible. He was a patient and efficient huntsman, a generous provider to his family and nation, and a loyal and thoughtful friend and clansman. He was also a stern and ruthless warrior in avenging any injury done to those under his care. And he was always stoical and indifferent to privation, pain, and even death. Special prominence could be achieved by those who, while adequate in all respects, were outstanding in one or another dimension of this ideal. The patient and thoughtful man with a skin "seven thumbs thick" (to make him indifferent to spiteful gossip, barbed wit, and social pressures generally) might become a sachem or a "distinguished name"—a "Pine Tree" chief. An eloquent man with a good memory and indestructible poise might be a council speaker and represent clan, nation, even the confederacy in far-flung diplomatic ventures. And the stern and ruthless warrior (always fighting, at least according to the theory, to avenge the death or insult of a blood relative or publicly avowed friend) might become a noted war-captain or an official war-chief. The war-captain ideal, open as it was to all youths, irrespective of clan lineage or of special intellectual qualifications, was perhaps the most emulated.

In the seventeenth century an Onondaga war-captain named Aharihon bore the reputation of being the greatest warrior of the country. He realized the ideal of autonomous responsibility to virtually pathological perfection. Let us note what is told of Aharihon in the *Jesuit Relations.*

Aharihon was a man of dignified appearance and imposing carriage, grave, polished in manner, and self-contained. His brother had been killed about 1654 in the wars with the Erie, a tribe westward of the Iroquois. As clansman and close relative, he was entitled—indeed obligated—either to avenge his brother's death by killing some Erie people or by adopting a war captive to take his place. Aharihon within a few years captured or had presented to him for adoption forty men. Each of them he burned to death over a slow fire, because, as he said, "he did not believe that there was any one worthy to occupy his [brother's] place." Father Lalemant was present when another young man, newly captured, was given to Aharihon as a substitute for the deceased brother. Aharihon let the young man believe that he was adopted and need have no further fear, and "presented to him four dogs, upon which to hold his feast of adoption. In the middle of the feast, while he was rejoicing and singing to entertain the guests, Aharihon arose, and told the company that this man too must die in atonement for his brother's death. The poor lad was astounded at this, and turned toward the door to make his escape, but was stopped by two men who had orders to burn him. On the fourteenth of February, in the evening, they began with his feet, intending to roast him, at a slow fire, as far up as the waist, during the greater part of the night. After midnight, they were to let him rally his strength and sleep a little until daybreak when they were to finish this fatal tragedy. In his torture, the poor man made the whole village resound with his cries and groans. He shed great tears, contrary to the usual custom, the victim commonly glorying to be burned limb by limb, and opening his lips only to sing; but, as this one had not expected death, he wept and cried in a way that touched even these Barbarians. One of Aharihon's relatives was so moved with pity, that he advised ending the sufferer's torments by plunging a knife into his breast—which would have been a deed of mercy, had the stab been mortal. However, they were induced to continue the burning without interruption, so that before day he ended both his sufferings and his life." Aharihon's career of death continued without interruption, and by 1663 he was able to boast that he had killed sixty men with his own hand and had burned fully eighty men over slow fire. He kept count by tattooing a mark on his thigh for each successive victim. He was known then as the Captain General of the Iroquois and was nicknamed Nero by the Frenchmen at Montreal because of his cruelty.

The French finally captured him near Montreal, but even in captivity his manner was impressive. "This man," commented Father Lalemant, "commonly has nine slaves with him, five boys and four girls. He is a captain of dignified appearance and imposing carriage, and of such equanimity and presence of mind that, upon seeing himself surrounded by armed men, he showed no more surprise than if he had been alone; and when asked whether he would like to accompany us to Quebec, he designed only to answer coldly that that was not a question to ask him, since he was in our power. Accordingly he was made to come aboard our Vessel, where I took pleasure in studying his disposition as well as that of an Algonquin in our company, who bore the scalp of an Iroquois but recently slain by him in war. These two men, although hostile enough to eat each other, chatted and laughed on board that Vessel with great familiarity, it being very hard to decide which of the two was more skillful in masking his feelings. I had Nero placed near me at table, where he bore himself with a gravity, a self-control, and a propriety, which showed nothing of his Barbarian origin; but during the rest of the time he was constantly eating, so that he fasted only when he was at table."

But this voracious captain was not renowned among the Onondaga as a killer only. He was, on the contrary, also a trusted ambassador, dispatched on occasion to Montreal on missions of peace. He was, in a word, a noted man. He was a killer, but he was not an indiscriminate killer; he killed only those whom it was his right to kill, tortured only those whom he had the privilege of torturing, always as an expression of respect for his dead brother. And although his kinfolk sometimes felt he was a little extreme in his stern devotion to his brother's memory, they did not feel that he was any the less a fine man, or that they had a right to interfere with his impulses; they were willing to entrust the business of peace, as well as war, to his hand. . . .

With this sort of man serving as an ego-ideal, held up by sanction and by praise to youthful eyes, it is not remarkable that young men were ambitious to begin the practice of war. All had seen captives tortured to death; all had known relatives lost in war whose death demanded revenge or replacement. The young men went out on practice missions as soon as they were big enough to handle firearms; "infantile bands, armed with hatchets and guns which they can hardly carry, do not fail to spread fear and horror everywhere." Even as late as the middle of the eighteenth century, Handsome Lake and his brothers and nephews were still busy at the old business of war for the sake of war. Cornplanter became a noted war-captain; Blacksnake, his nephew, was one of the official war-chiefs of the Seneca nation; and Handsome Lake himself took part in the scalping-party pattern as a young man. But Handsome Lake became a sachem and later a prophet, and he never gloried in the numbers of men he killed as his brother Cornplanter (somewhat guiltily) did. "While I was in the use of arms I killed seven persons and took three and saved their lives," said Cornplanter. And Blacksnake, in later life, told with relish of his exploits as a warrior. "We had a good fight there," he would say. "I have killed how many I could not tell, for I pay no attention to or kept [no] account of it, it was great many, for I never have it at all my Battles to think about kepting account what I'd killed at one time. . . ."

The cultivation of the ideal of autonmous responsibility—and the suppression of its antinomy, dependency—began early in life. Iroquois children were carefully trained to think for themselves but to act for others. Parents were protective, permissive, and sparing of punishment; they encouraged children to play at imitating adult behavior but did not criticize or condemn fumbling early efforts; they maintained a cool detachment, both physically and verbally, avoiding the intense confrontations of love and anger between parent and child to which Europeans were accustomed. Children did not so much live in a child's world as grow up freely in the interstices of an adult culture. The gain was an early self-reliance and enjoyment of responsibility; the cost, perhaps, was a lifelong difficulty in handling feelings of dependency.

The Seneca mother gave birth to her child in the privacy of the woods, where she retired for a few hours when her time came, either alone or in the company of an older woman who served as midwife and, if the weather was cold, built and tended a fire. She had prepared for this event by eating sparingly and exercising freely, which were believed (probably with good reason) to make the child stronger and the birth easier. The newborn infant was washed in cold water, or even in snow, immediately after parturition and then wrapped in skins or a blanket. If the birth were a normal one, the mother walked back to the village with her infant a few hours afterwards to take up the duties of housewife. The event was treated as the consummation of a healthful process rather than as an illness. The infant spent much of its first nine months swaddled from chin to toe and lashed to a craddleboard. The child's feet rested against a footboard; a block of wood was placed between the heels of a girl to mold her feet to an inward turn. Over its head stretched a hoop, which could be draped with a thin cloth to keep away flies or to protect the child from the cold. The board and its wrappings were often lavishly decorated with silver trinkets and beadwork embroidery. The mother was able to carry the child in the board, suspended against her back, by a tumpline around her forehead; the board could be hung from the limb of a tree while she hoed corn; and it could be converted into a crib by suspending it on a rack of poles laid horizontally on forks stuck in the ground. The mother was solicitous of the child's comfort, nursed it whenever it cried, and loosened it from the board several times a day to change the moss that served as a diaper and to give it a chance to romp. The children, however, tended to cry when released from the board, and their tranquility could often be restored only by putting them back. Babies were seldom heard crying.

The mother's feeling for her children was intense; indeed, to one early observer it appeared that "Parental Tenderness" was carried to a "dangerous Indulgence." Another early writer remarked, "The mothers love their children with an extreme passion, and although they do not reveal this in caresses, it is nevertheless real." Mothers were quick to express resentment of any restraint or injury or insult offered to the child by an outsider. During the first few years the child stayed almost constantly with the mother, in the house, in the fields, or on the trail, playing and performing small tasks under her direction. The mother's chief concern during this time was to provide for the child and to protect it, to "harden" it by baths in cold wather, but not to punish. Weaning was not normally attempted until the age of three or four, and such control as the child obtained over its excretory functions was achieved voluntarily, not as a result of consistent punishment for mistakes. Early sexual curiosity and experimentation were regarded as a natural childish way of behaving, out of which it would, in due time, grow. Grandparents might complain that small children got into everything, but the small child was free to romp, to pry into things, to demand what it wanted, and to assault its parents, without more hazard of punishment than the exasperated mother's occasionally blowing water in its face or dunking it in a convenient river.

The years between about eight or nine and the onset of puberty were a time of easy and gradual learning. At the beginning of this period the beginnings of the differentiation of the roles of boys and girls were laid down. The girls were kept around the house, under the guidance of their mothers, and assigned to the lighter household duties and to helping in the fields. Boys were allowed to roam in gangs, playing at war, hunting with bows and arrows and toy hatchets, and competing at races, wrestling, and lacrosse. The first successes at hunting were greeted with praise and boast of future greatness. Sometimes these roaming gangs spent days at a time away from the village, sleeping in the bush, eating wild roots and fruits, and hunting such small game as could be brought down by bow and arrow, blowgun, or snare. These gangs developed into war parties after the boys reached puberty. Among themselves, both in gangs and among siblings of the same family, the children's playgroups were not constantly supervised by parents and teachers, and the children governed themselves in good harmony. Said one close observer, "Children of the same family show strong attachments to each other, and are less liable to quarrel in their youthful days than is generally the case with white children."

The parents usually tried to maintain a calm moderation of behavior in dealing with their children, a lofty indifference alike to childish tantrums and seductive appeals for love. Hardihood, self-reliance, and independence of spirit were sedulously inculcated. When occasion presented itself, fathers, uncles, or other elder kinfolk instructed their sons in the techniques of travel, firemaking, the chase, war, and other essential arts of manhood, and the mothers correspondingly taught their daughters the way to hoe and plant the cornfields, how to butcher the meat, cook, braid corn, and other household tasks. But this instruction was presented, rather than enforced, as an opportunity rather than as a duty. On occasion the parent or other responsible adult talked to the child at length, "endeavoring," as a Quaker scribe gently put it, "to impress on its mind what it ought to do, and what to leave undone." If exhortation seemed inadequate in its effect, the mentor might ridicule the child for doing wrong, or gravely point out the folly of a certain course of action, or even warn him that he courted the rage of offended supernatural beings. Obedience as such was no virtue, however, and blows, whippings, or restraints of any kind, such as restriction to quarters, were rarely imposed, the faults of the child being left to his own reason and conscience to correct as he grew mature. With delicate perception the adults noted that childish faults "cannot be very great, before reason arrives at some degree of maturity."

Direct confrontation with the child was avoided, but when things got seriously out of hand, parents sometimes turned older children over to the gods for punishment. A troublesome child might be sent out into the dusk to meet Longnose, the legendary Seneca bogeyman. Longnose might even be impersonated in the flesh by a distraught parent. Longnose was a hungry cannibal who chased bad children when their parents were sleeping. He mimicked the child, crying loudly as he ran, but the parents would not wake up because Longnose had bewitched them. A child might be chased all night until he submitted and promised to behave. Theoretically, if a child remained stubborn, Longnose finally caught him and took him away in a huge pack-basket for a leisurely meal. And—although parents were not supposed to do this—an unusually stubborn infant *could* be threatened with punishment by the great False Faces themselves, who, when invoked for this purpose, might "poison" a child or "spoil his face." "I remember," recalled a Cayuga woman of her childhood, "how scared I was of the False-faces; I didn't know what they were. They are to scare away disease. They used to come into the house and up the stairs and I used to hide away under the covers. They even crawled under the bed and they made that awful sound. When I was bad my mother used to say the False-faces would get me. Once, I must have been only 4 or 5, because I was very little when I left Canada, but I remember it so well that when I think of it I can hear that cry now, and I was going along a road from my grandfather's; it was a straight road and I couldn't lose my way, but it was almost dark, and I had to pass through some timber and I heard that cry and that rattle. I ran like a flash of lightening and I can hear it yet."

At puberty some of the boys retired to the woods under the stewardship of an old man, where they fasted, abstained from any sort of sexual activity (which they had been free to indulge, to the limit of their powers, before), covered themselves with dirt, and mortified the flesh in various ways, such as bathing in ice water and bruising and gashing the shinbones with rocks. Dreams experienced during such periods of self-trial were apt to be regarded as visitations from supernatural spirits who might grant *orenda,* or magical power, to the dreamer, and who would maintain a special sort of guardianship over him. The person's connection with this supernatural being was maintained through a charm —such as a knife, a queerly shaped stone, or a bit of bone—which was connected with the dream through some association significant to the dreamer. Unlike many other tribes, however, the Iroquois apparently did not require these guardian-spirit visions for pubescent youths. Many youths were said not to have had their first vision until just before their first war party. Furthermore, any man could have a significant dream or vision at any time. Girls too went through a mild puberty ritual, retiring into the woods at first menstruation and paying particular attention to their dreams. With the termination of the menstrual period the girl returned to the household; but hereafter, whenever she menstruated, she would have to live apart in a hut, avoiding people, and being careful not to step on a path, or to cook and serve anyone's food, or (especially) to touch medicines, which would immediately lose their potency if she handled them.

The Europeans who observed this pattern of child experience were by no means unfavorably impressed although they were sometimes amazed. They commented, however, almost to a man, from early Jesuit to latter-day Quaker, on a consequence that stood out dramatically as they compared this "savage" maturation with "civilized." "There is nothing," wrote the Jesuit chronicler of the Iroquois mission in 1657, "for which these peoples have a greater horror than restraint. The very children cannot endure it, and live as they please in the houses of their parents, without fear of reprimand or chastisement." One hundred and fifty years later, the Quaker Halliday Jackson observed that "being indulged in most of their wishes, as they grow up, liberty, in its fullest extent, becomes their ruling passion." The Iroquois themselves recognized the intensity of their children's resentment at parental interference. "Some Savages," reported Le Mercier of the Huron, "told us that one of the principal reasons why they showed so much indulgence toward their children, was that when the children saw themselves treated by their parents with some severity, they usually resorted to extreme measures and hanged themselves, or ate of a certain root they call *Audachienrra*, which is a very quick poison." The same fear was recorded among the Iroquois, including the Seneca, in 1657. And while suicides by frustrated children were not actually frequent, there are nevertheless a number of recorded cases of suicide where parental interference was the avowed cause. And *mutatis mutandis*, there was another rationalization for a policy of permissiveness: that the child who was harshly disciplined might grow up, some day, to mistreat his parents in revenge.

This theory of child raising was not taken for granted by the Seneca; on the contrary, it was very explicitly recognized, discussed, and pondered. Handsome Lake himself, in later years, insisted that parents love and indulge their children.

. . .

IROQUOIS WARFARE:
THE STRATEGY OF THREAT AND RETALIATION

Whatever its philosophical rationalization and economic consequences might be, the actual mechanism of Iroquois warfare was the traditional process of blood feud. A family, one of whose members had been killed by an alien (i.e., a person who was not one of the five or, after about 1722, Six Nations or their allies), was morally obligated to avenge the death by killing, or capturing and adopting, one or more members of the "enemy" tribe. Friends of the injured family could help in the satisfaction of the score, but the feud was fundamentally a personal matter between the injured family and the alien group. Such a feud could begin from various incidental circumstances: a chance encounter with a trespassing stranger; a drunken brawl; involvement in a military campaign initiated by a third party. Over a period of time, however, a sequence of mutually vengeful killings could occur, involving an increasing number of members of the two groups, until finally there were so many unsettled scores left on both sides that a state of chronic "war" could be said to exist, justifying an endless exchange of forays, some of them involving large numbers of vengeance-seeking warriors on both sides. Inasmuch as these forays were technically intended by the participants not to acquire territory nor to establish political sovereignty but to even the score in a feud, good tactics required minimal loss of life by the avenging party. A victory with heavy casualties was, in effect, a defeat, since the score then remained uneven.

This mechanism was partially controlled by political policy, particularly as expressed and maintained by the Great League. The League itself had been explicitly designed to prevent the proliferation of blood feuds within and among the various member nations; this purpose was clearly stated both in the Dekanawidah myth, which described the origin of the League, and in the rituals of condolence that were held whenever one of the forty-nine members of the council died. Indirectly, no doubt, the League's ethical position on intra-Iroquois blood feuds influenced Iroquois warfare by maintaining a climate of mutual confidence among the tribes. In this climate it was more feasible to organize large-scale military enterprises than in an atmosphere of mutual fear and suspicion. But it should not be supposed that Iroquois warfare was merely activity of the League. The League—and probably tribal and village councils also—functioned more as a restraining than as an initiating body. The League as an entity and its several chiefs could urge upon the warriors the wisdom of holding back their striking arms; and their influence was such that raids could be postponed or put off indefinitely while diplomats negotiated issues for the common good. Conversely, the League organization could deliberately sit silent while the war captains prepared their campaigns. Furthermore, the council organization served as an information center, receiving, discussing, filtering, and disseminating news and opinion that could influence the military passions of the warriors and the women. Thus, while the League was in itself not a warmaking body, it could aim and time the unleashing of the war potential that, because of the wide ramification of the kinship-revenge motif, was always straining to burst into active hostilities. This process of control by restraining, directing, and timing the ever-ready mechanism of revenge operated most conspicuously in relations between the Iroquois and white groups, because the records of negotiations and of fighting are here more satisfactory; but the same process governed the relations of the Iroquois to other Indian tribes.

The major functions of Iroquois warfare—its consequences, both intended and unintended, for the Iroquois way of life and their situation in the world—were, in the early part of the century, three-fold: to maintain an emotional equilibrium in individuals who were strongly motivated to avenge, or replace, murdered kinfolk, and thereby to maintain the social equilibrium of kinship units; to extend, or at least maintain, Iroquois political influence over other tribal groups, and thus to provide access by trade or hunting to land rich in peltries; and to perpetuate a political situation in which the threat of retaliation against either party could be used to play off the British and the French against one another. Territorial immunity, military support, trade advantages, and outright gifts of food, dry goods, and hardware could be extorted from both sides under the asserted or implied threat that the Iroquois and their allies would abandon their neutral role and would join the generous party in an attack on the stingy one if their wants were not satisfied.

The equilibrium-maintaining function of Iroquois warfare requires some amplification. Certainly the Iroquois were not unique among Indian tribes, or even primitive peoples generally, in the importance of kinship in establishing the individual's social rights and obligations and in defining his image in his own eyes and the eyes of others. Such discipline and security as the individual enjoyed tended to be provided by his family (and by "family" we mean not merely the immediate household but the various and widely ramifying connections of the kinship system). In such a setting an injury to an Iroquois Indian's relatives became doubly significant, not only because it disturbed the integrity of the group with which he was identified, but also because the affected individuals could not depend upon obtaining redress through police and courts. It was thus a matter of honor for kinfolk to protect one another and, if necessary, to avenge injuries. In the case of a killing, the most immediately affected parties might well be women—mother, sisters, and wife of the lost person—who could demand either the torture and death of the offender or the adoption of a captive to take the departed person's place. (In a fundamental sense, even the dead offender was adopted, since the scalp torn from the slain foe was often ritually adopted into the bereaved family, and the bodies of captives who had been tortured to death were sometimes eaten ceremonially.) While women could hold the initiative in demanding redress and could determine the fate of captives, men were responsible for risking their lives to bring back scalps or prisoners. Joining a war party thereby became a test of manhood, conducted under the watchful eyes of bereaved women, and failure to participate in the revenge process would prejudice the reluctant youth's standing in the eyes of his own family and the community generally.

The effectiveness of the League in partially blocking the free exercise of the revenge process among the five participating tribes may therefore have been partly responsible for the implacability and ferociousness of the Iroquois in pursuing external enemies; with the intrusion of political influence into the revenge motif locally, it became even more essential for warriors to validate their moral stature in the eyes of kinsmen and community by allowing no slackness in the settling of external scores. If this interpretation is sound, then the Iroquois reputation for pertinacity and ruthlessness in fighting with their external enemies may be regarded as an indirect consequence of the blocking of the blood feud among the participating members of the League. The *pax Iroquois* resulted in the displacement of revenge motivations outward, onto surrounding peoples, Indian and European alike.

But this displacement brought new difficulties in turn, perhaps more clearly recognized by the sachems of the League than by the warriors. The intensification of external warfare—augmented in the seventeenth century by the abrasive circumstances of competition in the fur trade—meant ever more costly raids and counter-raids, in what seems to have been a rising crescendo of violence. The strain on the Iroquois themselves was great: serious loss of manpower, the need to replenish the population by mass adoption of captives, and the development of something like a chronic combat fatigue, the symptoms of which—preoccupation with death and misfortune, persistent nightmares of captivity, of being burned alive, of attack by enemy warriors—were vividly described by the Jesuits. Paradoxically, the League of peace had become a facility for destruction. Thus the League, lest the revenge process get out of hand, perforce had to expand so as to embrace under its sheltering branches, which precluded the blood feud, ever more of the Iroquois' traditional enemies. Each accretion to the League required the warriors to go farther and farther away to settle a score, and thereby reduced the total frequency of raids and their cost in terms of lives and human suffering. By the middle of the eighteenth century a rough equilibrium had been established: The nearby Indian nations had been brought by various mixtures of conquest, threat, and diplomatic persuasion into some sort of affiliation with the League. While killings and counterkillings still occasionally occurred, they no longer threatened the survival of the tribes; and there was still sufficient opportunity, in the raid exchanges with the southern Indians, for the revenge motif to exercise the kinship devotions of the warriors and women.

The social interests of the League sachems, on the one hand, and the warriors and the women, on the other, conflicted. Warriors and women formed a bloc composed of complementary roles in the revenge process, each dependent on the other for validation and fulfillment of status. The sachems, however, *as sachems* had to view the revenge process as potentially destructive. Thus one repeatedly finds sachems, or their representatives in contact with Europeans, complaining that they could not control their young men, that the warriors were apt to heed the women rather than the chiefs. While such statements were certainly true, for reasons given above, the situation that they reflected was also fruitful in insuring the successful fulfillment of the third function of Iroquois warfare. The chiefs of the League, or of any particular tribe, could at any time say that the warriors and the women could no longer be restrained from striking a blow against some enemy to gain revenge for some recent or ancient injury. Thus, while the League as such, by the treaties of 1701, remained committed to neutrality between the French and the English, groups of warriors—acting according to the code of revenge—could, if offended, at any time assail either party. It was always possible, of course, for the British to seduce some Mohawk into service against the French, and the French to persuade some Geneseo Seneca to strike the British, but these breaches of contract served more as an ever-present reminder of the importance of keeping the League itself neutral than as an excuse for terminating the agreement. Thus, without more duplicity than was characteristic of either the British or the French themselves, the League chiefs were able to orchestrate the revenge mechanism of warfare into the contrapuntal melody of extorting political and material gifts from both the French and the English. The importance of this theme in Iroquois life from 1701 to 1755 can hardly be overestimated: It gave them territorial security, a relatively high material culture, a continued ascendancy over neighboring peoples, and an enormous sense of their own importance.

THE RITUALS OF HOPE AND THANKSGIVING

In the course of trying to live up to the rigorous ideal of autonomy and responsibility, Iroquois men hunted, traded, fought, and negotiated at a high cost in loneliness and discomfort. They too on occasion yearned for someone's help to relieve pain and hardship, felt rage at insult and neglect, were jealous of others' success, were miserable when a loved one died. Even though their public behavior was stoic, they were underneath not nearly as insulated from one another, as self-sufficient and indifferent to human contact, as the overt fulfillment of the ideal of autonomy seemed to imply. Indeed, the severity of the ideal guaranteed an equal intensity of desire for its converse—dependency and lack of responsibility.

In general, Iroquois religion tended to be a means by which the disappointments and sacrifices entailed by living up to the ideal of autonomous responsibility could to some extent be compensated. Its rituals and beliefs were cathartic, satisfying the desperate needs for nurturance that could not be expressed, and might even be feared, in daily life. But the religion did its work in disguised, symbolic, and ceremonially insulated forms so that acting out normally disallowed wishes did not threaten self-respect. In the opinion of the Iroquois themselves, these rituals prevented both mental illness and social disorder.

The set of issues to which Iroquois religion addressed itself was unlike that to which contemporary European religions were oriented. European methods of social discipline in the main produced adults who were relatively tolerant of external restraint and whose typical problem was guilt, particularly over wishes for aggressive, dominant independence in matters of sex, politics, and human relations generally. The religious antihero of the Europeans was proud, independent Lucifer; of the Iroquois, it was the infantile, beggarly False Face. European religions provided a rich variety of ritual prescriptions for the management of guilt by confession, atonement, forgiveness, and absolution. Early Iroquois religion did not pay much attention to guilt of this kind because Iroquois people were not much bothered by it. But their religion did concern itself explicitly with cathartic ways of handling existential frustration. In general, these ways can be analytically separated into rituals of thanksgiving and hope and rituals of fear and mourning. The former—including particularly the communal thanksgiving festivals and the cult of dreams—worked to provide reassurance of continued protection and support from supernaturals and of ultimate impulse gratification, especially of desires for nurturance, within an indulgent earthly community. The latter—notably witchcraft, the masked medicine ceremonies, and the condolence rituals—attempted to cope with the consequences of loss: loss of love, loss of health, and loss of loved ones by death. Ultimately, of course, the two categories merge, for impulse gratification itself was believed to be prophylactic or even curative.

●   ●   ●

DREAMS AND THE WISHES OF THE SOUL

When the black-robed Jesuit fathers began the preaching of the gospel to the Seneca nation in the year 1668, they quickly found that the Seneca were rigidly attached to the Iroquoian religious traditions. Particularly obstinate were they in looking to their dreams for guidance in all the important affairs of life.

"The Iroquois have, properly speaking, only a single Divinity," wrote Father Fremin "—the dream. To it they render their submission, and follow all its orders with the utmost exactness. The Tsoanontouens [Seneca] are more attached to this superstition than any of the others; their religion in this respect becomes even a matter of scruple; whatever it be that they think they have done in their dreams, they believe themselves absolutely obliged to execute at the earliest moment. The other nations content themselves with observing those of their dreams which are the most important; but this people, which has the reputation of living more religiously than its neighbors, would think itself guilty of a great crime if it failed in its observance of a single dream. The people think only of that, they talk about nothing else, and all their cabins are filled with their dreams. They spare no pains, no industry, to show their attachment thereto, and their folly in this particular goes to such an excess as would be hard to imagine. He who has dreamed during the night that he was bathing, runs immediately, as soon as he rises, all naked, to several cabins, in each of which he has a kettleful of water thrown over his body, however cold the weather may be. Another who has dreamed that he was taken prisoner and burned alive, has himself bound and burned like a captive on the next day, being persuaded that by thus satisfying his dream, this fidelity will avert from him the pain and infamy of captivity and death—which, according to what he has learned from his Divinity, he is otherwise bound to suffer among his enemies. Some have been known to go as far as Quebec, travelling a hundred and fifty leagues, for the sake of getting a dog, that they had dreamed of buying there. . . ."

●   ●   ●

The theory of dreams among the Iroquois was in evident accord with the theme of freedom in the culture as a whole. The intolerance of externally imposed restraints, the principle of individual independence and autonomy, the maintenance of an air of indifference to pain, hardship, and loneliness—all these were the negative expression, as it were, of the positive assertion that wishes must be satisfied, that frustration of desire is the root of all evil. But men are never equally aware and equally tolerant of all their desires; and dreams themselves, carefully examined, are perhaps the quickest portal to that shadowy region where the masked and banished wishes exist in limbo. What then, if anything, can we learn about the unconscious of the Iroquois Indians from scattered dreams recorded by the Jesuits and other casual observers?

The manifest content of Iroquois dreams was as various, probably, as the wishes of mankind: There were dreams of love and hate, pleasure and pain, of lost loved ones and longed-for guardians; inconsequential and absurd things happened, and incidential objects were transfixed by the arrow of desire; abhorrent actions and repulsive thoughts plagued the restless sleeper. Dreams as reported in the literature seem to have held a prevailing anxious tone, ranging from nightmare fantasies of torture to the nagging need to define the unconscious wish and satisfy it before some disaster occurs. The most dramatic and most frequently mentioned dreams seem to come from three groups of people: pubescent youths (who must renounce childhood's indulgences); warriors (who feared capture and torture); and the sick (who feared death). These were, perhaps, the stress points that generated desire. Adolescent conflict, dreams of battle, and the silent panic of the sick; these are things of which many men of many cultures, including our own, have experience.

The manifest content and the conscious rationale the Seneca gave to dreams themselves were mainly in the active voices, and such passivity as showed itself was laden with pain unless it occurred in visitation dreams, where a man might be passive in relation to a god. But the latent content, representative of the underlying wish, may be seen in the *acting-out,* which was so often passive or self-destructive. Dreams were not to brood over, to analyze, or to prompt lonely and independent actions; they were to be told, or at least hinted at, and it was for other people to be active. The community rallied round the dreamer with gifts and ritual. The dreamer was fed, he was danced over, he was rubbed with ashes, he was sung to, he was given valuable presents, he was accepted as a member of a medicine society. The man whose dream manifested a wish to attack and kill was satisfied by being *given* a coat; the man who dreamed of sleeping with a woman did not attempt to woo his mistress, he was *given* an available female by the chief's council. Only in the personality-transformation dreams of pubescent boys and adult prophets was passivity accepted in the dream, and these were the dreams of men *in extremis.*

This observation suggests that the typical Iroquois male, who as a matter of fact in his daily life was an exceedingly brave, generous, active, and independent spirit, nevertheless typically cherished some strong, if unconscious, wishes to be passive, to beg, to be cared for. This unallowable passive tendency, so threatening to a man's sense of self-esteem, could not appear easily even in a dream, and when it did, it was either experienced as an intolerably painful episode of torture, or was put in terms of a meeting with a supernatural protector. The Iroquois themselves unwittingly made the translation, however: An active manifest dream was fulfilled by a passive receiving action. The arrangement of the dream-guessing rite, indeed, raised this dependency to an exquisite degree: The dreamer could not even *ask* for his wish; like a baby, he must content himself with cryptic signs and symbols, until someone guessed what he wanted and gave it to him.

The culture of dreams may be regarded as a necessary escape valve in Iroquois life. Iroquois men were, in their daily affairs, brave, active, self-reliant, and autonomous; they cringed to no one and begged for nothing. But no man can balance forever on such a pinnacle of masculinity, where asking and being given are unknown. Iroquois men dreamed; and without shame they received the fruits of their dreams, and their souls were satisfied.

2

Family Structure in Seventeenth-Century Andover, Massachusetts

PHILIP J. GREVEN, JR.

American historians have rediscovered the family. To be sure, they have always known it existed, and their suppositions about family life have seemed plausible and, indeed, self-evident. From bits and pieces of information, historians have assumed that in the colonial period both birthrates and infant-mortality rates were very high, that people married extremely young, that life expectancy was low—particularly for child-bearing women—although the survivors lived to a ripe old age, and that the family was "extended"—including nieces, nephews, and cousins as well as mature children—rather than "nuclear." Applying the technique of the historical demographer to long-ignored sources, Philip J. Greven, Jr., either modifies or denies these assumptions.

Surprisingly little is known at present about family life and family structure in the seventeenth-century American colonies. The generalizations about colonial family life embedded in textbooks are seldom the result of studies of the extant source materials, which historians until recently have tended to ignore. Genealogists long have been using records pre-

From the *William and Mary Quarterly*, 3d ser., 23 (1966):234–56. Footnotes omitted. Reprinted by permission of the author and the *William and Mary Quarterly*. An expanded version of this essay appears in Philip J. Greven, Jr., *Four Generations: Population, Land and Family in Colonial Andover, Massachusetts* (Ithaca: Cornell University Press, 1970).

served in county archives, town halls, churches, and graveyards as well as personal documents to compile detailed information on successive generations of early American families. In addition to the work of local genealogists, many communities possess probate records and deeds for the colonial period. A study of these last testaments and deeds together with the vital statistics of family genealogies can provide the answers to such questions as how many children people had, how long people lived, at what ages did they marry, how much control did fathers have over their children, and to what extent and under what conditions did children remain in their parents' community. The answers to such questions enable an historian to reconstruct to some extent the basic characteristics of family life for specific families in specific communities. This essay is a study of a single seventeenth-century New England town, Andover, Massachusetts, during the lifetimes of its first and second generations—the pioneers who carved the community out of the wilderness, and their children who settled upon the lands which their fathers had acquired. A consideration of their births, marriages, and deaths, together with the disposition of land and property within the town from one generation to the next reveals some of the most important aspects of family life and family structure in early Andover.

The development of a particular type of family structure in seventeenth-century Andover was dependent in part upon the economic development of the community during the same period. Andover, settled by a group of about eighteen men during the early 1640's and incorporated in 1646, was patterned at the outset after the English open field villages familiar to many of the early settlers. The inhabitants resided on house lots adjacent to each other in the village center, with their individual holdings of land being distributed in small plots within two large fields beyond the village center. House lots ranged in size from four to twenty acres, and subsequent divisions of land within the town were proportionate to the size of the house lots. By the early 1660's, about forty-two men had arrived to settle in Andover, of whom thirty-six became permanent residents. During the first decade and a half, four major divisions of the arable land in the town were granted. The first two divisions established two open fields, in which land was granted to the inhabitants on the basis of one acre of land for each acre of house lot. The third division, which provided four acres of land for each acre of house lot, evidently did not form another open field, but was scattered about the town. The fourth and final division of land during the seventeenth century occurred in 1662, and gave land to the householders at the rate of twenty acres for each acre of their house lots. Each householder thus obtained a minimum division allotment of about eighty acres and a maximum allotment of about four hundred acres. Cumulatively, these four successive divisions of town land, together with additional divisions of meadow and swampland, provided each of the inhabitants with at least one hundred acres of land for farming, and as much as six hundred acres. During the years following these substantial grants of land, many of the families in the town removed their habitations from the house lots in the town center onto their distant, and extensive, farm lands, thus altering the character of the community through the establishment of independent family farms and scattered residences. By the 1680's, more than half the families in Andover lived outside the original center of the town on their own ample farms. The transformation of the earlier open field village effectively recast the basis for family life within the community.

An examination of the number of children whose births are recorded in the Andover town records between 1651 and 1699 reveals a steady increase in the number of children being born throughout the period. (See Table I.) Between 1651 and 1654, 28 births are recorded, followed by 32 between 1655 and 1659, 43 between 1660 and 1664, 44 between 1665 and 1669, 78 between 1670 and 1674, and 90 between 1675 and 1679. After 1680, the figures rise to more than one hundred births every five years.

TABLE 1   The Numer of Sons and Daughters Living at the Age of 21 in Twenty-nine First-Generation Families

Sons	0	1	2	3	4	5	6	7	8	9	10
Families	1	2	7	1	6	6	3	3	0	0	0
Daughters	0	1	2	3	4	5	6	7	8	9	10
Families	0	2	7	6	11	2	0	0	0	1	0

The entire picture of population growth in Andover, however, cannot be formed from a study of the town records alone since these records do not reflect the pattern of generations within the town. Looked at from the point of view of the births of the children of the first generation of settlers who arrived in Andover between the first settlement in the mid-1640's and 1660, a very different picture emerges, hidden within the entries of the town records and genealogies. The majority of the second-generation children were born during the two decades of the 1650's and the 1660's. The births of 159 second-generation children were distributed in decades as follows: 10 were born during the 1630's, either in England or in the towns along the Massachusetts coast where their parents first settled; 28 were born during the 1640's; 49 were born during the 1650's;

43 were born during the 1660's; declining to 21 during the 1670's, and falling to only 8 during the 1680's. Because of this pattern of births, the second generation of Andover children, born largely during the 1650's and the 1660's, would mature during the late 1670's and the 1680's. Many of the developments of the second half of the seventeenth century in Andover, both within the town itself and within the families residing there, were the result of the problems posed by a maturing second generation.

From the records which remain, it is not possible to determine the size of the first-generation family with complete accuracy, since a number of children were undoubtedly stillborn, or died almost immediately after birth without ever being recorded in the town records. It is possible, however, to determine the number of children surviving childhood and adolescence with considerable accuracy, in part because of the greater likelihood of their names being recorded among the children born in the town, and in part because other records, such as church records, marriage records, tax lists, and wills, also note their presence. Evidence from all of these sources indicates that the families of Andover's first settlers were large, even without taking into account the numbers of children who may have been born but died unrecorded. An examination of the families of twenty-nine men who settled in Andover between 1645 and 1660 reveals that a total of 247 children are known to have been born to these particular families. Of these 247 children whose births may be ascertained, thirty-nine, or 15.7 per cent, are known to have died before reaching the age of 21 years. A total of 208 children or 84.3 per cent of the number of children known to be born thus reached the age of 21 years, having survived the hazards both of infancy and of adolescence. This suggests that the number of deaths among children and adolescents during the middle of the seventeenth century in Andover was lower than might have been expected.

In terms of their actual sizes, the twenty-nine first-generation families varied considerably, as one might expect. Ten of these twenty-nine families had between 0 and 3 sons who survived to the age of 21 years; twelve families had either 4 or 5 sons surviving, and six families had either 6 or 7 sons living to be 21. Eighteen of these families thus had four or more sons to provide with land or a trade when they reached maturity and wished to marry, a fact of considerable significance in terms of the development of family life in Andover during the years prior to 1690. Fewer of these twenty-nine families had large numbers of daughters. Fifteen families had between 0 and 3 daughters who reached adulthood, eleven families had 4 daughters surviving, and three families had 5 or more daughters reaching the age of 21. In terms of the total number of their children born and surviving to the age of 21 or more, four of these twenty-nine first-generation families had between 2 and 4 children

(13.8 per cent), eleven families had between 5 and 7 children (37.9 per cent), and fourteen families had between 8 and 11 children (48.3 per cent). Well over half of the first-generation families thus had 6 or more children who are known to have survived adolescence and to have reached the age of 21. The average number of children known to have been born to these twenty-nine first-generation families was 8.5, with an average of 7.2 children in these families being known to have reached the age of 21 years. The size of the family, and particularly the number of sons who survived adolescence, was a matter of great importance in terms of the problems which would arise later over the settlement of the second generation upon land in Andover and the division of the estates of the first generation among their surviving children. The development of a particular type of family structure within Andover during the first two generations depended in part upon the number of children born and surviving in particular families.

Longevity was a second factor of considerable importance in the development of the family in Andover. For the first forty years following the settlement of the town in 1645, relatively few deaths were recorded among the inhabitants of the town. Unlike Boston, which evidently suffered from smallpox epidemics throughout the seventeenth century, there is no evidence to suggest the presence of smallpox or other epidemical diseases in Andover prior to 1690. With relatively few people, many of whom by the 1670's were scattered about the town upon their own farms, Andover appears to have been a remarkably healthy community during its early years. Lacking virulent epidemics, the principal hazards to health and to life were birth, accidents, non-epidemical diseases, and Indians. Death, consequently, visited relatively few of Andover's inhabitants during the first four decades following its settlement. This is evident in the fact that the first generation of Andover's settlers was very long lived. Prior to 1680, only five of the original settlers who came to Andover before 1660 and established permanent residence there had died; in 1690, fifteen of the first settlers (more than half of the original group) were still alive, forty-five years after the establishment of their town. The age at death of thirty men who settled in Andover prior to 1660 can be determined with a relative degree of accuracy. Their average age at the time of their deaths was 71.8 years. Six of the thirty settlers died while in their fifties, 11 in their sixties, 3 in their seventies, 6 in their eighties, 3 in their nineties, and 1 at the advanced age of 106 years. The longevity of the first-generation fathers was to have great influence on the lives of their children, for the authority of the first generation was maintained far longer than would have been possible if death had struck them down at an early age. The second generation, in turn, was almost as long lived as the first generation had been. The average age of 138 second-generation men at the time of their deaths was 65.2 years, and the average age of sixty-two second-generation women at the time of their deaths was 64.0 years. (See Table 2.) Of the 138 second-generation men who reached the age of 21 years and whose lifespan is known, only twenty-five or 18.1 per cent, died between the ages of 20 and 49. Forty-two (30.3 per cent) of these 138 men died between the ages of 50 and 69; seventy-one (51.6 per cent) died after reaching the age of 70. Twenty-five second-generation men died in their eighties, and four died in their nineties. Longevity was characteristic of men living in seventeenth-century Andover.

TABLE 2   Second-Generation Ages at Death

Ages	Males		Females	
	Numbers	Percentages	Numbers	Percentages
20–29	10	7.3	4	6.1
30–39	9	6.5	4	6.1
40–49	6	4.3	6	9.1
50–59	16	11.5	10	15.2
60–69	26	18.8	13	19.7
70–79	42	30.4	16	24.2
80–89	25	18.1	8	12.1
90–99	4	3.1	5	7.5
Total	138	100.0%	66	100.0%

The age of marriage often provides significant clues to circumstances affecting family life and to patterns of family relationships which might otherwise remain elusive. Since marriages throughout the seventeenth century and the early part of the eighteenth century were rarely fortuitous, parental authority and concern, family interests, and economic considerations played into the decisions determining when particular men and women could and would marry for the first time. And during the seventeenth century in Andover, factors such as these frequently dictated delays of appreciable duration before young men, especially, might marry. The age of marriage both of men and of women in the second generation proved to be much higher than most historians hitherto have suspected.

Traditionally in America women have married younger than men, and this was generally true for the second generation in Andover. Although the assertion is sometimes made that daughters of colonial families frequently married while in their early teens, the average age of sixty-six second-generation daughters of Andover families at the time of their first marriage was 22.8 years. (See Table 3.) Only two girls are known to have married at 14 years, none at 15, and two more at 16. Four married at the age of 17, with a total of twenty-two of the sixty-six girls marrying before attaining the age of 21 years (33.3 per cent). The largest percentage of women married between the ages of 21 and 24, with twenty-four or 36.4 per cent being married during these years, making a total of 69.7 per cent of the second-generation daughters married before reaching the age of 25. Between the ages of 25 and 29 years, fourteen women (21.2 per cent) married, with six others marrying at the age of 30 or more (9.1 per cent).

TABLE 3   Second-Generation Female Marriage Ages

Age	Numbers	Percentages		
under 21	22	33.3	24 & under =	69.7%
21–24	24	36.4	25 & over =	30.3%
25–29	14	21.2	29 & under =	90.9%
30–34	4	6.1	30 & over =	9.1%
35–39	1	1.5		
40 & over	1	1.5		
	66	100.0%	Average age = 22.8 years	

Relatively few second-generation women thus married before the age of 17, and nearly 70 per cent married before the age of 25. They were not as young in most instances as one might have expected if very early marriages had prevailed, but they were relatively young nonetheless.

The age of marriage for second-generation men reveals a very different picture, for instead of marrying young, as they so often are said to have done, they frequently married quite late. (See Table 4.) The

TABLE 4   Second-Generation Male Marriage Ages

Age	Numbers	Percentages		
Under 21	4	4.3	24 & under =	39.4%
21–24	33	35.1	25 & over =	60.6%
25–29	34	36.2		
30–34	16	17.2	29 & under =	75.6%
35–39	4	4.3	30 & over =	24.4%
40 & over	3	2.9		
	94	100.0%	Average age = 27.1 years	

average age for ninety-four second-generation sons of Andover families at the time of their first marriages was 27.1 years. No son is known to have married before the age of 18, and only one actually married then. None of the ninety-four second-generation men whose marriage ages could be determined married at the age of 19, and only three married at the age of 20. The contrast with the marriages of the women of the same generation is evident, since only 4.3 per cent of the men married before the age of 21 compared to 33.3 per cent of the women. The majority of second-generation men married while in their twenties, with thirty-three of the ninety-four men marrying between the ages of 21 and 24 (35.1 per cent), and thirty-four men marrying between the ages of 25 and 29 (36.2 per cent). Nearly one quarter of the second-generation men married at the age of 30 or later, however, since twenty-three men or 24.4 per cent delayed their marriages until after their thirtieth year. In sharp contrast with the women of this generation, an appreciable majority of the second-generation men married at the age of 25 or more, with 60.6 per cent marrying after that age. This tendency to delay marriages by men until after the age of 25, with the average age being about 27 years, proved to be characteristic of male marriage ages in Andover throughout the seventeenth century.

Averages can sometimes obscure significant variations in patterns of behavior, and it is worth noting that in the second generation the age at which particular sons might marry depended in part upon which son was being married. Eldest sons tended to marry earlier than younger sons in many families, which suggests variations in their roles within their families, and differences in the attitudes of their fathers towards them compared to their younger brothers. For twenty-six eldest second-generation sons, the average age at their first marriage was 25.6 years. Second sons in the family often met with greater difficulties and married at an average age of 27.5 years, roughly two years later than their elder brothers. Youngest sons tended to marry later still, with the average age of twenty-two youngest sons being 27.9 years. In their marriages as in their inheritances, eldest sons often proved to be favored by their families; and family interests and paternal wishes were major factors in deciding which son should marry and when. More often than not, a son's marriage depended upon the willingness of his father to allow it and the ability of his father to provide the means for the couple's economic independence. Until a second-generation son had been given the means to support a wife—which in Andover during the seventeenth century generally meant land—marriage was virtually impossible.

Marriage negotiations between the parents of couples proposing marriage and the frequent agreement by the father of a suitor to provide a house and land for the settlement of his son and new bride are familiar facts. But the significance of this seventeenth-century custom is much greater than is sometimes realized. It generally meant that the marriages of the second generation were dependent upon their fathers' willingness to let them leave their families and to establish themselves in separate households elsewhere. The late age at which so many sons married during this period indicates that the majority of first-generation parents were unwilling to see their sons married and settled in their own families until long after they had passed the age of 21. The usual age of adulthood, marked by marriage and the establishment of another family, was often 24 or later. Since 60 per cent of the second-generation sons were 25 or over at the time of their marriage and nearly one quarter of them were 30 or over, one wonders what made the first generation so reluctant to part with its sons?

At least part of the answer seems to lie in the fact that Andover was largely a farming community during the seventeenth century, structured, by the time that the second generation was maturing, around the family farm which stood isolated from its neighbors and which functioned independently. The family farm required all the labor it could obtain from its own members, and the sons evidently were expected to assist their fathers on their family farms as long as their fathers felt that it was necessary for them to provide their labor. In return for this essential, but prolonged, contribution to their family's economic security, the sons must have been promised land by their fathers when they married, established their own families, and wished to begin their own farms. But this meant that the sons were fully dependent upon their fathers as long as they remained at home. Even if they wanted to leave, they still needed paternal assistance and money in order to purchase land elsewhere. The delayed marriages of second-generation men thus indicate their prolonged attachment to their families, and the continuation of paternal authority over second-generation sons until they had reached their mid-twenties, at least. In effect, it appears, the maturity of this generation was appreciably later than has been suspected hitherto. The psychological consequences of this prolonged dependence of sons are difficult to assess, but they must have been significant.

Even more significant of the type of family relationships emerging with the maturing of the second generation than their late age of marriage is the fact that paternal authority over sons did not cease with marriage. In this community, at least, paternal authority was exercised by the first generation not only prior to their sons' marriages, while the second generation continued to reside under the same roof with their parents and to work on the family farm, and not only at the time of marriage, when fathers generally provided the economic means for their sons' establishment in separate households, but also *after* marriage, by the further step of the father's withholding legal control of the land from the sons who had settled upon it. The majority of first-generation fathers continued to own the land which they settled their sons upon from the time the older men received it from the town to the day of their deaths. All of the first-generation fathers were willing to allow their sons to build houses upon their land, and to live apart from the paternal house after their marriage, but few were willing to permit their sons to become fully independent as long as they were still alive. By withholding deeds to the land which they had settled their sons upon, and which presumably would be theirs to inherit some-day, the first generation successfully assured the continuity of their authority over their families long after their sons had become adults and had gained a nominal independence. Since the second generation, with a few exceptions, lacked clear legal titles to the land which they lived upon and farmed, they were prohibited from selling the land which their fathers had settled them upon, or from alienating the land in any other way without the consent of their fathers, who continued to own it. Being unable to sell the land which they expected to inherit, second-generation sons could not even depart from Andover without their fathers' consent, since few had sufficient capital of their own with which to purchase land for themselves outside of Andover. The family thus was held together not only by settling sons upon family land in Andover, but also by refusing to relinquish control of the land until long after the second generation had established its nominal inde-pendence following their marriages and the establishment of separate households. In a majority of cases, the dependence of the second-generation sons continued until the deaths of their fathers. And most of the first generation of settlers was very long lived.

The first generations' reluctance to hand over the control of their property to their second-generation sons is evident in their actions. Only three first-generation fathers divided their land among all of their sons before their deaths and gave them deeds of gift for their portions of the paternal estate. All three, however, waited until late in their lives to give their sons legal title to their portions of the family lands. Eleven first-generation fathers settled all of their sons upon their family estates in Andover, but gave a deed of gift for the land to only one of their sons; the rest of their sons had to await their fathers' deaths before inheriting the land which they had been settled upon. Ten of the settlers retained the title to all of their land until their deaths, handing over control to their sons only by means of their last wills and testa-ments. For the great majority of the second generation, inheritances constituted the principal means of transferring the ownership of land from one generation to the next. The use of partible inheritances in Andover is evident in the division of the estates of the first generation. Twenty-one of twenty-two first-generation families which had two or more sons divided all of their land among all of their surviving sons. Out of seventy-seven sons who were alive at the time their fathers either wrote their wills or gave them deeds to the land, seventy-two sons received some land from their fathers. Out of a total of sixty-six sons whose inheritances can be determined from their fathers' wills, sixty-one or 92.4 per cent received land from their fathers' estates in Andover. Often the land bequeathed to them by will was already in their possession, but without legal conveyances having been given. Thus although the great majority of second-generation sons were settled upon their fathers' lands while their fathers were still alive, few actually owned the land which they lived upon until after their fathers' deaths. With their inheritances came ownership; and with ownership came independence. Many waited a long time.

The characteristic delays in the handng over of control of the land from the first to the second generation may be illustrated by the lives and actions of several Andover families. Like most of the men who wrested their farms and their community from the wilderness, William Ballard was reluctant to part with the control over his land. When Ballard died intestate in 1689, aged about 72 years, his three sons, Joseph, William, and John, agreed to divide their father's estate among themselves "as Equally as they could." They also agreed to give their elderly mother, Grace Ballard, a room in their father's house and to care for her as long as she remained a widow, thus adhering voluntarily to a common practice for the provision of the widow. The eldest son, Joseph, had married in 1665/6, almost certainly a rather young man, whereas his two brothers did not marry until the early 1680's, when their father was in his mid-sixties. William, Jr., must have been well over 30 by then, and John was 28. Both Joseph and William received as part of their division of their father's estate in Andover the land where their houses already stood, as well as more than 75 acres of land apiece. The youngest son, John, got all the housing, land, and meadow "his father lived upon except the land and meadow his father gave William Blunt upon the marriage with his daughter," which had taken place in 1668. It is unclear whether John lived with his wife and their four children in the same house as his parents, but there is a strong likelihood that this was the case in view of his assuming control of it after his father's death. His two older brothers had been given land to build upon by their father before his death, but no deeds of gift had been granted to them, thus preventing their full independence so long as he remained alive. Their family remained closely knit both by their establishment of residences near their paternal home on family land and by the prolonged control by William Ballard over the land he had received as one of the first settlers in Andover. It was a pattern repeated in many families.

There were variations, however, such as those exemplified by the Holt family, one of the most prominent in Andover during the seventeenth century. Nicholas Holt, originally a tanner by trade, had settled in Newbury, Massachusetts, for nearly a decade before joining the group of men planting the new town of Andover during the 1640's. Once established in the wilderness community, Holt ranked third among the householders, with an estate which eventually included at least 400 acres of land in Andover as a result of successive divisions of the common land. At some time prior to 1675, he removed his family from the village, where all the original house lots had been located, and built a dwelling house on his third division of land. Although a small portion of his land still lay to the north and west of the old village center, the greatest part of his estate lay in a reasonably compact farm south of his new house. Holt owned no land outside of Andover, and he acquired very little besides the original division grants from the town. It was upon this land that he eventually settled all his sons. In 1662, however, when Nicholas Holt received the fourth division grant of 300 acres from the town, his eldest son, Samuel, was 21 years old, and his three other sons were 18, 15, and 11. The fifth son was yet unborn. His four sons were thus still adolescents, and at ages which they could provide the physical labor needed to cultivate the land already cleared about the house, and to clear and break up the land which their father had just received. The family probably provided most of the labor, since there is no evidence to indicate that servants or hired laborers were numerous in Andover at the time. With the exception of two daughters who married in the late 1650's, the Holt family remained together on their farm until 1669, when the two oldest sons and the eldest daughter married.

By 1669, when Holt's eldest son, Samuel, finally married at the age of 28, the only possible means of obtaining land to settle upon from the town was to purchase one of the twenty-acre lots which were offered for sale. House-lot grants with accommodation land had long since been abandoned by the town, and Samuel's marriage and independence therefore depended upon his father's willingness to provide him with sufficient land to build upon and to farm for himself. Evidently his father had proved unwilling for many years, but when Samuel did at last marry, he was allowed to build a house for himself and his wife upon his father's "Three-score Acres of upland," known otherwise as his third division. Soon afterwards, his second brother, Henry, married and also was given land to build upon in the third division. Neither Samuel nor Henry was given a deed to their land by their father at the time they settled upon it. Their marriages and their establishment of separate households left their three younger brothers still living with their aging father and step-mother. Five years passed before the next son married. James, the fourth of the five sons, married in 1675, at the age of 24, whereupon he, too, was provided with a part of his father's farm to build a house upon. The third son, Nicholas, Jr., continued to live with his father, waiting until 1680 to marry at the late age of 32. His willingness to delay even a token independence so long suggests that personal factors must have played an important part in his continued assistance to his father, who was then about 77 years old. John Holt, the youngest of the sons, married at the age of 21, shortly before his father's death.

For Nicholas Holt's four oldest sons, full economic independence was delayed for many years. Although all had withdrawn from their father's house and had established separate residences of their own, they nonetheless were settled upon their father's land not too far distant from their family homestead, and none had yet been given a legal title to the land where they lived. Until Nicholas Holt was willing to give his sons deeds of gift for the lands where he had allowed them to build and to farm, he retained all legal rights to his estate and could still dispose of it in any way he chose. Without his consent, therefore, none of his sons could sell or mortgage the land where they lived since none of them owned it. In the Holt family, paternal authority rested upon firm economic foundations, a situation characteristic of the majority of Andover families of this period and these two generations.

Eventually, Nicholas Holt decided to relinquish his control over his Andover property by giving to his sons, after many years, legal titles to the lands which they lived upon. In a deed of gift, dated February 14, 1680/1, he conveyed to his eldest son, Samuel, who had been married almost twelve years, one half of his third division land, "the Said land on which the said Samuels House now Stands," which had the land of his brother, Henry, adjoining on the west, as well as an additional 130 acres of upland from the fourth division of land, several parcels of meadow, and all privileges accompanying these grants of land. In return for this gift, Samuel, then forty years old, promised to pay his father for his maintenance so long as his "natural life Shall Continue," the sum of twenty shillings a year. Ten months later, December 15, 1681, Nicholas Holt conveyed almost exactly the same amount of land to his second son, Henry, and also obligated him to pay twenty shillings yearly for his maintenance. Prior to this gift,

Nicholas had given his fourth son, James, his portion, which consisted of one-third part of "my farme" including "the land where his house now stands," some upland, a third of the great meadow, and other small parcels. In return, James promised to pay his father three pounds a year for life (three times the sum his two elder brothers were to pay), and to pay his mother-in-law forty shillings a year when she should become a widow. The farm which James received was shared by his two other brothers, Nicholas and John, as well. Nicholas, in a deed of June 16, 1682, received "one third part of the farme where he now dwells," some meadow, and, most importantly, his father's own dwelling house, including the cellar, orchard, and barn, which constituted the principal homestead and house of Nicholas Holt, Sr. In "consideration of this my fathers gift . . . to me his sone," Nicholas, Junior, wrote, "I doe promise and engage to pay yearly" the sum of three pounds for his father's maintenance. Thus Nicholas, Junior, in return for his labors and sacrifices as a son who stayed with his father until the age of 32, received not only a share in the family farm equal to that of his two younger brothers, but in addition received the paternal house and homestead. The youngest of the five Holt sons, John, was the only one to receive his inheritance from his father by deed prior to his marriage. On June 19, 1685, Nicholas Holt, Jr., at the age of 83, gave his "Lovinge" son a parcel of land lying on the easterly side of "my now Dwelling house," some meadow, and fifteen acres of upland "as yett unlaid out." One month later, John married, having already built himself a house upon the land which his father promised to give him. Unlike his older brothers, John Holt thus gained his complete independence as an exceptionally young man. His brothers, however, still were not completely free from obligations to their father since each had agreed to the yearly payment of money to their father in return for full ownership of their farms. Not until Nicholas Holt's death at the end of January 1685/6 could his sons consider themselves fully independent of their aged father. He must have died content in the knowledge that all of his sons had been established on farms fashioned out of his own ample estate in Andover, all enjoying as a result of his patriarchal hand the rewards of his venture into the wilderness.

Some Andover families were less reluctant than Nicholas Holt to let their sons marry early and to establish separate households, although the control of the land in most instances still rested in the father's hands. The Lovejoy family, with seven sons, enabled the four oldest sons to marry at the ages of 22 and 23. John Lovejoy, Sr., who originally emigrated from England as a young indentured servant, acquired a seven-acre house lot after his settlement in Andover during the mid-1640's, and eventually possessed an estate of over 200 acres in the town. At his death in 1690, at the age of 68, he left an estate worth a total of £327.11.6, with housing and land valued at £260.00.0, a substantial sum at the time. Although he himself had waited until the age of 29 to marry, his sons married earlier. His eldest son, John, Jr., married on March 23, 1677/8, aged 22, and built a house and began to raise crops on land which his father gave him for that purpose. He did not receive a deed of gift of his land, however; his inventory, taken in 1680 after his premature death, showed his major possessions to consist of "one house and a crope of corn" worth only twenty pounds. His entire estate, both real and personal, was valued at only £45.15.0, and was encumbered with £29.14.7 in debts. Three years later, on April 6, 1683, the land which he had farmed without owning was given to his three year old son by his father, John Lovejoy, Sr. In a deed of gift, the elder Lovejoy gave his grandson, as a token of the love and affection he felt for his deceased son, the land which John, Junior, had had, consisting of fifty acres of upland, a piece of meadow, and a small parcel of another meadow, all of which lay in Andover. Of the surviving Lovejoy sons only the second, William, received a deed of gift from the elder Lovejoy for the land which he had given them. The others had to await their inheritances to come into full possession of their land. In his will dated September 1, 1690, shortly before his death, Lovejoy distributed his estate among his five surviving sons: Christopher received thirty acres together with other unstated amounts of land, and Nathaniel received the land which his father had originally intended to give to his brother, Benjamin, who had been killed in 1689. Benjamin was 25 years old and unmarried at the time of his death, and left an estate worth only £1.02.8, his wages as a soldier. Without their father's land, sons were penniless. The youngest of the Lovejoy sons, Ebenezer, received his father's homestead, with the house and lands, in return for fulfilling his father's wish that his mother should "be made comfortable while she Continues in this world." His mother inherited the east end of the house, and elaborate provisions in the will ensured her comfort. With all the surviving sons settled upon their father's land in Andover, with the residence of the widow in the son's house, and with the fact that only one of the sons actually received a deed for his land during their father's lifetime, the Lovejoys also epitomized some of the principal characteristics of family life in seventeenth-century Andover.

Exceptions to the general pattern of prolonged paternal control over sons were rare. The actions taken by Edmund Faulkner to settle his eldest son in Andover are instructive precisely because they were so exceptional. The first sign that Faulkner was planning ahead for his son came with his purchase of a twenty-acre lot from the town at the annual town meeting of March 22, 1669/70. He was the only first-generation settler to purchase such a lot, all of the other purchasers being either second-generation sons or newcomers, and it was evident that he did not buy it for himself since he already had a six-acre house lot and more than one hundred acres of land in Andover. The town voted that "in case the said Edmond shall at any time put such to live upon it as the town shall approve, or have no just matter against them, he is to be admitted to be a townsman." The eldest of his two sons, Francis, was then a youth of about nineteen years. Five years later, January 4, 1674/5, Francis was admitted as a townsman of Andover "upon the account of the land he now enjoyeth," almost certainly his father's twenty acres. The following October, aged about 24, Francis married the minister's daughter. A year and a half later, in a deed dated February 1, 1676/7, Edmund Faulkner freely gave his eldest son "one halfe of my Living here at home" to be "Equally Divided between us both." Francis was to pay the town rates on his half, and was to have half the barn, half the orchard, and half the land about his father's house, and both he and his father were to divide the meadows. Significantly, Edmund added that "all my Sixscore acres over Shawshinne river I wholly give unto him," thus handing over, at the relatively young age of 52, most of his upland and half of the remainder of his estate to his eldest son. The control of most of his estate thereby was transferred legally and completely from the first to the second generation, Edmund's second and youngest son, John, was still unmarried at the time Francis received his gift, and waited until 1682 before marrying at the age of 28. Eventually he received some land by his father's will, but his inheritance was small compared to his brother's. Edmund Faulkner's eagerness to hand over the control of his estate to his eldest son is notable for its rarity and accentuates the fact that almost none of his friends and neighbors chose to do likewise. It is just possible that Faulkner, himself a young son of an English gentry family, sought to preserve most of his Andover estate intact by giving it to his eldest son. If so, it would only emphasize his distinctiveness from his neighbors. For the great majority of the first-generation settlers in Andover, partible inheritances and delayed control by the first generation over the land were the rule. Faulkner was the exception which proved it.

Embedded in the reconstructions of particular family histories is a general pattern of family structure unlike any which are known or suspected to have exsted either in England or its American colonies during the seventeenth century. It is evident that the family structure which developed during the lifetime of the first two generations in Andover cannot be classified satisfactorily according to any of the more recent definitions applied to types of family life in the seventeenth century. It was not simply a "patrilineal group of extended kinship gathered into a single household," nor was it simply a "nuclear independent family, that is man, wife, and children living apart from relatives." The characteristic family structure which emerged in Andover with the maturing of the second generation during the 1670's and 1680's was a combination of both the classical extended family and the nuclear family. This distinctive form of family structure is best described as a *modified extended family*—defined as a kinship group of two or more generations living within a single community in which the dependence of the children upon their parents continues after the children have married and are living under a separate roof. This family structure is a *modified* extended family because all members of the family are not "gathered into a single household," but it is still an *extended* family because the newly created conjugal unit of husband and wife live in separate households in close proximity to their parents and siblings and continue to be economically dependent in some respects upon their parents. And because of the continuing dependence of the second generation upon their first-generation fathers, who continued to own most of the family land throughout the better part of their lives, the family in seventeenth-century Andover was *partiarchal* as well. The men who first settled the town long remained the dominant figures both in their families and their community. It was their decisions and their actions which produced the family characteristic of seventeenth-century Andover.

One of the most significant consequences of the development of the modified extended family characteristic of Andover during this period was the fact that remarkably few second-generation sons moved away from their families and their community. More than four fifths of the second-generation sons lived their entire lives in the town which their fathers had wrested from the wilderness. The first generation evidently was intent upon guaranteeing the future of the community and of their families within it through the settlement of all of their sons upon the lands originally granted to them by the town. Since it was quite true that the second generation could not expect to acquire as much land by staying in Andover as their fathers had by undergoing the perils of founding a new town on the frontier, it is quite possible that their reluctance to hand over the control of the land to their sons when young is not only a reflection of their patriarchalism, justified both by custom and by theology, but also of the fact that they could not be sure that their sons would stay, given a free choice. Through a series of delays, however, particualrly those involving marriages and economic independence, the second generation continued to be closely tied to their paternal families. By keeping their sons in positions of prolonged dependence, the first generation successfully managed to keep them in Andover during those years in which their youth and energy might have led them to seek their fortunes elsewhere. Later generations achieved their independence earlier and moved more. It remains to be seen to what extent the family life characteristic of seventeenth-century Andover was the exception or the rule in the American colonies.

3

Underlying Themes
in the Witchcraft
of Seventeenth-Century
New England

JOHN DEMOS

Although historians have been fascinated by Salem witchcraft, they have generally agreed upon its relative unimportance and irrelevance and its aberrant nature. Social historian John Demos, however, has demonstrated that a close look at witchcraft affords valuable insights into New England culture. Without making judgments on the guilt of witches or witchhunters, Demos utilizes the techniques of anthropology and psychology to emphasize the patterns in seventeenth-century New England society, family life, and personality that witchhunts reveal.

It is faintly embarrassing for a historian to summon his colleagues to still another consideration of early New England witchcraft. Here, surely, is a topic that previous generations of writers have sufficiently worked, indeed overworked. Samuel Eliot Morison once commented that the Salem witch-hunt was, after all, "but a small incident in the history of a great superstition"; and Perry Miller noted that with only minor qualifications "the intellectual history of New England can be

From *American Historical Review* 75 (1970):1311–26. Footnotes omitted. Reprinted by permission of the author.

written as though no such thing ever happened. It had no effect on the ecclesiastical or political situation, it does not figure in the institutional or ideological development." Popular interest in the subject is, then, badly out of proportion to its actual historical significance, and perhaps the sane course for the future would be silence.

This assessment seems, on the face of it, eminently sound. Witchcraft was not an important matter from the standpoint of the larger historical process; it exerted only limited influence on the unfolding sequence of events in colonial New England. Moreover, the literature on the subject seems to have reached a point of diminishing returns. Details of fact have been endlessly canvassed, and the main outlines of the story, particularly the story of Salem, are well and widely known.

There is, to be sure, continuing debate over one set of issues: the roles played by the persons most directly involved. Indeed the historiography of Salem can be viewed, in large measure, as an unending effort to judge the participants—and, above all, to affix blame. A number of verdicts have been fashionable at one time or another. Thus the ministers were really at fault; or Cotton Mather in particular; or the whole culture of Puritanism; or the core group of "afflicted girls" (if their "fits" are construed as conscious fraud). The most recent, and in some ways most sophisticated, study of the Salem trials plunges right into the middle of the same controversy; the result is yet another conclusion. Not the girls, not the clergy, not Puritanism, but the accused witches themselves are now the chief culprits. For "withcraft actually did exist and was widely practiced in seventeenth-century New England"; and women like Goody Glover, Bridget Bishop, and Mammy Redd were "in all probability" guilty as charged.

Clearly these questions of personal credit and blame can still generate lively interest, but are they the most fruitful, the most important questions to raise about witchcraft? Will such a debate ever be finally settled? Are its partisan terms and moral tone appropriate to historical scholarship?

The situation is not hopeless if only we are willing to look beyond the limits of our own discipline. There is, in particular, a substantial body of interesting and relevant work by anthropologists. Many recent studies of primitive societies contain chapters about witchcraft, and there are several entire monographs on the subject. The approach they follow differs strikingly from anything in the historical literature. Broadly speaking, the anthropological work is far more analytic, striving always to use materials on witchcraft as a set of clues or "symptoms." The subject is important not in its own right but as a means of exploring certain larger questions about the society. For example, witchcraft throws light on social structure, on the organization of families, and on the inner dynamics of personality. The substance of such investigations, of course, varies greatly from one culture to another, but the framework, the informing purposes are roughly the same. To apply this framework and these purposes to historical materials is not inherently difficult. The data may be inadequate in a given case, but the analytic categories themselves are designed for any society, whether simple or complex, Western or non-Western, past or contemporary. Consider, by way of illustration, the strategy proposed for the main body of this essay.

Our discussion will focus on a set of complex relationships between the alleged witches and their victims. The former group will include all persons accused of practicing witchcraft, and they will be called, simply, witches. The category of victims will comprise everyone who claimed to have suffered from witchcraft, and they will be divided into two categories to account for an important distinction between different kinds of victims. As every schoolchild knows, some victims experienced fits—bizarre seizures that, in the language of modern psychiatry, closely approximate the clinical picture of hysteria. These people may be called accusers, since their sufferings and their accusations seem to have carried the greatest weight in generating formal proceedings against witches. A second, much larger group of victims includes people who attributed to witchcraft some particular misfortune they had suffered, most typically an injury or illness, the sudden death of domestic animals, the loss of personal property, or repeated failure in important day-to-day activities like farming, fishing, and hunting. This type of evidence was of secondary importance in trials of witches and was usually brought forward after the accusers had pressed their own more damaging charges. For people testifying to such experiences, therefore, the shorthand term witnesses seems reasonably appropriate.

Who were these witches, accusers, and witnesses? How did their lives intersect? Most important, what traits were generally characteristic and what traits were alleged to have been characteristic of each group? These will be the organizing questions in the pages that follow. Answers to these questions will treat both external (or objective) circumstances and internal (or subjective) experiences. In the case of witches, for example, it is important to try to discover their age, marital status, socioeconomic position, and visible personality traits. But it is equally important to examine the characteristics attributed to witches by others—flying about at night, transforming themselves into animals, and the like. In short, one can construct a picture of witches in fact and in fantasy; and comparable efforts can be made with accusers and witnesses. Analysis directed to the level of external reality helps to locate certain points of tension or conflict in the social structure of a community. The fantasy picture, on the other hand, reveals more directly the psychological dimension of life, the inner preoccupations, anxieties, and conflicts of individual members of that community.

Such an outline looks deceptively simple, but in fact it demands an unusual degree of caution, from writer and reader alike. The approach is explicitly cross-disciplinary, reaching out to anthropology for strategy and to psychology for theory. There is, of course, nothing new about the idea of a working relationship between history and the behavioral sciences. It is more than ten years since William Langer's famous summons to his colleagues to consider this their "next assignment"; but the record of actual output is still very meager. All such efforts remain quite experimental; they are designed more to stimulate discussion than to prove a definitive case.

There is a final point—about context and the larger purposes of this form of inquiry. Historians have traditionally worked with purposeful, conscious events, "restricting themselves," in Langer's words, "to recorded fact and to strictly rational motivation." They have not necessarily wished to exclude non-rational or irrational behavior, but for the most part they have done so. Surely in our own post-Freudian era there is both need and opportunity to develop a more balanced picture. It is to these long-range ends that further study of witchcraft should be dedicated. For witchcraft is, if nothing else, an open window on the irrational.

The first witchcraft trial of which any record survives occurred at Windsor, Connecticut, in 1647, and during the remainder of the century the total of cases came to nearly one hundred. Thirty-eight people were executed as witches, and a few more, though convicted, managed somehow to escape the death penalty. There were, of course, other outcomes as well: full-dress trials resulting in acquittal, hung juries, convictions reversed on appeal, and "complaints" filed but not followed up. Finally, no doubt, many unrecorded episodes touching on witchcraft, episodes of private suspicion or public gossip, never eventuated in legal action at all.

This long series of witchcraft cases needs emphasis lest the Salem outbreak completely dominate our field of vision. Salem differed radically from previous episodes in sheer scope; it developed a degree of self-reinforcing momentum present in no other instance. But it was very similar in many qualitative aspects: the types of people concerned, the nature of the charges, the fits, and so forth. Indeed, from an analytic standpoint, all these cases can be regarded as roughly equivalent and interchangeable. They are pieces of a single, larger phenomenon, a system of witchcraft belief that was generally prevalent in early New England. The evidence for such a system must, of course, be drawn from a variety of cases to produce representative conclusions. For most questions this is quite feasible; there is more evidence, from a greater range of cases, than can ever be presented in a single study.

Yet in one particular matter the advantages of concentrating on Salem are overwhelming. It affords a unique opportunity to portray the demography of witchcraft, to establish a kind of profile for each of the three basic categories of people involved in witchcraft, in terms of sex, age, and marital status. Thus the statistical tables that follow are drawn entirely from detailed work on the Salem materials. The earlier cases do not yield the breadth of data necessary for this type of quantitative investigation. They do, however, provide many fragments of evidence that are generally consistent with the Salem picture.

There is at least minimal information about 165 people accused as witches during the entire period of the Salem outbreak.

Sex	Total	Marital Status	Male	Female	Total	Age	Male	Female	Total
Male	42	Single	8	29	37	Under 20	6	18	24
Female	120	Married	15	61	76	21–30	3	7	10
Total	162	Widowed	1	20	21	31–40	3	8	11
		Total	24	110	134	41–50	6	18	24
						51–60	5	23	28
						61–70	4	8	12
						Over 70	3	6	9
						Total	30	88	118

These figures point to an important general conclusion: the witches were predominantly married or widowed women, between the ages of forty-one and sixty. While the exceptions add up to a considerable number, most of them belonged to the families of middle-aged, female witches. Virtually all the young persons in the group can be identified as children of witches and most of the men as husbands of witches. In fact this pattern conformed to an assumption then widely prevalent, that the transmission of witchcraft would naturally follow the lines of family or of close friendship. An official statement from the government of Connecticut included among the "grounds for Examination of a Witch" the following:

> if ye party suspected be ye son or daughter the servt or familiar friend; neer Neighbor or old Companion of a Knowne or Convicted witch this alsoe a presumton for witchcraft is an art yt may be learned & Convayd from man to man & oft it falleth out yt a witch dying leaveth som of ye aforesd. heirs of her witchcraft.

In short, young witches and male witches belonged to a kind of derivative category. They were not the prime targets in these situations; they were, in a literal sense, rendered suspect by association. The deepest suspicions, the most intense anxieties, remained fixed on middle-aged women.

Thirty-four persons experienced fits of one sort or another during the Salem trials and qualify thereby as accusers.

Sex	Total	Marital Status	Male	Female	Total	Age	Male	Female	Total
Male	5	Single	5	23	28	Under 11	0	1	1
Female	29	Married	0	6	6	11–15	1	7	8
Total	34	Widowed	0	0	0	16–20	1	13	14
		Total	5	29	34	21–25	0	1	1
						26–30	0	1	1
						Over 30	0	4	4
						Total	2	27	29

Here again the sample shows a powerful cluster. The vast majority of the accusers were single girls between the ages of eleven and twenty. The exceptions in this case (two boys, three males of undetermined age, and four adult women) are rather difficult to explain, for there is little evidence about any of them. By and large, however, they played only a minor role in the trials. Perhaps the matter can be left this way: the core group of accusers was entirely composed of adolescent girls, but the inner conflicts so manifest in their fits found an echo in at least a few persons of other ages or of the opposite sex.

Eighty-four persons came forward as witnesses at one time or another during the Salem trials.

Sex	Total	Marital Status	Male	Female	Total	Age	Male	Female	Total
Male	63	Single	11	3	14	Under 20	3	2	5
Female	21	Married	39	16	55	21–30	13	4	17
Total	84	Widowed	3	1	4	31–40	14	6	20
		Total	53	20	73	41–50	18	7	25
						51–60	11	1	12
						61–70	2	1	3
						Over 70	2	0	2
						Total	63	21	84

Here the results seem relatively inconclusive. Three-fourths of the witnesses were men, but a close examination of the trial records suggests a simple reason for this: men were more likely, in seventeenth-century New England, to take an active part in legal proceedings of any type. When a husband and wife were victimized together by some sort of witchcraft, it was the former who would normally come forward to testify. As to the ages of the witnesses, there is a fairly broad distribution between twenty and sixty years. Probably, then, this category reflects the generalized belief in witchcraft among all elements of the community in a way that makes it qualitatively different from the groupings of witches and accusers.

There is much more to ask about external realities in the lives of such people, particularly with regard to their social and economic position. Unfortunately, however, the evidence is somewhat limited here and permits only a few impressionistic observations. It seems that many witches came from the lower levels of the social structure, but there were too many exceptions to see in this a really significant pattern. The first three accused at Salem were Tituba, a Negro slave, Sarah Good, the wife of a poor laborer, and Sarah Osbourne, who possessed a very considerable estate. Elizabeth Godman, tried at New Haven in 1653, seems to have been poor and perhaps a beggar; but Nathaniel and Rebecca Greensmith, who were convicted and executed at Hartford eight years later, were quite well-to-do; and "Mistress" Ann Hibbens, executed at Boston in 1656, was the widow of a wealthy merchant and former magistrate of the Bay Colony.

What appears to have been common to nearly all these people, irrespective of their economic position, was some kind of personal eccentricity, some deviant or even criminal behavior that had long since marked them out as suspect. Some of them had previously been tried for theft or battery or slander; others were known for their interest in dubious activities like fortunetelling or certain kinds of folk-healing. The "witch Glover" of Boston, on whom Cotton Mather reports at some length, was Irish and Catholic, and spoke Gaelic; and a Dutch family in Hartford came under suspicion at the time the Greensmiths were tried.

More generally, many of the accused seem to have been unusually irascible and contentious in their personal relations. Years before her conviction for witchcraft Mrs. Hibbens had obtained a reputation for "natural crabbedness of . . . temper"; indeed she had been excommunicated by the Boston church in 1640, following a long and acrimonious ecclesiastical trial. William Hubbard, whose *General History of New England* was published in 1680, cited her case to make the general point that "persons of hard favor and turbulent passions are apt to be condemned by the common people as witches, upon very slight grounds." In the trial of Mercy Desborough, at Fairfield, Connecticut, in 1692, the court received numerous reports of her quarrelsome behavior. She had, for example, told one neighbor "yt shee would make him bare as a bird's tale," and to another she had repeatedly said "many hard words." Goodwife Clawson, tried at the same time, was confronted with testimony like the following:

> Abigail Wescot saith that as shee was going along the street goody Clasen came out to her and they had some words together and goody Clason took up stones and threw at her: and at another time as shee went along the street before sd Clasons dore goody Clason caled to mee and asked mee what was in my Chamber last Sabbath day night; and I doe afirme that I was not there that night: and at another time as I was in her sone Steephens house being neere her one hous shee folowed me in and contended with me becase I did not com into her hous caling of me proud slut what—are you proud of your fine cloths and you love to be mistres but you neuer shal be and several other provoking speeches.

The case of Mary and Hugh Parsons, tried at Springfield in 1651, affords a further look at the external aspects of our subject. A tax rating taken at Springfield in 1646 records the landholdings of most of the principals in the witchcraft prosecutions of five years later. When the list is arranged according to wealth, Parsons falls near the middle (twenty-fourth out of forty-two), and those who testified against him come from the top, middle, and bottom. This outcome tends to confirm the general point that economic position is not, for present purposes, a significant datum. What seems, on the basis of the actual testimonies at the trial, to have been much more important was the whole dimension of eccentric and anti-social behavior. Mary Parsons, who succumbed repeatedly to periods of massive depression, was very nearly insane. During the witchcraft investigations she began by testifying against her husband and ended by convicting herself of the murder of their infant child. Hugh Parsons was a sawyer and brickmaker by trade, and there are indications that in performing these services he was sometimes suspected of charging extortionate rates. But what may have weighed most heavily against him was his propensity for prolonged and bitter quarreling; many examples of his "threatening speeches" were reported in court.

One other aspect of this particular episode is worth noting, namely, the apparent influence of spatial proximity. When the names of Parsons and his "victims" are checked against a map of Springfield in this period, it becomes very clear that the latter were mostly his nearest neighbors. In fact nearly all of the people who took direct part in the trial came from the southern half of the town. No other witchcraft episode yields such a detailed picture in this respect, but many separate pieces of evidence suggest that neighborhood antagonism was usually an aggravating factor.

We can summarize the major characteristics of the external side of New England witchcraft as follows: First, the witches themselves were chiefly women of middle age whose accusers were girls about one full generation younger. This may reflect the kind of situation that anthropologists would call a structural conflict—that is, some focus of tension created by the specific ways in which a community arranges the lives of its members. In a broad sense it is quite probable that adolescent girls in early New England were particularly subject to the control of older women, and this may well have given rise to a powerful underlying resentment. By contrast, the situation must have been less difficult for boys, since their work often took them out of the household and their behavior generally was less restricted.

There are, moreover, direct intimations of generational conflict in the witchcraft records themselves. Consider a little speech by one of the afflicted girls during a fit, a speech meticulously recorded by Cotton Mather. The words are addressed to the "specter" of a witch, with whom the girl has been having a heated argument:

> What's that? Must the younger Women, do yee say, hearken to the Elder?—They must be another Sort of Elder Women than You then! they must not bee Elder Witches, I am sure. Pray, do you for once Hearken to mee.—What a dreadful Sight are You! An Old Woman, an Old Servant of the Divel!

Second, it is notable that most witches were deviant persons— eccentric or conspicuously anti-social or both. This suggests very clearly the impact of belief in witchcraft as a form of control in the social ordering of New England communities. Here indeed is one of the most widely-found social functions of witchcraft; its importance has been documented for many societies all over the world. Any individual who contemplates actions of which the community disapproves knows that if he performs such acts, he will become more vulnerable either to a direct attack by witches or to the charge that he is himself a witch. Such knowledge is a powerful inducement to self-constraint.

What can be said of the third basic conclusion, that witchcraft charges particularly involved neighbors? Very briefly, it must be fitted with other aspects of the social setting in these early New England communities. That there was a great deal of contentiousness among these people is suggested by innumerable court cases from the period dealing with disputes about land, lost cattle, trespass, debt, and so forth. Most men seem to have felt that the New World offered them a unique opportunity to increase their properties, and this may have heightened competitive feelings and pressures. On the other hand, co-operation was still the norm in many areas of life, not only in local government but for a variety of agricultural tasks as well. In such am-bivalent circumstances it is hardly surprising that relations between close neighbors were often tense or downright abrasive.

"In all the Witchcraft which now Grievously Vexes us, I know not whether any thing be more Unaccountable, than the Trick which the Witches have, to render themselves and their Tools Invisible." Thus wrote Cotton Mather in 1692; and three centuries later it is still the "invisible" part of witchcraft that holds a special fascination. Time has greatly altered the language for such phenomena—"shapes" and "spec-ters" have become "hallucinations"; "enchantments" are a form of "sug-gestion"; the Devil himself seems a fantasy—and there is a correspond-ing change of meanings. Yet here was something truly remarkable, a kind of irreducible core of the entire range of witchcraft phenomena. How much of it remains "unaccountable"? To ask the question is to face directly the other side of our subject: witchcraft viewed as psychic process, as a function of internal reality.

The biggest obstacles to the study of psycho-history ordinarily are practical ones involving severe limitations of historical data. Yet for witchcraft the situation is uniquely promising on these very grounds. Even a casual look at writings like Cotton Mather's *Memorable Provi-dences* or Samuel Willard's *A briefe account* etc. discloses material so rich in psychological detail as to be nearly the equivalent of clinical case reports. The court records on witchcraft are also remarkably full in this respect. The clergy, the judges, all the leaders whose positions carried special responsibility for combatting witchcraft, regarded publi-city as a most important weapon. Witchcraft would yield to careful study and the written exchange of information. Both Mather and Willard received "afflicted girls" into their own homes and recorded "possession" behavior over long periods of time.

A wealth of evidence does not, of course, by itself win the case for a psychological approach to witchcraft. Further problems remain, prob-lems of language and of validation. There is, moreover, the very basic problem of selecting from among a variety of different theoretical models. Psychology is not a monolith, and every psycho-historian must declare a preference. In opting for psychoanalytic theory, for example, he performs, in part, an act of faith, faith that this theory provides deeper, fuller insights into human behavior than any other. In the long run the merit of such choices will probably be measured on pragmatic grounds. Does the interpretation explain materials that would other-wise remain unused? Is it consistent with evidence in related subject areas?

If, then, the proof lies in the doing, let us turn back to the New England witches and especially to their "Trick . . . to render themselves and their tools Invisible." What characterized these spectral witches? What qualities were attributed to them by the culture at large?

The most striking observation about witches is that they gave free rein to a whole gamut of hostile and aggressive feelings. In fact most witchcraft episodes began after some sort of actual quarrel. The fits of Mercy Short followed an abusive encounter with the convicted witch Sarah Good. The witch Glover was thought to have attacked Martha Goodwin after an argument about some missing clothes. Many such examples could be accumulated here, but the central message seems immediately obvious: never antagonize witches, for they will invariably strike back hard. Their compulsion to attack was, of course, most dramatically visible in the fits experienced by some of their victims. These fits were treated as tortures imposed directly and in every detail by witches or by the Devil himself. It is also significant that witches often assumed the shape of animals in order to carry out their attacks. Animals, presumably, are not subject to constraints of either an internal or external kind; their aggressive impulses are immediately translated into action.

Another important facet of the lives of witches was their activity in company with each other. In part this consisted of long and earnest conferences on plans to overthrow the kingdom of God and replace it with the reign of the Devil. Often, however, these meetings merged with feasts, the witches' main form of self-indulgence. Details are a bit thin here, but we know that the usual beverage was beer or wine (occasionally described as bearing a suspicious resemblance to blood), and the food was bread or meat. It is also worth noting what did not happen on these occasions. There were a few reports of dancing and "sport," but very little of the wild excitements associated with witch revels in continental Europe. Most striking of all is the absence of illusions to sex; there is no nakedness, no promiscuity, no obscene contact with the Devil. This seems to provide strong support for the general proposition that the psychological conflicts underlying the early New England belief in witchcraft had much more to do with aggressive impulses than with libidinal ones.

The persons who acted as accusers also merit the closest possible attention, for the descriptions of what they suffered in their fits are perhaps the most revealing of all source materials for present purposes. They experienced, in the first place, severe pressures to go over to the Devil's side themselves. Witches approached them again and again, mixing threats and bribes in an effort to break down their Christian loyalties. Elizabeth Knapp, bewitched at Groton, Massachusetts, in 1671, was alternately tortured and plied with offers of "money, silkes, fine cloaths, ease from labor"; in 1692 Ann Foster of Andover confessed to being won over by a general promise of "prosperity," and in the same year Andrew Carrier accepted the lure of "a house and land in Andover." The same pattern appears most vividly in Cotton Mather's record of another of Mercy Short's confrontations with a spectral witch:

> "Fine promises!" she says, "You'l bestow an Husband upon mee, if I'l bee your Servant. An Husband! What? A Divel! I shall then bee finely fitted with an Husband: . . . Fine Clothes! What? Such as Your Friend Sarah Good had, who hardly had Rags to cover her! . . . Never Dy! What? Is my Life in Your Hands? No, if it had, You had killed mee long before this Time!—What's that?—So you can!—Do it then, if You can. Come, I dare you: Here, I challenge You to do it. Kill mee if you can. . . ."

Some of these promises attributed to the Devil touch the most basic human concerns (like death) and others reflect the special preoccupations (with future husbands, for example) of adolescent girls. All of them imply a kind of covetousness generally consistent with the pattern of neighborhood conflict and tension mentioned earlier.

But the fits express other themes more powerfully still, the vital problem of aggression being of central importance. The seizures themselves have the essential character of attacks: in one sense, physical attacks by the witches on the persons of the accusers and in another sense, verbal attacks by the accusers on the reputations and indeed the very lives of the witches. This points directly toward one of the most important inner processes involved in witchcraft, the process psychologists call "projection," defined roughly as "escape from repressed conflict by attributing . . . emotional drives to the external world." In short, the dynamic core of belief in witchcraft in early New England was the difficulty experienced by many individuals in finding ways to handle their own aggressive impulses. Witchcraft accusations provided one of the few approved outlets for such impulses in Puritan culture. Aggression was thus denied in the self and attributed directly to others. The accuser says, in effect: "I am not attacking you; you are attacking me!" In reality, however, the accuser is attacking the witch, and in an extremely dangerous manner, too. Witchcraft enables him to have it both ways; the impulse is denied and gratified at the same time.

The seizures of the afflicted children also permitted them to engage in a considerable amount of direct aggression. They were not, of course, held personally responsible; it was always the fault of the Devil at work inside them. Sometimes these impulses were aimed against the most important—and obvious—figures of authority. A child in a fit might behave very disobediently toward his parents or revile the clergy who came to pray for his recovery. The Reverend Samuel Willard of Groton, who ministered to Elizabeth Knapp during the time of her most severe fits, noted that the Devil "urged upon her constant temptations to murder her p'rents, her neighbors, our children . . . and even to make away with herselfe & once she was going to drowne herself in ye well." The attacking impulses were quite random here, so much so that the girl herself was not safe. Cotton Mather reports a slight variation on this type of behavior in connection with the fits of Martha Goodwin. She would, he writes, "fetch very terrible Blowes with her Fist, and Kicks with her Foot at the man that prayed; but still . . . her Fist and Foot would alwaies recoil, when they came within a few hairs breadths of him just as if Rebounding against a Wall." This little paradigm of aggression attempted and then at the last moment inhibited expresses perfectly the severe inner conflict that many of these people were acting out.

One last, pervasive theme in witchcraft is more difficult to handle than the others without having direct recourse to clinical models; the summary word for it is orality. It is helpful to recall at this point the importance of feasts in the standard imaginary picture of witches, but the experience of the accusers speaks even more powerfully to the same point. The evidence is of several kinds. First, the character of the "tortures" inflicted by the witches was most often described in terms of biting, pinching, and pricking; in a psychiatric sense, these modes of attack all have an oral foundation. The pattern showed up with great vividness, for example, in the trial of George Burroughs:

> It was Remarkable that whereas Biting was one of the ways which the Witches used for the vexing of the Sufferers, when they cry'd out of G.B. biting them, the print of the Teeth would be seen on the Flesh of the Complainers, and just such a sett of Teeth as G.B.'s would then appear upon them, which could be distinguished from those of some other mens.

Second, the accusers repeatedly charged that they could see the witches suckling certain animal "familiars." The following testimony by one of the Salem girls, in reference to an unidentified witch, was quite typical: "She had two little things like young cats and she put them to her brest and suckled them they had no hair on them and had ears like a man." It was assumed that witches were specially equipped for these purposes, and their bodies were searched for the evidence. In 1656 the constable of Salisbury, New Hampshire, deposed in the case of Eunice Cole,

> That being about to stripp [her] to bee whipt (by the judgment of the Court att Salisbury) lookeing uppon hir brests under one of hir brests (I thinke hir left brest) I saw a blew thing like unto a teate hanging downeward about three quarters of an inche longe not very thick, and haveing a great suspition in my mind about it (she being suspected for a witche) desiered the Court to sende some women to looke of it.

The court accepted this proposal and appointed a committee of three women to administer to Goodwife Cole the standard, very intimate, examination. Their report made no mention of a "teate" under her breast, but noted instead "a place in her leg which was proveable wher she Had bin sucktt by Imps or the like." The women also stated "thatt they Heard the whining of puppies or such like under Her Coats as though they Had a desire to sucke."

Third, many of the accusers underwent serious eating disturbances during and after their fits. "Long fastings" were frequently imposed on them. Cotton Mather writes of one such episode in his account of the bewitching of Margaret Rule: "tho she had a very eager Hunger upon her Stomach, yet if any refreshment were brought unto her, her teeth would be set, and she would be thrown into many Miseries." But also she would "sometimes have her Jaws forcibly pulled open, whereupon something invisible would be poured down her throat . . . She cried out of it as of Scalding Brimstone poured into her." These descriptions and others like them would repay a much more detailed analysis than can be offered here, but the general point should be obvious. Among the zones of the body, the mouth seems to have been charged with a special kind of importance for victims of witchcraft.

In closing, it may be appropriate to offer a few suggestions of a more theoretical nature to indicate both the way in which an interpretation of New England witchcraft might be attempted and what it is that one can hope to learn from witchcraft materials about the culture at large. But let it be said with some emphasis that this is meant only as the most tentative beginning of a new approach to such questions.

Consider an interesting set of findings included by two anthropologists in a broad survey of child-rearing practices in over fifty cultures around the world. They report that belief in witchcraft is powerfully correlated with the training a society imposes on young children in regard to the control of aggressive impulses. That is, wherever this training is severe and restrictive, there is a strong likelihood that the culture will make much of witchcraft. The correlation seems to suggest that suppressed aggression will seek indirect outlets of the kind that belief in witchcraft provides. Unfortunately there is relatively little concrete evidence about child-rearing practices in early New England; but it seems at least consistent with what is known of Puritan culture generally to imagine that quite a harsh attitude would have been taken toward any substantial show of aggression in the young.

Now, some further considerations. There were only a very few cases of witchcraft accusations among members of the same family. But, as we have seen, the typical pattern involved accusations by adolescent girls against middle-aged women. It seems plausible, at least from a clinical standpoint, to think that this pattern masked deep problems stemming ultimately from the relationship of mother and daughter. Perhaps, then, the afflicted girls were both projecting their aggression and diverting or "displacing" it from its real target. Considered from this perspective, displacement represents another form of avoidance or denial; and so the charges of the accusers may be seen as a kind of double defense against the actual conflicts.

How can we locate the source of these conflicts? This is a more difficult and frankly speculative question. Indeed the question leads farther and farther from the usual canons of historical explanation; such proof as there is must come by way of parallels to findings of recent psychological research and, above all, to a great mass of clinical data. More specifically, it is to psychoanalytic theory that one may turn for insights of an especially helpful sort.

The prominence of oral themes in the historical record suggests that the disturbances that culminated in charges of witchcraft must be traced to the earliest phase of personality development. It would be very convenient to have some shred of information to insert here about breast-feeding practices among early New Englanders. Possibly their methods of weaning were highly traumatic, but as no hard evidence exists we simply cannot be sure. It seems plausible, however, that many New England children were faced with some unspecified but extremely difficult psychic tasks in the first year or so of life. The outcome was that their aggressive drives were tied especially closely to the oral mode and driven underground. Years later, in accordance with changes normal for adolescence, instinctual energies of all types were greatly augmented; and this tended, as it so often does, to reactivate the earliest conflicts—the process that Freud vividly described as "the return of the repressed." But these conflicts were no easier to deal with in adolescence than they had been earlier; hence the need for the twin defenses of projection and displacement.

One final problem must be recognized. The conflicts on which this discussion has focused were, of course, most vividly expressed in the fits of the accusers. The vast majority of people in early New England—sub-

jected, one assumes, to roughly similar influences as children—managed
to reach adulthood without experiencing fits. Does this pose serious difficulties for the above interpretations? The question can be argued to a
negative conclusion, in at least two different but complementary ways.
First, the materials on witchcraft, and in particular on the fits of the accusers, span a considerable length of time in New England's early history.
It seems clear, therefore, that aggression and orality were more or less
constant themes in the pathology of the period. Second, even in the far
less bizarre testimonies of the witnesses—those who have been taken to
represent the community at large—the same sort of focus appears. It is,
above all, significant that the specific complaints of the accusers were so
completely credible to so many others around them. The accusers, then,
can be viewed as those individuals who were somehow especially sensitive to the problems created by their environment; they were the ones
who were pushed over the line, so to speak, into serious illness. But their
behavior clearly struck an answering chord in a much larger group of
people. In this sense, nearly everyone in seventeenth-century New England
was at some level an accuser.

4

The Agricultural Practices of National Groups in Eighteenth-Century Southeastern Pennsylvania

JAMES T. LEMON

.

Historical geographers are interested in far more than maps. They have abandoned their earlier rigid adherence to the notion that physical environment is the chief determinant of historical events and have exploited colonial statistical evidence to produce studies on population distribution, the rectangular land survey system, types of settlement, economic development, and social change. Concentrating on the relatively narrow area of southeastern Pennsylvania, James T. Lemon shows how attitudes and stereotypes influenced "unbiased" writers and historians. Based on tax lists and estate inventories, Lemon's statistical findings challenge the long-held view that Pennsylvania Germans were preeminent among colonial farmers.

The farming practices of the "Pennsylvania Dutch" in the eighteenth century have often been described as superior to those of settlers from the British Isles. Governor George Thomas, Lewis Evans, Benjamin Franklin, and Benjamin Rush, among others, believed that agricultural traditions of national groups were quite distinct. Thomas said the Ger-

Reprinted, with omissions, from the *Geographical Review*, 56 (1966):467–96. © by the American Geographical Society of New York.

mans were responsible for the high productivity of Pennsylvania. Franklin, despite his dislike of these Palatine "boors," expressed admiration for their "habitual industry and frugality," which permitted them to "underlive others." Rush, whose "Account of the Manners of the German Inhabitants of Pennsylvania" has been widely quoted, concluded that "a German farm may be distinguished from the farms of the other citizens . . . by . . . the fertility of their [sic] fields; the luxuriance of their meadows, and a general appearance of plenty and neatness in everything that belongs to them." Among modern commentators, Shryock has drawn a sharp distinction between German and British farming traditions, and a new general history of the people of the United States by Handlin has helped to nurture the belief. Dissenting voices have been few; recently Shoemaker, in a discussion of Pennsylvania barns, expressed doubt whether the Germans differed greatly from their neighbors from the British Isles.

Within the whole range of agricultural activities it is not possible to distinguish the Germans, English, and Scotch-Irish as national groups with distinctive cultural traits. The eighteenth-century record, including tax lists and estate inventories, makes it clear that most writers have been biased in characterizing the Germans as the best farmers. Conversely, on insufficient evidence the Scotch-Irish have been rated as inferior farmers but as typical "frontiersmen."

In an investigation of skill in selecting land, kinds of crops and livestock, techniques for improving yields, attitudes about work and saving, and degree of material success this lack of differentiation among groups becomes apparent. Many specific beliefs held by Rush and others —that Germans seldom incurred debts, for example, and that they cleared their lands in a more orderly fashion than others—are assessed here and found untenable. The attitudes about the Germans and Scotch-Irish seem to be based on widespread agreement on stereotypes of "national character." Some speculations are offered to account for the existence of such biases in America, because a study of spatial patterns undertaken by a historical geographer must consider the values both of those who interpret and of those who act.

NATIONAL GROUPS IN SOUTHEASTERN PENNSYLVANIA

Of the major national groups in southeastern Pennsylvania in 1730 and 1760 (Figs. 1 and 2), the English predominated in the east, the Germans in the north, and the Scotch-Irish in the west, but there were several areas of overlap, and a large number of the Scotch-Irish had settled among the English, and between the English and the Germans, in the south. In 1790, of the some 325,000 people living in the counties south and east of Blue

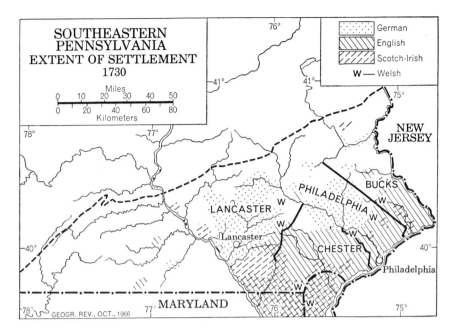

FIGURE 1

(North) Mountain, persons of German-speaking ancestry accounted for 40 to 45 percent, English and Welsh for slightly more than 30 percent, and the English-speaking Scotch-Irish, including some Scots and Irish, for nearly 20 percent. There were also a few Swedes, Dutch, and French.

Chester and Lancaster Counties provide a more precise view and warrant comparative treatment because of their mixed ethnic and religious populations and their high agricultural productivity. The predominantly English character of Chester, the Germanness of Lancaster, and the strong representation of Scotch-Irish in both are apparent in Table I. So, too, is the declining numerical importance of the non-Germans in Lancaster between 1760 and 1782 and of the Welsh in Chester between 1730 and 1760. In 1782 the Germans were prominent in the central and northern parts of Lancaster and on the northern edge of Chester, and the Scotch-Irish were most numerous in southwestern and western Chester and eastern, southern, and west-central Lancaster. The English were dominant in eastern and central Chester and were found also in Scotch-Irish areas. These distributions will be analyzed in relation to some of the problems raised below.

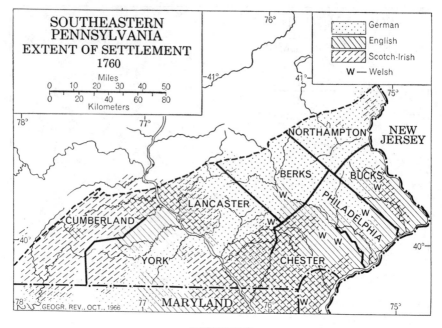

FIGURE 2

TABLE I   National Groups in Chester and Lancaster Counties
(In percentages of population)

	Lancaster			Chester		
	1730	1759	1782	1722	1759	1782
English	67	59	63 ⎫		⎧ 15	10
Welsh	17	8	7 ⎬	35	⎨ 1	1
Scotch-Irish, Scots, Irish	12	23	19 ⎭		⎩ 19	13
German-speaking	2	5	8	65	58	68
Other and unassigned	2	5	3	—	7	8
Approximate population	10,025	24,500	34,500	1,150	25,550	42,775

INITIAL SELECTION OF LAND

The selection of good-quality land accessible to markets is a mark of skillful farming. Greater perception of good land has been attributed to Germans. For example, some nineteenth-century writers believed that most Germans sought heavier limestone lowland soils covered with thick forests, and that the other national groups, especially the Scotch-Irish, desired lightly wooded but poorer-quality shale uplands. These choices were thought to have been a consequence of homeland experience. Similarly, many writers have held that as a consequence of Celtic restlessness and Teutonic stability the Scotch-Irish were frontiersmen par excellence and the Germans usually bought their land from others, notably the Scotch-Irish. These assumptions are unwarranted.

To assess the relationship of national groups to the land, the areal variations in its qualities must first be considered. The patterns of climate and vegetation were relatively uniform in southeastern Pennsylvania in the eighteenth century. The water supply was easily accessible only at streams and springs; indeed, some limestone areas had intermittent streams. But of greatest relevance to agricultural activity was the quality of the soil, a result of the kinds of parent materials and of the topography, specifically the degree of slope. Certainly, climate, natural vegetation, and, more recently, fertilizers have tended to make most soils loamy and productive; nevertheless, recent soil surveys of Lancaster, Chester, and Delaware Counties indicate that differences still occur because of parent materials and slope. The distribution of the three commonest kinds of parent materials—limestones, shales, and crystallines—and their relationship to the physiographic regions are shown in Figures 3 and 4. Gentle slopes (less than 3 percent) are much more frequent in limestone areas

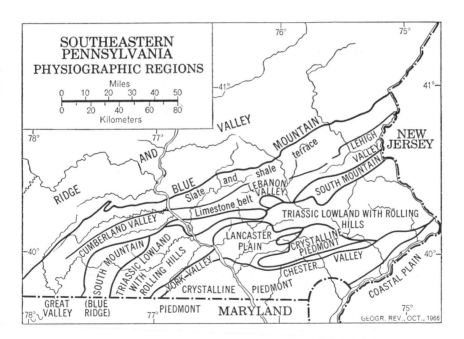

FIGURE 3

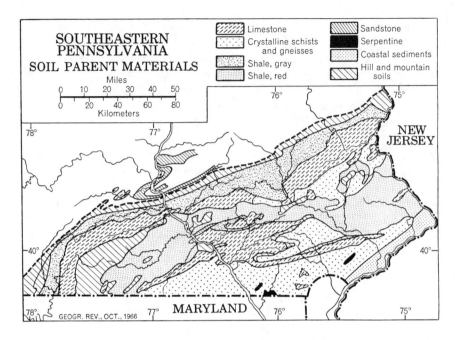

SOUTHEASTERN
PENNSYLVANIA
SOIL PARENT MATERIALS

Limestone
Crystalline schists and gneisses
Shale, gray
Shale, red
Sandstone
Serpentine
Coastal sediments
Hill and mountain soils

FIGURE 4

than in others; however, except in the hills, slopes are generally less than 8 percent. Gently sloping areas of limestone and crystalline soils are the most productive (Table II). Where slopes are between 3 and 6 percent,

TABLE II   Soil Fertility in Present-Day Lancaster County

Soil	% Slope	Condition	Productivity Index of Seven Kinds of Crops
Limestone loams	0–3	Little erosion	100
	3–6	Moderate erosion	90–100, mostly 98
Crystalline loams	0–3	Little erosion	97–100, mostly 100
	3–6	Moderate erosion	75–100, mostly 95 on deep soil, 85–87 on moderately deep
Shale loams	3–8	Moderate erosion	55–85, average 71

deep limestone and crystalline soils are about equally productive. Shale soils of moderate slope have only 55 to 85 percent of the fertility of the others.

No clear relationship is apparent between soils and the position of national groups in 1730 and 1760 (Figs. 1, 2, and 4). By 1760 the English and Welsh had settled on soils derived from crystalline bedrock (Chester and Lancaster Counties), from red shales (Bucks and York Counties), and from limestones (Chester Valley, Lancaster Plain, and Lebanon Valley). The Scotch-Irish had settled chiefly on crystalline soils (Chester, Lancaster, and York Counties), on limestone and shale soils (in the Cumberland and Lehigh Valleys and western York), and on limestones (eastern Lancaster County). Germans had settled on the limestone soils of Lancaster and York, and of the Lebanon and Lehigh Valleys, where they also occupied gray shales. Germans were the most prominent group on the extensive area of red shales in Montgomery County. The heavy settlement of Germans on shales clearly weakens the validity of the generalization that as a group they commonly sought lowland limestone soils. Furthermore, in 1759, after a generation of settlement, 49 percent of the 235 taxables in almost exclusively German Cocalico Township, Lancaster County, were on "poor" land, which constituted 33 percent of the 25,953 acres assessed. In short, Germans settled on all qualities of land.

Many areas of good soils were selected by individuals or religious groups. Mennonites occupied some of the best limestone land in Lancaster County in 1710, though others later took up poorer land in the same county and another large group settled on the red shales of Montgomery. The limestone soils of the Lancaster Plain and the Chester Valley attracted not only land speculators but some of the more affluent Quakers, Scotch-Irish Presbyterians, Welsh Anglicans, German Lutherans, and German and Huguenot Reformed folk.

Water supply was also a major consideration among the first settlers. Early survey drafts indicate that in newly opened areas the settlers took up land in stream bottoms or near springs, leaving the interfluves to those who followed. An example is found in a Scotch-Irish settlement in the Lebanon Valley. This evidence denies that these people invariably sought uplands.

"Frontier" locations were not the monopoly of any one national group. Before 1680 the Swedes were on the edge of European settlement, though confined to the margins of the Delaware River; by 1700 the English and Welsh were clearly the most numerous frontiersmen; and later the Germans dominated the northern line and the Scotch-Irish the western (Fig. 2). The north was as much a frontier as the west, and during the conflicts of the 1750's Scotch-Irish and Germans suffered equally from Indian attacks in the Great Valley. There seems little doubt that all groups had numerous representatives willing to live beyond areas already settled.

A detailed analysis of the distribution of national groups is not appropriate here, but the factors should be recognized in distinguishing

other aspects of cultural antecedency from so-called "national character."
Familiarity in the guise of the same language, the same religious denomi-
nation, kinfolk, and old neighbors, exerted a pull in the establishment of
initial nuclei of settlements and on subsequent settlers. These cultural
factors operated in conjunction with the time and place of entry into the
province, ability to pay for land, availability of land, and, in some instances, government policies.

CROPS AND LIVESTOCK

A superior approach to farming has been cited as a major reason for the
supposed greater productivity of German farms. To check this hypothesis,
the kinds of crops and livestock (though few writers made an issue of
these), the types of farming, and techniques related to the use of land will
be considered.

A large number of crops were produced in Pennsylvania in the
eighteenth century. Most were of European origin; maize was the major
addition from the Indians. As compared with the present time, alfalfa
was little used before 1800, and rye, buckwheat, flax, and hemp have
declined in importance. A complete inventory is unnecessary; crops have
been selected to provide adequate comparison among national groups.

Wheat both for domestic consumption and for export was "the grand
article of the province. They sow immense quantities," exclaimed the
anonymous author of "American Husbandry" in 1775, footnoting a fact
established by 1700. Rye was also a major crop, amounting to one-fifth to
one-third of the acreage of wheat. Differences in the amounts of crops
grown by national groups could not be established firmly because the assessment lists for the falls of 1759 and 1784, the only years for which these
amounts are available, combine rye and wheat as "winter grain."

The locations of average acreages sown with winter grain do not correlate with the locations of national groups. In a list of sample townships
(Table III) averages for every group fall above or below the township
averages. South-central Chester County and the Lancaster Plain had

TABLE III   Average Acreages Sown in Winter Grain, Lancaster County, Fall, 1759

Sample Townships	All Groups	German	English	Scotch-Irish	Welsh	Other and Unclassified
Bart	7.8	8.9	6.9	7.8	—	8.1
Caernarvon	11.3	10.1	10.4	5.2	14.8	5.5
Donegal	10.5	8.8	11.6	11.5	—	11.3
Lampeter	11.9	12.2	17.0	11.0	8.8	10.0

higher average acreages than elsewhere in the two counties (Fig. 6); the former area was identified chiefly with English Quakers, the latter with German-speaking Mennonites and a few persons of other national and religious groups (Fig. 5). Smaller acreages were found among Germans

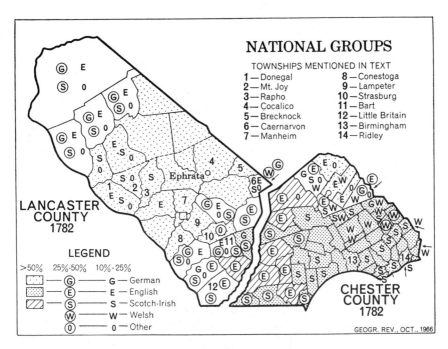

FIGURE 5

in the northern parts of the two counties and among Scotch-Irish and English in the southern parts. Generally it appears that this regional pattern was associated with affluence rather than with nationality (Fig. 9). Chester and Lancaster Counties had about the same average acreages (9½ in Chester, 10 in Lancaster), but Chester was mainly English-speaking and Lancaster about three-fifths German.

Information for other crops is sparse. Indian corn was widely grown, though perhaps less widely than in New England and the South. In 1805 the average Pennsylvania farm was thought to produce 100 to 150 bushels on five to ten acres. There was a slight, though hardly definite, tendency for non-Germans to produce more. Oats were also important, because of the relatively large number of horses in Pennsylvania. There is no evidence that the Scotch-Irish grew more oats than others. Hemp was localized on the Susquehanna River and Pequea Creek floodplains in Lancaster County. English, Scotch-Irish, and Germans sold large lots of hemp in the

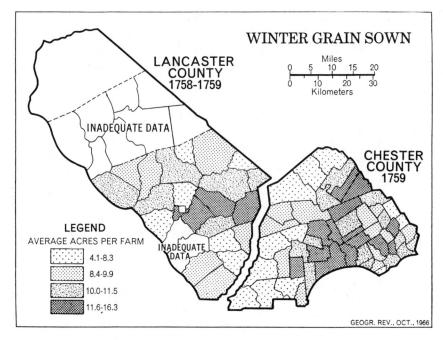

FIGURE 6

mid-sixties. Flax, for fiber and seed, was an important product for many farms, though grown on small acreages. No distinction between national groups can be made; both Scotch-Irish and Germans had used flax extensively in Europe. Among forage crops, white clover, red clover, bluegrass, and timothy were grown. Inventories and newspaper advertisements suggest that "English" grass and clover were grown fairly early in newly settled areas, indeed in poorer Scotch-Irish areas. Red clover was noted in several areas in 1790, and some comments indicate that it was being raised for seed in Lancaster County by 1750. Although this might suggest that Germans were ahead in the production of this superior forage crop, reports from Germans in Northampton and York Counties indicate little use until 1790. The only available information on the regionalization of fodder crops is associated with soils in York and Franklin (southern Cumberland before 1785) Counties and comes from a correspondent of Washington's in 1790; clover and bluegrass were more prevalent on limestone soils, and timothy in other areas. It is impossible to identify particular crops with national groups.

This is the case with livestock also, though with some qualifications about sheep. Oxen are noted only rarely in tax lists and estate inventories. Horses were without question the chief suppliers of locomotive power, both for plowing and for hauling wagons. Tradition has identified the Conestoga horses and wagon with the Germans of Lancaster County, but there is no justification for this association. The name "Conestoga" was given by Philadelphians who in early years considered the Conestoga area (Lancaster County) synonymous with backcountry. However, there are also references to "Dutch," "English," and even "Irish" wagons, and, in the inventories of Lancaster farmers, to "Philadelphia" wagons. There is little evidence from tax lists and inventories that any national group owned more horses than any other. This is also true for cattle, despite Rush's assertion that the Germans kept fewer. More affluent areas, such as parts of the Lancaster Plain, had more of both per farm. Quantitative data for swine are limited to inventories; most farms had between five and ten hogs, but no distinction by national groups can be hazarded. Despite the lack of information, it is clear that pigs were important in the rural economy of all groups.

Although sheep were less prominent in Pennsylvania than in the British Isles, there was a slight tendency for the Scotch-Irish and English to raise more than the Germans. The more affluent British in east-central Lancaster had the most sheep per taxable (Fig. 7); in the poorer southern end there were more farmers keeping sheep than elsewhere in the county

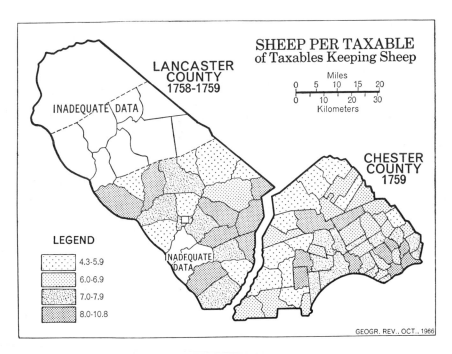

FIGURE 7

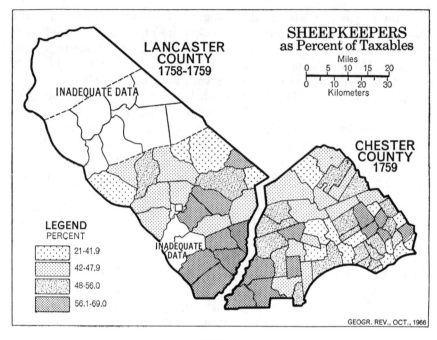

FIGURE 8

(Fig. 8). These English-speaking areas also contained more weavers than other rural areas in Lancaster according to the 1759 tax lists. The pattern for Chester was similar: poorer areas, more farmers with sheep; affluent areas, more sheep per taxable. The pattern related to ethnic groups is not nearly as apparent as the distinctions based on economic status. A breakdown of inventory data is by no means clear, though non-Germans held on the average slightly more sheep.

It should be apparent from this survey of a few crops and livestock that differences among national groups were slight or uncertain. Regional variations, noted for winter grain and sheep, were more clearly associated with affluence than with national groups.

FARMING TECHNIQUES

Good techniques are necessary for high productivity. The Germans have been praised as having superior skills; they were allegedly more sophisticated on arrival and were responsible for several innovations in Pennsylvania. Specifically, they have been credited with the cutting rather than the girdling of trees, the best horticultural ideas, stall-feeding, large bank barns, the watering of meadows, the use of gypsum fertilizer, the "Dutch" fan, and the Conestoga horses and wagon. Rush suggested that the Scotch-Irish of Donegal had learned their good farming techniques from the Germans. But the historical record is by no means clear as to who were the greatest innovators or who possessed superior skills.

Sometime it has been assumed that more German-speaking settlers than others had been farmers in Europe. However, a review of all available data does not clearly indicate differences among Ulstermen, English, and Germans. Even if differences existed, it is debatable whether a farming background would have provided the skills necessary in the husbandry of Pennsylvania. Undoubtedly many immigrant craftsmen became farmers, and perhaps these might have been more flexible in adopting Pennsylvania practices than immigrant farmers.

In Pennsylvania there were signs that innovations identified with the "Agricultural Revolution" in England in the century and a half following 1650 were recognized, if not consistently adopted. In England the key element was the introduction of forage crops—most notably red clover and, less widely, turnips—into rotation schemes. The increase in fodder production that was the direct effect resulted in more and fatter animals for human consumption. In addition, the soil was improved by the greater use of manure and by the more frequent cultivation of clover. German-speaking areas, including the Rhine, the area of origin of most immigrants into Pennsylvania, were not as inclined to change as England before 1750.

The "revolution" did not strike Pennsylvania farmers with the same degree of necessity that many English farmers felt. Because of persistent and successful marketing patterns, grain, and especially wheat, was relatively more important than livestock in Pennsylvania throughout much of the century. This resulted in a rather general pattern of extensive farming, which clearly did not call for the practices needed in more intensive use of the land, despite all the disparaging remarks about agriculture by travelers and the pleas of Philadelphia gentlemen farmers. Certain modifications were made, nevertheless, and certain practices did result in better land use by some farmers.

"The two principal links in good farming, are proper Rotation of Crops . . . and Manures," John Bordley asserted in 1792. Some concern was expressed about rotations from the earliest days of the province, beginning with William Penn. Mid-century tenant agreements specified that winter grain could be sown but once in every three or four years on any one field, and that one or two fields should be held for spring grain and one for fallow. Although red clover may have been sown in meadows as early as 1740, there is no evidence of its presence in rotations until about 1790. Upland meadows with other grasses may have been taken into the pattern earlier. In the 1790's records indicate that the number of fields in use had increased generally and that clover was being grown, possibly because the market patterns in the period 1775–1789 encouraged more meat production. Cazenove in 1794 reported rotations with clover in the Lehigh, Lebanon, and Cumberland Valleys; in Chester and Lancaster Counties and lands adjacent to Philadelphia similar plans with grass and clover were reported. There does not seem to be any evidence that the Germans practiced rotations with clover or grass earlier than others; indeed, in the Lehigh Valley, Cazenove said, clover was a recent acquisition.

Among fertilizers animal manure was the most prominent, though lime and, eventually, gypsum were used. The lack of manure and the failure to use it when available are mentioned from the beginning of Penn's colony. In 1684 Pastorius said that the Swedes made no use of manure. In 1733 Hassert, who had just arrived from Germany, asserted that farmers "know of no manuring." Kalm in 1749, Francis Alison in 1770, and postrevolutionary travelers commented on the neglect. An assertion by Hummel, who founded a town in Dauphin County (part of Lancaster until 1785), that manure was unnecessary brought the German traveler Schoepf in 1783 to reply: "Such over-confident opinions regarding the inexhaustible goodness of his soil gradually puts the farmer's industry to sleep, and when, finally, betterment is necessary many of them had rather move on to take up fresh land than to be at the trouble of improving the old." A correspondent to the *Germantauner Zeitung* on July 24, 1787, while praising Mennonites and other sectarians, indicated that farmers thought the use of manure unnecessary.

Despite these negative statements, manure was used by many farmers. Some rental agreements specified dunging. Part of the problem was the lack of dung because of a low ratio of cattle to land area, and the lack of fencing to keep animals from the woods. Often the grainlands had to do without manure. From the evidence it seems clear that the Pennsylvania Dutch shared these problems with their neighbors.

By mid-century lime, and toward the end of the century gypsum, had come to be rather widely used as fertilizer. Lewis Evans noted the number of kilns in the Chester Valley in 1754, and advertisements for land in this area and in Strasburg Township on the Lancaster Plain specified the use of lime on grainlands. Not all farmers thought lime was useful; John Adams found Germans in New Jersey who felt that "Lime makes the father rich, the Grandson poor,—i.e., exhausts the land." Some apparently learned that too much lime can suppress growth rather than improve it. Gypsum also may have been overdone, because it was used less after 1815. The introduction of gypsum, or plaster of Paris, was specifically identified with the Germans of Lancaster County by William Strickland of the British Board of Agriculture. However, Richard Peters claimed to have introduced it to that county before the Revolution. In any case, Schoepf in 1783 reported its use from Philadelphia to York. There does not seem to be any correlation of gypsum use with Germans alone.

The irrigation of meadows Strickland also attributed to the Germans of Lancaster County, perhaps because of Pownall's comment in 1754 that he had not seen irrigation with sluices in America (or England) until he reached a "Swisser's" farm in Lancaster County. The practice was widespread, however, and need not be identified with Germans. Strickland himself noted that it was common in Connecticut at an early date and also prevalent in the west of England, and recent evidence for the latter area suggests that sophisticated methods were practiced by 1700. A large number of English settlers in Pennsylvania and Connecticut came from this west country. In Pennsylvania, newspaper advertisements before 1730 cited watered meadows. In Lancaster County a number of wills specifying division of water among heirs indicate that Scotch-Irishmen had elaborate means of irrigation by 1757, and in 1770 the Gillespie farm in Little Britain Township had 900–1000 rods of sluices, which ran into the meadows every half acre. Ironically, the praise bestowed on the Germans by Strickland in 1801 was passé; a German at Bethlehem wrote to Richard Peters in 1797 stating that the use of gypsum on upland meadows had rendered watered meadows superfluous except as rough pasture.

Germans have been credited with introducing stall-feeding and with having more attractive animals. In the kinds of fodder used there seem to have been no distinction among groups. The use of forests by both cattle and pigs seems to have continued despite early prohibitions. Edward Shippen noted that the woods adjacent to the towns of Lancaster, an almost exclusively German area, were so used in 1769. Even Rush qualified his statement that Germans had better fences with a "sometimes." There is no evidence on who introduced pigs to maize, though by 1740 the practice was in use by Quakers.

Although stalls appear with greater frequency in newspaper advertisements after 1740, in the literature there is no evidence of stall-feeding until 1750. The desire for fatter animals that was apparent by 1770 may have indicated that stall-feeding was becoming prevalent by that time. However, the famous Pennsylvania large bank barn seems to have been rare until after the Revolution, and it was not until the last decade of the century that there were explicit discussions of this barn. In 1782 strongly Mennonite Conestoga Township had many more barns made of logs than stone or frame barns. Indeed, there were more stone houses than stone barns. In 1799 Lancaster County had more barns longer than one hundred feet than other counties, but the origin of the bank barn is obscure and cannot be attributed to the Germans with any degree of certainty.

If German farms were more productive than the farms of other groups, the reasons do not lie in the field of technology. The national origins of many techniques are obscure; and as for fertilizer, many Germans had a positive aversion to its use. Resistance to change, perhaps as much a consequence of market conditions as of conservatism, was widespread. On September 4, 1787, "Ein Bauer" in a letter to the *Germantauner Zeitung* complained about a columnist who on May 29 had suggested ways in which farmers might improve their land and production; farmers, he said, had always gotten along without this kind of help. That Germans were not then considered exemplary farmers is indicated by the absence of references to them in the agricultural writings of gentlemen farmers during the last two decades of the century. These experimenters strove constantly to emulate English farming practices.

Innovations did occur, however; the use of clover, lime, and gypsum, more fattening of livestock, and more sophisticated rotations were apparent by the end of the century. Instead of being attributable to any particular national groups or even chiefly to the gentlemen experimenters, it would seem likely that permanent improvements were the work of better-than-average ordinary farmers who could afford to risk some of their capital. Because the Mennonites and the Quakers were the most affluent farmers, they may well have been the chief innovators. How the innovative process worked among the Quakers is indicated by the gypsum-grinding records of a Birmingham Township mill in Chester County. In 1790 and 1792 a few persons bought some gypsum, but in 1793 twenty farmers, mostly Quakers, had several hundred pounds ground, even as much as four and one-half tons. Once the value of the practice had been proved, others would follow if they could afford the cost.

HABITS AND CUSTOMS

We have not been able to establish that German settlers were generally more perceptive in their initial selection of land or superior in the use of technical skills, but were they more industrious and frugal than others, as has been asserted? Work habits, food consumption, indebtedness, and locational stability need to be investigated.

Whether any national group worked harder than others cannot be answered with any degree of precision, though some comments can be made on land-clearance practices, labor-saving devices, and servants and slaves. Rush's suggestion that Germans were more diligent than the indolent English and Scotch-Irish because they cut rather than girdled trees can be neither denied nor confirmed. Many travelers thought American farms lacked neatness—an indication, perhaps, that girdling was ubiquitous. In 1780 Timothy Matlack speculated that girdling was commonplace because the first settlers, "full of *English* ideas of farming [his italics]," cleared by felling only, but this "broke their hearts with the labor"; poorer settlers "urged by necessity" to practice girdling got better yields. Thus the idea spread. As a confirmation of wastefulness among Germans at least, Peter Miller of Ephrata, speaking of predominantly German Cocalico Township, noted that farmers destroyed much timber each year.

The development and use of other labor-saving devices are also unclear. Cradles were discussed, and advertisements in newspapers indicate that new kinds of scythes and sickles appeared, but there are no indications of other new means of harvesting. The large amount of labor required in threshing led to the production of fans and threshing machines. Fans were noted as early as 1731. A threshing machine was specified in a German inventory in 1757, and John Clayton of Chester County was given the right by the Assembly to construct a threshing device in 1764. There is no clear indication that Germans were either more or less inclined than non-Germans toward labor-saving improvements.

Whether Germans were less inclined to use hired and indentured servants and slaves is likewise open to question. The presence of more Negro slaves among the Scotch-Irish and English has been cited as an indication of greater German self-reliance. However, most Quakers eschewed the use of slaves, after mid-century at least, and even in Scotch-Irish townships the percentage of servants and slaves on tax lists was very low—less than 4 percent of the population. Tax lists do not give the number of indentured servants, but German farmers used them. The whole question of labor in relation to the kind of agriculture practiced needs clarification. Except during harvesttime, possibly because of the greater emphasis on grain farming than on livestock, and because families averaged five or six members, hired labor was not needed continuously except on the largest farms. Certainly there are several notices in the agents' letters to the owners of the town lots of Lancaster that the poor were idle "for want of employment" except during harvest. Most of these poor were German in an area of German farms. As for the propensity for work, the Scotch-Irish women of Cumberland County were found

TABLE IV Proportions of Grains Cited in Widow's Dowers

Crop	Frequency	Average Allotment	Crop	Frequency	Average Allotment
Wheat	116 wills	13.2 bushels	Oats	11 wills	9.0 bushels
Rye	58	5.4	Buckwheat	4	4.8
Barley	17	3.8	Indian corn	13	6.3

to "do all the drugery [sic] of a family as well as any German woman you ever saw." The German women may have had the reputation, but their work load could be matched.

With respect to dietary habits, Rush asserted that the Germans were self-effacing in using cheaper grains rather than wheat for their own consumption, and that they were less inclined than others to imbibe liquor. The evidence does not support his view. Soon after Rush wrote his tract (1789) Phineas Bond reported that farmers in Pennsylvania ate rye bread when wheat prices were relatively high so that they could capitalize on the difference. But this was not stated as a general rule. In fact, when wheat was cheap in 1752, it was fed to livestock in Cocalico Township. An analysis of widow's dowers specified in the wills of farmers, chiefly "plain folk" (Table IV), indicated that generally wheat was the grain most preferred, echoing a German diarist who in 1728 noted that "wheat-bread is eaten in almost all places." Muhlenberg suggested that less palatable buckwheat was only for the poor, and corn may have been used more by non-German poor. However, Mennonites seem to have used corn as a breakfast food.

In the wills noted liquor was cited twenty-three times and cider forty-nine times. That the Germans were learning whiskey making from the Scotch-Irish in 1784, as Rush said, is without foundation; a cursory glance at tax lists and inventories indicates that reasonably affluent Germans had been distilling rye whiskey and brandy long before this. Therefore, to attribute to the Scotch-Irish the production of rye for whiskey, and to the Germans the use of rye for grain, has no empirical basis. In general, the dietary elements were similar among groups; all ate well, and the food included large amounts of meat.

Rush's statement that the Germans were "afraid of debt, and seldom purchase anything without paying cash for it," does not hold up under scrutiny, especially in view of the widespread scarcity of cash. Credit was the machinery of trade and the basis of capital. A glance at inventories listing debts, the mortgage deeds entered in deed books, and the mortgages held by the government loan office indicates widespread use of credit by Germans. In 1774, from a sample of 509 mortgagees, half of whom were farmers, 116 had German names, 249 English names, and 101 Scotch-Irish names. Bookkeeping was used as a major device to facilitate commerce.

Ownership and tenancy patterns do not show sharp differences among groups. From the tax lists it appears that tenancy was less common among English and Welsh than among Germans and Scotch-Irish (Table V), presumably a reflection of the earlier arrival of more of the English and Welsh than of the Scotch-Irish and Germans.

The degree of locational stability needs to be considered also.

TABLE V   Nonlandowners in Chester and Lancaster Counties *
(In percentages of taxable persons)

	German	English	Scotch-Irish	Welsh	Other	County
Chester 1758–1759	46	24	28	20	39	27
Chester 1782	35	26	31	20	30	27
Lancaster 1758–1759	36	27	39	14	37	36
Lancaster 1782 (present-day area)	31	36	34	18	37	32
Dauphin and Lebonon, part of Lancaster, 1782 (present-day area)	32	20	23	—	26	29

* Figures include those specified as tenants, sharecroppers, and "inmates," who generally did not work any land. In calculations the unmarried freeman was usually excluded.

Changing population distributions are shown in Table I. In both Chester and Lancaster Counties between 1760 and 1782 the majority group tended to gain at the expense of some minority groups. The tendency was most marked in the decrease of the Welsh in Chester and of the English-speaking people in Lancaster, particularly on the plain.

However, for several reasons the data in Table I cannot be used to support the contention that Germans as a national group were less mobile than others. First, the population densities in the two counties remained at about the same level between 1760 and 1790. Also, the Quakers of Chester County, like the Mennonites of Lancaster, showed a strong degree of stability. Moreover, instances of extreme German mobility can be cited. Henry Melchior Muhlenberg complained that only half of his congregation of 1742 in upper Philadelphia County (later Montgomery) were still there in 1747. On Richard Penn's "Manor of Andolhea" in the German Tulpehocken settlement in the Lebanon Valley, only three of sixteen persons who had originally settled in 1723 had lands warranted and surveyed in 1741. In Brecknock, a very poor German township in Lancaster County, less than 60 percent of the taxables of 1771 remained in 1782. These figures would seem to indicate that some Germans were highly mobile. Geographical mobility was a consequence of the desire for social and economic improvement; Germans had to deal with the problem of economical-sized farms as much as others.

In habits and customs, then, Germans do not seem to have been endowed with any more virtue than others. Two comments by the German traveler Schoepf are relevant. First, he conjectured that the Germans would have been absorbed by others had they been as small a group as

TABLE VI   Consolidated Statement of Values from a Sample of Inventories, 1713–1790*

	Inventories	Average Value (£)		Inventories	Average Value (£)
German names	160	254	Welsh names	23	261
English names	130	281	Other and		
Scotch-Irish			uncertain	51	325
names	83	254			

* An analysis of variance disclosed that at the 5 percent significance level differences among German, English, and Scotch-Irish samples were not statistically significant.

the Swedes in Berks County. Second, he told an anecdote about a German in the rather poor hilly country of northern Chester, who stated that he would rather live somewhere else, but he expressed a singular dislike for the famed Kentucky country on the Ohio, whither several of his friends were trying to persuade him to withdraw. He had heard that in Kentucky there is no real winter; and where there is no winter, he argued, people must work year in, year out, and that was not his fancy; winter, with a warm stove and sluggish days, being indispensable to his happiness.

SUCCESS IN AGRICULTURAL ACTIVITIES

Because of a paucity of data covering the productivity of farms, the best information is the economic worth of individuals as indicated in inventories and amount of taxes paid. From Table VI it appears that differences were insignificant, though a number of large inventories in the "Other and uncertain" category perhaps distort the picture. In average values of inventories English Chester and German Lancaster advanced at about the same rate between 1713 and 1790.

Corroboration can be found in tax lists. In 1758–1759 the average tax paid in Chester was 16s. 7d., as compard with 14s. 11d. in Lancaster; in 1782 the average tax was £7 18s. and £8 4s. respectively. Figures for other counties show that some strongly German counties were similar to strongly non-German ones—Berks and Cumberland for example. Moreover, among the most affluent persons, only the Welsh seem to have been excessively out of line with population distribution (Table VII). Detailed calculations for all income levels in a number of townships with mixed populations in both Chester and Lancaster also support the view that economic status did not vary greatly among national groups. Likewise, distributions of national groups did not correlate with affluence

(Figs. 5 and 9). Wealthy and poor townships were identified with each of the national groups.

The major distinction among religious groups should be noted: among the sixty wealthy Germans in Table VII nearly 60 percent were

TABLE VII   Proportions of Persons Paying Taxes of £40 or More in Lancaster County, 1782

	Number	% of Group	% of Population
German-speaking	60	67	67
English	6	7	10
Scotch-Irish	11	12	13
Welsh	6	7	1
Other and uncertain	7	8	9

Mennonites, yet Mennonites constituted only one-quarter of Lancaster's population. In Chester, Quakers headed list after list. Much of the explanation for the differential regional patterns of economic status (Fig. 9) lies in the presence of these two groups in the affluent areas. It is in part to them that credit for the productivity of Pennsylvania belongs. Of course, this should not be overstated; some Scotch-Irish Presbyterians, German Lutherans and Reformed folk, and Anglicans were also among those listed as paying more than £40 tax, and there were poor Mennonites and Quakers. What seems certain is that if the data from inventories and tax lists have a strong equivalence with productivity and success it is impossible to maintain that Germans as a national group were different from others.

PERSISTENT STEREOTYPES AND CONCEPTS

Reasonable doubt has been cast on the widespread belief that Germans were better farmers than others in eighteenth-century Pennsylvania. An obvious question that now arises is why the view was held in early Pennsylvania and why it has persisted to the present time. Fundamentally, one can speculate that many persons in the modern period of Western history have tended to differentiate national cultural traits rather sharply. The power of national states in Europe and the identification of citizens with them seem to bear witness to this view of culture. Stereotyped images of, for example, Irishmen and Frenchmen are widespread. More specifically, early Pennsylvanians inherited, I believe, a set of attitudes

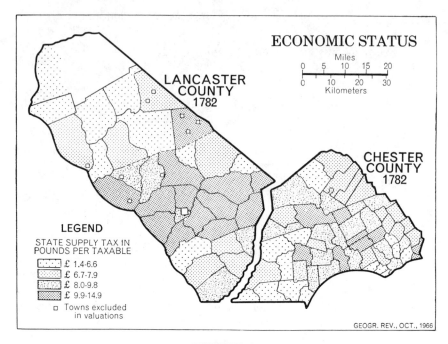

ECONOMIC STATUS

LANCASTER
COUNTY
1782

CHESTER
COUNTY
1782

LEGEND

STATE SUPPLY TAX IN
POUNDS PER TAXABLE

£ 1.4-6.6
£ 6.7-7.9
£ 8.0-9.8
£ 9.9-14.9
□ Towns excluded
  in valuations

GEOGR. REV., OCT., 1966

FIGURE 9

from England by which they judged other people. This contention is
supported by the general comments found in the literature. Rarely are
there references to "English" Pennsylvanians or "English" farming practices in America. Writers certainly spoke of Germans, Scots, and Irish,
but English Quaker farmers and other English settlers were, and still are,
largely unnoticed by scholars and others. It seems reasonable to assume
that historically we have tended to look through "English" eyes at our
society and to distinguish minority groups of Germans, Scotch-Irish, and
others in America more sharply than the "English." Given a set of stereotypes held by Englishmen about the German peasant and the Celtic
peoples, it is not surprising that these attitudes have been continued on
this side of the Atlantic.

Perpetuation of these beliefs has depended on reasons that need to
be considered briefly. Writers have generalized about a whole area from
images derived from particular regions and have adopted ideas from
other persons. Political circumstances have encouraged praise or deni-
gration of what have been thought to be distinct national groups.
Philosophical trends have also coincided with stereotypes of national

groups and have reinforced ideas about them. First, there is the transference of impressions from one area to the whole. For example, late-eighteenth-century writers regarded the well-traveled Lancaster Plain, an area inhabited by German-speaking Mennonites, as the most productive agricultural region in the state. Identification of all Germans with them, as is done today with the Amish, was easy, given a stereotyped belief in German agricultural superiority.

Similarly, eighteenth-century writers were prone to copy from others, frequently without credit. For example, Strickland in 1801 praised the German-speaking Swiss of Lancaster County for inventing meadow irrigation sluices. Because of internal contraditions in his work, noted earlier, it seems conceivable that he took this information from Thomas Pownall's description of America, first published in 1776. Pownall in turn relied heavily on correspondence and conversation with Lewis Evans. It seems, then, that ideas and information were perpetuated by writers and prominent Philadelphians. Despite the utility of travel accounts, they must be read with a discriminating eye. As for Benjamin Rush, Oliver Wendell Holmes wryly commented that he was "observing rather than a sound observer."

Travelers and others have also tended to uphold a view of German superiority for political and philosophical reasons. The editor of Rush's letters suggests that "The Manners of the German Inhabitants" was a tract designed to win the support of the German-speaking people for American nationalism and the Constitution. In the present century some works may have been written to prove that the Pennsylvania Dutch were loyal Americans. More subtle was the praise for Germans because they seemed best to exemplify rural life. Physiocratic doctrines were influential in the writings of gentlemen farmers and Philadelphians by the time Rush wrote his eulogy. Franklin, who never farmed, thought a life producing primary goods was "the only honest way." Jefferson believed that "those who labour in the earth are the chosen people of God." This praise of bucolic virtues served to strengthen support for the superiority of the German peasant, given the already existing bias that he was the best farmer.

In the late nineteenth century ethnic societies began to foster myths about their ancestors. Although the Scotch-Irish could not praise their forefathers' skill in farming, they could point to their courage and Calvinism. Of course, in excess this has resulted in attitudes of "racial" superiority. In the 1930's the Pennsylvania Dutch were identified with the wider German culture.

Ethnic superiority seems less of a live issue today. Yet the concept of "national character" is still widely used. Margaret Mead and Geoffrey Gorer, for example, have been strong proponents of the concept in general. Such an idea may be useful; in Pennsylvania certain architectural styles and food preparations had a traditional foundation in Europe, at least for a time. However, the concept has little validity for the comprehending of problems related to agriculture, or even to basic consumption habits. It seems more sensible to approach Pennsylvanians of the eighteenth century as Americans with a Western European background in which major differences in behavior and attitudes were the result of religious beliefs, social status, and economic circumstances, rather than attributable to a vague, elusive, and unchanging phenomenon called "national character." I agree with the writer in the *Pennsylvania Herald* of York in 1792, who, while referring specifically to the election of the sheriff of York County, perhaps had Rush in mind:

> [I] offer some observations on a dangerous prejudice, which has been actually fomented by a few designing men—I mean the distinction of *Dutch* and *Irish*—a distinction calculated to convulse our County—to raise and perpetuate national reflections, and to separate in interests and sentiments the nearest neighbors.
>
> What is it to me, when I am about to vote, whether the great grandmother of the candidate came from Germany or from Ireland—from the banks of the Rhine, or the Lake of Calarney—whether he and his ancestors have dined oftenest on cabbage or potatoes? . . . I don't think one of those vegetables more calculated to make an honest man or a rogue than the other. All national prejudices are the growth of a contracted mind or a silly head—it raises a distinction which destroys all enquiry into the merit of a candidate.

5

Awakening

RICHARD L. BUSHMAN

Historians have long appreciated the impact of the Great Awakening in undermining the authority of orthodox religion in particular and established institutions in general and even in creating a milieu in which revolutionary ideas could flourish. In his study of the growth of freedom in Connecticut and the impact of this freedom on human character, Richard L. Bushman places even greater emphasis on the Great Awakening. Utilizing the insights of psychology and sociology of religion, he plausibly explains the origins and success of that religious revival.

In 1721 an extraordinary number of conversions occurred in Windsor, Windham, and two parishes in Norwich. For the first time a rash of revivals occurred instead of individual instances spotted across the face of the colony at wide intervals in time. Another series, beginning in North-ampton in 1735, followed the same pattern on a much larger scale. Re-ligious excitement moved down the Connecticut Valley, eastward from the river into the back country, and in both directions along the coast.

The conversion spirit spread rapidly because religious tension was high. [Jonathan] Edwards said that news of the 1735 revival struck "like a flash of lightning, upon the hearts" of the people. Throughout the decade ministers often had to comfort "Souls in Distress under Inward Troubles." [Thomas] Clap found this pastoral work the most difficult of his duties:

Reprinted by permission of the publishers from Richard L. Bushman, *From Puritan to Yankee: Character and the Social Order in Connecticut, 1690–1795* (Cambridge, Mass.: Harvard University Press), pp. 183–95. © 1967 by the President and Fellows of Harvard College. Footnotes omitted.

"Persons are oftentimes under great Trouble and Distress of Mind," he wrote in 1732, "and sometimes brought almost to Despair." A colleague in 1737 offered suggestions on the best method of leading persons under concern "thro' the Work of Humiliation . . . unto Christ." The tide of conversions was already rising in 1740 when [George] Whitefield visited New England.

The need for an Awakening to heal society as well as to save men's souls was widely acknowledged. For eighty years the clergy had deplored the declension of piety. As vice, injustice, pride, contempt for authority, and contention in church and town became more prevalent, law after law was added to the books to restrain corruption but without appreciable effect. "There have been many Enquiries after the *Cause of our Ill State,*" lamented the election sermon of 1734, "and after proper *Means* and *Methods* of Cure: Yea, and many *Attempts,* but alas, to how little purpose!" Ministers pleaded with their congregations "*to awake out of Sleep.*" Privately they sought ways "to revive a Concern about religion." Congregations fasted and prayed to humble themselves "before God Under the sense of Leaness and bareness . . . and to Implore the divine Graces to be poured out." After the Windham revival in 1721, the pastor exclaimed, "Oh! that the same Good *Spirit from on High* were poured out upon the rest of the Country." Hearing of Whitefield's success in the middle and southern colonies, several leading New England ministers invited him to visit and preach, and Governor [Joseph] Talcott gratefully welcomed him to Connecticut in 1740.

For six weeks in September and October Whitefield toured New England, releasing a flood of religious emotions wherever he went. Along his route from Boston to Northampton, down the Connecticut Valley, and westward along the Sound hundreds were converted, and the itinerants Gilbert Tennent of New Jersey and James Davenport of Long Island continued the work through 1741 and 1742. Local ministers, adopting Whitefield's style of preaching, started revivals in their own congregations and aided neighboring pastors in theirs. The increase of admissions to full communion is a measure of the volume of religious experience.

The revivals occurred throughout the colony. Even though some areas, such as the first parish in Fairfield, did not respond, religious activity flourished all around them. Coast and inland towns, new and old towns, towns in the east and in the west participated in the Awakening. Although it was probably more intense in the east than in the west and on the coast and large rivers than inland, no area was immune to the contagion.

The Awakening affected people of all classes. One clergyman reported that men of "all orders and degrees, or all ages and characters" were converted. Edwards marveled that "some that are wealthy, and of a fashionable, gay education; some great beaus and fine ladies" cast off their vanities and humbled themselves. In town after town leading citizens participated along with more common people. A comparison of the taxes of persons admitted to communion in two Norwich parishes from 1740 to 1743 with the taxes of the town as a whole shows that economically the new converts represented an almost exact cross-section of the population.

The revivals Whitefield precipitated seemed to fulfill all the hopes placed in him. Vicious persons repented of their sins, inveterate absentees from worship returned, love for the minister waxed strong, contention in the town died away, and interest in worldly pursuits shifted to the scriptures and the state of one's soul. People could not get enough preaching: meetings were added to the regular schedule, and worshippers met privately to discuss religion. When the Hartford County Association in June 1741 urged ministers to hold extra meetings, preaching alternately for each other if necessary, it declared that the "awakening and Religious Concern, if duly cultivated and directed may have a very happy Influence to promote Religion and the Saving Conversion of Souls."

A few ministers were dubious from the start, however, and their doubts steadily darkened into dislike. The news of enthusiasm on Long Island made Daniel Wadsworth, pastor of the first church in Hartford, uncomfortable even before Whitefield arrived. Upon seeing him in October 1740, Wadsworth was uncertain "what to think of the man and his Itinerant preachings," and by the following spring "irregularities and disorders" in the town worried him. In August 1741 the Hartford Association declared against itinerants and their unjust censures of other ministers. The clergy agreed that no weight was to be given to "those screachings, cryings out, faintings and convulsions, which, sometimes attend the terrifying Language of some preachers," nor to the "Visions or visional discoveries by some of Late pretended to." The following month, after reports of Davenport's conduct had reached Hartford, Wadsworth concluded that "the great awakening etc. seemes to be degenerating into Strife and faction." Itinerants had turned people "to disputes, debates and quarrels." "Steady christians and the most Judicious among ministers and people," he observed at the end of September 1741, "generally dislike these new things set afoot by these Itinerant preachers." By the end of 1741 open opposition appeared to what had at first been considered to be a work of grace.

At the request of several ministers, the Assembly in October 1741 underwrote the expenses of a general convention of ministers to stop the "unhappy misunderstandings and divisions" in the colony and to bring about "peace, love and charity." Probably in response to the resolves of the clergy, the Assembly enacted a law in the spring of 1742 forbidding itinerants. Ministers were to obtain permission from the congregation and the pastor of a parish before preaching there. If a complaint was lodged against a pastor for preaching outside of his parish, the magistrates were not to enforce collection of his salary, and unordained persons and ministers without congregations or from other colonies were required to obtain permission before preaching. Realizing that one consociation might be more favorable to revival preachers or contentious individuals than another, the Assembly forbade any to advise or to license candidates to preach in the jurisdiction of another. Thus this act outlawed itineracy, the primary method of spreading the revival, and thereby officially denounced the Awakening. When Whitefield next visited Connecticut in 1744, most pulpits were closed to him.

Conversions waned after 1743. Only sporadic and isolated revivals occurred in the next fifty years, and none was comparable in size to the Great Awakening. But the impact of the experience was felt long afterwards. The converted were new men, with new attitudes toward themselves, their religion, their neighbors, and their rulers in church and state. A psychological earthquake had reshaped the human landscape.

What had happened to prepare so large a portion of the population for this momentous change? What power was there in the words of a sermon to plunge a person into the blackest despair and then bring him out into light and joy, a new man? The answer lay in the revivalist's message. He told his listeners that they were enemies of God and certain to be damned. When sufficiently crushed by their sinfulness, they learned that good works would never save them but that God's free grace would. This idea lifted men from their misery and restored them to confidence in God's love. Men who had come to believe that they were damnably guilty were ready to rely on unconditional grace.

The peculiarities of the Puritan personality partly account for the listeners' conviction that they were worthy only of damnation and hence wholly dependent on God's favor. Hypersensitive to overbearing authority, and always afraid of its destructive power, Puritans instinctively resisted whenever it threatened—but not without guilt. Since they could not avoid conflicts, surrounded as they were by rulers and laws, they lived in the consciousness of multiple offenses. They did not separate earthly clashes with authority from sins against God, for they believed the rulers and laws derived their power from the heavens. With life so structured, deep feelings of guilt inevitably grew.

These tensions had existed long before 1740, but despite pleas from the clergy, conversions had been few. Not until 1721 were any appreciable number of men sufficiently overpowered by their own sinfulness to rely wholly on God's grace and be converted. Two conditions prepared men for conversion: an increased desire for material wealth that ministers called worldly pride or covetousness, and the growing frequency of clashes with authority entailed in the pursuit of wealth. Both were the results of economic expansion, and both were, in the Puritan mind, offenses against God.

The Puritans' feelings about wealth were ambiguous. Even the most pious associated it with a secure place in the community and divine approval, and everyone accorded great respect to rich men, numbering them among the rulers of society. Prosperity was a sign of good character: all were expected to practice industry and thrift, the virtues that brought the rewards of wealth. To some extent worldly success was a token of God's favor: none felt constrained to stint their efforts to prosper in their callings.

Yet the dangers of riches also were well known. The rich were prone to *"fall into Temptation,"* Cotton Mather warned, and be *"drowned in Perdition."* "There is a venom in *Riches,"* he said, "disposing our depraved Hearts, to cast off their *Dependence* on *God."* It was a maxim of the Jeremiads that "where a Selfish, Covetous spirit and Love of this world prevails, there the Love of God decayeth." When Connecticut's first published poet, Roger Wolcott, occupied himself with the theme of the divine wrath visited on seekers of earthly honor and wealth, he explained that he might have chosen the path of pride himself, "but that I see Hells flashes folding through Eternities." In this world money answered everything but a guilty conscience.

The contradiction in the prevailing attitudes toward wealth perplexed both the ministers and the people. Pastors complained that men excused avarice as justifiable enterprise. "They will plead in defense of a Worldly Covetous spirit, under the colour or specious pretence of Prudence, Diligence, Frugality, Necessity." Cotton Mather lamented that even the farmer was grasped with worldliness, yet he turned away rebukes with the assertion that he was merely pursuing his calling as a husbandman. The people could not distinguish respectable industry from covetousness: their ambitions drove them on year after year, while self-doubts were never far below the surface. Robert Keayne, the wealthy Boston merchant of the early period, built a fine fortune, but at great cost. When censured by the clergy for acting against the public good, he was crushed and, in a document written to clear himself of guilt, poured out the tensions he had long felt.

Throughout the seventeenth century a few Puritans experienced Keayne's miseries, but the temptations of worldly pride were too remote to hurt the consciences of most. The opportunities for gain were largely inaccessible to ordinary men until after 1690, when economic expansion opened new prospects to many more farmers and merchants. Common men could take up a small trade or invest in a ship sailing to the West Indies, and land purchased in a new plantation doubled in value within a few years. The expansive economy of the early eighteenth century unleashed ambitions restrained by the absence of opportunity. Everyone hoped to prosper; the demand for land banks and the 300 percent increase in per capita indebtedness were measures of the eagerness for wealth. An indentured farmhand in the 1740's complained that his master never spoke about religion: "His whole attention was taken up on the pursuits of the good things of this world; wealth was his supreme object. I am afraid gold was his God."

In the midst of this economic growth, the ministers faithfully excoriated the spreading worldliness. It was obvious, one minister wrote, "that the Heart of a People is gone off from God and gone after the Creature; that they are much more concerned about getting Land and Money and Stock, than they be about getting Religion revived." "The Concern is not as heretofore to accommodate themselves as to the Worship of God," it was said in 1730, "but Where they can have most Land, and be under best advantages to get Money." These accusations were put aside with the usual rationalizations, but so long as the ministers reminded men that riches cankered their souls, a grave uncertainty haunted everyone who pursued wealth.

The desire to prosper also precipitated clashes with law and authority, adding to accumulating guilt. With increasing frequency after 1690 people fought their rulers or balked at the laws, usually as a consequence of their ambition. Such friction wore away confidence as it convinced men inwardly of their own culpability.

Under more peaceful circumstances law and authority protected the Puritan from the asperities of his own doctrines. Taken seriously, Puritan theology kept men in unbearable suspense about their standing with God: He chose whom He would to be saved, and the rest were cast into the fires of hell. But the founding fathers had qualified this pure conception of divine sovereignty by stressing the authority vested in the social order. Since civil and ecclesiastical rulers were commissioned by God and the laws of society were an expression of His will, obedience to Connecticut's government was in effect obedience to divine government, and the good will of the rulers was an omen of God's good will. So long as man complied with the law and submitted to authority, he was safe from divine punishment.

After 1690, in their ambition to prosper, people disregarded the demands of social order. Nonproprietors contested the control of town lands with proprietors, and outlivers struggled with the leaders in the town center to obtain an independent parish. In the civil government settlers fought for a clear title to their lands and new traders for currency. Church members resisted the enlargement of the minister's power or demanded greater piety in his preaching. All these controversies pitted common men against rulers and the laws.

Under these circumstances the social order became a menace to peace of mind rather than a shield against divine wrath. Just as conformity gave an inward assurance of moral worth, so resistance, even in spirit, was blameworthy. Dissenters, in politics or economics as well as religion, could not oppose the community fathers whom God had set to rule without feeling guilty. Even when a move to the outlands or complaints about a minister's arrogance were well justified, the participants in the action feared that they sinned in resisting.

Few men in 1740 were outright rebels, for strong loyalties still bound almost all to their communities. By comparison to their forebears of 1690, however, this later generation was estranged. It could not comfort itself in the recollection of a life of conformity to the divinely sanctioned order. In part it was emboldened by the wealth it had sought and often gained, but that provided an unsteady support when the pursuit of riches was so often condemned. However hardened the contentious appeared, guilt generated by an undue love of wealth and by resistance to the social order had hollowed out their lives.

East of the Connecticut River, in the most rapidly expanding section of the colony, turmoil was greatest. Extravagant growth plunged the towns into strife over land titles, currency, and religion. The party battles loosened the social structure and alienated men from their social and religious leaders. Economic opportunity also aroused the hunger for land and commercial success. Here the revival was noticeably most intense. "Whatever be the reason," Ezra Stiles commented later, "the eastern part of Connecticut . . . are of a very mixt and uncertain character as to religion. Exhorters, Itinerants, Separate Meetings rose in that part." Around three-quarters of the separations between 1740 and 1755 occurred east of the Connecticut River. The greatest number in any town —four—were in Norwich, the commercial center of the east. Nearby towns—New London, Groton, Stonington, Lyme, Windham, and Preston —had similarly prospered, and a third of the separations in the colony took place in these towns and Norwich. These departures, roughly measuring the fervor of the Awakening, were the outcome of the personal instability eastern men felt after a half-century of extraordinary expansion.

Before Whitefield arrived, ministers sensed the shaky state of their parishioners' confidence. One pastor noted the grave uncertainty of people under spiritual concern: "They want to know they shall be sure they believe, that they love God, that they are in the right way, are sincere and the like." As the ministers recognized, an outward show usually covered somber doubts: reprobates disguised or fled from their real condition while inwardly they suffered from a consciousness of guilt.

Whitefield broke through this facade. Though he stood apart from the established clergy, he was accepted by them. He did not represent the repressive ministerial rule which entered so largely into the conflicts of the period but nevertheless came clothed with acknowledged authority. The revivals he started in the middle colonies also imbued him with a reputation of extraordinary power. "Hearing how god was with him every where as he came along," one awakened person later reported, "it solumnized my mind and put me in a trembling fear before he began to preach for he looked as if he was Cloathed with authority from the great god." Besides, he was an impassioned and fluent preacher.

Whitefield moved his hearers because excessive worldliness and resistance to the divinely sanctioned social order had already undermined their confidence. He told men what they already knew subconsciously: that they had broken the law, that impulses beyond their control drove them to resist divine authority, and that outward observance did not signify loving and willing submission. Confronted with truth, his listeners admitted that they were "vile, unworthy, loathsom" wretches. "Hearing him preach," a converted man said, "gave me a heart wound. By gods blessing my old foundation was broken up and i saw that my righteousness would not save me."

This confrontation of guilt, the first part of conversion, drove men to despair, but the revivalists did not leave their hearers there to suffer. By publicly identifying the sources of guilt and condemning them, the preachers also helped to heal the wounds they first inflicted. Converts were persuaded that by acknowledging and repudiating their old sins, they were no longer culpable. The reborn man was as joyful and loving when the process was completed as he was miserable at its start.

Converts were told, for instance, that wealth held no attractions for the saintly. The business of Christ's disciples, one preacher taught, "is not to hunt for Riches, and Honours, and Pleasures in this World, but to despise them, and deny themselves, and be ready to part with even all the lawful Pleasures of Comforts of the World at any Time." In a dramatic gesture expressing a deep impulse, Davenport had his followers gather the symbols of worldliness—wigs, cloaks, hoods, gowns, rings, necklaces—into a heap and burn them.

Converts responded eagerly, casting off with great relief their guilt-producing ambition. The pious David Brainerd spontaneously broke into poetry:

> Farewell, vain world; my soul can bid Adieu:
> May Saviour's taught me to abandon you.

After Isaac Backus was converted, he felt that he "should not be troubled any more with covetousness. The earth and all that is therein appeared to be vanity." His mother, also a convert, felt ready to "give up my name, estate, family, life and breath, freely to God." She would not relinquish her peace of soul "no, not to be in the most prosperous condition in temporal things that ever I was in." For many the choice was to enjoy peace of soul or prosperity. The pursuit of wealth and an easy conscience were incompatible. Jonathan Edwards noted a temptation among converts to go to extremes and "to neglect worldly affairs too much." They were unwilling to jeopardize their newfound peace by returning to worldliness.

The revivalists undermined the social order, the other main source of guilt, not by repudiating law and authority, but by denying them sanctifying power. Estrangement from rulers and the traditional patterns of life was demoralizing as long as the social order was considered divine, but Awakening preachers repeatedly denied that salvation came by following the law. No amount of covenant owning, Sabbath observance, moral rectitude, or obedience to rulers redeemed the soul. Praying, Bible study, and attendance at worship might result solely from worldly motives, to avoid disgrace or to pacify a guilty conscience. "Civility and external Acts belonging to Morality," one revivalist taught, "are no Part of the Essence of the Religion of Christ." Without grace, "tho men are adorn'd with many amiable qualities, and lead sober, regular, and to all appearance religious lives, yet they remain under the condemning sentence of the Law, and perish at last in a state of unsanctified nature." Reborn men were expected to practice moral virtues, but their salvation was not at stake. Obedience brought no assurance of grace, and disobedience did not entail damnation. Though still driven to resist rulers or to depart from the approved pattern of community life, believers in the revival message felt little guilt.

In this fashion the Awakening cleared the air of tensions. Men admitted that they had lusted after wealth, condemned themselves for it, and afterwards walked with lighter hearts. They ended the long struggle with the social order by denying its power to save and hence to condemn. After a century of Puritan rule, law and authority were burdens too heavy to bear. All the anxiety they evoked was released when men grasped the idea that salvation came not by obedience to law.

In the converts' minds the escape from guilt was possible because of God's grace. The idea that the law could not condemn if God justified contained the deepest meaning of the Awakening. The rules and rulers, who governed both externally and in the conscience, had judged men and found them wanting until God out of His good grace suspended the sentence of damnation. The authority of Christ nullified earthly authority. Edwards said that converted men exulted that "God is self-sufficient, and infinitely above all dependence, and reigns over all." In the inward struggle with guilt, God's infinite power overruled the older authority that had stood over every Puritan conscience, judging and condemning.

In that moment of grace the Awakening worked its revolution. Henceforth a personal relation with God governed reborn men who were empowered by faith to obey the God they knew personally above the divine will manifest in earthly law and authority. It was characteristic of the converted to "renounce all confidence in everything but Christ, and build all their hopes of happiness upon this unalterable Rock of Ages." "I seemed to depend wholly on my dear Lord," Brainerd reported following his conversion. "God was so precious to my soul that the world with all its enjoyments was infinitely vile. I had no more value for the favor of men than for pebbles. The Lord was my ALL." Though the old authority was still a substantial force in every life, it did not structure the identity of converts as much as their own bright picture of God.

Under the government of this personal, internal authority, converts experienced a peace and joy unknown under earthly fathers and their old conscience. God's grace dissolved uncertainty and fear. The convert testified to the "sweet solace, rest and joy of soul," the image of God bestowed. "The thought of having so great, so glorious, and excellent a Being for his Father, his Friend, and his Home, sets his heart at Ease from all his anxious Fears and Distresses." The power to replace oppressive authority figures with faith in a loving God was the ultimate reason for the revivalists' success.

Thus the men affected by the Awakening possessed a new character, cleansed of guilt and joyful in the awareness of divine favor. Unfortunately for the social order, however, their personal redemption did not save society. In making peace with themselves, converts inwardly revolted against the old law and authority, and, as time was to show, they would eventually refuse to submit to a social order alien to their new identity. Conservative suspicions of the revival were confirmed when reborn men set out to create a new society compatible with the vision opened in the Great Awakening.

6

Economic Development
and Social Structure
in Colonial Boston

JAMES A. HENRETTA

The traditional notion that colonial New England fostered political and economic democracy through its town meetings and its system of adequate property holdings received a tremendous boost from Robert E. Brown's *Middle-Class Democracy and the Revolution in Massachusetts, 1691-1780* (1955). Brown's carefully documented work argued that, with its strong middle class, Massachusetts—and perhaps all the colonies—was democratic before the Revolution and that the Revolution grew out of that democracy. Since no place in America was more important to the revolutionary movement than Boston, an analysis of its social structure helps evaluate democracy's role in bringing on the Revolution. By comparing the quantitative data afforded by 1687 and 1771 tax lists, James A. Henretta measures the changes in Boston's social structure and finds them anything but democratic.

A distinctly urban social structure developed in Boston in the 150 years between the settlement of the town and the American Revolution. The expansion of trade and industry after 1650 unleashed powerful economic forces which first distorted, then destroyed, the social homogeneity and cohesiveness of the early village community. All aspects of town life were affected by Boston's involvement in the dynamic, competitive world of

From *William and Mary Quarterly*, 3d ser., 22 (January 1965):75–92. Footnotes omitted. Reprinted by permission of the author.

Atlantic commerce. The disruptive pressure of rapid economic growth, sustained for over a century, made the social appearance of the town more diverse, more complex, more modern—increasingly different from that of the rest of New England. The magnitude of the change in Boston's social composition and structure may be deduced from an analysis and comparison of the tax lists for 1687 and 1771. Containing a wealth of information on property ownership in the community, these lists make it possible to block out, in quantitative terms, variations in the size and influence of economic groups and to trace the change in the distribution of the resources of the community among them.

The transformation of Boston from a land-based society to a maritime center was neither sudden nor uniform. In the last decade of the seventeenth century, a large part of the land of its broad peninsula was still cultivated by small farmers. Only a small fraction was laid out in regular streets and even less was densely settled. The north end alone showed considerable change from the middle of the century when almost every house had a large lot and garden. Here, the later-comers—the mariners, craftsmen, and traders who had raised the population to six thousand by 1690—were crowded together along the waterfront. Here, too, in the series of docks and shipyards which jutted out from the shore line, were tangible manifestations of the commercial activity which had made the small town the largest owner of shipping and the principal port of the English colonies. Over 40 per cent of the carrying capacity of all colonial-owned shipping was in Boston hands.

Dependence on mercantile endeavor rather than agricultural enterprise had by 1690 greatly affected the extent of property ownership. Boston no longer had the universal ownership of real estate characteristic of rural Massachusetts to the end of the colonial period. The tax list for 1687 contained the names of 188 polls, 14 per cent of the adult male population, who were neither owners of taxable property of any kind nor "dependents" in a household assessed for the property tax. Holding no real estate, owning no merchandise or investments which would yield an income, these men constituted the "propertyless" segment of the community and were liable only for the head tax which fell equally upon all men above the age of sixteen. Many in this group were young men, laborers and seamen, attracted by the commercial prosperity of the town and hoping to save enough from their wages to buy or rent a shop, to invest in the tools of an artisan, or to find a start in trade. John Erving, a poor Scotch sailor whose grandson in 1771 was one of the richest men in Boston, was only one propertyless man who rose quickly to a position of wealth and influence.

But many of these 188 men did not acquire either taxable property or an established place in the social order of Boston. Only sixty-four, or

35 per cent, were inhabitants of the town eight years later. By way of contrast, 45 per cent of the polls assessed from two to seven pounds on the tax list, 65 per cent of those with property valued from eight to twenty pounds, and 73 per cent of those with estates in excess of twenty pounds were present in 1695. There was a direct relation between permanence of residence and economic condition. Even in an expanding and diversifying economic environment, the best opportunities for advancement rested with those who could draw upon long-standing connections, upon the credit facilities of friends and neighbors, and upon political influence. It was precisely these personal contacts which were denied to the propertyless.

A second, distinct element in the social order consisted of the dependents of property owners. Though propertyless themselves, these dependents—grown sons living at home, apprentices, and indentured servants—were linked more closely to the town as members of a tax-paying household unit than were the 188 "unattached" men without taxable estates. Two hundred and twelve men, nearly one sixth of the adult male population of Boston, were classified as dependents in 1687. The pervasiveness of the dependency relationship attested not only to the cohesiveness of the family unit but also to the continuing vitality of the apprenticeship and indenture system at the close of the seventeenth century.

Yet even the dependency relationship, traditionally an effective means of alleviating unemployment and preventing the appearance of unattached propertyless laborers, was subjected to severe pressure by the expansion of the economy. An urgent demand for labor, itself the cause of short indentures, prompted servants to strike out on their own as soon as possible. They became the laborers or semiskilled craftsmen of the town, while the sons of the family eventually assumed control of their father's business and a share of the economic resources of the community.

The propertied section of the population in 1687 was composed of 1,036 individuals who were taxed on their real estate or their income from trade. The less-skilled craftsmen, 521 men engaged in the rougher trades of a waterfront society, formed the bottom stratum of the taxable population in this pre-industrial age. These carpenters, shipwrights, blacksmiths, shopkeepers owned only 12 per cent of the taxable wealth of the town. Few of these artisans and laborers had investments in shipping or in merchandise. A small store or house, or a small farm in the south end of Boston, accounted for their assessment of two to seven pounds on the tax list. (Table I)

Between these craftsmen and shopkeepers and the traders and merchants who constituted the economic elite of the town was a middle group of 275 property owners with taxable assets valued from eight to twenty

TABLE I   Distribution of Assessed Taxable Wealth in Boston in 1687

Total Value of Taxable Wealth	Number of Taxpayers in Each Wealth Bracket	Total Wealth in Each Wealth Bracket	Cumulative Total of Wealth	Cumulative Total of Taxpayers	Cumulative Percentage of Taxpayers	Cumulative Percentage of Wealth
£ 1	0	£ 0	£ 0	0	0.0%	0.0%
2	152	304	304	152	14.6	1.8
3	51	153	457	203	19.5	2.7
4	169	676	1,133	372	35.9	6.8
5	33	165	1,298	405	39.0	7.8
6	97	582	1,880	502	48.5	11.3
7	19	133	2,013	521	50.2	12.1
8	43	344	2,357	564	54.4	14.2
9	22	198	2,555	586	56.6	15.4
10	45	450	3,005	631	60.9	18.1
11	17	187	3,192	648	62.5	19.2
12	30	360	3,552	678	65.4	21.4
13	13	169	3,721	691	66.6	22.4
14	12	168	3,889	703	67.9	23.4
15	22	330	4,219	725	69.9	25.4
16	21	336	4,555	746	72.0	27.5
17	1	17	4,572	747	72.0	27.6
18	18	324	4,896	765	73.8	29.5
19	1	19	4,915	766	73.9	29.6
20	30	600	5,515	796	76.8	33.2
21–25	41	972	6,487	837	80.7	39.0
26–30	48	1,367	7,854	885	85.4	47.3
31–35	29	971	8,825	914	88.2	53.1
36–40	21	819	9,644	935	90.2	58.1
41–45	19	828	10,472	954	92.1	63.1
46–50	16	781	11,253	970	93.6	67.8
51–60	16	897	12,150	986	95.1	73.2
61–70	19	1,245	13,395	1,005	97.0	80.7
71–80	7	509	13,904	1,012	97.8	83.8
81–90	3	253	14,157	1,015	97.9	85.3
91–100	7	670	14,827	1,022	98.6	89.3
100–	14	1,764	16,591	1,036	100.0	100.0

TABLE II   Distribution of Assessed Taxable Wealth in Boston in 1771

Total Value of Taxable Wealth	Number of Taxpayers in Each Wealth Bracket	Total Wealth in Each Wealth Bracket	Cumulative Total of Wealth	Cumulative Total of Taxpayers	Cumulative Percentage of Taxpayers	Cumulative Percentage of Wealth
£ 3–30	78	£ 1,562	£ 1,562	78	5.0%	0.3%
31–40	86	2,996	4,558	164	10.6	0.9
41–50	112	5,378	9,936	276	17.9	2.2
51–60	74	4,398	14,334	350	22.6	3.5
61–70	33	3,122	17,456	383	24.7	3.8
71–80	165	12,864	30,320	548	35.4	6.5
81–90	24	2,048	32,368	572	36.9	7.0
91–100	142	13,684	46,052	714	46.1	10.0
101–110	14	494	46,546	728	47.1	10.1
111–120	149	17,844	64,390	877	56.7	13.9
121–130	20	2,570	66,960	897	58.0	14.5
131–140	26	4,600	71,560	923	59.7	15.5
141–150	20	2,698	74,258	943	60.9	16.1
151–160	88	14,048	88,306	1,031	66.6	19.1
161–170	11	1,846	90,152	1,042	67.4	19.6
171–180	18	3,128	93,280	1,060	68.6	20.3
181–190	10	1,888	95,168	1,070	69.2	20.7
191–200	47	9,368	104,536	1,117	72.2	22.7
201–300	126	31,097	135,633	1,243	80.4	29.4
301–400	60	21,799	157,432	1,303	84.2	34.1
401–500	58	24,947	182,379	1,361	88.0	39.6
501–600	14	7,841	190,220	1,375	88.9	41.3
601–700	24	15,531	205,751	1,399	90.4	44.6
701–800	26	19,518	225,269	1,425	92.2	48.9
801–900	20	17,020	242,289	1,445	93.4	52.6
901–1,000	16	15,328	257,617	1,461	95.4	55.9
1,001–1,500	41	48,364	305,963	1,502	97.1	66.4
1,501–5,000	37	85,326	391,289	1,539	99.5	84.9
5,001–	7	69,204	460,493	1,546	100.0	100.0

pounds. Affluent artisans employing two or three workers, ambitious shopkeepers with investments in commerce, and entrepreneurial-minded sea masters with various maritime interests, bulked large in this center portion of the economic order. Of the 275, 180 owned real estate assessed at seven pounds or less and were boosted into the third quarter of the distribution of wealth by their holdings of merchandise and shares in shipping. (Table III) The remaining ninety-five possessed real estate rated at eight pounds or more and, in addition, held various investments in trade. Making up about 25 per cent of the propertied population, this middle group controlled 22 per cent of the taxable wealth in Boston in 1687. Half as numerous as the lowest group of property owners, these men possessed almost double the amount of taxable assets. (Table I)

Merchants with large investments in English and West Indian trade and individuals engaged in the ancillary industries of shipbuilding and distilling made up the top quarter of the taxable population in 1687. With taxable estates ranging from twenty to 170 pounds, this commercial group controlled 66 per cent of the town's wealth. But economic development had been too rapid, too uneven and incomplete, to allow the emergence of a well-defined merchant class endowed with a common outlook and clearly distinguished from the rest of the society. Only eighty-five of these men, one third of the wealthiest group in the community, owned dwellings valued at as much as twenty pounds. The majority held landed property valued at ten pounds, only a few pounds greater than that of the middle group of property holders. (Table III) The merchants had not shared equally in the accumulated fund of capital and experience which had accrued after fifty years of maritime activity. Profits had flowed to those whose daring initiative and initial resources had begun the exploitation of the lucrative colonial market. By 1687, the upper 15 per cent of the property owners held 52 per cent of the taxable assets of the town, while the fifty individuals who composed the highest 5 per cent of the taxable population accounted for more than 25 per cent of the wealth. (Table I)

By the end of the seventeenth century widespread involvement in commerce had effected a shift in the locus of social and political respectability in Boston and distinguished it from the surrounding communities. Five of the nine selectmen chosen by the town in 1687 were sea captains. This was more than deference to those accustomed to command. With total estates of £83, £29, £33, £33, and £24, Captains Elisha Hutchinson, John Fairweather, Theophilus Frary, Timothy Prout, and Daniel Turell were among the wealthiest 20 per cent of the population. Still, achievement in trade was not the only index of respectability. Henry Eames, George Cable, Isaac Goose, and Elnathan Lyon, the men appointed by the town to inspect the condition of the streets and roads, had the greater part of their wealth, £105 of £130, invested in land and live-

TABLE III   Real Estate Ownership in Boston in 1687 and 1771

1687			1771		
Assessed Total Value of Real Estate	Number of Owners	Cumulative Total of Owners	Assessed Annual Worth of Real Estate	Number of Owners	Cumulative Total of Owners
£ 1	0	0	£ 1	0	0
2	168	168	2	1	1
3	75	243	3	9	10
4	203	446	4	49	59
5	85	531	5	22	81
6	167	698	6	79	160
7	3	701	7	0	160
8	54	755	8	115	275
9	2	757	9	3	278
10	107	864	10	91	369
11	0	864	11	4	373
12	24	888	12	43	416
13	0	888	13	163	579
14	3	891	14	10	589
15	25	916	15	3	592
16	8	924	16	148	740
17	0	924	17	6	746
18	7	931	18	7	753
19	1	932	19	5	758
20	46	978	20	236	994
21–30	25	1,003	21–25	41	1,035
31–40	11	1,014	26–30	163	1,198
41–50	2	1,016	31–35	93	1,291
			36–40	92	1,383
			41–45	5	1,388
			46–50	42	1,430
			51–60	32	1,462
			61–70	10	1,472
			71–80	9	1,481
			81–90	3	1,484
			91–100	3	1,487

stock. And the presence of Deacon Henry Allen among the selectmen provided a tangible indication of the continuing influence of the church.

These legacies of an isolated religious society and a stable agricultural economy disappeared in the wake of the rapid growth which continued unabated until the middle of the eighteenth century. In the fifty years after 1690, the population of the town increased from 6,000 to 16,000. The farms of the south end vanished and the central business district became crowded. In the populous north end, buildings which had once housed seven people suddenly began to hold nine or ten. Accompanying this physical expansion of Boston was a diversification of economic endeavor. By 1742, the town led all the colonial cities in the production of export furniture and shoes, although master craftsmen continued to carry on most industry on a small scale geared to local needs. Prosperity and expansion continued to be rooted, not in the productive capacity or geographic position of the town, but in the ability of the Boston merchants to compete successfully in the highly competitive mercantile world.

After 1750, the economic health of the Massachusetts seaport was jeopardized as New York and Philadelphia merchants, exploiting the rich productive lands at their backs and capitalizing upon their prime geographic position in the West Indian and southern coasting trade, diverted a significant portion of European trade from the New England traders. Without increasing returns from the lucrative "carrying" trade, Boston merchants could no longer subsidize the work of the shopkeepers, craftsmen, and laborers who supplied and maintained the commercial fleet. By 1760, the population of Boston had dropped to 15,000 persons, a level it did not exceed until after the Revolution.

The essential continuity of maritime enterprise in Boston from the late seventeenth to the mid-eighteenth century concealed the emergence of a new type of social system. After a certain point increases in the scale and extent of commercial endeavor produced a new, and more fluid, social order. The development of the economic system subjected the family, the basic social unit, to severe pressures. The fundamental link between one generation and another, the ability of the father to train his offspring for their life's work, was endangered by a process of change which rendered obsolete many of the skills and assumptions of the older, land-oriented generation and opened the prospect of success in new fields and new places. The well-known departure of Benjamin Franklin from his indenture to his brother was but one bright piece in the shifting mosaic of colonial life.

The traditional family unit had lost much of its cohesiveness by the third quarter of the eighteenth century. The Boston tax lists for 1771 indicate that dependents of property owners accounted for only 10 per cent of the adult male population as opposed to 16 per cent eighty-five years earlier. Increasingly children left their homes at an earlier age to seek their own way in the world.

A second factor in the trend away from dependency status was the decline in the availability of indentured servants during the eighteenth century. Fewer than 250 of 2,380 persons entering Boston from 1764 to 1768 were classified as indentured servants. These were scarcely enough to replace those whose indentures expired. More and more, the labor force had to be recruited from the ranks of "unattached" workers who bartered their services for wages in a market economy.

This laboring force consisted of the nondependent, propertyless workers of the community, now twice as numerous relative to the rest of the population as they had been a century before. In 1687, 14 per cent of the total number of adult males were without taxable property; by the eve of the Revolution, the propertyless accounted for 29 per cent. The social consequences of this increase were manifold. For every wage earner who competed in the economy as an autonomous entity at the end of the seventeenth century, there were four in 1771; for every man who slept in the back of a shop, in a tavern, or in a rented room in 1687, there were four in the later period. The population of Boston had doubled, but the number of propertyless men had increased fourfold.

The adult males without property, however, did not form a single unified class, a monolithic body of landless proletarians. Rather, the bottom of society consisted of a congeries of social and occupational groups with a highly transient maritime element at one end of the spectrum and a more stable and respected artisan segment at the other. Although they held no taxable property, hard-working and reputable craftsmen who had established a permanent residence in Boston participated in the town meeting and were elected to unpaid minor offices. In March 1771, for instance, John Dyer was selected by the people of the town as "Fence Viewer" for the following year. Yet according to the tax and valuation lists compiled less than six months later, Dyer was without taxable property. At the same town meeting, four carpenters, Joseph Ballard, Joseph Edmunds, Benjamin Page, and Joseph Butler, none of whom was listed as an owner of taxable property on the valuation lists, were chosen as "Measurers of Boards." That propertyless men should be selected for public office indicates that the concept of a "stake in society," which provided the theoretical underpinning for membership in the community of colonial Boston, was interpreted in the widest possible sense. Yet it was this very conception of the social order which was becoming anachronistic under the pressure of economic development. For how could the growing number of propertyless men be integrated into a social order based in the first instance on the principle that only those having a tangible interest in the town or a definite family link to the society would be truly interested in the welfare of the community?

Changes no less significant had taken place within the ranks of the propertied groups. By the third quarter of the eighteenth century, lines of economic division and marks of social status were crystalizing as Boston approached economic maturity. Present to some degree in all aspects of town life, these distinctions were very apparent in dwelling arrangements. In 1687, 85 per cent of Boston real estate holdings had been assessed within a narrow range of two to ten pounds; by the seventh decade of the eighteenth century, the same spectrum ran from twelve to two hundred pounds. (Table III) Gradations in housing were finer in 1771 and had social connotations which were hardly conceivable in the more primitive and more egalitarian society of the seventeenth century. This sense of distinctiveness was reinforced by geographic distribution. Affluent members of the community who had not transferred their residence to Roxbury, Cambridge, or Milton built in the spacious environs of the south and west ends. A strict segregation of the social groups was lacking; yet the milieu of the previous century, the interaction of merchant, trader, artisan, and laborer in a waterfront community, had all but disappeared.

The increasing differences between the social and economic groups within the New England seaport stemmed in part from the fact that craftsmen, laborers, and small shopkeepers had failed to maintain their relative position in the economic order. In the eighty-five years from 1687 to 1771, the share of the taxable wealth of the community controlled by the lower half of the propertied population declined from 12 to 10 per cent. (Table II) If these men lived better at the end of the century than at the beginning, it was not because the economic development of Boston had effected a redistribution of wealth in favor of the laboring classes but because the long period of commercial prosperity had raised the purchasing power of every social group.

The decline in the economic distinctiveness of the middle group of property holders, the third quarter of the taxable population in the distribution of wealth, is even more significant. In 1771, these well-to-do artisans, shopkeepers, and traders (rising land values had eliminated the farmers and economic maturity the versatile merchant-sea captain) owned only 12½ per cent of the taxable wealth, a very substantial decrease from the 21 per cent held in 1687. These men lived considerably better than their counterparts in the seventeenth century; many owned homes and possessed furnishings rarely matched by the most elegant dwellings of the earlier period. But in relation to the other parts of the social order, their economic position had deteriorated drastically. This smaller middle group had been assessed for taxable estates twice as large as the bottom 50 per cent in 1687; by 1771 the assets of the two groups were equal.

On the other hand, the wealthiest 25 per cent of the taxable population by 1771 controlled 78 per cent of the assessed wealth of Boston. This represented a gain of 12 per cent from the end of the seventeenth century. An equally important shift had taken place within this elite portion of the population. In 1687, the richest 15 per cent of the taxpayers held 52 per cent of the taxable property, while the top 5 per cent owned 26.8 per cent. Eighty-five years later, the percentages were 65.9 and 44.1. (Tables I and II and Chart A)

Certain long-term economic developments accounted for the disappearance of a distinct middle group of property owners and the accumulation of wealth among a limited portion of the population.

CHART A *Lorenz Curves Showing the Distribution of Wealth in Boston in 1687 and 1771 (Drawn from data in Tables I and II.)*

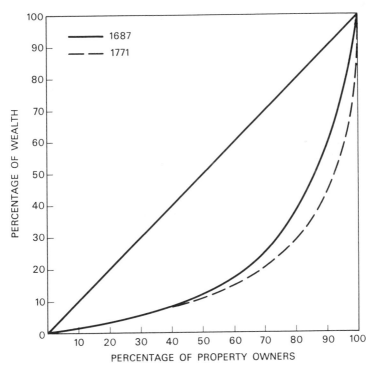

The scarcity of capital in a relatively underdeveloped economic system, one in which barter transactions were often necessary because of the lack of currency, required that the savings of all members of the society be tapped in the interest of economic expansion. The prospect of rapid commercial success and the high return on capital invested in mercantile activity attracted the small investor. During the first decade of the eighteenth century, nearly one of every three adult males in Boston was involved directly in trade, owning at least part of a vessel. In 1698 alone, 261 people held shares in a seagoing vessel. Trade had become "not so much a way of life as a way of making money; not a social condition but an economic activity." This widespread owner-ship of mercantile wealth resulted in the creation of a distinct economic "middle class" by the last decades of the seventeenth century.

A reflection of a discrete stage of economic growth, the involve-ment of disparate occupational and social groups in commerce was fleeting and transitory. It lasted only as long as the economy of the New England seaport remained underdeveloped, without large amounts of available capital. The increase in the wealth and resources of the town during the first half of the eighteenth century prompted a grow-ing specialization of economic function; it was no longer necessary to rely on the investments of the less affluent members of the community for an expansion of commerce. This change was slow, almost imper-ceptible; but by 1771 the result was obvious. In that year, less than 5 per cent of the taxable population of Boston held shares in shipping of ten tons or more, even though the tonnage owned by the town was almost double that of 1698. Few men had investments of less than fifty tons; the average owner held 112 tons. By way of contrast, the average holding at the end of the seventeenth century had been about twenty-five tons. Moreover, on the eve of the Revolution ownership of shipping was concentrated among the wealthiest men of the community. Ninety per cent of the tonnage of Boston in 1771 was in the hands of those whose other assets placed them in the top quarter of the population. With the increase in the wealth of the town had come a great increase in the number of propertyless men and a bifocalization of the property owners into (1) a large amorphous body of shopkeepers, artisans, and laborers with holdings primarily in real estate and (2) a smaller, somewhat more closely defined segment of the population with exten-sive commercial investments as well as elegant residences and personal possessions.

A similar trend was evident in other phases of town life. In the transitional decades of the late seventeenth and early eighteenth cen-tury, the fluidity inherent in the primitive commercial system had produced a certain vagueness in the connotations of social and economic status. Over 10 per cent of the adult males in Boston designated themselves as "merchants" on the shipping registers of the period from 1698 to 1714, indicating not only the decline in the distinctiveness of a title traditionally limited to a carefully defined part of the community but also the feeling that any man could easily ascend the mercantile ladder. Economic opportunity was so evident, so promising, that the social demarcations of the more stable maritime communities of England seemed incongruous. By the sixth decade of the eighteenth century, however, rank and order were supplanting the earlier chaos as successful families tightened their control of trade. The founding in 1763 of a "Merchants Club" with 146 members was a dramatic indication that occupations and titles were regaining some of their traditional distinctiveness and meaning.

An economic profile of the 146 men who composed this self-constituted elite is revealing. Of those whose names appeared on the tax and valuation lists of 1771, only five had estates which placed them in the bottom three quarters of the distribution of wealth. Twenty-one were assessed for taxable property in excess of £1,500 and were thus in the top 1 per cent of the economic scale. The taxable assets of the rest averaged £650, an amount which put them among the wealthiest 15 per cent of the population.

That 146 men, 6½ per cent of the adult male population, were considered eligible for membership in a formal society of merchants indicates, however, that mercantile activity was not dominated by a narrow oligarchy. The range of wealth among the members of the top quarter of the propertied population was so great and the difference of social background so large as to preclude the creation of a monolithic class or guild with shared interests and beliefs.

Yet the influence of this segment of society was pervasive. By the third quarter of the eighteenth century, an integrated economic and political hierarchy based on mercantile wealth had emerged in Boston to replace the lack of social stratification of the early part of the century and the archaic distinctions of power and prestige of the religious community of the seventeenth century. All of the important offices of the town government, those with functions vital to the existence and prosperity of the town, were lodged firmly in the hands of a broad elite, entry into which was conditioned by commercial achievement and family background. The representatives to the General Court and the selectmen were the leaders of the town in economic endeavor as well as in political acumen. John Hancock's taxable wealth totaled £18,000; James Otis was assessed at £2,040, while Colonel Joseph Jackson had property valued at £1,288. Other levels of the administrative system were reserved for those whose business skills or reputation provided the necessary qualifications. Samuel Abbot, John Barrett, Benjamin Dolbeare, John Gore, William Phillips, William White, and William Whitewell, Overseers of the Poor in 1771, had taxable estates of £815, £5,520, £850, £1,747, £5,771, £1,953, and £1,502 respectively. All were among the wealthiest 7 per cent of the property owners; and Barrett and Phillips were two of the most respected merchants of the town. John Scollay, a distiller with an estate of £320, and Captain Benjamin Waldo, a shipmaster assessed at £500, who were among those chosen as "Firewards" in 1771, might in an earlier period have been dominant in town affairs; by the seventh decade of the century, in a mature economic environment, the merchant prince had replaced the man of action at the apex of the social order.

Gradations continued to the bottom of the scale. Different social and occupational levels of the population were tapped as the dignity and responsibility of the position demanded. It was not by accident that the estates of the town assessors, Jonathan Brown, Moses Deshon, and John Kneeland, were £208, £200, and £342. Or that those of the "Cullers of Staves," Henry Lucas, Thomas Knox, and Caleb Hayden, totaled £120, £144, and £156. The assumption of a graded social, economic, and political scale neatly calibrated so as to indicate the relation of each individual to the whole was the basic principle upon which the functioning of townmeeting "democracy" depended. William Crafts, with a taxable estate of £80, was elected "Fence Viewer." Half this amount qualified William Barrett to be "Measurer of Coal Baskets," while Henry Allen and John Bulfinch, "Measurers of Boards," were assessed at £80 and £48. The design was nearly perfect, the correlation between town office and social and economic position almost exact.

As in 1687, the distribution of political power and influence in Boston conformed to the standards and gradations of a wider, more inclusive hierarchy of status, one which purported to include the entire social order within the bounds of its authority. But the lines of force which had emerged on the eve of the American Revolution radiated from different economic and social groups than those of eighty-five years before, and now failed to encompass a significant portion of the population. The weakening of the "extended" family unit and the appearance of a large body of autonomous wage earners, "proletarians" in condition if not in consciousness, had introduced elements of mobility and diversity into the bottom part of society. Equally significant had been the growing inequality of the distribution of wealth among the propertied segment of the community, notably the greater exclusiveness and predominance of a mercantile "elite." Society had become more stratified and unequal. Influential groups, increasingly different from the small property owners who constituted the center portion of the community, had arisen at either end of the spectrum. Creations of the century-long development of a maritime economy in an urban setting, these "merchant princes" and "proletarians" stood out as the salient characteristics of a new social order.

7

The Growth of American Community

RICHARD L. MERRITT

Content analysis is a method of systematically examining style in communications. Quantitative symbol analysis, a form of content analysis, concentrates on how often key words or phrases symbolizing a concept are used. In his study, Richard L. Merritt tabulates how often place names appear in the news items of a random sample (one issue every three months) of the *Massachusetts Gazette* (1735-1775), the *Boston Gazette* (1762-1775), the *New-York Weekly Journal* (1735-1751), the *New-York Mercury* (1752-1775), the *Pennsylvania Gazette* (1735-1775), the *Virginia Gazette* (1736-1775), and the *South-Carolina Gazette* (1735-1775). In addition to dividing place names into home colony symbols, other colony symbols, British symbols, Canadian symbols, Caribbean symbols, other symbols and, most important, symbols of common identity (continental symbols, or terms referring to the entire area and people that subsequently revolted), Merritt further divides continental symbols to determine whether they identify with the British community or with a "distinctly" American community. Merritt's resulting analysis sharply questions assumptions concerning American community awareness prior to 1775 and the influence of the Stamp Act upon its development.

In evaluating the alternative theories about the integration of the American political community, it is necessary first of all to correlate the three sets of evidence outlined . . . graphically in Figures 1 and 2. At the base of the charts are listed the various formative events. . . . The words "functional amalgamation" appear under the year 1775,

From Richard L. Merritt, *Symbols of American Community, 1735–1775* (New Haven: Yale University Press, 1966), pp. 142–47, 156–58, 160–64, 167–82. Reprinted with omissions by permission of the publisher.

the year in which the colonists formed a military alliance and in which the colonies first developed a set of unified structures performing a major portion of the functions of a national government—in short, the year in which the colonists crossed the threshold of functional amalgamation. The curved lines summarize the changing patterns of symbol usage in the colonial press, presented year by year in Figure 1 and as moving averages in Figure 2.

These three curved lines . . . will be used as indicators of the growth of an American sense of community awareness in the eighteenth century. The first (a solid line) . . . represents the American share of the total number of symbols appearing in the newspapers, that is, the relative amount of attention the colonial press devoted to events taking place in the area that later became the United States of America. As is true of the others, this curve shows the composite or average distribution of symbols of all newspapers (excluding the *Boston Gazette*). The second curve (a broken line) is a partial analysis of the American symbols, showing the percentage devoted to the continent as a whole or, as we have also termed them, to symbols of common identity. . . . Finally, the dotted line represents the share of symbols of common identity (appearing in items of both British and American as well as foreign origin) identifying the population inhabiting the American colonies as members of an American political community. Examples of such symbols would be "Americans," "American colonists," "continentals," and so forth.

The curves shown in Figures 1 and 2 are strikingly similar. Instead of rising evenly and slowly, or sharply, the curves all incline somewhat fitfully, suggesting the cycles of the learning curve. There is also a certain congruence in their patterns of fluctuation: the peak and trough years are almost identical in all the curves. In fact, looked at from a statistical point of view, the degree of correlation or association among the three curves is highly significant.

FUNCTIONAL AMALGAMATION AND COMMUNITY AWARENESS

The first of the theories offered by students of political communities, and which has been used to analyze the American example of the eighteenth century, emphasizes the importance of amalgamated political structures, arguing that a community awareness follows rather than precedes the process of amalgamation. What does the evidence of the newspapers tell us about this thesis?

During the four decades prior to the year in which the colonists crossed the threshold of functional amalgamation, the embryo Ameri-

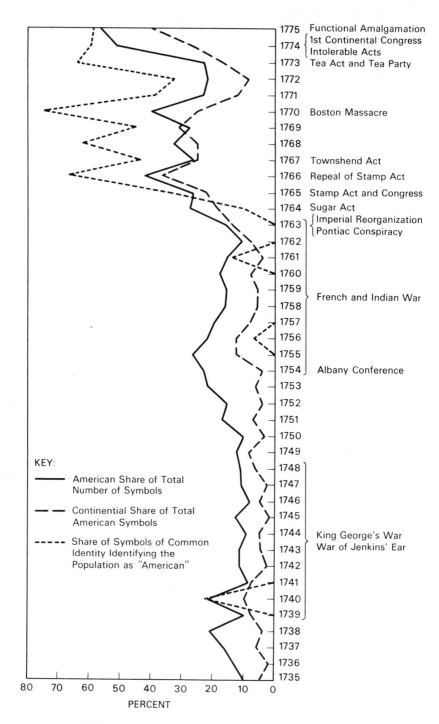

1775   Functional Amalgamation
1774 { 1st Continental Congress / Intolerable Acts
1773   Tea Act and Tea Party
1772
1771
1770   Boston Massacre
1769
1768
1767   Townshend Act
1766   Repeal of Stamp Act
1765   Stamp Act and Congress
1764   Sugar Act
1763 { Imperial Reorganization / Pontiac Conspiracy
1762
1761
1760
1759
1758 } French and Indian War
1757
1756
1755
1754 } Albany Conference
1753
1752
1751
1750
1749
1748
1747
1746
1745
1744 } King George's War / War of Jenkins' Ear
1743
1742
1741
1740
1739
1738
1737
1736
1735

KEY:

——— American Share of Total Number of Symbols

— — Continential Share of Total American Symbols

- - - - Share of Symbols of Common Identity Identifying the Population as "American"

80   70   60   50   40   30   20   10   0

PERCENT

FIGURE 1 *Functional Amalgamation, Formative Events, Curves of American Community Awareness, 1735–1775— a Comparison*

104

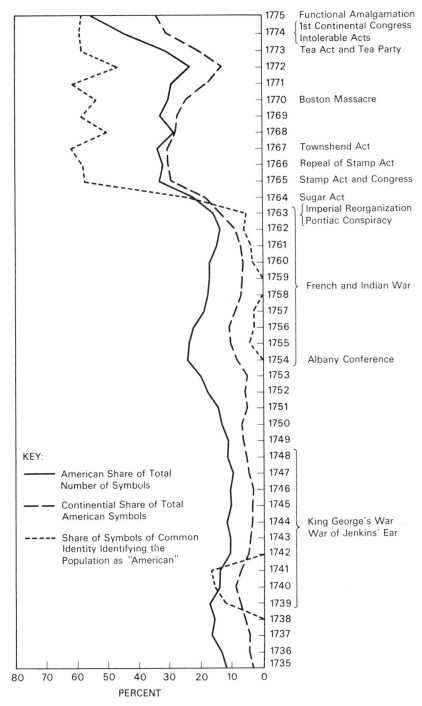

1775		Functional Amalgamation
1774	{	1st Continental Congress
		Intolerable Acts
1773		Tea Act and Tea Party
1772		
1771		
1770		Boston Massacre
1769		
1768		
1767		Townshend Act
1766		Repeal of Stamp Act
1765		Stamp Act and Congress
1764		Sugar Act
1763	{	Imperial Reorganization
		Pontiac Conspiracy
1762		
1761		
1760		
1759	}	French and Indian War
1758		
1757		
1756		
1755		
1754		Albany Conference
1753		
1752		
1751		
1750		
1749		
1748		
1747		
1746		
1745		
1744		King George's War
1743		War of Jenkins' Ear
1742		
1741		
1740		
1739		
1738		
1737		
1736		
1735		

80 70 60 50 40 30 20 10 0

PERCENT

KEY:

——— American Share of Total
Number of Symbols

— — Continential Share of Total
American Symbols

- - - - Share of Symbols of Common
Identity Identifying the
Population as "American"

FIGURE 2 *Functional Amalgamation, Formative Events,
Curves of American Community Awareness, 1735–1775—
a Comparison, Using "Moving Averages"*

105

can community found a constant place in the colonial press. More than one in five symbols pertained to America during these years; and in the critical decade from 1765 to 1775 the newspapers devoted one third of their symbol space to American events. In 1774 alone—the year before the colonists set up common political structures—one half of the symbols in the colonial press referred to American news.

Although the share or symbol space devoted to the mother country remained fairly constant over the 41-year period, it declined sharply relative to emphasis upon the American community. From 1735 to 1750 almost twice as many British as American symbols appeared in the colonial press; together these two categories comprised one third of the total number of symbols appearing in the newspapers. The last dozen pre-Revolutionary years saw the ratio of British to American symbols reversed. In fact, during the years from 1764 to 1775, the American community captured as great a share of symbol space as the Anglo-American community did between 1735 and 1763.

The American symbols appearing in the colonial press did not refer solely to local events but were intercolonial to a considerable degree. Well over one half of these American symbols pertained to occurrences in colonies other than the newspapers' home colonies. And during the course of the 41 years from 1735 to 1775, the home colony share of the American symbols decreased from about 40 to about 25 per cent. In the last 14 years of this period, one quarter of the total American symbol space was devoted to the colonies as a whole. Thus, by the end of the four decades, the individual colonies were not only paying more attention to other colonies than to themselves, but they were also paying substantially more attention to symbols of common identity than to home colony symbols.

The symbols of common identity appearing in the colonial press— whether of British or American origin, whether referring to the land or to the inhabitants of that land—were more likely to emphasize the American rather than the British tie long before 1775. Considered as a whole, the colonial press crossed this threshold in symbol usage a dozen or more years before the colonists successfully amalgamated some of their more important political institutions.

The evidence of the newspapers, then, renders it very difficult to maintain the belief of such writers as Merrill Jensen, Kenneth C. Wheare, John C. Ranney, Edward Frank Humphrey, and Esmond Wright, the belief that, prior to their unification, the colonies were by and large self-centered, indifferent to one another's existence and problems, and more interested in their connections to the mother country than in intercolonial affairs. Even before they crossed the threshold of extensive functional amalgamation, the colonists—at least as readers of the newspapers—had developed a fairly high degree of community awareness. However much the amalgamation of some of their political institutions may have affected the news patterns and symbol distributions in the newspapers after 1775, the assertion that no community awareness existed prior to that date is massively contradicted by the evidence surveyed in this study.

. . .

At best, the colonial wars postponed the emergence of sentiments of national separateness in America. In looking at the testimonials of the colonists themselves (or at the judgments of more recent students of the American political community) about the effect of these wars upon the moods and perceptions of the colonists, it is necessary to place such remarks and opinions in sequence. During the initial phase of the French and Indian War, for example, when the image of an American separateness was rising, a haughty attitude toward British methods of warfare may have been in keeping with the prevailing mood. We would not expect to find a similar attitude among the colonists toward General James Wolfe's victory on the Heights of Abraham in 1759, when the mood of Anglo-American solidarity was predominant in the colonies. But regardless of shifts in prevailing moods, the ultimate effect of the cycles left the colonists, at the end of the wars, using essentially the same symbol patterns in existence at the outset of the wars.

. . .

THE STAMP ACT CRISIS:
THE JUNCTURE OF EVENTS AND INTEGRATIVE PROCESSES

The formative event most often singled out by historians and political scientists in accounting for the growth of an American sense of community is the Stamp Act crisis. And, as may be seen in Figures 1 and 2, it is indeed undeniable that the sharpest upward swings of the curves of American community awareness, as well as their highest points in the 1760s, seem to coincide with the development of the Stamp Act crisis.

Two sets of facts, however, one to be found in the quantitative data analyzed in this study and the other implicit in the standard, nonquantitative interpretations of American history, argue against a causal relationship between the crisis and the growth of community awareness in the colonies.

The first set of evidence has been discussed: the Stamp Act crisis took place after the curves of community awareness had already begun to ascend, and the curves turned downward immediately after the repeal of the measure. If the crisis had in fact set the symbol revolution of the early 1760s in motion, we would expect that the force of inertia alone in the colonists' patterns of self-imagery and attention would have carried this revolution forward at least to some extent in the months after March 1766. Insead, there was a sharp drop in all of the curves that continued until 1768.

The second fact is that the parliamentary measures of 1764 and 1765, the Sugar Act and the Stamp Act, were not unique events in colonial history. Nor were they the first such measures to arouse the ire of the colonists.

. . .

What was it about the Sugar and Stamp Acts of 1764 and 1765 that was not present in the '30s and '50s and that now led the colonists to meet in joint congress in New York City and protest loudly? Why was the conflict over these measures of a magnitude never attained during previous periods of stress in the relations between the colonies and the mother country?

The Events of 1763

One possible explanation of the increased degree of colonial sensitivity to parliamentary interference in what the colonists felt were their rights in 1764 and 1765 pertains to the discrete and yet not unrelated events preceding the enactment of the Sugar and Stamp Acts. The fact that major shifts in symbol usage took place during the latter half of 1763 lends considerable plausibility to this explanation.

. . .

As a formative event capturing the imagination of the colonists, the effect of the Treaty of Paris seems to have been short-lived indeed. At best, its influence upon the distribution of symbols in the colonial press produced only a brief flurry of interest in American and continental symbols. . . .

PONTIAC'S CONSPIRACY was one of the most important colonial foci of attention during the latter half of 1763. Not only did this event find a prominent place in the newspapers from all of the colonies, but the different journals shared a common perception of the uprising. . . .

The role played by Pontiac's Conspiracy in the growth of an American political community is not at all clear. On the one hand, the colonists never developed a sense of involvement matching the amount of attention that they paid to the uprising; the colonial governments, while most assuredly deploring the butcheries on the western frontier, were for the most part unwilling to allocate men or other resources to quell the rebellion. This inability to act or cooperate in the face of a common threat dealt a severe blow to the cause of intercolonial integration.

On the other hand, however, Pontiac's Conspiracy made crystal clear certain aspects of divergent colonial and British perceptions and interests. Newspaper articles reprinted from British journals seemed unanimous in blaming the uprising upon the colonists' abuse of the Indians, and condemned the colonists for encroaching upon the Indian territories.

. . . .

Although the loss of life and the devastation of settled areas in the French and Indian War were more extensive, and the threat to the colonies greater, than in the Indian uprising of 1763, the war of the late 1750s did not occasion the dramatic shifts in attention and American community awareness that accompanied the latter event. . . .

THE ROYAL PROCLAMATION OF OCTOBER 1763 has also been cited by some scholars as an important source of irritation between the colonists and the mother country—an irritation that, they believe, developed into the Revolutionary War. . . .

In looking at the later colonial years as a whole, it seems somewhat difficult to justify the importance that has been assigned to the Royal Proclamation as a formative event in the embryo American political community. The months prior to its enunciation found rumors circulating throughout the colonies about its content—the press took notice of reports that 10,000 men were to be stationed in America at the colonists' expense —but, after its appearance, discussion of the measure in the colonial press quietly disappeared. The consensus among modern historians of colonial America seems to be that its provisions were generally unenforceable and for the most part left unenforced. It is probably also true, however, that the Proclamation caused some inconvenience to some colonists, who had to find ways of evading its provisions. Whatever the inconveniences, though, the westward advance of the colonists across the Proclamation Line continued, and the colonists continued to trade with the Indians, probably cheating and otherwise taking advantage of them to no lesser degree than before October 1763.

The events of 1763, then, no not explain the critical nature of the Stamp Act crisis. Clearly these events "caused" neither the Stamp Act crisis nor the symbol revolution that took place in the colonial press in the early 1760s. We must look elsewhere for clues about the timing of changes in symbol usage. And we must look elsewhere for answers to certain types of questions about these events. If, for example, a newly found sense of security emboldened the colonists to make demands of the mother country after the Paris Treaty of 1763, why did not a similar sense of security lead them to make similar demands after the Peace of Aix-la-Chapelle in 1748? What had intervened in the sixteen years from 1747 to 1763 that made news of Pontiac's Conspiracy in the northwest so important in the colonial press, while earlier French depredations in the northeast had failed to secure widespread newspaper coverage? Notice was scarcely taken of the Iron Bill of 1750 during the year of its passage. "Iffing" is always dangerous in analyzing historical events and processes, but I would suggest that, if the Iron Bill had been enacted in 1767 or even 1764, it would have met with vociferous colonial opposition. Instead of a "Stamp Act crisis," the colonists would have rallied to the clarion call for intercolonial cooperation in the midst of an "Iron Bill crisis." A spark that would have gone unnoticed in the previous decade could have kindled the flames of patriotism in the 1760s.

Changing Levels of American Community Awareness

A second approach to the question of increased colonial sensitivity to parliamentary measures of control in the 1760s centers on the growth of habits and facilities of intercolonial communication. Attention to American events and problems is an important aspect of this approach, as is the emergence of trading patterns, communication systems, and intercolonial contacts.

THE LEVELS OF ATTENTION paid to American symbols and the collective concept (the solid and broken lines, respectively, in Figures 1 and 2) increased steadily if somewhat fitfully throughout the twenty-eight years preceding the Treaty of Paris and Pontiac's Conspiracy. The level of attention paid to American symbols increased by 49 per cent from 1735 to 1762 (based on a linear trend line), while the level of attention paid to continental symbols increased by 77 per cent.

Taking the fluctuations in the curves of American community awareness into account does not alter our conclusion about the increased levels of attention to American symbols. In fact, the cycles of the curves shown in Figures 1 and 2 took place on progressively higher planes. And even the low points in 1761 and 1762 were at higher levels than the lowest points of previous cycles.

Two other facts about the level of attention will also be recalled from earlier sections of this study. First, the symbol distributions of the newspapers from different colonies became increasingly congruent as the colonial years passed. And, second, by 1763, references to the colonies as a whole were more likely than not to identify them as an area separate from the British political community.

Expanding facilities of intercolonial communication characterized the context in which changes in the levels of attention took place. Illustrative of this expansion is the colonial press itself. The number of newspapers, for example, mushroomed in the decades between 1735 and 1775. At the time of John Peter Zenger's trial for seditious libel there were only nine newspapers in all America; by the end of the French and Indian War their number had more than doubled, and 38 were in existence on the eve of the Revolution. Furthermore, the size and news coverage of the journals kept pace with their numbers: the linage in the average newspaper doubled, and the number of symbols increased almost threefold, from the 1730s to the 1760s.

Another indication of the colonists' changing patterns of communication lies in their choice of trading partners. The number of ships plying between the major American ports of New York, Philadelphia, Hampton, and Charleston, on the one hand, and harbors in Great Britain or Ireland, on the other hand, doubled from 1734 to 1772 (increasing from 264 to 556), but the number of ships engaged in the coasting trade quadrupled (from 402 to 1,750) during the same period. Comparable figures for the port of Boston are even more dramatic. . . . In short, although the shipping facilities of the colonies expanded generally during the course of the eighteenth century, coastal shipping grew at a much more rapid rate than did trade with the mother country.

Population expansion accompanied the growing intercolonial commercial ties. From 1700 to 1775, the American population multiplied tenfold. Along with a general movement west, people began to fill in the gaps separating the urban clusters scattered along the Atlantic seaboard. By the middle of the 1770s, according to census data currently available, a fairly continuous line of settlement ran from Penobscot Bay to Savannah.

With the expansion of the population came the construction of post roads, ferries, and other means to facilitate intercolonial travel and communication. This is not to say that the transportation system was complete or ideal; some of the roads were almost impassable in bad weather. But two facts stand out: the roads multiplied and were considerably improved during the eighteenth century (a good indication of this fact is the amount of time it took to travel between two cities: post office records report that a letter required three days to go from Philadelphia to New York in 1720, but only one day in 1764); travel between colonies was often faster and cheaper than that between coastal and inland population clusters within the same colony.

Intercolonial mobility made increasingly possible the exchange of ideas among the colonists. Among the many colonial travelers, one of the more notable was the evangelist George Whitefield. From 1738 until his death in 1770, he made seven journeys throughout the colonies, five of them extending from Georgia to New England. The religious revival that he occasioned, termed the "Great Awakening," was perhaps the first mass movement to sweep America. It was the spirit engendered in this movement that helped Whitefield to collect money throughout the colonies (and even in England) for such worthy causes as an orphanage in Georgia, the construction of Dartmouth and Princeton colleges, and the reconstruction of the Harvard College library after a fire in 1764.

The end of the French and Indian War found the colonists with communication habits and facilities considerably better than those of the 1730s or even the early 1750s. The politically relevant strata of colonial society had a wider range of opportunities to learn about events and attitudes affecting and influencing their fellow colonists than had been possible prior to that time.

And, if we are to judge from symbol usage in the colonial press, a new set of perceptions and foci of attention accompanied these changed habits and facilities of communication. American events were becoming increasingly more important in the attention patterns. The idea of referring to the colonies as a single unit was gaining favor. The newspapers began separating the colonies from the mother country through their symbol usage more often than identifying the colonies as a part of a British political community. Slow to develop, the trends toward increased American community awareness and an enhanced sense of American community were well under way.

With their changing self-images and attention patterns, the colonists began to perceive new common interests. Events that in earlier years might have seemed unimportant took on a new aura of significance in the context of changing perceptions and new trends toward intercolonial habits and facilities of communication. The grumbling responses in the 1730s and 1750s that the Molasses Act and the Iron Bill may have elicited from the colonists were isolated, and hence to a large measure ineffective. As the facilities for intercolonial communication improved, however, and as the colonists began to focus more and more of their attention upon the American community, such tones of dissatisfaction could find echoes throughout the continent. An Indian uprising in 1763, much less threatening than other attacks upon the colonists during the course of the previous two decades, could become a major topic of discussion in the press. The rapidly expanding newspapers could spend a larger amount of space on differences between the perspectives and interests of the colonists and those of the mother country. Given these circumstances, then, it seems less likely that the Stamp Act crisis itself generated bonds of community awareness among the colonists than that the rapidly growing ties of communication and community enabled the colonists to voice the effective opposition to parliament that has come to be called the "Stamp Act crisis"—which, in its turn, made a further contribution to the developing sense of American community.

The Interaction of Formative Events and Levels
of Community Awareness

The evidence does not bear out a direct causal relationship between any *single* event and trends in American community awareness. Could it be, however, that it was the *cumulative impact* of the colonial wars or of the events in the years from 1763 to 1765 that created ties of community among the colonists? To what degree did the "formative events" of the pre-Revolutionary era interact with levels of American community awareness?

By the summer of 1763, judging from their symbol usage, the colonists had reached what might be described as the "takeoff" stage of political integration—"a period in which small, scattered, and powerless movements" directed toward integration "change into larger and more coordinated ones with some significant power behind them." Before those crucial months, the colonial press revealed a slow and often unsteady—but nonetheless increasing—interest in American events, a growing interest in events affecting the colonies as a whole, and an ever greater tendency to identify the colonies as American rather than as British.

The significance of these trends lies in the realm of inference and judgment. It is by no means clear, for example, that the colonists' moods and perceptions in the spring of 1763, although considerably different from previous decades, committed them irrevocably to a course ultimately leading to rebellion and independence. A more accurate appraisal of the Americans' mood might have led parliament to alter its own attitude and policy. But the order of magnitude of any parliamentary shifts would have to have been commensurate with the order of magnitude of the cumulative changes in the colonial mood and perceptions that had already occurred. It would have required major concessions to reverse the trend of a growing American sense of community. It would have required, for instance, substantial concessions in terms of the arguments then current in the colonies: freer trade, defense against the Indians, "no taxation without representation," and so forth. And it would have required substantial changes in the imperial policy-making mechanism to accommodate greater colonial participation.

However justified its reasons may have been, Great Britain rejected the path of conciliation. At a time of changing moods and perceptions in the colonies, the mother country instituted measures that underscored the cross-pressures already existent in the imperial system. By April 1763 the colonists had read rumors that 10,000 British regulars were to be posted in America, with "every Article of Expence" after the first year "to be defrayed by the Colonies." Three months later followed the publication of "An Act for the further Improvement of His Majesty's Revenue of Customs; for the Encouragement of Officers making Seizures; and for the Prevention of the clandestine Running of Goods into any Part of His Majesty's Dominions." There could have been little doubt that the act was aimed in large part at the rum, molasses, and sugar trade carried on between the colonies and the French Caribbean islands. Lest there be any doubt, however, many newspapers also published lists of British naval vessels ordered to the American station—45 newcomers in all, of which 17 were to range off the coast between Canso and Cape Florida. Nor could British accounts of Pontiac's Conspiracy have provided pleasant reading for the colonists. The solution to the Indian problem? Articles of British origin appearing in the colonial press generally envisioned curbs to be imposed upon the colonists, not the Indians! The Royal Proclamation of October 1763, which reached colonial ears some two months later, incorporated these ideas and went one step further: it verified the rumors, circulating since the spring of 1763, and provided for the stationing of 10,000 Redcoats in America at the colonists' expense. These British measures and sentiments, coming at a time of accelerating trends toward higher levels of community awareness among the colonists, gave impetus to a moving political force already under way.

In analyzing the psychological basis of opinion change, Carl I. Hovland, Irving L. Janis, and Harold H. Kelley write that "heightened conflict" at the time of a communication designed to change a person's mind "can lead to certain types of resolution which increase long-term effectiveness." This relationship of communication, persuasion, and counterpressures in personal behavior is extremely pertinent to the situation of the American colonies in 1763. Each new measure instituted by the British government in the latter half of that year (and in the subsequent years) constituted a challenge to the colonists' changing set of moods, images, habits, and attitudes. Each new measure, in effect, was a counterpressure that in the long run only served to increase the persistence with which the colonists clung to their new perceptions and patterns of behavior. And, as Merle Curti has written, "when the shoe began to pinch, the conviction that British and American interests differed became an important factor in the growth of American self-consciousness."

By the end of 1763 the colonists' takeoff toward political integration was well under way. The movement toward an American political community waxed strong during the years of the Stamp Act crisis. The repeal of that act, while removing the most immediate cause of colonial grievance, did little to alter the basic moods and perceptions that in large part had been responsible for the crisis, and which had conditioned the colonists' responses during the struggle itself. That the levels of American community awareness dropped off after the repeal of the

Stamp Act does not mean that American community awareness sank to the level prevalent during the 1740s: in most cases, the curves after 1766 were higher than in any year prior to the Stamp Act crisis.

Judging from symbol usage in the newspapers, the remaining decade of the colonial era witnessed an intense interaction of increasing American community sentiments and events. On the one hand, the colonists' mood became increasingly more sensitive to actual or perceived abridgments of their rights, or what they perceived their rights to be. Milder provocations began to arouse stronger responses. And, on the other hand, each new event—the Townshend Act, the Boston Massacre, the Tea Act, the Intolerable Acts—only served to bring the complex of images and attitudes into sharper focus.

THE GROWTH OF AMERICAN COMMUNITY

The data surveyed in this study tell us much about the timing and patterns of growing national consciousness in the eighteenth-century American colonies. They indicate, for instance, the more significant changes in the colonists' perceptions of and attitudes toward their community. Some were essentially quantitative: the amount of intercolonial news carried by the newspapers increased sixfold and more from the late 1730s to the early 1770s; the distributions of symbols in the newspapers of different colonies were increasingly parallel (even if not always symmetrical); the major shifts in symbol usage occurred during the latter half of 1763. A change in quality attended these changes in quantity: a growing propensity to pay attention to American events, an ever greater willingness to refer to Americans as a single group, the increasing use of terms identifying the colonists as Americans rather than as members of a British political community—all these suggest aroused expectations about group membership in a distinctly American political community.

Second, concomitant changes in the structure of intercolonial communication, such as the expansion of trade among the colonies, the emergence of interlocking elites, and the construction of post roads and other means to facilitate communication and transportation, reinforced the developing image of an American community. Which came first—the ties of social communication and identity, or improved facilities—is a chicken-and-egg question that must remain unanswered for now.

Third, the growth of far-reaching habits of and facilities for intercolonial communication preceded the creation of unified political institutions among the colonists. However much the structures created in 1775 and later may have furthered a sense of Americanism and given the colonists a concrete as well as symbolic focus around which to rally, the structures themselves did not generate this Americanism; more probably, it was the changed climate of opinion that permitted the institutions to be created in the first place.

Fourth, the emergence of American community consciousness seems to explain, rather than to be explained by, the occurrence of single, dramatic events in the later colonial years. Wars against the French and their Indian allies merely postponed the emergence of sentiments of Americanism. Other "formative" events, such as the Stamp Act crisis, came well after American community awareness had begun to increase. Such events as these, however, even if they did not furnish the original impetus, most assuredly reinforced the colonists' growing sense of American separatism. It was this interplay that, more than anything else, led to the Revolution and the formation of the American Union.

What the data surveyed in the study cannot do is to account for such changes in the colonists' communication patterns. They cannot answer the question: What impulses led the eighteenth-century Americans to pay more rather than less attention to one another as time passed, to trade, correspond, and visit more with one another, to view themselves as a community apart from the British or even the Anglo-American political community? Neither can they give us clues about the motivations of His Majesty's Government in London. What was it, for instance, that prompted the Royal ministers to institute such measures as the Stamp Act and the Boston Port Bill which, in retrospect at least, seem to have been calculated to stir up colonial hostility and resistance? The answers to such questions do not lie in the raw data but in inference and interpretation based upon the information they supply, as well as in the confrontation of these data with other types of information about community sentiments in colonial America. Some of these interpretations and analyses lie outside the scope of this study; others have been discussed briefly in the preceding pages.

The increasing intercolonial communication load accompanied extensive changes in the colonists' habits of and facilities for intercolonial communication and decision-making. The data surveyed above indicate growing colonial interaction from 1735 to 1775, together with a high rate of mutually beneficial transactions, compared to the total number of intercolonial transactions of all sorts. To be sure, they indicate that the emergence of an American community consciousness was a slow process, retarded at times by developments that emphasized the colonists' psychic distance from one another and their reliance upon the mother country, and occasionally hastened by developments highlighting conflicts within the imperial relationship. But, what is more important, these data indicate that, by the early 1770s, the colonists were sufficiently different from their English contemporaries that they comprised a political community—embryonic in some respects, perhaps, but nonetheless a distinct American political community.

We, Some of the People: Apportionment in the Thirteen State Conventions Ratifying the Constitution

CHARLES W. ROLL, JR.

Until Charles Beard wrote *An Economic Interpretation of the Constitution* (1913), historians agreed with Thomas Jefferson that the Constitutional Convention was "an assembly of demigods." Beard, however, knocked the Founding Fathers from their pedestals by arguing that they were a powerful minority who wrote both an economic document designed to enhance their own interests (by giving the central government the power to tax and to control commerce and by depriving the states of power over currency and contracts) and an antidemocratic document designed to perpetuate their reactionary power and to frustrate the democratic majority (by building in a system of checks and balances and elaborate electoral machinery).

Although Beard had his critics, his thesis held sway until Robert E. Brown in his careful analysis, *Charles Beard and the Constitution* (1956), argued that the Constitution was democratic, and Forrest McDonald in *We the People* (1958), having painstakingly examined the sources, insisted that the Constitution was not, as Beard had declared, "an economic document" drawn up by a "consolidated economic group whose property interests were immediately at stake."

Charles W. Roll, Jr., has recognized that ratification was only as democratic as apportionment of ratifying convention delegates was equal. His careful comparison of the population of various convention districts within states suggests that some of

From *The Journal of American History*, 56 (1969):21–40. Footnotes omitted. Reprinted by permission of the author and *The Journal of American History*.

Beard's critics have exaggerated the democratic methods pursued in adopting the Constitution. Since convention districts approximated state assembly districts, these critics may also have exaggerated the democratic nature of late eighteenth-century American society.

On June 15, 1964, the Supreme Court in *Reynolds* v. *Sims* ruled that members in a house of a state legislature must represent districts substantially equal in population. This so-called "one-man, one-vote" decision (and its companion decisions) resulted in extensive litigation and intensive judicial examination of one house (or both) of nearly every state's legislative branch. The constitutional ground for the "one-man, one-vote" decision is found in a clause in the Fourteenth Amendment: "nor [shall any state] deny to any person within its jurisdiction the equal protection of the laws."

The state conventions which ratified the federal Constitution in the years 1787-1790 are here placed under the same districting microscope as the Supreme Court used for its 1964 decision. How equal, or unequal, in population were the several districts represented in these conventions? Which states had the most unequal system of representation, which had the least?

Delegates to the thirteen conventions were elected and met between late 1787 and May 1790. The census of 1790 provides an almost perfectly timed guide for determining the population of the convention districts. Population movement within a state or between states—particularly the westward movement—and the time differential between the earlier conventions and the census may account for some slight systematic bias because the population of interior districts may be overestimated at the expense of seaboard districts. This bias, however, should not be significant. Calculations are based on the 1790 census; but because the time differential is small, they can be considered to be close approximations of the situation at the time of the state conventions.

Only Delaware, where apportionment was virtually equal, and possibly Pennsylvania could have met the standards applied by today's Court. The Georgia and South Carolina conventions were the most unequally districted, with about 13 percent of each of these states' population able to control the convention. All of the remaining states can be placed somewhere in between these extremes (see Table I).

An analysis of the three regions as a whole discloses that the general system of districting in the Middle Atlantic area was much more nearly equal than in either of the other two regions. The districting situation in the South was especially distorted.

TABLE I   Apportionment   in   State   Ratifying   Conventions   (1787–1790)

Middle Atlantic States	Minimum Percentage of Population Represented by Majority of Delegates	Ratio of Smallest District to Largest District in State
Delaware	52.6	1: 1.0
Pennsylvania	47.2	1: 1.7
New Jersey	40.2	1: 7.8
Maryland	37.6	1: 9.4
New York	35.6	1: 6.7
New England		
Massachusetts	38.4	1: 21.7
New Hampshire	36.3	1: 7.7
Connecticut	34.0	1: 8.1
Rhode Island	31.5	1: 6.2
South		
North Carolina	32.1	1: 15.9
Virginia	28.1	1: 30.9
South Carolina	13.1	1: 91.0
Georgia	12.8	1:122.4

As a result of population variations between states and the degree of unequal districting within states, delegates representing 14.7 percent of the thirteen-state population theoretically could have combined to put nine states in the ratification column, as required by the Constitution, to launch the new ship of state. Furthermore, because the refusal of five states could have blocked this change, the votes of delegates representing about 96 percent of the nation's population in the most over-represented districts of the eight most populous states theoretically could have been overridden by the votes of majorities composed of delegates representing 4 percent of the nation's population in the remaining five states (see Table II).

The foregoing statistical configurations are theoretical. It is clear, however, that from the standpoint of "majority rule" a situation quite below today's acceptable standards was a possibility. It is equally clear that very difficult hurdles, both the required approval of nine states and the unequal systems of districting in most states, were placed on the ratification track.

Did inequalities in the apportionment of delegates to the state conventions affect the outcome? If so, did these inequalities benefit the highly organized pro-Constitution faction or help the less well-organized Antifederalists? And if so, to what degree did they have an effect?

TABLE II   State-by-State Distribution of Population and Voting Strength

State	Percent of Thirteen-State Population	Minimum Percent of Thirteen-State Population Represented by Delegate Majority
Delaware	1.6	.9
Georgia	1.7	.2
Rhode Island	2.2	.7
New Hampshire	4.5	1.6
South Carolina	4.5	.6
Subtotal (five states to defeat)	14.5	4.0
New Jersey	5.5	2.2
Connecticut	7.5	2.6
Maryland	6.9	2.6
North Carolina	10.3	3.3
Subtotal (nine states to approve)	44.7	14.7
New York	10.1	3.6
Pennsylvania	13.9	6.6
Massachusetts	14.8	5.7
Virginia	16.5	4.6
Total (thirteen states)	100.0	35.2

By June 21, 1788, delegates representing 40.2 percent of the thirteen-state population had voted in their respective state conventions to cause nine states to ratify the Constitution. This is nearly three times the minimum 14.7 percent possible; but it was not until July 26, 1788, when the eleventh state, New York, ratified, that delegates representing a clear majority of the thirteen-state population had voted for ratification. By May 29, 1790, when the thirteenth state, Rhode Island, finally ratified, convention delegates representing 59.3 percent of the population had voted in support of the Constitution (see Table III).

In eight states distorted apportionment benefited the proponents of ratification (See Table IV).

As it turned out, therefore, the principle of majority rule was not so flagrantly violated (on a country-wide basis) as it might have been. This is the result of the fact that, country-wide, the average number of people represented by each "anti" delegate was only slightly higher than the average number of people represented by each delegate voting for the Constitution. In the South and in the Middle Atlantic states, the population per "anti" delegate was nearly half again as large as the

TABLE III   Actual Voting Strength in the Ratification Process

Ratifying State	Date of Ratification	Percent of Thirteen-State Population	Percent of Thirteen-State Population Actually Represented by Delegates Voting for Constitution
Delaware	December 7, 1787	1.6	1.6
Pennsylvania	December 12, 1787	13.9	9.2
New Jersey	December 18, 1787	5.5	5.4
Georgia	January 2, 1788	1.7	1.5
Connecticut	January 9, 1788	7.5	5.8
Massachusetts	February 6, 1788	14.8	7.2
Maryland	April 28, 1788	6.9	5.5
South Carolina	May 23, 1788	4.5	1.8
New Hampshire	June 21, 1788	4.5	2.2
		60.9	40.2
Virginia	June 25, 1788	16.5	8.3
New York	July 26, 1788	10.1	3.4
North Carolina	November 21, 1789	10.3	6.4
Rhode Island	May 29, 1790	2.2	1.0
		100.0	59.3

population per "pro" delegate; in New England, however, the population per "pro" delegate was slightly larger than the population per "anti" delegate (see Table V).

In fact, the most under-represented districts sending delegates to the ratifying conventions in each state—the towns in New England and counties elsewhere—tended to be more evenly divided in their delegate sentiment than the most over-represented districts (see Table VI). In other words, according to the way the delegate (or the majority of delegates) of each district ultimately voted, the most over-represented districts favored the Constitution by a margin of nearly 25 percentage points, while the most under-represented districts favored the Constitution side by a margin of only 14 percentage points.

The results of this district-by-district analysis are not heightened, but minimized, by the fact that the eight states with small numbers of districts—and hence having a less than proportional effect on the total results—tended to have delegates from the more under-represented districts more closely divided in sentiment than were the delegates from the more under-represented districts in the five states with large numbers

TABLE IV   Distribution of Vote on Ratification

| State | Percent of Delegates Voting for Constitution | Percent of Population Represented by Delegates | | | Degree Apportionment Aided Constitution in Delegate Voting (Points)† |
		Voting For	Voting Against	Not Voting	
Delaware	100.0	100.0	—	—	—
Pennsylvania	66.7	65.7	34.3	—	+ 1.0
New Jersey	97.4	98.0	—	2.0	− 0.6
Georgia	78.8	88.9	—	11.1	−10.1
Connecticut	74.0	78.0	19.1	2.9	− 4.0
Massachusetts	51.3	53.5	44.2	2.3	− 2.2
Maryland	82.9	79.6	18.2	2.2	+ 3.3
South Carolina	62.8	39.0	52.2	8.8	+23.8
New Hampshire	50.5	49.8	42.5	7.7	+ 0.7
Virginia	52.3	50.3	48.3	1.4	+ 2.0
New York	46.2 *	33.7	49.7	16.6	+12.5
North Carolina	66.0	62.6	30.2	7.2	+ 3.4
Rhode Island	48.6 *	44.1	51.4	4.5	+ 4.5

    * A majority of delegates voting.
    † A point represents the difference between the percentage of delegates voting for the Constitution and the percentage of the state's population they represented. The percentages for Massachusetts and New Hampshire are based on represented population.

TABLE V   Population Per Delegate

Delegate Position	Thirteen States	New England (Four States)	Middle Atlantic (Five States)	South (Four States)
Voting for Constitution	1,727.4	1,244.0	3,771.9	1,235.1
Voting against Constitution	1,886.7	1,127.7	5,653.4	1,834.6
Not voting either way	1,566.3	1,116.5	6,019.3	1,066.6

of districts. Had the former eight states had greater numbers of districts, the effect of unequal apportionment would be even more pronounced in this analysis. In the Middle Atlantic region and in the South, delegate sentiment was considerably more evenly divided in the most under-represented districts than in the most over-represented districts, where delegate sentiment was overwhelmingly in favor of the Constitution. In New England, the tendency was the reverse, but less pronounced.

TABLE VI   Overall District Sentiment as Reflected by Delegate(s)

	No. of Districts	Districts with Delegate or More Delegates on "Yes" Side (Percent)	Districts with Delegate or More Delegates on "No" Side (Percent)	Districts with Delegate or Delegates Not Voting or Evenly Divided (Percent)	Net "Yes" Margin (Percentage Points) *
⅓ most over-represented districts in each state	255	59.2	34.5	6.3	+24.7
⅓ most nearly average districts in each state	258	55.1	39.9	5.0	+15.2
⅓ most under-represented districts in each state	255	54.9	41.2	3.9	+13.7

* Points represent the difference in percentage points between percent of districts whose delegate (or a majority of whose delegates) voted for ratification and percent of districts whose delegate (or a majority of whose delegates) voted against ratification.

The impetus of the early ratification by a number of states gave the pro-Constitution forces an important advantage over their adversaries in the battles in the other states. Under-representation in pro-Constitution areas in the first seven states to ratify clearly benefited opponents of the Constitution, but not enough to be a factor in these generally one-sided states. It was in those six states which ratified last—omitting Pennsylvania and Massachusetts, the same states in which sentiment as reflected by delegate voting was about two-to-one or closer—where under-representation of anti-Constitution areas most dramatically aided Federalist forces.

Little Delaware rushed to become the first state to ratify and did so unanimously. Even before receiving official notice of the new plan of government, Pennsylvania called a ratification convention; and delegates ratified by a two-to-one margin. New Jersey was the third state to ratify. Georgia, like New Jersey, voted unanimously to ratify (if one counts those who actually voted). Connecticut became the fifth state to ratify when her delegates voted three-to-one to accept the Constitution.

The march toward ratification by the required nine states thus got underway early and in earnest. Each state's ratification made it easier for the ratification forces in neighboring states. But the forward motion slowed to a crawl at the time of the election of delegates in Massachusetts and the meeting of that state's convention. Finding themselves outnumbered by opponents of the new Constitution, Massachusetts Federalists thought it necessary to make a "conciliatory proposition"— to propose that the new government, as soon as possible after its establishment, consider and adopt a number of amendments, of which three out of ten later became part of the Bill of Rights. Thus Massachusetts became the sixth state to ratify and did so by the close vote of 187 to 168, with nine abstentions.

The importance of the Massachusetts decision cannot be exaggerated. During the five weeks that the Massachusetts convention was in session, the New Hampshire convention met. The pro-Constitution delegates, finding themselves outnumbered by over two-to-one, largely because of anti-Constitution instructions from a number of towns, were able to effect a postponement to await the outcome in neighboring Massachusetts. Three months later, the New Hampshire delegates reconvened after there had been much work done to reverse or vacate antifederalist instructions. With the additional goad of South Carolina's becoming the eighth state to ratify, New Hampshire, in the words of George Bancroft, "grew restless to be the state yet needed to assure the new bond of union." New Hampshire, by a delegate vote of fifty-seven to forty-seven, with nine abstentions, won the race with Virginia to be the ninth state to ratify.

In the chain of events of ratification, South Carolina becomes a particularly important link. George Washington wrote: "An event similar to this (postponement in New Hampshire of which great use is made by the opposition) in Maryland, would have the worst tendency imaginable; for indecision there w[ou]ld. have considerable influence upon South Carolina, the only other State which is to precede Virginia, and submits the question almost wholly to the determination of the latter." South Carolina happens to have been one of the three states in which a thoroughly unequal apportionment of delegates resulted in ratification. But a more equitable districting, for example along the lines called for by recent Supreme Court decision, would have resulted in rejection of the Constitution. While 63 percent of South Carolina's delegates voted to ratify the Constitution, they represented only 39 percent of the non-slave population. Opposed to the Constitution were 31 percent of the delegates representing 52 percent of the population (see Table VII).

Coastal areas, including Charleston, Beaufort, and Georgetown, overwhelmingly favored the Constitution. Up-country areas just as over-

TABLE VII   South Carolina Ratification

	Percent of Delegates	Percent of Non-slave Population Represented by Delegates So Voting
Voting for Ratification (149 delegates)	62.8	39.0
Voting against Ratification (73 delegates)	30.8	52.2
Not Voting (15 delegates)	6.4	8.8
	100.0	100.0

whelmingly opposed it. The less populated coastal areas, however, had 151 delegates to the up-country's eighty-six. The Charleston district alone was allocated 109 delegates. As for South Carolina, Charles A. Beard was aware that "the seventy-three votes cast in the convention against ratification may in fact have represented a majority of the white inhabitants and voters in the state." Just as the decision in *Reynolds* v. *Sims* notes that "Citizens, not history or economic interests, cast votes . . . [and] people, not land or trees or pastures, vote," both Beard and the census provide figures showing that tax payments and slave property were more equitably represented at the South Carolina convention than were the state's white inhabitants (see Table VIII).

TABLE VIII   Taxes, Slaves, and Delegates in South Carolina

	White In-habitants, 1790 (Percent)	Delegate Representa-tion in 1788 Convention (Percent)	No. of Slaves, 1790 (Percent)	Amount of Taxes Paid, 1794 (Percent)
Coastal area: Charleston, Beaufort, Georgetown	21.0	60.8	72.9	77.0
Up-country area	79.0	39.2	27.1	23.0
	100.0	100.0	100.0	100.0

The psychological effect of the South Carolina ratification on the key state of Virginia was all the more important because it eliminated the possibility of an attractive alternative. In the words of George Bancroft, "the plan for a southern confederacy was crushed by the fidelity of South Carolina . . . . [which] dashed the hope of proselyting Virginia to propose [it]."

With the way paved by South Carolina's action, Virginia ratified by the very close vote of eighty-nine to seventy-nine; and the spotlight then turned upon New York, whose size made her as important as Virginia. "Our only chance of success depends on you," wrote Alexander Hamilton to James Madison before he received news of Virginia's action. "[S]ymptoms of relaxation in some of the [Antifederalist] leaders authorises a gleam of hope, if you do well; but certainly I think not otherwise."

New York Federalists had found themselves outnumbered in their convention by an estimated ratio of nineteen to forty-six. However, as Bancroft says: "On the third of July, while the convention was still engaged in considering the constitution, and noting the propositions of amendments, the decisive news of the unconditional ratification of the constitution by Virginia broke on its members; and from that moment it was certain that they would not venture to stand alone against the judgment of every state in New England except Rhode Island, and every other state except North Carolina."

This news led twelve delegates elected by the Antifederalists to vote for ratification and six more not to vote at all, and this produced a Federalist victory by another close vote—thirty to twenty-seven. Of the eighteen pivotal delegates, nine were from the most under-represented counties, another five were from the most nearly average counties, and only four from an over-represented county. Even with the switching of these delegates and the addition of the large blocs of people represented by them to the Federalist side of the ledger, the delegates voting to ratify the Constitution represented a minority of the people of New York—fewer people than the losing delegates represented (see Table IX).

TABLE IX   New York Ratification

	Percent of Delegates	Percent of Population Represented by Delegates So Voting
Voting for Ratification (30 delegates)	46.2	33.7
Voting against Ratification (27 delegates)	41.5	49.7
Not Voting (8 delegates)	12.3	16.6
	100.0	100.0

At this point, two of the thirteen states remained out of the Union. North Carolina was to hold two conventions, one during the summer of 1788, when ratification was defeated 84 to 184, and another in the fall of 1789, when the impossibility of continuing as an independent republic led to a vote for ratification of 194 to 77.

Rhode Island, such a maverick at the time that it was frequently called "Wrong Island," defeated or postponed numerous efforts to call a ratifying convention. By 1790, however, it was possible to hold a convention for this purpose, largely because of the threat that Providence and possibly other pro-Constitution towns would withdraw from the state and join the Union. The delegates voted for ratification by the closest vote of any of the twelve previous state tallies—thirty-four to thirty-two, with four abstaining. By so doing, Rhode Island became the third state in which the delegates voting their state into the Union represented fewer people than those delegates voting against the Constitution (see Table X).

TABLE X   Rhode Island Ratification

	Percent of Delegates	Percent of Population Represented by Delegates So Voting
Voting for Ratification (34 delegates)	48.6	44.1
Voting against Ratification (32 delegates)	45.7	51.4
Not Voting (4 delegates)	5.7	4.5
	100.0	100.0

The unequal apportionment of districts for the state ratifying conventions theoretically could have brought about a situation wherein delegates representing a small minority of the people in the nation could have enacted the Constitution. Similarly, delegates representing an even smaller minority could have defeated the new plan of government. As it worked out, unequal districting, though not resulting in such an extreme violation of the concept of majority rule, did immeasurably benefit the pro-Constitution forces. Three states—two of which were very important states either because of the effect on the forward-moving chain of events (South Carolina) or because of size and location (New York) —undoubtedly would have rejected the Constitution if their system of representation had been based on more equal districts. This would have seriously endangered the success of the Union.

The political behavior and economic motivations underlying the formulation and ratification of the Constitution have been thoroughly researched. Several of these interpretations (and critiques of interpretations) should be reconsidered in the light of the present apportionment analysis.

Orin Grant Libby, the first historian to analyze the subject systematically, concludes that it "was carried . . . by the influence of those classes along the great highways of commerce, the sea-coast, the Connecticut river, the Shenandoah valley and the Ohio river." "In proportion as the material interests along these arteries of intercourse were advanced and strengthened," he adds, "the Constitution was most readily received and most heartily supported." He emphasizes the point that "the areas of intercourse and wealth carried the constitution" and says that opposition to ratification was "confined to those interior or sparsely settled districts that were the last to receive population, and whose interests were agricultural as opposed to commercial; rural as opposed to urban."

When all the districts are classified according to Libby's dichotomy, there is a clear tendency for the "interior or sparsely settled districts" to be among the most under-represented districts in each state and for the coastal districts (as well as those Libby described as "along the great highways of commerce") to be among the most over-represented districts in each state (see Table XI). In contrast with today's situation,

TABLE XI   Libby Classification

	Total		Along Coast and Arteries of Commerce		In Interior Reigons	
	Number	Percent	Number	Percent	Number	Percent
⅓ most over-represented districts in each state	255	33.2	139	39.0	116	28.2
⅓ most nearly average districts in each state	258	33.6	112	31.5	146	35.4
⅓ most under-represented districts in each state	255	33.2	105	29.5	150	36.4
	768	100.0	356	100.0	412	100.0

districting for the state conventions tended to favor the cities and commercial centers. A similarity of the two periods, however, is the over-representation of areas which, though non-urban, are more easily dominated by commercial interests.

Charles A. Beard, writing in 1913, twenty years after the publication of Libby's monograph, examined the types of property held by delegates to the Philadelphia convention and to the various state ratifying conventions. Agreeing that the ratification movement "centered particularly in the regions in which mercantile, manufacturing, security, and personalty interests generally had their greatest strength," Beard finds it ". . . impossible to escape the conclusion that holders of personalty saw in the new government a strength and defence to their advantage." He adds, "inasmuch as so many leaders in the movement for ratification were large security holders, and inasmuch as securities constituted such a large proportion of personalty, this economic interest must have formed a very considerable dynamic element, if not the preponderating element, in bringing about . . . the new system." Not differing from Libby on the regional sources of the opposition, Beard finds that it "almost universally came from the agricultural regions. . . ."

Beard carefully studied the popular vote for delegates in districts where figures were available. He found that, "of the estimated 160,000 who voted in the election of delegates, not more than 100,000 men favored the adoption of the Constitution at the time it was put into effect—about one in six of the adult males." This estimate by Beard of a maximum of 62.5 percent favoring the Constitution, based on his estimate of the popular vote on contested delegates in the first eleven states to ratify, as well as his estimates of sentiment in North Carolina and Rhode Island, proved amazingly close to the present finding that 59.3 percent of the total population was represented by delegates voting the thirteen states into the new system of government.

"The disenfranchisement of the masses through property qualifications and ignorance and apathy," he found, "contributed largely to the facility with which the personalty-interest representatives carried the day." While aware of some degree of unequal apportionment of districts in South Carolina and also New York, Beard seemed unaware of the degree to which malapportionment, as a general situation, also "contributed largely to the facility with which" ratification forces "carried the day" in all states where there was delegate division—except Massachusetts and Connecticut.

In a critique of the Beard thesis, Robert E. Brown quite accurately points out the preponderance of agricultural areas over the commercial areas; and he then asks how there could have been decisions for ratification in the case of no less than seven states—South Carolina, Virginia, Maryland, Pennsylvania, Connecticut Massachusetts, and New Hampshire—if all the farmers, or most of them, opposed ratification. There would appear, however, to be two reasons why the simple addition of agrarians to one side and of commercial men to the other is a less than accurate index to interpretation of ratification. First, as indicated here, especially in South Carolina, but also in the other states (except Massachusetts and Connecticut), the agrarian influence was under-represented and the commercial influence was over-represented in the ratification conventions. Second, Brown does not give sufficient consideration to the degree to which commercial centers could extend their influence over nearby agrarian areas, through such devices as trade with commercial agriculturists.

Forrest McDonald found approximately equal proportions of holders of personalty—including securities, Beard's "dynamic element"—and of farmers or noncommercialists on each side in delegate roll calls. McDonald's alternative interpretation of the ratification movement, set forth as a hypothesis, is based on the consecutive stages of a developing mercantilism. "Mercantilism was geared to the economic needs of the community comprising the sovereign jurisdiction," he writes, "and those needs were not the same in different communities at a given time. . . ." Since "mercantilism had always engendered a wide range of regulatory and promotional measures" and since the various states were at various stages of mercantilist development, there were different legislative needs in different states and, therefore, different needs among the same types of economic groups in different states. Whether to ratify or reject the Constitution "depended . . . upon . . . the endowments with which a state could expect to cope with its particular problems of sovereign existence, and the skill with which its people had met the problems that had faced them during the brief period of the experiments in independence."

McDonald suggests that "five states (Delaware, New Jersey, Georgia, Connecticut, and Maryland) had faced problems that had proved unsurmountable to them . . . [and] . . . ratified quickly. . . . Four states (Pennsylvania, Massachusetts, South Carolina, and New Hampshire) were considerably better equipped for sovereign existence than the first five. . . . [But] each . . . was dissipating its energies in internal factional or areal disputes, ranging from legislation designed by one group for the destruction of another to organized physical violence. . . . Four states (Virginia, New York, North Carolina, and Rhode Island) were successful enough as sovereign entities to satisfy the greater part of their populations."

Curiously, the more likely a state was able to stand on its own—according to McDonald's hypothesis—the more likely it was that unequal apportionment benefited the pro-Constitution forces in that state —according to the present technique of evaluating districting. Conversely, the more likely a state was facing insurmountable problems in existing on its own, the less likely it was that unequal apportionment benefited the ratification campaign in that state (see Table XII).

Thus, in McDonald's four states which "were successful enough as sovereign entities," the pro-Constitution margin drops off from 50.2 points among delegates from over-represented districts to 6.3 points among delegates from under-represented districts. For his second grouping of states, the pattern is the same, but the dropoff is less precipitous. For the five states with insurmountable problems, the pro-Constitution margin remains constant, regardless of the number of people represented by delegates.

In a critique of Beard, as well as of Beard's critics, Lee Benson broadened the motivation from economic to social. There are two rival

TABLE XII   Net "Yes" Margin in Percentage Points Among Delegates

	States Successful as Sovereign Entities (Va., N. Y., N. C., R. I.)	States With Factional or Areal Disputes (Pa., Mass., S. C., N. H.)	States With Insurmountable Problems (Del., N. J., Ga., Conn., Md.)
Delegates from the ⅓ most over-represented districts in each state	+50.2	+26.2	+65.0
Delegates from the ⅓ most nearly average districts in each state	+12.1	+18.9	+69.5
Delegates from the ⅓ most under-represented districts in each state	+ 6.3	+ 3.4	+65.5

motivating ideas. On the one hand, there is the Agrarian Society, called Arcadia, "sparsely settled, localistic, self-contained," supported by the *agrarian-minded* who desired a system that "allocated to the State relatively slight, widely-dispersed, strictly limited powers and located those powers 'close to the people.'" On the other hand, there is the Commercial Society, as envisioned during the 1780s, which contained a substantial majority of farmers and was supported by the *commercial-minded* who, being more cosmopolitan in outlook, "had a more positive and optimistic view of State power than localistic agrarians."

Benson says that while there was a "marked tendency" for "agrarians to be federalists" (that is, for stronger state and local power) "and for commercialists to be nationalists" (that is, for stronger central government power), "social ideologies and opinions on the Constitution were mainly determined by the combined effects of three related, somewhat overlapping factors: men's roles within the existing economic structure which strongly influenced their roles within the social structure; the degree of urbanization of the areas in which they lived; and the ties which linked their communities with seaboard cities and interior large towns."

And why did the pro-Constitution forces win? Benson suggests they won because "men who strongly favored a Commercial Society were also likely to possess the personal and social attributes needed to win political power." This enabled "them to join forces with others of like mind, including some even inclined to agrarianism," and they were more likely than their opponents to possess the resources—including financial and propagandistic—needed for victory. It might well be that, among the resources possessed by these forces, especially in the most difficult states, a firm understanding of how to make use of unequally apportioned districts to achieve their goal of a Commercial Society was not the least important weapon in their arsenal!

Any interpretation—whether hypothesized or methodologically produced—must take into consideration the inequalities in the apportionment of delegates. McDonald notes, "No single system of interpretation can explain all historical phenomena; it is even unlikely that a single system can adequately explain all aspects of a single historical event." Though not a "system of interpretation" in and of itself, malapportionment in the Constitution ratification conventions is such an important element in the dynamics of the ratification movement that it should be an integral part of any sound interpretation; but, instead, it has been virtually overlooked. For a historian to look at the ratification process step-by-step without considering the systematic distortions caused by this malapportionment is somewhat like a botanist examining a leaf under a microscope with a very distorting lens.

Borrowing an image from the Benson hypothesis, one finds that the agrarian supporters of Arcadia tended to lose out in their pursuit of "widely-dispersed, strictly-limited powers, located close to the people" largely because of unfairly diminished representation at the ratifying conventions. In the retrospect of 180 years, historians can see that Arcadia's later adherents have felt that they have been able to fight a rearguard, holding action against the complete destruction of their idea largely because, somehow in the interim, they had gained the representation advantage—to an almost equally distorted degree. With the recent Supreme Court decisions taking this superiority in representation strength from them, their concern for the future of the idea for which they have so bitterly fought through the years can be more readily understood by friend and foe alike.

Party Formation in the United States Congress, 1789 to 1796: A Quantitative Analysis

MARY P. RYAN

For a generation most historians have agreed that the first American party system had its beginnings in the introduction of the Hamiltonian program in 1790 and 1791 and that this party system emerged full-blown during the 1795 to 1796 Jay Treaty controversy. Mary P. Ryan, who has used a computer to analyze all congressional roll call votes during the first four Congresses, questions both when voting blocs and parties formed and how much the origin of the first party system owed to specific issues.

. . . An accurate measure of party activity in Congress, and its relationship to political issues, must be a comprehensive one. It should include all roll call votes, not just those issues which loom large in American historiography. The hundreds of roll calls in the early American congresses, however, cannot be easily encompassed by a single human mind. Moreover, the historian can make order out of this maze of yeas and nays only by a preconceived idea of who was a Federalist and who was a Republican. These limitations do not pertain to the computer. Therefore, this study has used a computer to define voting blocs in the first four American congresses. The strength of these voting groups has been

From *William and Mary Quarterly*, 3d ser., 28 (1971):525–27, 531–42. Reprinted with omissions by permission of the author.

related to all the issues which arose in national congressional bodies (both the House and the Senate) between 1789 and 1796. In this way it is possible to avoid some of the historical hindsight which has marked much of the investigation of early American political parties. Ironically, computer technology may bring us closer to the world of Thomas Jefferson.

Before proceeding, however, some clarification of the term party is necessary. In a democratic system the concept of party generally denotes a union of like-minded people for the long-range implementation of political principles and programs. One indication of party activity in the early Republic, for example, is the set of partisan principles held by noteworthy public officials. Yet this is but one ingredient of a party system. The electioneering and officeseeking aspects of political parties, as described by Noble Cunningham, often undercut questions of principle. Moreover, Alfred Young's study disclosed the subversion of the national Republican program at the state level. This paper focuses on still another manifestation of party—the coalition and opposition of members of the national legislature. The United States Congress is but one forum of party activity. A systematic treatment of this dimension of partisanship, however, will facilitate investigation of the overall nature and function of early American parties.

In this investigation the computer was used for mammoth but simple mathematical tasks. The first problem was to devise a measure of cohesiveness or "voting-togetherness" in Congress. This was accomplished by instructing the computer to compare all the votes of an individual member of Congress with all the votes of each of his peers. The number of agreements in each comparison, reduced by the probable number of chance agreements given the division of votes on the particular issue considered, was divided by the number of times this pair of congressmen voted on the same issue. The result of this calculation was designated by the Greek letter mu.* These simple mu scores usually fell

* The mu score was devised by Lynn L. Marshall. He defines it as follows: "The μ index for a pair of legislators is calculated by the following formula: $\mu = \dfrac{2(a-p)}{N}$. "N" is the number of roll calls on which both voted, "a" is the actual number of roll calls on which they agreed, and "p" is the probable agreement level or the level of agreement one would expect by chance given the divisions on each roll call. The "p" factor is computed by summing, for all roll calls on which the pair voted, the probability that both voted either with the majority or the minority. The index expresses a normalized variation from the probable agreement level, and may be either positive for an agreeing pair or negative for a disagreeing pair. The "2" factor is inserted in order to make the index vary from 0 to 1.00 on the positive side. It may vary from 0 to −2.00 on the negative side since "p" may vary from $\dfrac{N}{2}$ to N, if all roll calls are unanimous." (Only positive μ values were used in this paper.)

within the range of +.5 and —.5. All the positive mu scores for each member of Congress (i.e., his agreement ratio with each of his peers) were then averaged to give the individual's average positive mu. These scores for all members of a particular House or Senate were again averaged to yield the positive congressional mu. These scores, ranging from .232 to .396, provided a measure of general voting cohesiveness in the first four congresses.

The congressional mu provided only a measure of general voting cohesiveness; it did not isolate specific party division. By analyzing the individual average mus, however, it was possible to divide the congressional membership into two voting blocs. Upon comparing the simple mu scores of high-scoring legislators (when paired with one another), they were found to relate highly either positively or negatively, that is, to be either allies or foes. On this basis leaders were assigned to either one party or another. All lower scoring congressmen were then compared with these leaders and assigned to the voting bloc with which they related positively. Thus two voting parties were isolated.

. . .

The fundamental discovery of this study was the emergence in the first session of the United States Congress of two voting blocs which remained remarkably stable in the eight sessions that followed. Of the sixty-five legislators who entered the United States Senate between 1789 and 1796, only eighteen changed their bloc membership in a subsequent session. Of these, nine senators moved only into the lower echelons of the other party, voting with the new party less than two-thirds of the time. Three other senators were mavericks, switching from party to party recurrently. Of the six remaining defectors, four changed blocs for only one session and returned promptly to the party fold. Only two, Bradley of Vermont and Ross of Pennsylvania, actually shifted their party allegiance. The defection pattern in the House was similar. Among hundreds of representatives in this period, only twenty-four altered their bloc alignment. Nine of these defections were of a low order; two were by mavericks; ten were one session in duration; and only six were genuine changes in party allegiance.

Most members of the first American congresses quickly identified with one or two voting blocs and maintained this affiliation throughout the period. Moreover, newly elected congressmen clustered around the earliest voting configurations. For convenience these two voting blocs will be assigned the titles which they ultimately accepted—Republicans (Bloc A) and Federalists (Bloc B). The permutations in party consciousness, and the growing suitability of this nomenclature, will be apparent in the course of this paper.

136   Ryan

The most immediately apparent characteristic of these voting blocs was their sectional composition, as revealed in the following table. According to Table I New Englanders were predominantly Federalist and

TABLE I Sectional Character of Parties, First to Fourth Congresses

Congress: Session	Federaltists			Republicans		
	New England	Middle a	South b	New England	Middle	South
Senate						
1:1	4	4	0	0	2	7
1:2	4	6	2	0	2	5
1:3	4	6	0	0	1	10
2:1	10	2	0	0	2	10
2:2	9	5	0	0	7	7
3:1	4	6	3	2	2	8
3:2	5	3	1	2	1	3
4:1	8	5	3	1	1	8
4:2	6	7	2	1	1	7
House						
1:1	11	14	1	1	1	20
1:2	14	9	4	0	11	20
1:3	14	13	0	1	0	19
2:1	13	8	3	0	13	14
2:2	15	3	5	0	3	12
3:1	22	13	4	2	8	29
3:2	24	14	6	3	7	20
4:1	18	11	4	5	16	38
4:2	18	12	6	4	12	31

Notes: a New York, New Jersey, Pennsylvania, and Delaware.
b Includes Kentucky and Tennessee after admission to the Union in 1792 and 1796.

southerners largely Republican, while the congressional delegation from the middle states tended to divide its votes between the two parties. In the first two Senates this pattern was almost perfect. In the third and fourth Senates it began to break down as southerners appeared in the Federalist bloc and significant numbers of New Englanders voted with the Republicans. In the House this pattern was less clear, but nonetheless was in evidence. Those southerners in the Federalist camp in the first two congresses were primarily from South Carolina. It was not until the Third and Fourth Congresses that Virginia congressmen cast their votes with the Federalists. Given the tenacity of individual party allegiances described earlier, these slight changes in the sectional contours of party membership can be attributed primarily to the voting behavior of either marginal party members or of newly elected congressmen. Thus the early congressional parties had a clear sectional base which became somewhat less distinct in the Third and Fourth Congresses.

Needless to say, this sectional cleavage did not preclude party differences based on political programs and principles. The personal leadership of the two voting blocs disclosed their policy differences. For example, unflinching supporters of the policies of the Washington administration, such as Rufus King and Fisher Ames, consistently maintained the highest mu scores among the Federalists. While Virginia congressmen were the mainstay of Republicanism, staunch antifederalists like William Maclay, and hard core party organizers like Aaron Burr, also scored high in Republican loyalty. James Madison voted with the Republicans regularly. Yet it is interesting to note that the acknowledged founder of the Republican party did not score particularly high in voting cohesiveness, and on this measure of party loyalty surrendered leadership to others. The polarization of congressional voting grew in strength as the blocs expanded in membership. The increase in general voting cohesiveness as measured by the average congressional mu scores is demonstrated by the following table. This table indicates a significant increase in congressional voting cohesiveness over time. The agreement ratios,

TABLE II   Average Mu Scores, First to Fourth Congresses

Congress	Senate	House
1	.232	.300
2	.270	.320
3	.352	.386
4	.321	.396

which record degrees of loyalty to specific parties, revealed the same upward trend. The agreement ratios were calculated from party votes only. Since a diminishing number of nonparty votes in itself can be a measure of growing partisanship, Table III records both agreement ratios and the percentage of the total number of roll calls from which they were calculated.

Both the mu scores and the agreement ratios revealed a trend toward party activity which escalated in the Third Congress. Changes in

TABLE III   Party Agreement Ratios, First to Fourth Congresses

A. Senate

Congress	Total Number of Roll Calls	Percentage of Partisan Votes	Agreement Ratios Federalist	Republican	Average
1	78	69	.64	.49	.57
2	46	74	.66	.77	.70
3	75	72	.70	.81	.75
4	57	74	.72	.69	.71

B. House

Congress	Total Number of Roll Calls	Percentage of Partisan Votes	Agreement Ratios Federalist	Republican	Average
1	109	67	.62	.67	.64
2	96	78	.62	.62	.62
3	68	85	.74	.61	.67
4	82	71	.78	.67	.73

the number of party votes in each session were more ambiguous. Yet this amorphous pattern may have stemmed from the varying number of inconsequential issues before a given congress and may therefore be a poor index of party strength. As noted earlier, the Third Congress also marked a slight breakdown in the sectional contours of party membership. The geographical distribution of party membership, however, was not the only measure of the cogency of sectionalism. The quality of issues before Congress must also be considered. Strong cohesiveness, even within a sectionally skewed voting alignment, may indicate increasing loyalty to national party programs as well as agreement on matters of immediate sectional interest. Therefore, sectional as well as party consciousness can best be analyzed in relation to the particular issues which provoked strong voting cohesiveness at different times. Depending on the quality and context of the issue being voted upon, high cohesiveness may indicate sectional interest, opposition to a single proposal, or loyalty to a set of policies which identify a Federalist or a Republican party.

This kind of information was extrapolated from the final data matrix. In order to illustrate this procedure the matrices for the second session of the first House of Representatives, and for the first session of the fourth House, will be analyzed in detail. Although the party agreement ratios for these two sessions were similar, they illustrate different stages in party development. First of all, these sessions varied in the number and types of nonparty votes. Of the eighteen nonparty votes in the second session of the First Congress, four were on minute issues such as relief for an individual war widow. An additional vote was the lone exception to a series of partisan votes on the selection of a national capital. The thirteen remaining nonparty votes were on more significant and dormantly partisan issues such as the United States debt, spirit duties, and Indian policy. Of the ten nonparty votes in the first session of the Fourth Congress nine were on minute or procedural questions. Only one vote on a significant question, the fortification of harbors for a possible war with England, failed to divide Congress along partisan lines. Moreover, issues which failed to provoke a partisan response in the First Congress, such as Indian policy and the debt, had become the foci of party voting patterns by the Fourth Congress.

Thus, the particular issues which summoned high party cohesiveness further differentiated these two sessions of Congress. Table IV lists

TABLE IV   Party Voting First Congress, Second Session, House

Issue	Number of Partisan Roll Calls	Average Party Agreement Ratios	
		Federalists	Republicans
Location of capital	20 of 22	.84	.89
Spirit duties	1 of 3	.92	.94
Report on public credit	4 of 4	.48	.78
Funding of national debt	5 of 11	.46	.66
Post office	1 of 1	.31	.79
Salt duty	1 of 1	.19	.10

all the partisan votes of the second session of the First Congress along with their respective agreement ratios in decreasing order of magnitude. Both the majority of partisan roll calls and the consistently highest party agreement ratios of this session concerned the selection of a national capital. Therefore the high partisanship of the second session of the First Congress can be attributed to a single issue.

The partisanship of the Fourth Congress, on the other hand, expressed itself on a whole variety of issues, as Table V indicates. Tables IV and V not only illustrate the data and analysis upon which this study was based, but also intimate its major findings. Between the First and Fourth Congresses partisanship had grown both stronger and more comprehensive, until Federalists and Republicans forcefully opposed one another on a great variety of issues.

Evidence of this development in the remaining sessions of Congress will be presented in a summary manner. In this study an issue was categorized as highly partisan when both parties achieved an agreement ratio of .75 or above on the pertinent votes. In addition, the issues around which party identities might form were arranged into four categories. The first category included governmental organization, administration, and procedure—for example, the selection of a national capital or the admission of new states. Second were questions of finance, particularly Hamilton's plans for assumption of the state debts by the national government and the establishment of the Bank of the United States. The third category included foreign policy and military affairs, which came

TABLE V   Party Voting Fourth Congress, First Session, House

Issue	Number of Partisan Roll Calls	Average Party Agreement Ratios	
		Federalists	Republicans
Treaty with Spain	1 of 2	1.00	.95
Tennessee statehood	3 of 4	.94	.91
Jay Treaty	8 of 8	.94	.85
Israel Smith's seat	1 of 1	.92	.86
Sale of pirated goods	1 of 1	1.00	.74
National debt	3 of 3	.92	.70
Appropriations for foreign trade	1 of 1	.86	.65
Frontier protection	4 of 4	.64	.88
Indian trade	1 of 1	1.00	.50
Seamen relief	1 of 2	.52	.79
Appropriations for 1796	1 of 1	.93	.41
Land sales	2 of 2	.68	.45
Naval armaments	3 of 3	.82	.30
Cabinet salaries	2 of 2	.86	.17

to center around relations with the belligerents, England and France. Last was a collection of matters which arose from domestic controversies and popular demands, including perennial issues like the protection of the frontiers as well as unique manifestations of popular discontent such as the Whiskey Rebellion.

At different times, and with varying intensity, these four categories of issues became the battleground of two tenacious voting blocs. The general pattern was quite simple. In the First and Second Congresses the first category of issues, establishing the government and its procedures, accounted for most voting cohesiveness. In the Third and Fourth Congresses partisanship spread to all four categories. Moreover, in the early congresses votes on administrative and procedural questions stimulated a sectional response, while at the close of the period such questions brought into play attitudes toward the Washington administration as well as conscious party identities. Evidence of this transformation will be presented as it developed in both houses of Congress.

In the First Congress two voting blocs arose from the debate over the permanent seat of government. Sectional loyalties determined most congressmen's choice of a site for the nation's capital. In the Second Congress the seminal issue was again of an organizational nature: deciding the ratio of a state's population to its congressional representation. The sectional polarization of votes on apportionment reflected regional, and particularly southern, population expectations and the consequent geographical concentration of national power. Other procedural questions—constitutional amendments, contested elections, and the formation of executive departments—produced unanimity rather than partisanship in the first two congresses.

The remaining categories of issues were generally immune to partisanship in the first two congresses. The establishment of a department of foreign affairs and a national military failed to evoke a partisan voting pattern, as did policy toward the frontier, fisheries, and Indian affairs. Two persistent voting blocs formed around financial questions during the first two congresses, but these were temporary alignments outside the dominant party formation, that is, a voting pattern maintained only during a series of roll calls on a single issue, the assumption of state debts by the federal government. Voting cohesiveness on that issue reflected the persistent monetary interests of the different states. As legislators registered their votes according to the size of the debt within their respective states, Federalists like Rufus King of New York and Oliver Ellsworth of Connecticut found themselves in opposite camps. Voting on this issue did not indicate the formation of party opposition to the financial policies of the Washington administration. When in the Second Congress James Madison called upon his colleagues to condemn the architect of the Federalist financial system, Alexander Hamilton, only a slim majority of Republicans joined him.

Although the voting on nonprocedural and nonsectional issues in the first two congresses never constituted a consistent and forthright party conflict, it did display the rudiments of party consciousness. For example, Federalists united in support of administration policies such as establishing a national military, the Bank of the United States, and shipping regulations. Although the Republicans never strongly challenged these programs, they were developing their own positive party identity. The Republican bias in foreign policy was foreshadowed by opposition to stipulations in the peace treaty with Great Britain in the Senate and sympathetic endorsement of France's republican constitution in the House. The popular and anti-aristocratic image of the Republican party was also evidenced at this time. The Republicans championed the common farmer by opposing a tax upon his medium of exchange, "spirits." By the second session of the second Senate Republicans summoned the majority of its membership in support of the anti-aristocratic measure of opening their chamber to the public.

When the third Senate convened in December 1793 this embryonic partisanship within sectional voting blocs escalated to forceful party conflict. The very first issue before the Senate, the incorporation of the Bank of the United States, embroiled that body in partisan controversy. The procedural category followed finance into the fray as the Federalists stood their ground against seating the Republican stalwart Albert Gallatin. High partisanship also colored voting on domestic issues, the excise tax, and Indian policy. This upsurge in partisanship, the confrontation of two cohesive parties on a variety of issues, occurred a session later in the House of Representatives. The first issue before the second session of the third House was the Whiskey Rebellion. On the three votes which contested the legitimacy of this popular uprising and its relationship to the Democratic Societies which so alarmed the Federalists, both parties demonstrated nearly perfect solidarity. Voting on the related domestic issues of the frontier and Indian affairs manifested the same party cohesion. Moreover, extraneous and previously nonpartisan issues such as the United States debt now pitted unified Republicans against unified Federalists. Thus, by the close of the Third Congress congressional responses to popular events, as well as questions of national finance and procedural matters, had become objects of partisan dispute.

The third Senate had also exhibited strong partisanship in the category of foreign policy when unified Republicans and Federalists clashed over the embargo on British goods. The Republicans' hard line toward Great Britain was overruled when Washington affixed his signature to the Jay Treaty in August 1795. Once the conciliatory measures of the treaty were exposed it became another object of party antagonism. Thus, partisan foreign policy found its fullest expression in the first session of the fourth House of Representatives, which debated appropriations to enforce the Jay Treaty. Yet the abrasive partisanship around the Jay Treaty was not an isolated phenomenon. Members of the Fourth Congress aligned themselves in the same highly partisan manner when voting on routine government procedures. The Federalists strongly opposed the admission of Tennessee to the Union and the additional Republican votes it portended. The seating of Republican congressman Israel Smith also became a partisan ploy. Although the fourth Senate was not a forum for the debate of the Jay Treaty, high partisanship periodically greeted all categories of issues before that body. Moreover, even such trivial matters as establishing the time of the next Congress and relief for individual petitioners conformed, although imperfectly, to the partisan pattern.

By 1796 all classes of issues before Congress had become foci of party loyalty. While in the First Congress procedural issues summoned local and sectional interests, by the Fourth they evoked party identifications. Pitched battles over the seats of new congressmen attested to the party identification of even prospective legislators. The first session of the fourth Senate opened with a remarkable display of party consciousness, one which demonstrated the complex process of party maturation. The issue seemed a perfunctory procedure, the endorsement of the annual presidential address. Yet on this occasion, Washington had referred to the partisan issue of the Whiskey Rebellion and made his celebrated condemnation of the "self-created" Democratic Societies. The Republican bloc summoned the vast majority of its membership to express formal disagreement with these sentiments. Their temerity before the executive was in marked contrast to the behavior of the first Senate. At that time William Maclay's proposal to delete the words "most gracious" from the senatorial thanks to Washington did not even come to a vote. Within eight years of the founding of the Republic a routine communication to the president had become the focus of opposition and the manifestation of an already seasoned voting alliance.

This analysis of voting behavior with quantitative techniques and computer tools has confirmed the rapid formation and steady growth of congressional parties. It has disclosed two voting blocs—forged out of sectional interest and maintaining a basically sectional distribution of membership—growing into alliances which expressed party loyalties on a great variety of issues, of national as well as regional import. This process was subtler and more complex than the consolidation of voting patterns around seminal issues of finance and foreign policy. Partisan coalitions garnered substance and strength from more sources than resistance to the Hamiltonian system and the Jay Treaty. The two voting blocs which were forged in the First Congress had reached maturity by the Third, well before the Jay Treaty controversy. By 1795 not only dramatic foreign policy decisions, but also domestic matters and governmental routine, had become the objects of systematic party dispute.

Such were the manifestations of party formation in early American congresses. Speculation as to the origins and function of the first American party system is beyond the scope of this study. Yet the relationship between particular issues and mounting partisanship, as presented here, suggests some further lines of inquiry.

Party formation was not inherent in the issues or the interests which confronted the first congresses. Extracongressional political organizations contributed to the development of two parties. Most likely the partisanship of newspaper propaganda, political societies, and local electioneering had penetrated Congress by this time. What else but his Republican reputation denied Albert Gallatin of Pennsylvania a seat in the third Senate? The daily interaction of public officials further enhanced the possibility of party formation. The stability of the earliest voting alliances suggests the role played by personal allegiances and habits of communication. Moreover, the constitutional system within which congressmen operated seems to have conditioned the development of a two-party system. Section and local alliances seem to have given way, not to pluralism, but to a dualism of support or opposition to the policies of the executive branch. It would appear that the organizational and procedural context in which national officials operated played a significant part in party development.

Not all the provocations of partisanship, however, can be traced to the maneuvers of politicians. It was an uprising of Pennsylvania farmers which stimulated forthright party opposition in the House of Representatives. Moreover, the foreign policy debates of this period did not transpire in a congressional vacuum. Antagonism to British policy was a popular cause, the vehemence of which was illustrated by mob action in Boston and New York. Direct expression of popular discontent, as well as the behavior of political elites, stimulated party formation, and now call forth efforts to write history "from the bottom up." Jefferson's equivocal view of early parties rings true. If these infant parties had a democratic function it was to prevent executive indifference to the widespread complaints of the American people. This lesson was taken to heart by Fisher Ames as his party was ousted from executive office in 1800: "We should, I am sanguine enough to believe, throw upon our antagonists the burdens of supporting and vindicating government, and enjoy their late advantages of finding fault, which popular prejudice is ever prone to listen to."

Thomas Jefferson:
Self and Society

WINTHROP D. JORDAN

No one debates Thomas Jefferson's monumental impact on his time, nor does anyone deny Jefferson's profound effect on subsequent generations. Above all Jefferson is revered as the apostle and symbol of liberty. Yet the demigod is flawed by the nagging fact that he held slaves and by the gnawing knowledge that he believed blacks inferior. Historians have generally attributed the former to conditions in Jefferson's day and have ignored the latter. Winthrop D. Jordan, however, has explored Jefferson's racism both because it contrasts sharply with his love of freedom and because Jefferson's private torment reflects the dilemma of the larger society. Jordan's exploration reveals a close connection between Jefferson's personal life and his attitudes toward Negroes.

Against the backdrop of changing attitudes and actions concerning Negroes and Negro slavery, the writings of one man become a fixed and central point of reference and influence. In the years after the Revolution the speculations of Thomas Jefferson were of great importance because so many people read and reacted to them. His remarks about Negroes in the only book he ever wrote were more widely read, in all probability, than any others until the mid-nineteenth century. In addition

From Winthrop D. Jordan, *White Over Black: American Attitudes Toward the Negro, 1550–1812*, pp. 429–30, 457–81. © 1968 by the University of North Carolina Press. Footnotes omitted. Reprinted by permission of the publisher for the Institute of Early American History and Culture of Williamsburg, Va.

to his demonstrable impact upon other men, Jefferson is important—or perhaps more accurately, valuable to historical analysis—because he permits (without intending to) a depth and range of insight into the workings of ideas about Negroes within one man as he stood in relationship to his culture. Jefferson's energetic facility with the pen makes it possible, uniquely so in this period of history, to glimpse some of the inward springs of feeling which supported certain attitudes towards Negroes. It then becomes possible to see the intricate interlacing of one man's personality with his social surroundings, the values of his culture, and the ideas with which he had contact. Thomas Jefferson was not a typical nor an ordinary man, but his enormous breadth of interest and his lack of originality make him an effective sounding board for his culture. On some important matters, therefore, he may be taken as accurately reflecting common presuppositions and sensitivities even though many Americans disagreed with some of his conclusions.

To contemplate any man-in-culture is to savor complexity. It will be easiest to start with Jefferson's central dilemma: he hated slavery but thought Negroes inferior to white men. His remarks on the Negro's mental inferiority helped kindle a revealing public controversy on the subject which deserves examination. But it will also be necessary to return again to Thomas Jefferson, to his inward world where Negro inferiority was rooted. There it is possible to discern the interrelationship between his feelings about the races and his feeling about the sexes and thence to move once again to the problem of interracial sex in American culture. Finally, by tacking back to Jefferson and to the way he patterned his perceptions of his surroundings, it becomes easy to see how he assimilated the Indian to his anthropology and to America. His solution with the Negro was very different.

.   .   .

JEFFERSON: PASSIONATE REALITIES

Jefferson started, in fact, with a brief assertion of the necessity for colonizing Negroes elsewhere once they had been freed. "Why not retain and incorporate the blacks into the state?" Only later did his answer find wide acceptance in Virginia, especially after September 1800. "Deep rooted prejudices entertained by the whites; ten thousand recollections, by the blacks, of the injuries they have sustained; new provocations; the real distinctions which nature has made; and many other circumstances, will . . . produce convulsions which will probably never end but in the extermination of the one or the other race." His ensuing remarks made evident which factor carried greatest weight with him, for he immediately entered into a long discussion of other "objections" which were "physical and moral." "The first difference which strikes us," he wrote in accurate summary of his countrymen's perceptions, "is that of colour." Accepting the chromatically inaccurate but universally accepted metaphor of the Negro's "black" color, he continued, "Whether the black of the negro resides in the reticular membrane between the skin and scarf-skin, or in the scarf-skin itself; whether it proceeds from the colour of the blood, the colour of the bile, or from that of some other secretion, the difference is fixed in nature, and is as real as if its seat and cause were better known to us." For Jefferson, the overwhelming aspect of the Negro's color was its *reality;* he simply shelved the important scientific question of its cause. Even when he considered the question in a more neutral context, in his discussion of albino Negroes in the section on "Productions Mineral, Vegetable and Animal," he refused (or perhaps was unable) to offer a word of speculation about a matter on which other scientists speculated freely. Instead he rushed on, spilling forth words which revealed what the "reality" of the "difference" was for Thomas Jefferson. The passionate underpinnings of his feelings were laid bare.

> And is this difference of no importance? Is it not the foundation of a greater or less share of beauty in the two races? Are not the fine mixtures of red and white, the expressions of every passion by greater or less suffusions of colour in the one, preferable to that eternal monotony, which reigns in the countenances, that immoveable veil of black which covers all the emotions of the other race? Add to these, flowing hair, a more elegant symmetry of form, and their own judgment in favour of the whites, declared by their preference of them, as uniformly as is the preference of the Oran-ootan for the black women over those of his own species. The circumstances of superior beauty, is thought worthy attention in the propagation of our horses, dogs, and other domestic animals: why not in that of man?

With this geyser of libidinal energy Jefferson recapitulated major tenets of the American racial complex. Merely on a factual level he passed along several notions which had long been floating about, some since the first years of confrontation in Africa. Red and white were the ingredients of beauty, and Negroes were pronouncedly less beautiful than whites; Negroes desired sexual relations especially with whites; black women had relations with orang-outangs. On a deeper level the pattern of his remarks was more revealing of Jefferson himself. Embedded in his thoughts on beauty was the feeling that whites were subtler and more delicate in their passions and that Negroes, conversely, were more crude. He felt Negroes to be sexually more animal—hence the gratuitous intrusion of the man-like ape. His libidinal desires, unacceptable and inadmissible to his society and to his higher self, were effectively transferred to others and thereby drained of their intolerable immediacy. Having allowed these dynamic emotions perilously close to the surface in the form of the orang-outang, he had immediately shifted to the safe neutral ground of horse-breeding, thus denying his exposure by caricaturing it. Without fully recognizing the adversary within, he continued to flee, taking refuge on higher and higher ground. "They have less hair on the face and body." Not quite safe enough, but he was reaching the safe temple of science. "They secrete less by the kidnies, and more by the glands of the skin," he wrote, carefully placing the rationale before the important fact, "which gives them a very strong and disagreeable odour." Having taken as given the facts of Negro secretion, about which many contemporaries were uncertain, he applied them as proof to a less emotion-laden folk belief. "This greater degree of transpiration renders them more tolerant of heat, and less so of cold, than the whites." He came to rest finally in convoluted speculation. "Perhaps too a difference of structure in the pulmonary apparatus, which a late ingenious experimentalist [Adair Crawford, *Experiments . . . on Animal Heat*] has discovered to be the principal regulator of animal heat, may have disabled them from extricating, in the act of inspiration, so much of that fluid from the outer air, or obliged them in expiration, to part with more of it."

Yet Jefferson was never completely at rest. His picture of Negroes as crudely sensual beings, which was at once an offprint of popular belief and a functional displacement of his own emotional drives, kept popping up whenever Negroes came to mind. That it did not appear on other, irrelevant occasions indicated that there were limits to its personal importance, yet most of Jefferson's widely-read remarks on the Negro were tinged by it. When discussing the Negro's over-all temperament he wrote, "They are more ardent after their female: but love seems with them to be more an eager desire, than a tender delicate mixture of sentiment and sensation." In the original manuscript he had stated this even more baldly. Elsewhere in the *Notes* he commented in defense of the masculinity of Indian men despite the sparsity of their hair: "Negroes have notoriously less hair than the whites; yet they are more ardent."

Jefferson had framed old beliefs about the Negro's sexuality in newly deprecatory terms, and defenders of the Negro rose in his behalf. Gilbert Imlay laid his finger on the core of Jefferson's argument with acute intuition but faltering analysis:

> Were a man, who, with all the ardour of a youthful passion, had just been gazing upon the fair bosom of a loved and beautiful mistress, and afterwards marked the contrast of that paradise of sublunary bliss, to the African or Indian hue, to exclaim in the terms which Mr. Jefferson has used, he might be judged excusable on account of the intoxication of his

heated senses—But when a grave philosopher, who has passed the meridian of life, sits down to meliorate, by his writings and opinions, the condition of the slaves of his country, whose fetters have fixed an obliquity upon the virtue and humanity of the southern Americans, I confess it appears to me not a little jejune and inconsistent.

The Reverend Samuel Stanhope Smith of Princeton, however, was affronted by Jefferson's assertions of ardency which kindled "the senses only, not the imagination," and seized the opportunity of reading an environmentalist lecture in morals to slaveowners. "With what fine tints can imagination invest the rags, the dirt, or the nakedness so often seen in a quarter of negro labourers? Besides, to awaken the exquisite sentiments of a delicate love, and to surround it with all the enchantment of the imagination, this passion requires to be placed under certain moral restraints which are seldom formed in the coarse familiarity, and promiscuous intercourse permitted, and too often encouraged among the American slaves." Smith was careful to discharge the other barrel by declaring that he had seen many instances of the highest sentiments of love among Negroes. Jefferson never replied to these attacks.

While the depth of emotional intensity underlying his thinking about the Negro seems sufficiently evident, the sources of his feeling remain obscured by his unsurprising failure to articulate emotional patterns and processes of which he was unaware. As has often been remarked about him, few men have written so much yet revealed so little of themselves. This fact is in itself enormously suggestive, though it has been a disappointment to historians that he did not include in his papers some remarks on parents and childhood, some few letters to his beloved wife. Yet if one draws back the velvet curtain of his graceful style to regard the *pattern* of his life and thought, it is possible to detect certain of the currents running beneath the structure of his intellect.

JEFFERSON: WHITE WOMEN AND BLACK

Two interrelated currents seem especially relevant to his thoughts on the Negro, the more deep-seated one having to do with his relationships with members of the opposite sex. Jefferson grew up in a world of women. His father, a man of more imposing physique even than Jefferson, died when his son was fourteen. At that critical age he was left with a mother about whom we know almost nothing, four sisters, and one brother. He was never really congenial with his brother, and their infrequent correspondence in later life merely exposed the enormous gulf between them in interests and talents. He never said much concerning his mother and sisters. As a young man, leading a life thoroughly lacking in direction, he filled his letters with talk about girls, but his gay chitchat ended abruptly after a keenly disappointing one-sided romance with Rebecca Burwell, an attractve sixteen-year-old orphan. Consoling himself with outbursts of misogyny, Jefferson turned to the companionship of men. Nearly ten years later he made a level-headed match with Martha Skelton Wayles, a twenty-three-year-old widow whose young son died shortly before the wedding. On the marriage bond he at first inserted the word "spinster" but then corrected himself with "widow." The marriage lasted from 1772 until her death in 1782, but again Jefferson left no picture of the woman sharing his life. She bore him six children: three girls died in infancy, as did their only son (whom Jefferson referred to as such before the birth!), and two daughters survived. His wife's failing health worried him terribly—it was in this period that he wrote the *Notes*—and her death left him shattered with grief, not untinged, as so often happens, with self-pity.

Throughout his life after the Burwell affair, Jefferson seemed capable of attachment only to married women. Several years before his marriage he had made, on his own much later admission, improper advances to the wife of a neighboring friend. In Paris, as a widower, he carried on a superficially frantic flirtation with Mrs. Maria Cosway, a "love affair" in which the "love" was partly play and the "affair" nonexistent. The only woman outside his family for whom he formed some attachment was John Adams's remarkable wife, Abigail; with good reason he admired her intellect. With women in general he was uneasy and unsure; he held them at arm's length, wary, especially after his wife's death, of the dangers of over-commitment. Intimate emotional engagement with women seemed to represent for him a gateway into a dangerous, potentially explosive world which threatened revolution against the discipline of his higher self. His famous "Dialogue of the Head and the Heart," written to Maria Cosway, revealed his dim awareness of the struggle within, for beneath its stiltedness one senses a man not naturally cool but thoroughly air-conditioned. Of necessity, the Head emerged victorious in the dialogue, just as it did in real life, declaring pontifically to the Heart, "This is not a world to live at random in as you do." The sentence might have served as a motto for his life.

As Jefferson matured, he seems to have mitigated this inner tension by imputing potential explosiveness to the opposite sex and by assuming that female passion must and could only be controlled by marriage. Not long after the Burwell affair, he wrote or copied a solemn passage which characterized marriage as best founded on a wife's self-restraint and constant attentiveness to the wishes of her husband: "marriage, be a husband what he may, reverses the prerogative of sex." Certainly Jefferson lived in a culture which assumed dutiful wifely submission, but there was a particular urgency in his stress upon the necessity of female decorum. In any age, his strictures on toilet and dress to his unmarried daughter would seem egregiously detailed. "Nothing is so disgusting to our sex," he warned her, "as a want of cleanliness and delicacy in yours." It is scarcely surprising, therefore, that when living in Paris, Jefferson dashed off frequent warnings of the sexual corruptions awaiting American youths in Europe: "in lieu of this ["conjugal love"] are substituted pursuits which nourish and invigorate all our bad passions, and which offer only moments of extasy amidst days and months of restlessness and torment." And, he added, characteristically seizing an opportunity to salute republican virtue, "Much, very much inferior this to the tranquil permanent felicity with which domestic society in America blesses most of its inhabitants." If unrestrained sex seemed a dangerous trap to Jefferson, he was deeply certain which sex had set it. On one occasion, in his rough "Notes on a Tour of English Gardens," he jotted down an arresting mental picture, in an otherwise matter-of-fact account, of "a small, dark, deep hollow, with recesses of stone in the banks on every side. In one of these is a Venus pudique, turned half round as if inviting you with her into the recess." It was a revealing description, as much of Jefferson as of the statue. Most revealing of all was a letter to James Madison in 1786. The recent revisal of Virginia laws had included mitigation of criminal punishments, but the *lex talionis* had been preserved in two cases, death for treason or murder and castration for rape and buggery, etc. Jefferson wrote from Paris an interesting commentary. "The principle of retaliation is much criticised here, particularly in the case of Rape. They think the punishment indecent and unjustifiable. I should be for altering it, but for a different reason: that is on account of the temptation women would be under to make it the instrument of vengeance against an inconstant lover, and of disappointment to a rival." Evidently women loomed as threats to masculinity, as dangerously powerful sexual aggressors.

Jefferson's transferal of sexual aggressiveness to women helps explain certain otherwise puzzling aspects of his expressions on the Negro. He was greatly concerned with the Negro's lack of beauty—in his culture a highly feminine attribute—and it was with some justification that a political opponent charged that "The desire of preserving the beauty of the human race predominates . . . in the mind of our philosopher." Moreover, Jefferson failed to offer even a hint concerning the Negro male's supposedly large organ, and though this failure may have stemmed from an understandable reluctance to broach the matter publicly, he gave no suggestion even indirectly of the sexual aggressiveness of Negro men; nor did he ever do so privately. In fact—and it is an arresting one upon re-reading the passage—his previously quoted remarks concerning beauty and breeding had reference not to Negro men, nor to Negroes in general, but, in implicit yet highly specific fashion, to Negro women!

It is in the light of this emotional pattern that Jefferson's widely discussed relationship with the Hemings family should be considered. The subject is an unpalatable one for many Americans: the assertion that a great national figure was involved in miscegenation—this is the central supposed "fact" of the Hemings matter—is one that Americans find difficult to treat as anything but a malicious accusation. Malice *was*, indeed, the animating force behind the original claim, but we need to brace ourselves into an intellectual posture from which we can see that the importance of the stories about black Sally Hemings and Thomas Jefferson lies in the fact that they seemed—and to some people still seem—of any importance. The facts of the matter require attention not because Jefferson's behavior needs to be questioned but because they are of some (but not very much) help in understanding Jefferson's views about miscegenation and, far more, because they shed light on the cultural context in which he moved and of which we are heirs. Viewed in the context of his feelings about white women, the problem of Jefferson's actual overt behavior becomes essentially irrelevant to the subject of this book; it is to the inner world of his thought and feeling that we must look for significant behavior and, even more, to his culture for the larger significance of the matter.

In 1802 James T. Callender charged in the Richmond *Recorder* that it was "well known" that Jefferson kept Sally, one of his slaves, as concubine and had fathered children by her. The features of "Tom," the eldest offspring, were "said to bear a striking although sable resemblance to those of the president himself." Callender was a notorious professional scandalmonger who had turned upon Jefferson when the President had disappointed his hope for federal office. Despite the utter disreputability of the source, the charge has been dragged after Jefferson like a dead cat through the pages of formal and informal history, tied to him by its attractiveness to a wide variety of interested persons and by the apparent impossibility of utterly refuting it. Ever since Callender's day it has served the varied purposes of those seeking to degrade Jefferson for political or ideological reasons, of abolitionists, defamers of Virginia, the South, and even America in general, and both defenders and opponents of racial segregation. Jefferson's conduct has been attacked from several angles, for in fact the charge of concubinage with Sally Hemings constitutes not one accusation but three, simultaneously accusing Jefferson of fathering bastards, of miscegenation, and of crassly taking advantage of a helpless young slave (for Sally was probably twenty-two when she first conceived). The last of these, insofar as it implies forced attentions on an unwilling girl, may be summarily dismissed. For one thing, indirect evidence indicates that Sally was happy throughout her long period of motherhood, and, more important, Jefferson was simply not capable of violating every rule of honor and kindness, to say nothing of his convictions concerning the master-slave relationship.

As for bastardy and miscegenation, the known circumstances of the situation at Monticello which might support the charges were, very briefly as follows. The entire Hemings family seems to have received favored treatment. Sally's mother was mulatto and had come to Jefferson with her still lighter children from the estate of his father-in-law, John Wayles, in 1774. Most of Sally's siblings were personal servants; one brother became a skilled carpenter and two of Sally's children were eventually charged to him for training. Sally herself and her mother were house servants, and Sally (described as very fair) was sent as maid with Jefferson's daughter to Paris. All the slaves freed by Jefferson were Hemingses, and none of Sally's children were retained in slavery as adults. She bore five, from 1795 to 1808; and though he was away from Monticello a total of roughly two-thirds of this period, Jefferson was at home nine months prior to each birth. Her first child was conceived following Jefferson's retirement as Secretary of State with nerves raw from political battling with Hamilton. Three others were conceived during Jefferson's summer vacations and the remaining child was born nine months after his very brief return to Monticello for the funeral of his daughter. In short, Jefferson's paternity can be neither refuted nor proved from the known circumstances or from the extant testimony of his overseer, his white descendants, or the descendants of Sally, each of them having fallible memories and personal interests at stake.

If we turn to Jefferson's character we are confronted by evidence which for many people today (and then) furnished an immediate and satisfactory refutation. Yet the assumption that this high-minded man *could not* have carried on such an affair is at variance with what is known today concerning the relationship between human personality and behavior. If the previous suggestions concerning his personality have any validity, Jefferson's relations with women were ambivalent, and in the Hemings situation either tendency could have prevailed.

Assuming this ambivalence in Jefferson, one can construct two reasonable (though not equally probable) and absolutely irreconcilable cases. It is possible to argue on the one hand, briefly, that Jefferson was a truly admirable man if there ever was one and that by the time he had married and matured politically, in the 1770's, his "head" was permanently in control of his "heart." Hence a liaison with a slave girl would have been a lapse from character unique in his mature life. It would have represented, on a deeper level, abandonment of the only grounds on which he was able to maintain satisfactory relations with women, their safe incarceration in the married state. It would have meant complete reversal of his feelings of repulsion toward Negroes and a towering sense of guilt for having connected with such sensual creatures and having given free rein to his own libidinous desires, guilt for which there is no evidence. On the other hand, however, it is possible to argue that attachment with Sally represented a final happy resolution of his inner conflict. This would account for the absence after his return from Paris in 1789 of evidence pointing to continuing high tension concerning women and Negroes, an absence hardly to be explained by senility. Sally Hemings would have become Becky Burwell and the bitter outcome of his marriage erased. Unsurprisingly, his repulsion toward Negroes would have been, all along, merely the obverse of powerful attraction, and external pressures in the 1790's would easily have provided adequate energy for turning the coin of psychic choice from one side to the other. One is left fully persuaded only of the known fact that any given pattern of basic personality can result in widely differing patterns of external behavior.

The question of Jefferson's miscegenation, it should be stressed again, is of limited interest and usefulness even if it could be satisfactorily answered. The *Notes* had been written years before, and Jefferson never deviated from his "aversion," as he wrote just before he died, "to the mixture of colour" in America. One aspect of the history of the Hemings family, however, offers possible clarification on several points. It appears quite probable that Sally and some of her siblings were the children of his father-in-law, John Wayles. It must have been a burden indeed for Jefferson, who probably knew this, to have the Hemingses in the same house with their half-sister and aunt, his beloved wife, who almost certainly was ignorant of the situation. This burden might well have embittered his thoughts on miscegenation in general and have helped convince him to his dying day that it was a social evil. It would also have heightened his conviction that slavery was degrading to white men. And while it does not settle anything concerning his relations with Sally, it would explain the favored treatment the Hemings family received at Monticello.

For many people it seems to require an effort of will to remember that the larger significance of the Hemings matter lay not in Jefferson's conduct but in the charges themselves. Callender's words went echoing through the anti-Jefferson press (with help from Callender) because they played effectively upon public sentiment. The motivation underlying the charges was undoubtedly political; some of his opponents were willing to seize any weapon, no matter how crude, for berating Jefferson, but that a white man's sleeping with a Negro woman should be a weapon at all seems the more significant fact. It is significant, too, that the charge of bastardy was virutally lost in the clamor about miscegenation. Hamilton's admission of sexual transgressions with a white woman had done little to damage *his* reputation. Jefferson's offense was held to be mixture of the races, and Callender and his fellow scandalmongers strummed the theme until it was dead tired.

> In glaring red, and chalky white,
>   Let others beauty see;
> Me no such tawdry tints delight—
>   No! *black's* the hue for me!
>
> Thick pouting lips! how sweet their grace!
>   When passion fires to kiss them!
> Wide spreading over half the face,
>   Impossible to miss them.
>
> Oh! Sally! hearken to my vows!
>   Yield up thy sooty charms—
> My best belov'd! my more than spouse,
>   Oh! take me to thy arms! °

The same theme could easily be transformed into ridicule of Jefferson's equalitarianism.

> For make all like, let blackee nab
>   De white womans. . . . dat be de track!
> Den Quashee de white wife will hab,
>   And massa *Jefferson shall hav de black.*
> Why should a judge, (him alway white,)
>   'Pon pickaninny put him paw,
> Cause he steal little! dat no rite!
>   No! Quashee say he'll hab no law.†

Jefferson's personal transgression could be handsomely enlarged to represent a threat to society, according to what might be called the law of gross expansion. "Put the case that every white man in Virginia had done as much as Thomas Jefferson has done towards the utter destruction of its happiness, that eighty thousand white men had; each of them, been the father of five mulatto children. Thus you have FOUR HUNDRED THOUSAND MULATTOES in addition to the present swarm. The coutry would be no longer habitable, till after a civil war, and a series of massacres. We all know with absolute certainty that the contest would end in the utter

---

° Reprinted from *Boston Gazette* in Richmond *Recorder*, Dec. 1, 1802.
† *Ibid.*, Sept. 1, 1802.

extirpation both of blacks and mulattoes. We know that the continent has as many white people, as could eat the whole race at a breakfast." *

INTERRACIAL SEX: THE INDIVIDUAL AND HIS SOCIETY

Callender's grossness should not be allowed to obscure the fact that he was playing upon very real sensitivities. American tenderness on mixture of the races had been unrelieved by the Revolutionary upheaval of thought concerning the Negro. Indeed certain shifts in thought in the latter part of the eighteenth century may have served to deepen objection to inter-mixture. While conceiving of man's social and political activities as taking place within the ordered realm of nature (most obviously in the natural rights philosophy), Americans also brought biological preconceptions to the consideration of human beings. In nature, likes begat likes in ordered succession. Could Americans be entirely happy, then, with even the super-ficial confusion of appearances brought about by miscegenation? The "mulatto breed" was an affront to anyone with a sense of tidiness. In the 1790's, too, the Negro rebellions added urgency to all consideration of interracial relationships, and the growing sense of the separateness of Negroes meant more frequent expressions of alarm concerning mongreliza-tion. Given a new nation, with a slavery now recognized as a national concern, the omnipresent fact of miscegenation was perforce seen in a somewhat different light than in earlier years. Cases of intermixture once of only local pertinence had now become ingredients in the larger prob-lem of the integrity of the blood of the national community. Hence national councils became forums for denunciation of intermixture. Penn-sylvania's James Wilson announced during discussion of the three-fifths clause in the Constitutional Convention that he "had some apprehensions also from the tendency of the blending of the blacks with the whites, to give disgust to the people of Pena." William Loughton Smith, defending slavery in the congressional debate of 1790, declared that any "mixture of the races would degenerate the whites" and that as far as the future of America was concerned if Negroes intermarried "with the whites, then the white race would be extinct, and the American people would be all of the mulatto breed." And a nationalistic President Jefferson remarked concerning the Negro's future that "it is impossible not to look forward to distant times, when our rapid multiplication will expand itself beyond those [present] limits, and cover the whole northern, if not the southern continent, with a people speaking the same language, governed in similar forms, and by similar laws; nor can we contemplate with satisfaction either blot or mixture on that surface."

* *Ibid.*, Sept. 22, 1802.

This theme was to emerge as a dominant one especially in his own state during his presidency; by that time many other important individuals throughout the nation were speculating upon matters concerning the Negro. Important intellectual changes took place during the thirty years after he wrote the *Notes*, but Jefferson grew increasingly silent and depressed about the future of Africans in America. For the moment these individuals and changes may be held aside so as to permit concentration upon the problem of the relationship of one individual's attitudes to those of his society.

Beneath all pronouncements on the undesirability of racial mixture lay a substructure of feeling about interracial sex. Jefferson's feelings were of course partially molded by specific beliefs about Negroes which constituted readily visible manifestations of feelings prevailing in his culture not merely about Negroes but about life in general. It seems legitimate and profitable to speak of an entire culture as having feelings, partly because every society demands—and gets—a large measure of the behavior it "wants" (i.e., needs) from individuals and partly because in a literate culture expressions of individual feeling accrete through time, thus forming a common pool of expressed feelings. Usually, but by no means always, these expressions are highly intellectualized, that is, detached from direct functional connection with powerful emotional drives. Sometimes they are not, as they sometimes were not when Thomas Jefferson wrote about Negroes. It seems evident that his feelings, his affective life, his emotions —whatever term one prefers—were being expressed in some of his beliefs or opinions about the Negro. His opinions were thus sometimes quite directly the product of his repressions. And it seems axiomatic, given the assumptions about the nature of culture prevailing in the twentieth century, that variants of his repressions operated in so many individuals that one can speak of deep-seated feelings about the Negro as being social in character, that is, as characterizing an entire society. It seems important to remember that the explicit *content* of social attitudes stemmed not directly from the emotions being repressed but from the mechanisms of repression. The resultant attitudes, moreover, through constant communication within society, acquired autonomous energy and a viability independent of emotional underpinnings. Hence many individuals subscribed to beliefs about Negroes which performed no very vital function in their personality, and these beliefs may be considered as being part of the cultural environment.

It is with this final consideration in mind that such manifestations of attitudes as laws on interracial sexual relations must be considered; it saves us from despair at being unable to obtain much personal information on individual legislators. Again, it constitutes a useful way of looking at sectional differences in attitudes. Differences between North and South concerning interracial sex were not in kind but in vehemence, if vehemence is defined as the product of the degree of individual involvement and proportion of people involved. In New York in 1785, for example, the assembly passed a gradual emancipation bill which would have barred Negroes from the polls and from marrying whites. The senate objected to the intermarriage clause because "in so important a connection they thought the free subjects of this State ought to be left to their free choice." The assembly again voted narrowly to retain the clause and then, after conference with the senate, finally receded on it by a narrow margin, though later for other reasons the entire bill was lost. In Massachusetts, however, an act of 1786 on the "Solemnization of Marriage" voided marriages between whites and Negroes. Rhode Island passed a similar law in 1798. The Pennsylvania emancipation bill also contained a similar provision which was dropped before final passage. On the whole, this random pattern in the North suggests both the existence of sentiment against intermixture and a lack of great vehemence underlying it.

In the South, on the other hand, where there were more Negroes (wearing fewer clothes) there is evidence suggesting greater tension. For the most part laws prohibiting racial mixture were already on the books and nobody wanted them off. The Virginia legislature's refusal to accept Jefferson's provision in the revisal for banishment of white women bearing mulattoes stemmed more from objection to the harsh penalty than from willingness to countenance interracial matches. One foreign traveler observed that the unusually large number of mulattoes in the state was occasioned only by greater length of settlement and that public opinion was firmly set against interracial unions. Liaisons were carried on in secrecy, he explained, for "no white man is known to live regularly with a black woman." The converse relationship was of course another matter; though white women still occasionally slept with Negro men, southern society was as determined as ever to punish rigorously any Negro sexual attacks on white women. In 1769, Virginia had excluded castration from the penal code except as punishment for that offense. The brutality of castration had become offensive to humanitarian sentiment, however, and the legislature refused to enact Jefferson's revisal bill based on the lex talionis. Yet as late as 1792 emasculation was specifically declared by the legislature to be permissible punishment for any slave "convicted of an attempt to ravish a white woman." In practice the courts seem usually to have hanged such offenders but there was at least one case of sentence to castration, in 1797. The penalty was finally abolished in a general amendment to the penal code in 1805. Despite tension on the matter, some Virginians refused to be blinded by their feelings. In the 1800's several petitions to the governor asked clemency for Negroes condemned for rape on grounds that the white woman involved was of low character. Elsewhere in the South, however, there was evidence of smoldering emotion. In North Carolina a tradition was inaugurated at the turn of the century when lynching parties burned a Negro for rape and castrated a slave for remarking that he was going to have some white women. Georgia in 1806 enacted a mandatory death penalty for any Negro raping or attempting to rape a white woman. As late as 1827 a Georgia court sentenced a Negro to castration and deportation for attempted rape, and the *Macon Telegraph* castigated the court for its leniency.

The dynamics of the interracial sexual situation did not, of course, invariably tend toward emotional abandon. For one thing, in regions where slavery was firmly rooted in a high proportion of Negroes, the traditional European double standard for the sexes was subject to caricatural polarization. More sexual freedom for white men meant less for white women. Throughout the eighteenth century South Carolina had shown the effects of this tendency, though far less than the British West Indian societies. Despite difficulties created by the biases of travelers, it seems clear that the same tendency still operated in the deep South in the early years of the nineteenth century. One American traveler, the prominent ornithologist of Philadelphia, Alexander Wilson, described his unfavorable impressions by first lamenting that the "superabundance of Negroes" had "destroyed the activity of the whites," who "stand with their hands in their pockets, overlooking their negroes." In his letter to William Bartram in 1809 (here given as published much later in the century), Wilson went on to say,

These, however, are not one-tenth of the curses slavery has brought on the Southern States. Nothing has surprised me more than the cold, melancholy reserve of the females, of the best families, in South Carolina and Georgia. Old and young, single and married, all have that dull frigid insipidity, and reserve, which is attributed to solitary old maids. Even in their own houses they scarce utter anything to a stranger but yes or no, and one is perpetually puzzled to know whether it proceeds from awkwardness or dislike. Those who have been at some of their Balls [in Charleston] say that the ladies hardly even speak or smile, but dance with as much gravity, as if they were performing some ceremony of devotion. On the contrary, the negro wenches are all sprightliness and gayety; and if report be not a defamer—(*here there is a hiatus in the manuscript*) which render the men callous to all the finer sensations of love, and female excellence.

While one suspects that the "hiatus" may not have been the author's, the description clearly points to deep alienation on the part of white women. Their rightful consorts were often otherwise engaged, and their resulting shell of "dull frigid insipidity" was hardened by the utter necessity of avoiding any resemblance to women of the other race. Perhaps they sensed, too, that the protection they received against Negro men constituted a very perverse variety of affection. Their proper function, moreover, was to preserve the forms and symbols of civilization—they were, after all, bearers of white civilization in a literal sense—and to serve as priestesses in the temples, performing, in Wilson's preceptive phrase, a "ceremony of devotion."

The relationship between miscegenation and society was intricately reciprocal. While miscegenation altered the tone of society, the social institution of slavery helped reshape the definition of miscegenation from fusion of that which was different to fusion of higher and lower; hence slavery was of course responsible for much of the normative judgment implied in the concept of miscegenation. Yet both slavery and miscegenation rested, in the final analysis, upon a *perception of difference* between the races, a perception founded on physiognomic fact. When Jefferson, for example, set out to prove that emancipated Negroes must be removed from white society he predicated "the real distinctions nature has made," moved immediately into a discussion of appearance, and only then went on to less tangible differences in temperament and intellect. Underlying his discussion of the Negro, and everyone else's, was an axiomatic separation of Negroes from white men based on appearance.

JEFFERSON: A DICHOTOMOUS VIEW OF TRIRACIAL AMERICA

Yet two puzzles present themselves, the one concerning an individual's unusually extreme views and the other a more general problem of illogical perception. As for the first, Jefferson laid uncommonly great stress on the physical distinction between Negroes and whites. This emphasis derived partly from his emotional responses to women but also from a pervasive temperamental characteristic, a habit of mind not unconnected with his views of the opposite sex. He always regarded the world of men as utterly distinct from the strange world of women in which he could never feel at ease; his division was even sharper than that of the culture in which he lived, which was sharp enough, to be sure. (The English word *sex* itself derived from terms indicating cutting, separation, division.) On a different level, in terms of his "thought," Jefferson gave every evidence of a predilection for bifurcating men and issues and even his perceptual environment, for thinking of the world in terms of—it is significant that we cannot avoid a play on words here—black or white. His approach to the external world became most obvious perhaps during his involvement in the stormy partisan politics which elicited in so many Americans a tendency to regard the political world as composed of two conflicting opposites, Republican and Federalist, France and England, honest men and knaves. Jefferson pressed this tendency as far as anyone, and he may be said to bear some responsibility for the cleancut division of domestic politics in the 1790's, however much he deplored it. He always insisted that hard-core Federalists were "monocrats," i.e., utterly antirepublican, and that, on the other hand, the great body of Federalists were really Republicans at heart. This inability to admit a possible middle ground assumed only slightly different shape in his famous optative statement in the First Inaugural—"We are all republicans: we are all federalists"; here he resolved wide differences by a doubly incorrect denial of their existence. This was partly a matter of shorthand phrasing, but no terminology is innocent of meaning; earlier Jefferson had frequently described European social and political conflicts with such pairs as "hammer and anvil" and "sheep and wolves." He never shared in the contemporary enthusiasm for a balance of powers in government; indeed his picture of society as composed of the people and their enemies precluded any necessity for balancing various interests. It is virtually impossible, for example, to imagine Jefferson as author of the Federalist No. 10; Madison's stress on a multiplicity of factions was entirely foreign to him. Jefferson was at his best on occasions calling for the vigor of simple dichotomy, as in 1776 when he contrasted the virtues of a free people to the crimes of a tyrannical King.

A similar penchant for orderly division became apparent in his relations with individual persons. With a mind too intelligent to classify all men as good or bad, Jefferson nonetheless was temperamentally incapable of subtle analysis of other men's character, incapable of restraining himself from an all-inclusive value judgment. Gouverneur Morris sensed this quality when he wrote in his diary after a call upon Jefferson in Paris, "I think he does not form very just estimates of character, but rather assigns too many to the humble rank of fools, whereas in life the gradations are infinite and each individual has his peculiarities of fort and feeble." For his most famous love letter Jefferson seized upon the one literary form which could most adequately convey his conception of his own personality, a "dialogue" between "the head and the heart."

Jefferson's pervasive temperamental bent for order, symmetry, and normative dichotomy was nowhere more obvious than in his anthropolgy. Entirely aside from helping to clear the way for his seemingly paradoxical denunciation of both slavery and Negroes, it resulted in what was for Jefferson a highly satisfying resolution of the problem posed by the American Indian. Here his individual temperament came into contact with his society's perception of Indians as being utterly distinct from Negroes. Indians did not in fact look like white persons, yet Americans evinced either indifference or downright unwillingness to admit the fact. With Jefferson the unwillingness was monumental. Confronted by three races in America he determinedly turned three into two by transforming the Indian into a degraded yet basically noble brand of white man. Some of the most heartfelt passages in the *Notes on Virginia* were devoted to a defense of the Indian against the famous French naturalist, Buffon, whose aspersions Jefferson declared to be "just as true as the fable of Æsop." Indians, he asserted, were actually brave and manly and by no means deficient in attachment to family and friends. They were notably eloquent, Jefferson claimed in an extravagant panegyric climaxed by the announcement that the speech of Chief Logan was not in the least inferior to the "whole orations of Demosthenes and Cicero." In contrast with Negroes "they astonish you with strokes of the most sublime oratory; such as prove their reason and sentiment strong, their imagination glowing and elevated." Unlike the Negroes, he explained, "They will crayon out an animal, a plant, or a country, so as to prove the existence of a germ in their minds which only wants cultivation." Physically, too, Jefferson argued, the Indian was by no means inferior to the white man. Buffon had claimed that "The savage is feeble, and has small organs of generation; he has neither hair nor beard, and no ardor whatever for his female." Stung, like other Americans, by this slander on the natives of his own environment, Jefferson responded with the sharp rejoinder that the Indian "is neither more defective in ardor, nor more impotent with his female, than the white reduced to the same diet and exercise." Their natural supply of hair was the same "as with the whites" but they "pluck the hair as fast as it appears," considering it "disgraceful to be hairy on the body." Indian women, Jefferson continued, did indeed "raise fewer children than we do," but the causes lay "not in a difference of nature, but of circumstance." When married to white traders and leading a suitably regular life, Indian women "produce and raise as many children as the white women."

Jefferson thus rescued the Indian from his detractors by appealing to the "circumstances" of their life and, wherever possible, by outright denial of difference from the white man. In appropriately altered circumstances Indians would become white men, a happy transformation indeed. It was precisely this transformation which Jefferson thought the Negro could never accomplish. By constantly referring to environment for one group and to nature for the other he effectively widened the gap which Americans had always placed between the two. While stressing the "reality" of the Negro's blackness he denied the Indian's tawny color by not mentioning it, not even venturing the usual suggestion that the Indian's tawniness came not from nature but from bear grease. With both Indians and Negroes Jefferson appealed decisions on mental powers to the court of facts, but he clearly expected radically differing verdicts. In contrast to his "suspicion" concerning Negroes, he announced that with the Indians "we shall probably find that they are formed in mind as well as in body, on the same module with the 'Homo sapiens Europaeus.'" Nothing could demonstrate more clearly Jefferson's prejudgment of the verdict than the different slants with which he made his appeal to environmental influences.

While comparing Negroes unfavorably with Roman slaves, he declared that a comparison of Indians "in their present state with the Europeans North of the Alps" during the Roman Empire "would be unequal" because of the greater density of European population. The only "respectable evidence" which might be said to militate against Indian equality, Jefferson wrote in 1785, was that of Don Antonio de Ulloa. Jefferson's method of refuting this evidence was, in light of his passage on the Negro, little short of extraordinary.

> But he [Don Ulloa] saw the Indian of South America only, and that after he had passed through ten generations of slavery. It is very unfair, from this sample, to judge of the natural genius of this race of men: and after supposing that Don Ulloa had not sufficiently calculated the allowance which should be made for this circumstance, we do him no injury in considering the picture he draws of the present Indian of S. America as no picture of what their ancestors were 300 years ago. It is in N. America we are to seek their original character: and I am safe in affirming that the proofs of genius given by the Indians of N. America, place them on a level with Whites in the same uncultivated state.

Consistency of argument was no barrier when the final judgment had already been made.

In defending the Indian Jefferson was vindicating the American environment, for his remarks on the Indian in the *Notes* formed only part of his refutation of Buffon's claim that animals in the New World were smaller and weaker than in the Old and of Abbé Raynal's extension of that claim to white Americans. These charges stung Jefferson not only as nationalist but also as scientist, since they imputed inferiority to his natural laboratory equipment. In employing an environmentalist defense of the Indian he had to work carefully, however, since the Indian was both a portion of the American environment and the product of it. In order not to disparage his own natural environment he was careful to avoid any suggestion that the backwardness of the Indians was the effect of their surroundings and to attribute it (where he could not deny it) to the "circumstances of their situation," that is, to the way they lived. Unfortunately, this attribution left him completely unable to explain why Indians lived that way. At any rate, he was not prepared to let the Indians be subjected to the indignity of being called recent immigrants to America. Appealing the question of Indian origins to the evidence of language, he called for compilation of Indian vocabularies, collected many himself, and concluded categorically as early as 1781 that the wide disparity of Indian tongues "proves them of greater antiquity than those of Asia." Neither Jefferson nor anyone else tried to gain knowledge of Negro languages.

Nowhere was Jefferson's effort to Americanize the Indian more apparent than in his reiterated hope for cultural and physical amalgamation of Indians with white Americans. Together they formed one nation: "We, like you," he once addressed an Indian chief, "are Americans, born in the same land, and having the same interests." His purchase of Louisiana raised the possibility of encouraging the Indians to remove beyond the Mississippi, but he preferred that they be encouraged to give up hunting for farming and cede the resultant surplus of land to the United States. "In truth," he wrote, "the ultimate point of rest and happiness for them is to let our settlements and theirs meet and blend together, to intermix, and become one people." This would "best promote the interests of the Indians and ourselves, and finally consolidate our whole country to one nation only." Ten years later in 1813 he wrote regretfully that war had now intervened: "They would have mixed their blood with ours, and been amalgamented and identified with us within no distant period of time."

Amalgamation and identification, welcomed with the Indian, were precisely what Jefferson most abhorred with the Negro. The Indian was a brother, the Negro a leper. While Africans had always regarded the two peoples as very different, Jefferson underlined the dichotomy with a determined emphasis not matched by other men. His derogation of the Negro revealed the latent possibilities inherent in an accumulated popular tradition of Negro inferiority; it constituted, for all its qualifications, the most intense, extensive, and extreme formulation of anti-Negro "thought" offered by any American in the thirty years after the Revolution. Yet Thomas Jefferson left to Americans something else which may in the long run have been of greater importance—his prejudice for freedom and his larger equalitarian faith. It was this faith which must have caused him to fall gradually more silent on a subject which many of his fellow intellectuals were taking up with interest. For Jefferson more than for any of his known contemporaries, the subject was not an easy or a happy one.

11

Christians Versus Pagans

ROBERT F. BERKHOFER, JR.

From 1787 to the Civil War, missionaries spearheaded the process of Indian acculturation (the "drastic" modification of an Indian culture to conform to the dominant white
culture) that rapidly followed a tribe's loss of political autonomy. Focusing on the
Indian reaction to missionary activities and utilizing the insights of sociology and
anthropology, Robert F. Berkhofer, Jr., enumerates the limited range of responses open
to a tribe undergoing acculturation.

Conversion for the Christian Indians meant not only the transformation
of their values and their life ways but also the desire to impose the same
ideals and behavior upon their benighted neighbors. Inevitably such
attempts to reform their fellow tribesmen lead to intratribal conflict over
religion. Religious differences in turn focused attention upon governmental control and even form, for government by definition, even in
American Indian tribes, gives those in power legitimate coercion over
others within the society. The converted Indians desired possession of
their tribal government to protect themselves and to expand civilization
through the allotment of annuities for schools, farm implements, and
other aids. These Indians, frequently at the behest of missionaries, often
favored new government forms which imitated white political institutions. Control of these new forms supposedly gave the Christian Indians

From Robert F. Berkhofer, Jr., *Salvation and the Savage: An Analysis of Protestant
Missions and American Indian Response, 1787–1862* (Lexington: University of Ken-
tucky Press, 1965), pp. 125–43, 151. Reprinted with omissions by permission of
The University Press of Kentucky.

more opportunity and power to change those aspects of their neighbors' behavior that they regarded as primitive, hence shameful. Because of the interconnectedness of all social institutions, one of the best indexes of responses to missionary operations and to white culture in general, therefore, is the struggle over governmental position and structure.

Indian Christianization and tribal response to it depended upon the entire contact situation and the overall stage of acculturation in a given tribe. While for the seventy-five years under study the missionaries were a relatively homogeneous group in their ways of thinking and acting, not only were the Indians they met divided into diverse tribal cultures, but also the content of any one specific culture varied over time under the impact of white contact. Thus a tribe's reaction to missionary endeavor might be quite different in 1850 than fifty years earlier due to acculturation. From research into various tribal reactions, four basic sequences emerge depending upon the stage of acculturation and the degree of Indian autonomy. By examining the simple reactions under conditions of nondirected contact before proceeding to the more complex sequences after autonomy is lost, the clearest view can be obtained.

When the missionary entered a new field in a relatively unacculturated tribe, he settled among a local band or in a village. His efforts were not directed at the whole tribe because of the nature of social relations in a tribe. Before white contact, the tribe was composed of small communities that managed their own affairs to a very large extent. A community was characterized by face-to-face relationships among a small group of extended families. Individual rights and obligations were determined in the main by familial bonds. Such a community was highly integrated because the people shared common values and goals. In itself the societal unit, the cultural unit, and the community coincided, for the people possessing the culture were the same as those constituting the social relationships.

Though such an Indian community possessed a culture and social structure similar to other communities composing the tribe, it acted as an independent unit politically. In most actions affecting the missionary and his converts, the local chiefs or those of the neighboring villages were the only participants as government. Local autonomy was great. In the tribes under study, the authority of the chiefs was noncoercive and local. Without the support in opinion and action of his fellow Indians, the chief had no power and his decisions were lost. Such a situation did not mean the absence of law so much as there was little need for it in the community where consensus reigned and all decisions were unanimous in the sense that all capitulated to the proposed action or inaction. Such was the political situation facing the entering missionary.

By the time the Protestant missionary arrived at such a village or band, much acculturation had occurred, but in most cases the change had not affected the basic social structure or cultural patterning inherited from aboriginal times As the missionary gained adherents to his program of Christian civilization, more and more Indians accepted new values and aspired to a new way of life. As the missionary succeeded in his efforts, the Indians who retained the older customs realized their way of life was a system in opposition to his system. In fact, the very words and methods of the missionary called this idea to their attention, and they realized they must meet the challenge.

The repudiation of much of American civilization, including the missionary, forms the first sequence. Under the threat of a cultural division in the community, the native-oriented Indians persecuted the missionary to cause his voluntary withdrawal or, in the extreme, massacred him and other whites. At this stage of contact, the Indians frequently failed to differentiate between missionary and other American contact, and so pique, whether at government agent or God, led to slaughter of mission cattle, stolen clothes, burned mission fences, and sabotaged gristmills and sawmills. At the same time, the opposition employed the methods of social control normally used to correct any deviation within the community to bring them back into line with old ways. Social pressure ranged from the mild derision to the threats of personal violence. . . . After the elimination or withdrawal of the whites, the native-oriented group hoped to achieve the old cultural and social coincidence again. A simple diagram will clearly illustrate this sequence.

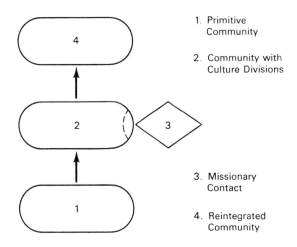

1. Primitive
   Community

2. Community with
   Culture Divisions

3. Missionary
   Contact

4. Reintegrated
   Community

The massacre of the Reverend Marcus Whitman and a few other Americans in Oregon during 1847 seems to be the most dramatic and straightforward example of this sequence. The increasing number of Americans entering Indian territory as well as the disruption threatened by the success of the mission caused the massacre. This possibility was open only to a tribe when American society was weak in the area of contact and the tribe's political autonomy was accordingly great.

Somewhat more complicated is the second possible sequence, which involved a social as well as a cultural division. Societal disruption naturally followed from missionization, for the acceptance of new values as well as pagan persecution demanded new social relationships. Sometimes conversion merely meant the end of polygamy. At other times couples separated because one spouse had converted. In still other instances, people left their villages to settle in places more favorable to Indian Christianity. In extreme cases new villages or bands were formed entirely of white-oriented Indians. Thus in this sequence, after the initial cultural divisions, the cleavage worsened, and instead of reuniting as in the first sequence, the community broke into two physically separate groups which enabled each one to live in its own community in which culture and social structure coincided. The process might repeat itself several times within the same original population. To continue the use of diagrams, this sequence may be represented under ideal conditions thusly:

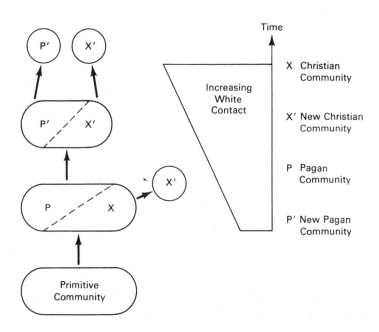

This sequence occurred about the time of the loss of political autonomy. Perhaps the most famous example of the formation of a new community was the deliberate practice of Moravian missionaries in separating their converts from the tribe in order to practice white man's ways in white man's social relationships. While the Moravians frequently operated in the period of permissive contact, Samuel Kirkland's work among the Oneidas in central New York illustrates this sequence after loss of autonomy.

Following the American Revolution, the Oneidas were confined to a reservation that rapidly dwindled as a result of land sales. By this time Kirkland's efforts, which had begun in the late 1760s, had produced the usual Pagan and Christian parties. In the 1790s the main Oneida village, which contained almost the entire tribal population, was divided between the two parties: the Christians lived in the western end and the Pagans in the eastern end. The Quakers commenced work in the Pagan section of the village in 1796 to at first the delight and then the chagrin of Kirkland. The Quaker work demonstrates that the differences between the two parties was not a complete dichotomy in regard to the adoption of white civilization but rather the extent of that adoption and the specific elements. After the Quakers left, the Pagans apparently revived some of their old ceremonies. They ate roasted dog and held various ceremonies in the fall of 1799. Visions were frequent, and the Pagans gained some adherents from the Christian party. In mid-1800 both parties after a six-day council agreed religion should no longer interfere with political affairs.

The agreement was short-lived, and finally in 1805, the two parties divided the reservation between them in order to "preserve the peace of the greater part of the nation." This was the first of many divisions of the reservation. In 1816 and 1817 Eleazar Williams, the famous Indian Episcopalian who was later presumed the lost dauphin, converted many of the Pagan party, which became known as the Second Christian party, and won the Christian party from Presbyterianism to Episcopalianism. Under the leadership of Williams, the Oneidas began to move to Wisconsin during the 1820s. Thereafter, blocs of First and Second Christian party Indians sold their lands separately in order to emigrate. In 1826 a Methodist missionary converted some of the remaining Pagans, who assumed the name of the Orchard party. The next year some of this party sold their land in order to go to Wisconsin. This fragmentation process continued well into the 1840s.

The Oneidas' attempt in 1805 to separate religious and political concerns points to the third possible sequence. As more and more missionaries arrived and more whites settled around the reservation, the coincidence between culture, social structure, and community broke down not only in one village as in the preceding sequence but in many towns in the tribe. To heal the divisions, attempts were made at political organization on the tribal level. Such attempts were reinforced by the activities of government agents and missionaries. Since the Indians bordered on rapidly expanding white settlements, the governmental authorities constantly bargained for tribal lands. The peculiar ethical views of the dominant society necessitated the signing of a contract by the tribe as a whole through some legal representatives and thus fostered the notion of a more elaborate tribal government. At the same time the ever-diminishing reservation impressed the concept of territoriality, which is so essential to the modern idea of the state, upon Christian and Pagan alike. Further, the idea of more formal government was assisted by the missionaries, who not only trained Indians in governance through church and voluntary associations organized by this time along tribal lines, but who had always strongly advocated better Indian government, that is, white law and organization. With missionary encouragement and the experience gathered in church societies, the members of the Christian party naturally attempted to form a tribal government in order to force their new culture and social relations upon their fellow tribesmen. In order to counter this move, the Pagans were compelled to expand the traditional political system in functions and authority, if not in offices. The dynamics of this sequence may be seen in the diagram below. The new government was an attempt at societal integration without the cultural integration of the whole population.

In the ideal development of this sequence, the form of government presented by the Christians for tribal use was modeled after that of the dominant society: a written constitution provided for elective officers to fill positions in a government of divided powers. Though the Pagans

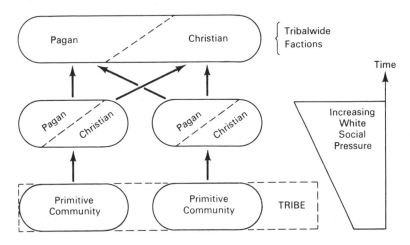

opposed the aims and even the mechanism of the Christians' political system, they would be forced at this stage to gain power through elections and capture the new government established by the Christians. If all had gone well, genuine political parties would have arisen. Yet a smoothly functioning political party system was never realized, for neither Christians nor Pagans consented to the other faction controlling the government in this period. The Pagans, when they won an election, dedicated themselves to destroying the government—or they paid no attention to the new government at all!

The classic example of this sequence and its attendant troubles is seen in Seneca history between the Revolution and the Civil War. Until 1790 the tribe was still trying to play off British and American officials to gain favors, as had been Iroquois custom. With the decisive defeat of the Western Confederates at Fallen Timbers and the British evacuation of the frontier forts in 1796, the Senecas soon found themselves on reservations formed around their villages in scattered locations in western New York State. As soon as all had quieted, the Philadelphia Friends, who had always been interested in Cornplanter on his visits to the young United States Capital, established a mission on his reservation. Not long after, Cornplanter's stepbrother, Handsome Lake, awoke from a two-hour trance, uttered the first of the "good words," and founded the synchretized pagan religion which soon spread to the other reservations. Although Presbyterian missionaries attempted to enter other reserves as early as the Quakers, none successfully overcame opposition until 1811. Community divisions were prevalent on the four major reserves by the eve of the War of 1812. The full development of a tribewide split along Pagan and Christian lines is marked by a council in 1819, which was called to consider other questions but actually debated whether the tribe should adopt white customs and institutions. This intratribal bickering was exacerbated by the Ogden Land Company's attempt to purchase the Seneca reservations in the 1820s and the federal government's efforts to remove the tribe in the following decade, which culminated in the Buffalo Creek Treaty of 1838. Many members claimed this treaty, by which the tribe ceded all their lands, was fraudulent, and they and the Quakers only obtained its repudiation after a four-year struggle. Dissatisfaction with the chiefs' role in this affair brought forth experiments in tribal government, again with the help of the Quakers. Finally in the famous year of revolution, 1848, dissatisfied Senecas declared in solemn constitutional convention: "We, the people of the Seneca nation of Indians . . . do hereby *abolish, abrogate* and annul our form of government by chiefs, because it has failed to answer the purposes for which all governments should be created." These failures were listed as lack of security for property, no laws for the institution of marriage, no provision for the poor, no provision for education, and no judiciary or executive depart-ments—all Christian and white-oriented demands. This declaration served as the preamble to a constitution which provided for a government of three branches: a legislature composed of eighteen members elected annually, an executive, and a judiciary of three peacemakers for each reservation. Other tribal officers elected annually by all males over twenty-one were the clerk, treasurer, superintendent of schools, over-seers of the highway, as well as a marshal and two deputies for each reserve. This revolution was no more successful (although less bloody) than its more important counterparts overseas, for the "Old Chiefs" party fought this government till the end of the period under discussion and secured modifications.

Certainly it is evident, even in this brief analysis, that the mission-aries were only a partial cause of the Seneca Revolution and that govern-mental pressures and other acculturative forces played a large part. After 1819, the difference between Pagan and Christian no longer revolved about the acceptance of white ways so much as the speed and degree of adoption. Some of the Pagan party, in fact, allied with the Quakers in the 1820s after the Christian party had turned to the Presbyterians. Surely as time went on, Christian civilization which had formed the focus of the conflict between divisions of the tribe in the earlier period was superseded by political divisions concerned with many other issues. In other words, the missionaries were thrown into both sides of the politi-cal division, depending upon whom they befriended. The Indian culture and social relations had become so fragmented under white contact that the natives could perceive the subtle differences in the views and be-havior of the whites and classify them accordingly.

This points up the last possible sequence of missionization. Given conditions of advanced acculturation and tribal division, missionaries entering a tribe were thrown into an already existing faction rather than aiding in the creation of one. Such a possibility is seen in Cherokee and Choctaw history, where missionaries were automatically involved in fac-tional politics revolving about removal and later slavery, in spite of their efforts at dissociation. Under these circumstances, Indian church mem-bers switched religious affiliation according to politics.

By the time the American Board missionaries entered the Cherokee Nation in 1817, that tribe had adopted a written law code with enforce-ment by the "Light Horse Guard" and eliminated blood revenge (perhaps with Gideon Blackburn's aid). Shortly after their arrival, the Chero-kees established bicameral legislature. Further centralization of govern-ment, the establishment of a court system, and a written constitution providing for the division of powers among the executive, legislature, and judiciary rapidly followed in the succeeding decade. Opposition to these developments came from the fullbloods, who led an abortive attempt against the progressive halfbreeds to eliminate these innovations. In these circumstances the missionaries of all denominations were thrown into already existing factions rather than creating them. Here unlike in most other tribes, the missionaries could deal with the entire tribe or large districts for prompt action. In return for this convenience they were dealt with by the larger political units and so brought more directly under the control of the Indians than was the usual case. When removal sharpened the political divisions in the tribe and when these divisions evolved into factions seeking control of the governmental structure in the West, the missionaries were automatically placed in factional politics in spite of their protests. These factions were no longer based upon the acceptance of civilization, but other issues. For instance, the misssionaries of northern societies were denied privileges on the basis of their abolitionist views. Some Indian church members switched membership from the northern to southern branches of churches over the question of slavery. The Cherokees received encouragement from white proslavery sympathizers in surrounding states. In other words, religious affiliation became a matter of political expediency.

When Kingsbury founded the American Board mission in the Choctaw Nation, the tribe was divided into three districts. Each district was headed by a chief called a "Mingo." Clan leaders under him were called captains since their service with the United States Army against the Creeks during the War of 1812. Soon after the missionaries arrived, a young Choctaw, who became a prominent chief later, expressed the conviction that only by the overthrow of the present chiefs could the tribe advance in civilization. Incipient factionalism seemed present. The division was over the degree of acceptance of civilization rather than any acceptance, for even the old chiefs favored schools. In late 1822 a captain in the Southeastern District, which was closest to white settlement, promulgated the first code of written laws, which provided punishment for theft, infanticide, adultery, and lack of industry. The halfbreeds were active in obtaining these laws. By mid-1826 the many halfbreeds and Christians in the General Council of the Choctaw Nation pushed a constitution through which regularized the existing government of principal chiefs and captains and the enforcement agency, the Light Horse Guard. Ardent factionalism did not break out until the great revival sparked by Alexander Talley in 1828. As thousands converted, the conservatives became alarmed and those in the Southeastern District attempted to rally around the old chief, who was subsequently deposed and replaced by a Christian. Immediately the successor called a council to adopt the laws and regulations already passed in the other two districts, headed by progressives.

To complicate the results of the revival, the removal question, injected in 1830, fanned the flames of factionalism higher. Greenwood LaFlore, an ardent Methodist chief who was anxious for political advancement, got the other two district chiefs to accept him as the chief of the entire tribe. Then at a council during which LaFlore and Talley played leading roles, a treaty was drafted in favor of removal. The opposition to emigration immediately crystallized around the former chiefs, Mushulatubbee and Nitakechi, and identified the Gospel with the loss of their homeland. Mushulatubbee and Nitakechi immediately replaced all the Christian captains by Pagans in their respective districts. Schools became unpopular and books were destroyed. At annuity time, civil war almost broke out. When the removal treaty was finally signed, leaders of both factions received presents for their acquiescence, although only LaFlore, Mushulatubbee, and Nitakechi signed. Resentment toward the signers caused the election of opposition chiefs in each of the districts. After emigration, party feeling continued strong until at least the end of the decade, and the missionaries encountered much opposition, for Christianity was linked with removal after Talley's efforts.

Among the Choctaws as among the Cherokees the slavery issue interfered with missionary labors. In 1848 Choctaws owned a thousand to twelve hundred slaves. Most of the owners were halfbreeds. A prominent Choctaw left an American Board mission church because of that society's view on slavery and established a Cumberland Presbyterian church in his neighborhood. He gathered a group of leading Choctaws about him who opposed the efforts of northern-based societies till the Civil War. This group pushed a law through the National Council in 1853 to prevent slaves' children from receiving an education and to remove all missionaries who preached abolitionism. Allied with but not caused by the slavery issue was the conflict over governmental structure in the late 1850s. Here the fullbloods opposed a new constitution that would have provided for the extension of territorial or state government over the tribe. Again civil war seemed to threaten, but compromise averted the clash. The agitation over slavery and politics hindered the spread of Christianity and forced the missionaries to take sides they did not want.

In both of these tribes by the 1850s the missionaries observed a widening cleavage between the English-speaking and native-speaking Indians. This tendency had gone so far in the Cherokee Nation that the two language groups were settling in different areas. The English-speaking Cherokees eagerly adopted white civilization, owned most of the slaves, and dominated the government and the school system. The other Indians resisted white innovations and opposed changes in the government that looked to a more modern state. Actually then, most of the political struggles recorded in the documents reflected the divisions in the elite rather than the cleavage between the more basic language groupings. In some ways this society is similar to Redfield's concept of the peasant society in which there is "a relatively stable and very roughly typical adjustment between local and national . . . life, a developed larger social system in which there are two cultures of upper and lower halves." Intermediate between the national American culture and the modified native culture is the elite which possesses its own distinct way of life which is the life of the peasant carried to another level of development. Further comparative work must be done before Cherokee and Choctaw society at the midcentury may safely be characterized as peasant. If it was, was it due to size and/or factions? One definite conclusion, however, is that as factionalism continued, religious affiliation frequently became a matter of mere political expediency. In other words, the Indians had acculturated to the point where they could not only differentiate the various elements of American civilization, but were themselves divided according to their perceptions of the various elements.

.   .   .

Although the . . . third and fourth sequences in general point to the eventual and complete assimilation of the American Indian, such was not to happen after the Civil War. Rather, greater fragmentation followed acculturation, and Americans always have refused final acceptance of the Indian because of racial prejudice. Furthermore, as the government took over work in the field, the missionary became less significant as the major acculturative force. The missionary had spearheaded acculturation in the seventy-five years under study only in the absence of government activity, though he was always within federal control. Yet, when the missionary was the chief force, he and the response to him provide many clues to understanding the nature of cultural change as well as Indian history of the period.

HOW DIFFERENT WAS THE SECOND PARTY SYSTEM,
AND WHY DID IT FAIL?

12

Political Development
and the Second Party System

RICHARD P. MC CORMICK

Richard P. McCormick based his *The Second American Party System: Party Formation in the Jacksonian Era* (1966) on massive research—including analysis of election data—on a state level. He summarized his conclusions for a Conference on American Political Party Development at Washington University, St. Louis, and a significant portion of those conclusions are reprinted here. After comparing the first two American party systems, McCormick argues that the crucial stage in forming the second party system occurred considerably later than commonly supposed. He also offers a plausible explanation for its ultimate failure.

·   ·   ·

III

It would seem to be quite clear that the stimulus for the formation of the second party system was supplied by the revival of the contest for the presidency in 1824. With the expiration of Monroe's second term there was no notable Virginian to take his place; the weak and discredited Republican congressional caucus was unable to produce a disci-

From *The American Party Systems: Stages of Political Development*, edited by William Nisbet Chambers and Walter Dean Burnham, pp. 97–114. © 1967 by Oxford University Press, Inc. Reprinted by permission. Footnotes renumbered.

plined solution to the problem of succession; and soon there were four candidates—all self-styled Republicans—contending for the presidency. Except in New England, where John Quincy Adams had virtually no opposition, the contest was extremely confused and did not at once produce new party alignments. Because it was so chaotic, and also because in many states one or another of the candidates enjoyed overwhelming support from local political leaders, voter participation was remarkably low.

The most important consequence of 1824, in terms of party formation, was that it projected Andrew Jackson to the fore as the rival to Adams. Looking ahead to 1828, rival political leaders from state to state began to calculate their courses of action with respect to what was termed the "presidential question." Obviously, many considerations entered into their appraisals, but the fact that loomed largest, no doubt, was the highly sectional nature of the appeal of the two candidates.

This sectional bias was clearly revealed in the election of 1828. Adams swept New England, securing majorities of three-to-one or better in four of the six states. Jackson was equally impressive in the South, and won commanding majorities in most of the newer states of the West. Having no sectional candidate of their own in the race, the Middle States provided the major battleground of the election, and—except in Pennsylvania—the vote was extremely close. The party alignments that formed in the Middle States by 1828 tended to be durable, as Table 1 shows,[1] although in both New York and Pennsylvania the anti-Jackson forces lacked cohesion and were distracted by Antimasonry. With these important exceptions, we could say that a new two-party system had emerged in the Middle States by 1828 and that it had been given definition by the presidential contest. In New England, because of the overwhelming loyalty to the sectional favorite, the opposition Jacksonian parties were able to make little headway until after Adams had been defeated. But by 1829 the political balance had altered considerably, and the Jacksonians rapidly moved into a competitive position in most states. In the South and West—except for the very special case of Kentucky—the election of 1828 stimulated the temporary formation of parties. Once the election was over, however, the alignments did not persist and politics continued to be conducted in what was essentially an unstructured fashion.

Despite the large issues that presumably were involved, the election

---

[1] See Table 1 for an index of the balance—or imbalance—of parties in each state for the presidential elections from 1828 through 1844. It will be observed that the average differential between the total vote obtained by the presidential candidates in 1828 was 36 points, which would mean an average percentage of 68 for the victor and 32 for the defeated candidate.

TABLE 1   Differential between Percentages of Total Vote Obtained by Major Presidential
Candidates, 1828–44

State	1828	1832	1836	1840	1844
Maine	20	10	20	1	13
New Hampshire	7	13	50	11	19
Vermont	50	10	20	29	18
Massachusetts	66	30	9	16	12
Rhode Island	50	14	6	23	20
Connecticut	50	20	1	11	5
New York	2	4	9	4	1
New Jersey	4	1	1	4	1
Pennsylvania	33	16	4	1	2
Delaware	—	2	6	10	3
Maryland	2	1	7	8	5
Virginia	38	50	13	1	6
North Carolina	47	70	6	15	5
Georgia	94	100	4	12	4
Kentucky	1	9	6	29	8
Tennessee	90	90	16	11	1
Louisiana	6	38	3	19	3
Alabama	80	100	11	9	18
Mississippi	60	77	2	7	13
Ohio	3	3	4	9	2
Indiana	13	34	12	12	2
Illinois	34	37	10	2	12
Missouri	41	32	21	14	17
Arkansas	—	—	28	13	26
Michigan	—	—	9	4	6
Average Differential	36	36	11	11	9

of 1832 had remarkably little effect on party formation. In the South and
West there were feeble efforts to organize support for Henry Clay, but
in most states he fared even less well than had Adams in 1828. In the
Middle States, the close balance that had become evident in 1828 persisted. The most striking shift occurred in New England, where in every
state the Jacksonians made tremendous gains and captured Maine and
New Hampshire. Perhaps this remarkable upheaval can be attributed
to the popularity of Jackson's policies regarding the bank, tariff, and internal improvements. Yet I am inclined to believe that the explanation is
to be found quite simply in the fact that Clay lacked the strong sectional
appeal that Adams had possessed.

How well developed, then, was the new party system by the end of 1832? In broad terms, it was well established in New England and the Middle States, despite the complications of Antimasonry. In every state the Jacksonians had acquired recognized leaders, constructed an elaborate party apparatus, and enlisted in their ranks multitudes of voters who identified with the Jackson party. The opposition, plagued by the lack of a persistent standard bearer, nevertheless managed to maintain a competitive position, whether under the Adams, National Republican, or Antimasonic label. The South, except for Kentucky, could best be described as politically monolithic. Where nearly all political leaders and candidates were nominally, at least, of the Jacksonian persuasion, there could scarcely be a functioning two-party system. In certain of the newer states of the West what can only be described as a dual party system existed. There were temporary party formations in 1828 and 1832 for the purpose of contesting the presidential election, but in state and congressional elections the contests were either conducted on a non-party basis or, in some instances, on the basis of alignments quite different from those that obtained in the presidential elections. It is common, in describing American politics in this era, to assert that by 1828 or by 1832 a functioning party system existed; but it would be my contention that in many states the crucial stage of party formation had not yet been reached.

Slight as was the effect of the election of 1832 on party formation, it did reveal an undercurrent that was soon to assume the proportions of a tidal wave. Although Jackson retained, and even increased, his huge majorities throughout the South, there were strong manifestations of dissatisfaction with his running mate and heir-apparent, Martin Van Buren of New York. In Virginia, North Carolina, Georgia, and Alabama, factions that professed loyalty to Jackson also launched organized efforts to oppose Van Buren's candidacy for the vice-presidency, and there were similar signs of restiveness in other Southern states as well. Some of these early anti-Van Burenites were admirers of John C. Calhoun, and others were appalled at the prospect of having to support a Northerner for the presidency. Still others, no doubt, were calculating how they might exploit anti-Van Buren sentiment to advance their political fortunes within their particular states.

What can best be characterized as a political explosion rocked the South from Virginia to Mississippi in 1834 and 1835. With Jackson nearing the end of his tenure, the political consensus that seemingly had prevailed was abruptly replaced by a sharp cleavage in almost every state. Those who remained loyal to the Jackson party found themselves confronted with a virulent opposition that shared a common antagonism to Martin Van Buren. While some of those "antis" continued to profess their undying loyalty to Old Hickory and his policies, others declaimed against executive usurpation, the removal of bank deposits, and the tariff, or sounded the changes on states' rights. The new sides were drawn in the state and congressional elections of 1834 and 1835, and by 1836 the Southern opposition parties—often bearing the name Whig—had found their standard bearer in Hugh Lawson White of Tennessee.

In the Western states, too, the approach of the election of 1836 spurred the slow process of party formation. More-or-less well-organized Van Buren-Democratic parties faced bitter struggles with opposition parties pledged variously to a local hero—William Henry Harrison of Ohio—or to mixed White-Harrison tickets. In part because of the unprecedented personal campaign waged by Harrison, the election aroused considerable interest. The alignments that emerged in this election persisted, even though state elections in Illinois, Indiana, and Missouri continued for a few years to bear only a vague resemblance to party contests.

The least studied of all our presidential elections, the election of 1836, was of crucial importance in determining the ultimate outlines of the second party system. In marked contrast to the situation that had existed in 1832, there were now two parties contesting elections in every state, and—no less significantly—in the large majority of the states the parties were competitive. Although Van Buren eked out a victory in the 1836 election, the party that he headed had very different dimensions from the one that had twice swept Jackson into office. In the South, where Jackson had encountered little more than token opposition, Van Buren polled slightly less than 50 per cent of the popular vote. Jackson had won 100 per cent of the votes in Georgia and 95 per cent of the votes in Tennessee in 1832; Van Buren lost both of these states in 1836. In the West, too, Van Buren's strength was far less than that of Jackson. Only in New England did Van Buren enhance the strength of the Democratic party. In the evenly balanced Middle States there was no large shift.

In brief, the effect of Van Buren's candidacy was to end the monolithic character of Southern politics and delineate and strengthen alignments in the West, thereby giving a truly national dimension to the second party system. While in 1832 the victorious candidate had secured a two-to-one margin in eleven states, only one state remained in that category in 1836: New Hampshire, which Van Buren carried by a three-to-one margin. Fittingly enough, the state in which Van Buren found his weakest support was Vermont. Here, indeed, is a conundrum for political analysts.

The anti-Van Buren or Whig parties that had formed in the several states between 1834 and 1836, together with those in New England and the Middle States that had originated earlier, had yet to develop national cohesion and leadership. Such an achievement would be essential if they were to contest successfully for the presidency. Meeting at Harrisburg in December 1839, in one of the most astutely contrived conventions ever held, they performed the difficult feat by agreeing to unite on the best available hero, Old Tippecanoe Harrison, and by sedulously avoiding any semblance of a party platform. Thus effectively mobilized, the Whigs proceeded to put on a spectacular campaign that was to fix a new style in American political drama.[2] The exciting contest, waged furiously now in every state, stimulated an unprecedented outpouring of voters and sent Van Buren down to a crushing defeat in the electoral college, although the popular vote was far less lopsided.

The campaign of 1840 brought the second American party system at last to fruition. In every region of the country, and indeed in every state, politics was conducted within the framework of a two-party system, and in all but a handful of states the parties were so closely balanced as to be competitive.[3] In broad terms, it was the contest for the presidency that shaped this party system and defined its essential purpose. The same party system, however, was to be utilized as the framework within which competition for office at all other levels of government would be conducted. The two parties were similar in structure, employed similar campaign techniques, and performed similar functions. Although in specific features the parties remained somewhat differentiated from state to state, there had in fact occurred a nationalization of institutional forms and political styles. There was also a nationalization of poltical identities. Voters everywhere would respond to candidates and issues as Whigs or Democrats.

IV

With this brief and even partial synopsis of party development in mind, it becomes possible to attempt some analyses of what it all signifies. We can approach this question by attempting some broad comparisons between the first and second party systems. But before engaging in this exercise, we might well pause to consider how politics was conducted in the absence of parties, for only with some understanding of this phase of our political history can we measure and evaluate the effects of parties.

Even after the appearance of the first party system, many states con-

---

[2] The story of this memorable campaign is ably detailed in Robert G. Gunderson, *The Log Cabin Campaign* (Lexington, Ky., 1957).

[3] See Table 1. In twenty of the states in 1840 the margin between the two parties was 15 points or less and the average differential was only 11 points. Note the contrast between 1832 and 1840.

tinued to conduct politics on a non-party basis. An example is Tennessee, which did so for roughly forty years.[4] With no vestige of political parties, the Tennessee brand of politics featured hard-fought contests for seats in the legislature and in Congress that not uncommonly brought over 70 per cent of the electorate to the polls. In the process, the state produced a host of outstanding political figures, including not only Andrew Jackson but James K. Polk, Hugh Lawson White, John Bell, and Felix Grundy as well. Reference could readily be made to a dozen other states where as late as the 1820's, or even 1830's, political parties were nonexistent. Leaving aside the intriguing question of why parties were not formed, at least for the purpose of conducting state politics, it would no doubt be illuminating if we could answer the question of what functions usually ascribed to political parties were not being performed in some manner in Tennessee and other non-party states. Probably none of us would insist that representative government was inconceivable without political parties, but we may readily err in attributing to parties a larger and more comprehensive role in the American political process than they in fact deserve. Unfortunately, we know even less about pre-party politics in the United States than we do about party politics, with the result that as yet we are not well prepared to make reliable comparisons between the two systems.

We are on slightly firmer ground when we endeavor to compare the first and the second party systems, although admittedly our knowledge of both is inadequate and the conceptual framework within which we structure our comparisons is incomplete. For the purposes of this essay, the comparative analysis must necessarily be kept within brief limits and deal only with large and readily visible attributes.

The first and second American party systems did not have precisely the same origins. It would seem that cleavages within Congress preceded and even forecast the formation of parties in the 1790's. In theoretical terms, it would be extremely important to be able to affirm that the first party system represented an "internally created" or "interior" type of party formation. Unfortunately, we cannot be sure how far this interior process of party formation might have proceeded, for superimposed on the impulse supplied by the congressional parties was the mobilization for the presidential contests in 1796 and 1800. It is my view that these contests for the presidency supplied a greater stimulus to party formation than did the congressional groupings. Nevertheless, the early existence of congressional alignments in the 1790's has no counterpart in the 1820's. Moreover, the parties of the 1790's possessed at the outset an issue-orientation that can hardly be discerned

---

[4] Tennessee might be called a "one-party" state in the sense that nearly all public figures, as well as voters, identified themselves as Jeffersonian Republicans, or —after 1824—as Jacksonians. But there was no formal party structure, and vigorously contested elections were conducted without relevance to parties.

in 1824 or 1828. Finally, the first party system had a relatively rapid emergence, whereas the second was formed in stages over a period of roughly sixteen years.

Both party systems, the second more clearly than the first, were oriented toward contesting presidential elections. This orientation presents a striking contrast to the situation in other Western political systems, where parties have been oriented toward securing as large a representation as possible in the national legislature (although it must be noted that in most cases it has been the legislature that names the functioning executive in such systems). It is this peculiarity, among others, that makes it so difficult to conceptualize American party systems in terms that would be relevant to other nations. In organizational terms, the congressional district has presented awkward problems for our parties, quite unlike the parliamentary constituencies in Europe. Why should the executive rather than the legislative branch have been the focal point for the party system, especially in the first half of the nineteenth century? No doubt an extended answer to this question could tell us much about the special character of American parties.

There were pronounced differences in the organizational structures of parties in the first and second party systems. The caucus reflected in part the prominent role taken by legislators—national and state—in guiding early party development, and it was extensively employed as a management device under the first party system.[5] In most states, as well as at the national level, party members within the legislature, often joined by non-legislators, performed extensive nominating functions and —usually through such agencies as central committees—directed party affairs generally. In many states, conspicuously in New England and Virginia, the caucus and its agencies operated a highly centralized party apparatus, although in time local party units increasingly employed delegate conventions to nominate candidates for lesser offices. Two states, New Jersey and Delaware, were exceptional in that they instituted the state convention. Because of the great variations in constitutional structures from state to state, the precise forms of party organization and even the functions performed by the caucus differed widely; but in its most highly developed form—notably in Massachusetts—the caucus structure was highly integrated and extremely efficient. At the national level, party management was relatively weak. The Republican congressional caucus was a promising institution, which under slightly altered circumstances might have exerted a lasting influence on the structure of Amer-

---

[5] For interesting material on the caucus-style party organization under the first party system, see Noble E. Cunningham, Jr., *The Jeffersonian Republicans: The Formation of Party Organizations 1789–1801* (Chapel Hill, 1957), 162–6; Cunningham, *The Jeffersonian Republicans in Power: Party Operations 1801–1809* (Chapel Hill, 1963), 111–12, 127, 133, 137, 142, 145–6; and David Hackett Fischer, *The Revolution of American Conservatism: The Federalist Party in the Era of Jeffersonian Democracy* (New York, 1965), 69–90 *passim*.

ican parties, but for reasons that must be passed over it failed to develop and maintain its authority and grew increasingly ineffective, especially after 1816. The Federalists, with their small and geographically unrepresentative delegation in Congress, could scarcely use the caucus as an authoritative national agency, and they had little success in developing the convention as an alternative.

Under the second party system, the caucus was almost completely replaced by the convention as the characteristic device for party management. The changeover, which has not yet been studied thoroughly, had great theoretical significance. In addition to reflecting demands for popular participation in party affairs the convention also represented a highly practical solution to problems facing party leaders at a time when party identities in legislative bodies were extremely confused, or when incipient parties had too few legislative representatives to organize a respectable caucus. Much might be made of the fact that the Antimasonic party, the first clear example of what Maurice Duverger calls an "externally created" or "exterior" type of party in the United States, was especially zealous in developing the convention technique and, as we know, held the first national party convention. Whether the extralegislative origins of the Jackson and Adams parties in most—but not all —states would justify our describing them as "exterior" parties could lead to considerable debate. What would seem to be indisputable is that the shift from caucus to convention implied a loss in the political authority of legislative bodies. While they were suffering this loss, they were also experiencing general curtailment of their elective functions, as evidenced by the trend toward the popular choice of electors, governors, and other state officials. Again, one would like to be able to understand fully why this downgrading of the legislative branch occurred and what implications it had for our system of politics.

The widespread adoption of the convention system in the 1830's, with its hierarchy of delegate conventions and party committees extending from the smallest electoral unit up to the national conventions, made for an exceedingly elaborate and complex organizational structure. Because candidates had to be nominated at so very many different levels of government, elections were held so frequently, and the party system embraced the entire range of offices, the organizations that had evolved in most states by the 1840's were marvels of ingenuity and intricacy and required enormous manpower to staff them. In contrast to the diversity of organizational forms under the first party system, there was now a high degree of uniformity throughout the nation and in both major parties.

It is possible that the shift from the caucus to the convention may have tended greatly to emphasize the purely electoral functions of the party apparatus. The members of a caucus, in their dual capacity as legislators and party managers, may have been more concerned with matters of program and policy than were the members of conventions. It would also appear that in its most centralized form, the caucus structure imposed a much higher degree of discipline than was to prevail under the convention system. Despite their elaborate organization, the new parties of the second party system were actually decentralized structures. The party apparatus at each level of government, or within each type of constituency, possessed considerable autonomy. Party mechanisms were better designed for achieving agreement on nominations than for formulating policies. Perhaps the very complexity and magnitude of the formal organizational structure contributed to the rise of the professional party manager and the informal leader, or boss.

In discussing any formal party structures, whether of the caucus or convention type, the problem inevitably arises as to whether the formal structure reflected the actual locus of power or influence. Superficially, the delegate convention system of the 1830's and 1840's resulted in the "democratization" of parties, but we have yet to determine the degree to which conventions were genuine decision-making bodies. Perhaps they were, but they must also be viewed as having what might be termed a cosmetic function; that is, they gave a democratic appearance to what might in fact have been decisions determined by a party oligarchy. Indeed, Ostrogorski used the term "democratic formalism" to describe the convention structure.

The two party systems could also be compared with respect to participation. The installation of the convention party structure unquestionably multiplied opportunities for party followers to assume roles as activists. This development was especially prominent in those states where previously there had been little or no formal party organization, but its effects could be noted everywhere. Moreover, intense inter-party competition stimulated unprecedented levels of voter participation, not uncommonly rising to 80 per cent of the electorate, whereas prior to 1824 in a very large number of states it was exceptional for half of the eligible voters to participate regularly in elections.[6] Both in the compre-

---

[6] See my "New Perspectives on Jacksonian Politics," *American Historical Review*, LXV (1960), 288–301, for illustrative data on the increase in voter participation. In those states where the parties were competitive after 1800, it was not uncommon for 70 per cent or more of the adult white males to vote, and on occasion higher levels were reached. But in states where the parties were unbalanced, or where elections were not contested on a party basis, participation would usually be under 50 per cent. There are, however, curious exceptions to these generalizations. Alabama recorded the suspiciously high figure of 97 per cent in a gubernatorial election in 1819, and Tennessee reached 80 per cent in the gubernatorial election of 1817. These, and other data that could be cited, suggest that high participation could be achieved in the absence of parties, and even in the absence of the stimulus of a presidential contest.

hensiveness of their structures and in the universality of their appeal, then, the new parties could truly be characterized as mass parties.

One may properly speculate as to whether the measurable increase in voter participation had a direct influence on party programs and governmental actions. To put the question differently, when vast numbers of men who had formerly lacked the franchise or who had been apathetic entered the electoral arena, were there discernable shifts in party attitudes or public policy? Did the parties and the governments become more "democratic"? This would be an extremely difficult question to answer, but I have the impression that the "new" voters tended to divide between the two parties in much the same proportion as the "old" voters.[7] We might conclude that both parties accommodated the new voters by modifying their appeals and their programs. An alternative conclusion could be that because the new voters did not enter predominantly into one party and make it the instrument for achieving their political goals, they had no great effect on the parties. Any sure evaluation of the effects of enlarged participation must depend on further studies, but at least we might agree that the mass participation that we associate with the second party system did affect the style of politics.

The extended form of participation in politics in the era of the second party system can scarcely be comprehended in purely political terms—that is, only in terms of rivalry between opposing power elites or interest groups for dominance in the state and for control over public policy. It would be difficult to account for all the phenomena of the system within these limited concepts, and the varieties of experiences that parties in this era afforded to the electorate went beyond the political sphere.[8] Those tens of thousands of men and women who attended the mammoth Whig festival at Nashville in 1840; those untold millions who carried torches, donned uniforms, chanted slogans, or cheered themselves hoarse at innumerable parades and rallies; those puffed-up canvassers of wards, servers of rum, and distributors of largesse; and all those simple folk who whipped themselves into a fury of excitement and anxiety as each election day approached, were thrilling to a grand dramatic experience, even a cathartic experience. There was no spectacle, no contest, in America that could match an election campaign, and all could identify with and participate in it.

Innumerable foreign observers saw clearly this amazing dimension of American politics. As Michael Chevalier perceived it, the political

[7] See my "Suffrage Classes and Party Alignments: A Study in Voter Behavior," *Mississippi Valley Historical Review*, XLVI (1959), 397–410.

[8] M. Ostrogorski, among other foreign observers, has some extremely perceptive comments on the "ritual character" of American parties in *Democracy and the Party System in the United States* (New York, 1910), 408–12.

campaign and all its attendant pageantry and exaltation meant to Americans what religious festivals had meant to the peoples of Catholic Europe. Witnessing a post-election celebration of New York City Democrats, he was struck by the resemblance.

> The procession was nearly a mile long; the democrats marched in good order to the glare of torches; the banners were more numerous than I had ever seen them in any religious festival; all were in transparency, on account of the darkness. On some were inscribed the names of the democratic societies or sections, . . . others bore imprecations against the Bank of the United States; *Nick Biddle* and *Old Nick* here figured largely and formed the pendant of our *libera nos a malo*. Then came portraits of General Jackson afoot and on horseback . . . Those of Washington and Jefferson, surrounded with democratic mottoes, were mingled in all tastes and of all colors. Among these figured an eagle, not a painting, but a real live eagle, tied by the legs, surrounded by a wreath of leaves, and hoisted upon a pole, after the manner of the Roman standards. The imperial bird was carried by a stout sailor, more pleased than ever was a sergeant permitted to hold one of the strings of the canopy, in a Catholic ceremony. From further than the eye could reach, came marching on the democrats. I was struck with the resemblance of their air to the train that escorts the *viaticum* in Mexico or Puebla. . . . The democratic procession, also, like the Catholic procession, had its halting places; it stopped before the house of the Jackson men to fill the air with cheers, and halted at the doors of the leaders of the Opposition, to give three, six, or nine groans.
>   . . . If these scenes were to find a painter, they would be admired at a distance, not less than the triumphs and sacrificial pomps, which the ancients have left us delineated in marble and brass; for they are not mere grotesques after the manner of Rembrandt, they belong to history, they partake of the grand; they are the episodes of a wondrous epic which will bequeath a lasting memory to posterity, that of the coming of democracy.[9]

Finally, the first and second party systems exhibited pronounced differences in their extent and their alignment. The parties of the 1790's had never really been extended to more than fifteen states, and in several of those they scarcely became rooted. The second party system comprehended every state, although there might well be some reservations about South Carolina. The first party system was, from one point of view, very badly aligned. Early in its history the New England states were heavily inclined toward the Federalist party, while in the South the Republicans possessed a lopsided supremacy. Although New England in time achieved a brief balance of parties, the South became virtually a one-party region. The second party system was extraordinary in that the two parties were

[9] Michael Chevalier, *Society, Manners and Politics in the United States* (Boston, 1839), 318–19.

fairly evenly balanced in every region.[10] Between 1836 and 1852, as in no other period in our history, each of the parties was truly national in its extent.

V

It would be possible and even profitable to explain why the two party systems differed in so many attributes, but such a disquisition would probably have to be very lengthy if it were to be at all persuasive. Within the limited compass of this essay it is appropriate to attempt no more than a brief reference to the most salient factors.

Of foremost importance in affecting the structures of parties as well as the specific tasks that elements within the party organization had to perform were certain fundamental changes in the constitutional and legal environment.[11] To put the matter simply, the rules under which the political game was to be played changed greatly between 1800 and 1840. The most obvious development was a trend from diversity to uniformity in governmental structures and electoral procedures from state to state. The magnitude and significance of this quiet revolution in the electoral environment has generally been ignored, except for a curious preoccupation with modifications in suffrage qualifications.[12] We have yet to assess adequately the relevance to our party system of the movements toward the popular, at-large election of presidential electors, the choice of congressmen by districts, the popular election of governors, and the multiplication in numbers of locally elected officials. In a related realm, the adoption of printed ballots, the creation of small voting districts, and the consolidation of elections on a single day had enormous consequences for political parties.

One general effect of this quiet revolution was to complicate the tasks of the parties. In a situation where, for example, members of a legislature were elected from the county as a unit and where the legislature in turn appointed the governor, presidential electors, and county officials, parties would have limited tasks, as contrasted with a situation where

---

[10] See Table 1.

[11] Constitutions and electoral laws, as demonstrated by the studies of Duverger and others, strongly conditioned the nature of party systems. This is not to maintain that all attributes of parties are explainable in these terms, and in seeking to account for cleavages between parties, political styles, or the characteristics of political elites, for example, relevant social factors must be considered. But I would agree with Lipset that "electoral laws determine the nature of the party system as much as any other structural variable." See Seymour Martin Lipset, *The First New Nation* (New York, 1963), 293.

[12] There have been scarcely any comparative studies of constitutional change at the state level, although this field offers rich opportunities for scholars. For a pioneering study, which still stands alone, see Fletcher M. Green, *Constitutional Development in the South Atlantic States, 1776–1860* (Chapel Hill, 1930).

members of each house of the legislature were chosen from different constituencies, and presidential electors, the governor, and county officials were popularly elected. Compelled to elaborate an intricate organization capable of making nominations and conducting campaigns within a bewildering variety of constituencies, and obliged at the same time to appeal for the broadest possible base of support, the new parties confronted a staggering challenge, especially when they might be called upon to engage in electoral combat two or three times within a single year. It is no wonder that they were reduced to little more than electoral machines.

If one change in the electoral environment loomed larger than all the rest it was the shift to the popular, at-large election of presidential electors. This development gave a popular dimension to the contest for the presidency, reduced the political authority of the state legislatures, called forth elaborate and intensive campaign efforts, facilitated the building of national parties, reduced the effectiveness of third parties, and made the presidential election the focal point of the party system—to suggest but a few consequences. How and through what influences this transformation of the process of choosing electors was brought about has yet to be studied, but a complete understanding of its implications might well be crucial to any conceptualization of the American party system.

The political environment was profoundly influenced not only by these constitutional and legal developments, but also by fairly obvious technological, economic, and social changes. Revolutionary improvements in means of transportation and communication made it feasible, for example, for parties to hold state and even national conventions and conduct nationwide campaigns. Rising economic expectations associated with the transformation and expansion of the economy gave new energy to democratic dogmas and spurred mass participation in politics. The entrance of new states into the union broadened the spatial dimensions of the party system, and the growth of urban areas and the sharp rise in immigration created new challenges. Above all, the increasingly egalitarian flavor of American society, now given voice in an incontestable rhetoric, compelled both parties to project the same democratic image.

These briefly enumerated changes in the constitutional and cultural environment may account for certain fairly obvious differences in organization and style between the first and second party systems. But they do not fully explain what was most distinctive about the latter, namely, its lack of sectional bias. As the second party system reached maturity in the 1840's, it scarcely reflected the fact that the basic cleavage within the nation, transcending all others, was that which may be vaguely defined as North-South sectionalism. The first party system had mirrored this tension to the degree that after 1800 the Federalists were very largely a Northern party. The third party system as it finally became aligned in the 1870's also contained a decided sectional bias, with its solidly Democratic South and its Northern-oriented Republican party. In attempting to explain how the second party system produced not sectional parties but parties that were remarkably well balanced throughout the nation, we are confronted with a paradox. In the successive contests for the presidency between 1824 and 1836 strong sectional loyalties shaped the responses of political leaders and voters in each region to the opposing candidates. But by 1836 the end result of the series of realignments was a sectionally balanced party system. In brief, the explanation for the paradoxical character of the second party system is to be found in the peculiar circumstances associated with the contests for the presidency.

To recapitulate, the second party system did not emerge suddenly; it developed in a series of stages, and at each stage it was shaped by the sectional identifications of the candidates. With Andrew Jackson and John Quincy Adams as the candidates in 1828, a highly sectionalized vote resulted; New England went almost as overwhelmingly for Adams as the South did for Jackson; only the Middle States were evenly divided. When Henry Clay was substituted for Adams, New England was no longer held together by its loyalty to a sectional favorite, and parties throughout the North came into balance. When Martin Van Buren was substituted for Jackson—and opposed by White and Harrison—the South and much of the new West ceased to be politically monolithic, as anti-Van Buren parties quickly mobilized. These sectional responses to the presidential candidates were crucial at the time of party formation. Once the parties had been formed and identities had been acquired by the voters, alignments tended to remain relatively firm. Thus highly sectional responses in a series of presidential elections resulted in the formation of non-sectional parties.

Merely to emphasize their distinctiveness, I have chosen to call these national parties "artificial" because their ultimate alignments bore no direct relationship to the realities of sectional antagonism. At maturity, each party sought to aggregate interests that were national in scope; and within each party almost equally powerful Northern and Southern wings contested for supremacy. Intra-party tensions were greater than the tensions between the two parties. The federalized character of our constitutional structure and the inability of any national party agency to exercise firm discipline made it all but impossible to restrain the intra-party tensions. Responsible leaders of both parties understood that such parties could be destroyed by issues that were sectional in character. The parties could indulge themselves in furious controversies over the "Monster Bank," but they might be rent asunder by such issues as expansionism or the status of slavery in the territories.

The second American party system was truly a wondrous creation. Emerging over a period of sixteen years from the circumstances associated with the successive contests for the presidency, it elaborated a complex organizational structure within which there could be orderly competition for offices at all levels of government. It also provided maximal opportunities for mass participation and produced a political style that took on the aspects of a democratic religion. It could perform a wide range of electoral functions, and it could resolve conflicts that were not highly charged with sectional antagonisms. But, like the first party system, it, too, met with failure.

Apparently it was still in a healthy condition down to about 1850. Then, under the strain of the sectional issues confronting the nation, it began to crumble. The first sign was the collapse of the Whig party in the lower South, and by 1856 the already altered Democratic party was confronted by the newly marshalled Republican party and, in some areas, by the short-lived American, or "Know-Nothing," party as well. At last, in 1860, the Democrats succumbed to a fateful division and the Civil War followed. Although in the North a viable new party system operated, it was not until the 1870's, with the nation reunited and the South released from the abnormal years of Reconstruction, that the third party system assumed national dimensions.

Why did the second party system fail? One answer could be that it was inadequate to cope with conflicts that arrayed section against section. The first party system had come perilously close to foundering on this rock in 1814; but the second party system, for the reason that its parties were truly national in scope and lacked a pronounced sectional bias, was presumably better designed to manage divisive pluralism. Here we face a dilemma. If in a democratic two-party system the parties became so aligned as to reflect crucial ideological, class, social, or sectional cleavages, and they therefore present the electorate with drastic alternatives, the strain on the political system as a whole, and particularly at the level of government, may be disruptive. If, on the other hand, each party is expected to mediate conflicting interests by aggregating the broad spectrum of those interests, the strain on the political system at the level of the parties may be disruptive. I have no solution to propose to this dilemma, other than to suggest that a party system that is *too* comprehensive—as was the second party system—may be potentially as explosive as a party system that is polarized around drastic alternatives—as was the third party system in its formative years.[13] Perhaps this is to say that threatening problems or the strains of crises must be shared between the party system and the government.

[13] For an interesting discussion of the conditions under which a two-party system may be less able to resolve conflict than a multi-party system, see Lipset, *The First New Nation,* 308–12.

13

Interpreting New York Voting

LEE BENSON

To determine "who voted for whom" in the 1844 New York election, Lee Benson computed percentages of the party vote in all units in all counties, ranked those units according to support of the Democratic party, and compared the variables in the rural towns and urban wards most committed or most hostile to the Democrats. Borrowing heavily from sociology, Benson's multivariate analysis determines not only who voted for whom in 1844 but questions long-held assumptions about the socio-economic base of Jacksonian politics.

PATTERNS IN NEW YORK VOTING BEHAVIOR

To get down to cases: Before we can regard any interpretation of 1844 New York voting behavior as "potentially verifiable," we must show that it conforms to all known facts and credible inferences about what happened and who voted for whom. Once we recognize that the Jacksonians won either by narrow majorities before 1837 or by narrow pluralities after that date, or frequently failed to win by any margin, it will surely become apparent that there is no basis for explanations that tell why they were the "popular party." Similarly, explanations of why the Jacksonians won strong support from low-status socioeconomic groups or classes become incredible once we recognize that, in fact, they did not win such support. This . . . interpretation of New York voting behavior,

From Lee Benson, *The Concept of Jacksonian Democracy: New York as a Test Case*, pp. 289–93, 317–28. © 1961 by Princeton University Press; Princeton Paperback, 1970. Reprinted by permission of Princeton University Press.

therefore, has been developed from the group patterns that have been established with *reasonable* credibility and *reasonable* accuracy. Further research may modify or discredit those patterns, but at the moment they appear to possess substantial credibility.

Polarity in Voting

New York voters did not divide along class lines. Other nonpolarized voting patterns are also evident. Major party strength varied considerably in the rural counties and, to a lesser extent, in the cities, but an urban-rural cleavage had not yet materialized; that is, neither the Democrats nor the Whigs drew disproportionately from urban or rural voters. Though political cleavages had developed between free thinkers and orthodox believers and between puritans and non-puritans, and though we can say that a "Catholic vote" apparently existed by 1844, a "Protestant vote" had not yet manifested itself. There are some indications of sectarian political divisions, but none that members of that broad group generally showed any preferences *as Protestants* for either major party. Similarly, native groups, with the exception of Negroes and Huguenots, had not yet developed polarized voting patterns, although perceptible differences existed among them. . . . With the exception of free thinkers, puritans, Negroes and Huguenots, post-1790 immigrants were the only groups who displayed sharply polarized voting patterns in New York. All the New British groups overwhelmingly voted Whig; all the New non-British groups overwhelmingly voted Democratic.

Viewed superficially, these nonpolarized voting patterns might seem to support the argument that voting behavior cannot be interpreted objectively. It might be argued that the historian, confronted with an apparently random distribution of behavior, must either eschew interpretation or stress some motive (or variable) that derives from his subjective frame of reference. And that argument might seem to be strengthened when we recall that content analyses revealed distinct differences in the principles and policies of the major parties in New York. If the party differences were distinctly different, and yet the great bulk of the electorate distributed their ballots at random, how then can we expect to reconstruct objectively men's motives for voting?

But the operative words in the above paragraph are "viewed superficially." Even if we exclude areas where immigrants tended to live in significant numbers, when we get down to the *town and ward level*, it becomes evident that voting patterns actually were sharply polarized rather than evenly divided. That is, many rural towns and urban wards cast very heavy Democratic or Whig votes. In different counties, and freqently within the same county, members of the same native group did vote strongly Democratic in some towns and strongly Whig in others. But since *polarized local* voting patterns did exist, *the absence of political polarization among native groups identified by widely inclusive group attributes* (ethnocultural, religious, class, residence) is highly significant; this is in effect the same kind of observation that Sherlock Holmes made when he recognized the significance of the finding, "the dog *didn't* bark."

For example, recognition that revived nativist, anti-Catholic movements scored impressive political successes during the 1850's tells us much about the failure of the American Republicans to receive support in 1844 (except in areas with relatively large percentages of Catholic and New non-British immigrants). Seen in that perspective, the failure of the American Republicans shows that the conditions which would lead the native Protestant electorate to respond politically to nativist, anti-Catholic issues had not yet developed during the 1840's. It is not surprising, therefore, that perceptible Democratic-Whig differences over those issues should have had relatively little impact upon voting behavior patterns firmly fixed before 1844. Similarly, the failure of the Liberty Party to receive support except from a small number of "ultraist" Whigs testifies to the limited political impact of issues connected with slavery. Under those conditions, our theory would predict that a "wide variety of factors" influenced native Protestant voters throughout the state—a prediction consonant with the marked variations in major party strength evident on the level of rural towns and urban wards.

It is true that the major New York parties differed distinctly over principles and policies, but seen in perspectives, their differences were relatively narrow in scope. That is, the differences manifested themselves within the framework of deep agreement on political fundamentals. Despite their clashes over the positive state, locus of government power, role of different goverment branches, and foreign policy, both the Democrats and Whigs stood firmly committed to political democracy (for white men) and to liberal capitalism. And both were committed at least officially to separation of church and state—although . . . the Whigs projected an image calculated to win support from pious Protestants. Significantly, the only really sharp cleavages evident among native voters in 1844—the orthodox-free thinker and puritan-nonpuritan splits—related to fundamental church-state issues.

The above "facts" seem to warrant the inference that party differences over *socioeconomic* issues did not have sufficient impact to alter voting patterns already fixed by 1832; some localized, minor shifts and some temporary fluctuations occurred, but the patterns remained essentially unchanged. Irreconcilable with the Jacksonian Democracy assumption that socioeconomic principles and policies primarily determined political cleavages, this finding "fits" the theory of voting behavior derived from the Hofstadter-Hartz thesis. In the absence of intense, widespread ethnocultural and religious conflicts, the theory predicts that American voting patterns will vary widely among members of native groups identified by any of the broad attributes noted above. Instead of dividing into solid blocs, voters are likely to be more or less influenced by: 1) long-established political associations and loyalties (going back decades and, in some places, generations); 2) local leadership and local antagonisms having nothing properly to do with politics, according to the Horace Greeley definition of political propriety; 3) local historical traditions, conflicts, needs, and issues; 4) differences in party organization and control over communication media, as well as differences in control over ostensibly nonpolitical institutions.

In short, the theory leads to this prediction: unless very intense ethnocultural and religious antagonisms fuse members of the dominant native Protestant group into solid blocs, a multiplicity of "localistic" factors will produce wide variations in their voting patterns.

. . .

NEGROES, IRISH CATHOLICS, "NEW BRITISH"

Chautauqua Yankees and Rockland Dutch tended to polarize politically, but in general members of white native Protestant ethnocultural groups tended to divide evenly (that is, not more than 60-40). In contrast, Negroes, Huguenots, and immigrant groups voted as solid blocs. We can infer that ethnocultural groups who voted as solid blocs were influenced by special factors which aroused intense emotions and tended not to influence other groups. It also seems reasonable to infer that those factors did not relate to socioeconomic issues. Why, for example, should party differences over the tariff have led Negroes in 1844 to vote 95 per cent Whig and Irish Catholics 95 per cent Democratic? Their opposite patterns become logical, however, when we view them as having been influenced primarily by their positive and negative orientations to reference groups and their subsequent fulfillment of political roles. To support this interpretation, we focus attention upon three ethnocultural groups who voted as blocs.

The Negroes

As we have seen, the Van Buren faction wrote into the 1821 Constitution the provision requiring property qualifications for Negro voters.

The provision did more than limit the number of Negroes who could vote: it simultaneously increased their isolation within New York society and their dependence upon those whites who accepted them at least as members of the political community. An appeal later made by "colored men" conveys the symbolic importance of their political segregation: "Think not that we are over anxious or that we set too high a value on the ballot-box. You can imagine its worth to yourselves—can you not faintly conceive of its worth to us? True, we are colored men; but have not colored men eyes, hands, organs, dimensions, senses, affections, passions? Are we not fed with the same food, hurt with the same weapons, subject to the same diseases, healed by the same means, warmed and cooled by the same Winter and Summer as yourselves? If then, we are like you in those things, remember the golden rule, and vote for us, that we may become like you in others."

The colored men made their appeal during the campaign to elect delegates to the New York Constitutional Convention of 1846, which would decide whether political equality applied to Negroes. On that question the major parties differed radically. To quote the *Morning News*, a leading organ of the Radical Democracy opposed to equality for "Blacks," "The principal object of the Whigs who have participated in the movement for a Convention to revise the Constitution of this State, has been to procure the right of suffrage for the Negroes to the same extent that it is enjoyed by white citizens." The *New York Tribune*, engaged in a running debate with the *Morning News*, stated the Whig position as follows: "This question of Suffrage is in truth fundamental to all others. On the one side stand Equality, Reason, Justice, Democracy, Humanity; on the other are a base, slavery-engendered prejudice and a blackguard clamor against 'Niggers.'"

In essence, the *Tribune* accurately stated the different party positions on Negro equality—positions which stemmed from the different attitudes Whigs and Democrats had long held and expressed toward Negroes. Because of the Constitutional Convention, the differences were expressed particularly sharply in 1846 and indicate clearly why Negroes voted so solidly against the New York Jacksonians' version of democracy.

The *Morning News* did not adopt the anti-Negro vocabulary of abuse employed by less "high toned" Democratic papers, but it expressed the same underlying attitudes. Urging support for Democratic candidates to the Constitutional Convention, it observed that the equal suffrage issue formed only part of a larger subject: "The subject resolves into the question, not merely whether we shall give negroes the right of suffrage, but whether we shall endeavour to overcome the great laws of nature, which do not permit two distinct and uncongenial races of men to mingle together in harmony or in mutual self-government. Holding the opinion that such a result is impossible, and undesirable if it were otherwise, we can see no useful object to be attained by trying to effect it; and we are confident that any attempt to do so by allowing Negro suffrage, would be attended with evils and disasters which would be deplored when too late."

When he was attacked by the *Tribune* for advocating views antithetical to his professed belief in democracy, the editor of the *News* replied by noting that though he had not written the articles, their general doctrines "met our entire approval." "It is a pity they [the 'superior' and the 'inferior' race] are united together in the same community at all. It is no good policy to attract more and more of the Black Race by such political bounties on their entrance and residence among us. Their augmentation in number ought to be rather discouraged than favored."

Two quotations from *Tribune* editorials represent Whig views and further point up the difference between Whig and Democratic attitudes toward Negroes. ". . . The pandering of the Loco-Foco Party, in utter contempt of their own avowed principles, to this vulgar and hateful Prejudice [against 'Blacks'], cherished mainly by the weakest or worst of our own Race, *will* be remembered, because it ought to be, by the Blacks, when it will not be so fashionable and Democratic to insult or kick a Black man at the Polls as it now is."

In effect, the *Tribune* claimed that the Democrats used Negroes as a negative reference group: "Wherever in our State there is no pervading Anti-Slavery sentiment, there the Loco-Focos are red-mouthed and vociferous against Black Suffrage at all hazards. Hostility to 'Niggers' is their great card, by which they hope to carry their Delegates [to the Convention] in this City and all the close [Hudson] River Counties."

Since the Whigs had favored equal suffrage before 1846, the Negroes' solid vote can partly be attributed to their pursuing a political goal. But, as the quotations above show, the different party positions on the suffrage issue stemmed from their fundamentally different attitudes toward Negroes as members of society. Thus it seems reasonable to say that Negro voting behavior in New York was primarily determined by this factor: men most hostile to them tended to be Democrats, men most favorable to them tended to be Whigs. Put another way, once we find that Democrats were considerably more likely to be "Nigger-Haters," we can deduce from our theory of American voting behavior that Negroes would range themselves solidly against the Democratic Party. And, as we shall see, because essentially the same kind of factors influenced their behavior, the theory also helps to account for the bloc votes cast by Irish Catholics and New British.

Irish Catholics

Unlike Negroes, Irish Catholics had white skins and had never been slaves; thus no political party or faction stigmatized them as being incapable of becoming members of the community. But as early as 1827, their capacity and right to become *full-fledged* members of the community were denied by leading organs of the Adams faction—and affirmed by leading organs of the Van Buren-Jackson faction.

Supporters of Adams were disheartened by the 1827 election returns which added up to victory for their Republican opponents. Regarding the returns as ominous for the 1828 presidential contest, the *New York American* argued, "It appears as a general proposition, both plain and just, that political privileges should belong exclusively to the natives of the country." The *New York National Advocate* stated the same proposition in these words: "It is time to cease to make citizens of the subjects of European governments." In the *Advocate's* view, the half-million Irishmen in the United States particularly threatened the nation's well-being, for their voting behavior showed they lacked the qualities necessary to participate intelligently in American politics. In the recent New York election, "Everything in the shape of an Irishman, was drummed to the polls and their votes made to pass. . . . It was emphatically an *Irish triumph*." As might be expected from the election returns, the Regency's *Albany Argus* took a different view of the voting of naturalized citizens and strongly defended their "rights of Citizenship."

By 1832 the Antimasons had created a militant, *Protestant* "Church and State Party." And Irish Catholic voting patterns had crystallized along the lines feared by the Adamsites and anticipated by the Jacksonians. After the election returns were in, the leading Antimasonic paper, Thurlow Weed's *Evening Journal,* denounced and ridiculed the "multitude of Foreigners . . . chiefly Irishmen" who had been fraudulently naturalized. "The Foreigners who have voted away our rights, and assaulted and maimed our citizens, will soon be calling for Charity to support themselves and their families." According to the *Journal:* "Jacksonism, in its most ferocious and appalling aspects, was displayed at our Polls yesterday! Axes, Knives, Paving Stones, and Bricks were the *arguments* used by the FOREIGN Mercenaries who were under pay by the Albany Regency. . . . Such are the legitimate fruits of Jacksonism! Our rights and liberties are not only gone, but our LIVES are at the mercy of abandoned FOREIGNERS, instigated by the still more abandoned office-holders."

Before the election the *Argus* had appealed to Irishmen to vote for the democratic Jacksonians who welcomed them into the community

and defended them from the autocratic hypocrites who were their enemies: "Remember, that four years ago, the aristocrats, who now cajole
you, accounted your support a disgrace, and reproached the Jackson
Democratic Party as being composed of 'homebred villains and renegade
Irishmen.' "

After the election the *Argus* pointed to unrestrained attacks against
the Irish by anti-Jacksonians. It triumphantly observed: "Nothing can
exceed the virulence and malignity of the Coalition [Antimasons-National
Republicans] journals towards our Irish population, except the assiduous
and disreputable but vain efforts of the same factions to win them over
to the support of the Aristocracy."

In later years Thurlow Weed experienced a change of heart—or at
least advocated a change of tactics. And, as we have seen, his wing of
the Whig Party continued to court Irish Catholics, even when they persisted in voting Democratic. To no avail. The Irish Catholic pattern set
by 1832 prevailed in 1844. No doubt the pattern prevailed partly because
New York Democrats bestowed petty favors upon Irish Catholics, continued to oppose changes in the naturalization laws, and continued to
preach "Jeffersonian principles" in relation to immigration and matters
of conscience. But that does not satisfactorily explain why Democrats
and Whigs tended to take opposite positions on issues of deep concern
to Irish Catholics (and other New non-British).

A more satisfactory and comprehensive explanation emerges when
we recognize that immigrant Irish Catholics and native puritanical Protestants viewed each other as negative reference groups whose values,
beliefs, attitudes, and ways of life clashed fiercely. Since our theory assumes that antagonisms in nonpolitical spheres of American life find expression in American politics, we can say that Irish Catholic voting
behavior in New York was primarily determined by their reactions to
the men generally most hostile to them (puritanical Protestants), who
tended to be Whigs, and to the men generally most favorable to them
("Jeffersonian liberals"), who tended to be Democrats.

Of course, as we have seen, hostility to Irish Catholics cut across
party lines. But two deductions seem reasonable: 1) More than any other
sizeable groups, militant puritanical Protestants were likely to express
hostility to immigrants whose religious beliefs differed so sharply from
their own. 2) In turn, the Irish Catholics reciprocated their hostility and
aligned themselves with men opposed to the Protestant "Church and
State Party." In politics, as in other spheres of life, "The enemy of my
enemy is my friend."

Our interpretation of bloc voting receives further support when we
observe that Irish Catholic-Negro conflicts shaped and reinforced the
political patterns of both low-status groups. We need not discuss those

conflicts in detail, for historians have documented them. And we need not rely solely upon twentieth century theory to deduce the political consequences of Irish Catholics and Negroes regarding each other as negative reference groups. In 1846 the *Tribune* in effect invoked that theory to explain the defeat in New York City of Whig candidates to the state Constitutional Convention: "The polls were given up almost wholly to the Adopted citizens of German or Irish birth, who are always on hand (to their praise be it spoken and the shame of our born Freemen!) but who on this occasion were called out by skillful appeals to their hatred of the unfortunate African Race. It was mournful to see hundreds who have not been six years in the Country earnestly and abusively clamorous for the disfranchisement of men whose fathers' fathers were born here, and many of them shed their blood for the defense of our liberties in the war of the Revolution."

The *Tribune's* analysis is particularly convincing, and illuminating, because it rejected the argument of Whig nativists that the "adopted citizens"—the New non-British—had shown themselves to be unfit for full membership in the community. "That the Adopted Citizens generally manifested a most discreditable, unjust disposition to deprive the Colored Race of Equal Rights is most true. . . . Yet Truth compels us to add this base, aristocratic clamor against 'Niggers' originated not with Adopted but with Native Citizens, and was potent in influencing the votes of one class as well as the other [in various parts of the state]."

New British

Although the statement drastically oversimplifies complex phenomena and processes, we can say that in essence the New British voted Whig because the Irish Catholics voted Democratic. And our interpretation gains comprehensiveness when we say that the positive as well as the negative reference groups of the New British influenced their political behavior.

To a greater or lesser extent, all immigrants belonged to "outgroups" and faced difficult social and psychological problems upon arrival in the United States as strangers and aliens. The dictionary defines an alien not only as "one born in or belonging to another country who has not acquired citizenship by naturalization and is not entitled to the privileges of a citizen," but as "one who has been estranged or excluded." To overcome their estrangement, and their exclusion, and become members of the American community, in spirit as in law, aliens had to do more than receive naturalization papers. They had to win acceptance by the native "in-group." But their eventual success in becoming "assimilated" depended largely upon their initial desire and capacity to become acculturated.

Acculturation, a relatively recent term, is generally credited to American anthropologists. A satisfactory definition of the concept has not yet been developed, but we quote the one most widely used: "Acculturation comprehends those phenomena which result when groups of individuals having different cultures come into continuous first-hand contact, with subsequent changes in the original cultural patterns of either or both groups."

Surveying the literature on the acculturation of American ethnic groups, one anthropologist suggests a crucial difference between acculturation and assimilation: "The acculturation of an ethnic group in the United States—its acquisition of the culture of the dominant group—is an exclusive function of the group's desire and capacity for acculturation; but assimilation—the disappearance of group identity through nondifferential association and exogamy [marriage 'outside the tribe or blood group']—is a function of both dominant and ethnic group behavior. And in some instances, even when the ethnic group desires assimilation, *the dominant group prevents it* [italics added]."

Compared to the Irish Catholics (and other immigrants), the New British possessed greater desire and capacity for acculturation. Moreover, their aspirations for assimilation received warmer, more positive response from the dominant group. Essentially, the American cultural pattern was British in origin and Protestant in faith; as a result, although the cultural patterns of English, Scottish, Welsh, and Protestant Irish immigrants differed significantly from the American, they differed in degree, not kind. This relative lack of differentiation from native white Protestants simultaneously encouraged and permitted the New British to acquire the culture of the dominant group; in other words, the New British could become Americanized more easily than could the Irish Catholics.

Two closely related processes hastened the Americanization of the New British and their conversion into staunch Whigs: 1) They distinguished themselves from low-status immigrants, in part by expressing hostility to them—especially to the Irish Catholics. 2) They identified themselves with natives whom they regarded as exemplifying *the* American cultural pattern, in part by expressing hostility to low-status immigrants—especially Irish Catholics.

To a considerable extent, of course, conflicts between New British and Irish Catholics simply represented the transplantation to the New World of conflicts long fought in the Old World. In 1844, for example, the *Freemen's Journal*, "read chiefly by the Irish or American of Irish parentage," described nativism as follows: "The truth is, there are too many reasons to believe that the present movement is but a British attempt to engraft insidiously on the hated stock of American Republicanism, the principles of the Irish Orangeman—[Protestant Irish]. . . . The most active, though not the most prominent of the *Native* Americans in New York, and probably in Philadelphia also, have been Irish Orangemen."

Similarly, early in 1845 the *New York Evening Post* emphasized that the "so-called American Party" had more ancient and deeprooted sources than the desire to "put civil disabilities on the population of foreign birth": "There is also connected with the present controversy, a religious persecution, far more to be deprecated than any attempt at political disfranchisement, and which proposes to re-enact among us the bloody contests that disgraced the sixteenth century, between the Catholics and Protestants, or at least to introduce into this country the Orange processions, so long the scourge of Ireland.—Why was it that so many foreigners enrolled themselves among the *professed* [italics added] nativists and were among the most clamorous of their party? It was not that they desired their own proscription, but that they were willing to jeopard [*sic*] their own political rights to gratify their religious hate."

We can go beyond the *Post* to suggest that, for the New British, hostility to Irish Catholics did more than gratify ancient religious and ethnic hates; it identified them with and earned them the approval of contemporaries who belonged to the dominant group and who claimed the right to define Americanism. Thus another Democratic paper, the *Brooklyn Eagle,* charged that when Whig "natives" decried "foreign influence in American politics," their real target was not foreigners in general, but those "born in Ireland." In fact, according to the *Eagle* any immigrants who voted Democratic were subjected to attack by men whose sympathy was with the few, not the many. "No exception" was taken to the English and the Scotch, for example, because they "make good Whigs."

The *American Republican,* the leading organ of the nativist, anti-Catholic movement, provides even more convincing evidence that the New British acted politically in order to differentiate themselves from Irish Catholics (and other low-status immigrants) and to identify themselves with the dominant group. Its editor reported that an "Englishman told us that he had concluded not to take out his naturalization papers as he did not want to have his name published in a list of newly naturalized Irishmen." Moreover, he observed, "It is well known that a large portion of the intelligent English naturalized citizens will vote the American Republican ticket, and we trust, that other enlightened and patriotic adopted citizens will do the same."

It is not important whether the *American Republican* and the *Post* exaggerated the number of New British who voted for the nativist-Whig coalition in 1844; what is important is this: if adopted citizens—could there be a more revealing term—voted Democratic, they ranged themselves with Irish Catholics and exposed themselves to charges that they were unenlightened, unpatriotic "foreigners"; if they voted Whig, they ranged themselves against Irish Catholics and, at worst, exposed themselves to Democratic charges that they supported "the aristocratic party" —charges not likely to diminish seriously their self-esteem or lessen their chances of winning acceptance by the dominant group and thereby accelerating their upward social mobility. In fact, identification with "aristocrats" might well have pleased immigrants striving to climb the American social ladder.

Having examined the political behavior of the New British, the Irish Catholics, and the Negroes, we can reasonably conclude that the stand of the major parties on socioeconomic issues had *relatively* little effect upon bloc voting in New York; we must attribute that phenomenon more to factors initially associated with positive and negative reference groups and subsequently with fulfillment of political roles. Party differences on certain political issues of deep interest to nonmembers of the dominant group did exist; but these differences, I suggest, stemmed from differences originating outside the political sphere. They were less a cause than a consequence of voting behavior. (For example, largely because Irish Catholics had long voted Democratic, in 1844 the major parties took different positions on naturalization laws.)

14

The Egalitarian Myth and the American Social Reality: Wealth, Mobility, and Equality in the "Era of the Common Man"

EDWARD PESSEN

Above all others, the age of Jackson has been regarded as an egalitarian age. It has been lauded as the common man's era—a time when fortunes were won and lost and wealth was distributed more equally. After examining tax data of Northeastern cities and ransacking all available sources for biographical information, Edward Pessen has assessed the social mobility and stratification of that age with striking results.

"In America," wrote Tocqueville, "most of the rich men were formerly poor." The idea that, in the words of Henry Clay, the wealthy and successful were "self-made men," came close to being an article of faith, so widely was it subscribed to by Americans during the era. The common man was constantly reminded that "the most exalted positions" or great wealth were accessible to men of humble origin, since in this country "merit and industry" rather than "exclusive privileges of birth" determined the course of

From *American Historical Review* 76 (1971):1004–6, 1012–27. Reprinted with omissions by permission of the author. © 1971 by Edward Pessen.

one's career. The merchant prince, William E. Dodge, offered the estimate that seventy-five per cent of the era's wealthy men "had risen from comparatively small beginnings to their present position." If few modern historians would commit themselves to a precise ratio, many have nevertheless agreed that a remarkable movement up the social and economic ladder characterized the second quarter of the nineteenth century. We have evidently convinced our colleagues in sociology, including some of the leading students of social mobility and stratification, that for the Jacksonian period the facts are in: intergenerational economic and occupational mobility were the rule. Actually it is not the facts that are in but rather a continuing series of firmly stated generalizations that essentially do nothing more than assume that the facts would bear them out.

That Tocqueville in some instances was ready to spin his marvelous social theorems by reference more to logic than to pedestrian data is well known. What is fascinating is the extent to which scholars, ordinarily skeptical of unverified observation, have relied on it in discussing the origins of the rich in the "age of the common man."

The social origins and parental status of wealthy citizens of Boston, Philadelphia, New York City, and Brooklyn have been investigated in order to test the belief that typically they were born poor. Information has been gathered on the several hundred wealthiest citizens in each of these great cities. The evidence indicates that some of the best known among the wealthy citizens did in fact have the kind of background ascribed to them by the egalitarian thesis.

John Jacob Astor's story is perhaps improperly described as a rise from rags to riches. There is some question as to precise wealth or status of his father. Whether the latter was a "very worthy" minor officeholder, as some described him, or a poor man devoted more to tippling than to industry, as he was depicted by others—for the moment I am prepared to regard the two judgments as contradictory—it seems fairly certain that the great merchant was indeed a self-made man of humble origin. The same can be said, with even more certainty, of his sometime partner, Cornelius Heeney, who migrated from Ireland apparently with less than a dollar in his pockets, to become one of the wealthiest residents in Brooklyn. Lewis A. Godey, publisher of the popular *Ladies' Book*, John Grigg, and Joseph Sill were wealthy Philadelphians of humble beginnings, while Daniel P. Parker, Ebenezer Chadwick, John R. Adan, and the three Henshaw brothers in Boston also appear to have been of poor or humble birth, as were such New York eminences as Anson G. Phelps, Marshall O. Roberts, Gideon Lee, Saul Alley, and possibly the Lorillard brothers. Stephen Girard's claim that he, too, had been a destitute youth was evidently accepted by most contemporaries, although there is some doubt as to whether it was well founded. Evidence is thus not lacking that some rich men had in fact been born poor. The most interesting feature of such evidence, however, is its uncommonness.

During the age of alleged social fluidity, the overwhelming majority of wealthy persons appears to have been descended of parents and families who combined affluence with high social status. The small number of these families that had been less than rich had typically been well to do. Only about two per cent of the Jacksonian era's urban economic elite appear to have actually been born poor, with no more than about six per cent of middling social and economic status. Included in the middle are the families of Peter Cooper, William E. Dodge, Gerard Hallock, Joseph Sampson, Cornelius Vanderbilt, Moses Yale Beach, Peter Chardon Brooks, Amos and Abbot Lawrence, Thomas H. Perkins, George C. Shattuck, George Hall, Thomas Everitt, Jr., Samuel R. Johnson, Cyrus P. Smith, and Samuel Smith, all of whom appeared to have been both better off and of higher status occupations than the mechanics, cartmen, milkmen, and laborers who predominated in the cities. The middle category was composed of ministers, petty officials, professionals other than successful lawyers and doctors, shopkeepers, skilled artisans who doubled as small tradesmen, and independent or moderately prosperous farmers. The evidence for these generalizations, inevitably imperfect, requires explanation.

It was of course impossible to obtain reliable information on the family status of all persons, but fortunately abundant evidence exists on the backgrounds of most of the wealthiest persons in the great cities. Data were secured on ninety per cent of the more than one hundred New Yorkers who in 1828 were assessed for $100,000 and upward, and in 1845 at $250,000 or more; on eighty-five per cent of the more than one hundred Bostonians worth $100,000 or better in 1833, and $200,000 or more in 1848; and on about ninety per cent of the seventy-five Brooklynites who in 1841 were evaluated at $60,000 or more. For Philadelphia . . . the nature of the tax records does not permit them to be used to disclose the assessed total wealth of individuals. One can differentiate the "super rich" of that city from other rich or well-to-do persons only by accepting at face value the sums attributed in the anonymous *Memoirs and Auto-Biography of Some of the Wealthy Citizens of Philadelphia.* (Information was obtained on seventy per cent of the 365 persons each claimed by the *Memoirs* to be worth $100,000 or more.) The pattern of the social backgrounds of the urban rich was strikingly similar for all the Northeastern cities. About ninety-five per cent of New York City's one hundred wealthiest persons were born into families of wealth or high status and occupation; three per cent came of "middling" background; only two per cent were born poor. As small a portion of Boston's one hundred wealthiest citizens started humble, with perhaps six per cent originating from middling families. Philadelphia's statistics differ from

Boston's only in that four per cent of the former city's 365 richest citizens were born into families of middling status; two per cent of her wealthiest citizens started poor. Cornelius Heeney and John Dikeman were the only wealthy Brooklynites of truly humble origins, with sixteen per cent born into middling status, and the remaining eighty-one per cent of wealthy or high-status families.

Evidence was not as freely available for the "lesser rich" of the great cities. Data were obtained on about seventy per cent of the more than 450 New Yorkers assessed at between $25,000 and $100,000 in 1828, and for sixty-three per cent of the 950 New Yorkers who in 1845 were worth between $45,000 and $250,000; on close to sixty-five per cent of the 260 Bostonians evaluated at between $50,000 and $200,000, in 1833, and on the same percentage of the four hundred Bostonians similarly assessed in 1848; and sixty-three per cent of the one hundred Brooklynites assessed in 1841 at $30,000 to $60,000. It is of course possible that the backgrounds of the "missing persons" were unlike those of the much larger number of persons for whom information was obtained. It could be argued that the omissions concern less eminent persons, whose families probably were not as wealthy or of as high status as the families whose careers and records are better publicized. Yet a significant feature of the evidence is its disclosure that there appeared to be no difference in the patterns of social origin among the "lesser wealthy" as against the "super rich"; or in the patterns of family background of the relatively little known or unknown rich for whom information was obtained as against the eminent rich.

Many of the era's richest men, while born into relative affluence, managed to carve out fortunes that far surpassed their original inheritances. Such persons were self-made only in a special sense, their careers hardly illustrating what publicists of the era meant by that term. That the children of high-status parents, living in an age of dynamic growth, convert their original advantages into fortunes of unprecedented scope is—as Jackson Turner Main has noted in another context—hardly a sign of social mobility. A family whose adult heads for four or five generations were among the economic elite of their city or community cannot be said to have experienced upward social movement because their always inordinate wealth kept increasing.

The rags-to-riches ideology had so penetrated American thought during the era that publishers whose own compilations contradicted the thesis could manage to convince themselves that it was nevertheless true. Freeman Hunt, devoted and enthusiastic admirer of America's merchants, whom he extolled in his charming *Merchants' Magazine*, could somehow describe Walter Restored Jones of the old, eminent, and wealthy family of Cold Spring, Long Island, truly one of fortune's favorites, as a "self-taught and self-made man." Popular ideology notwith-standing, the era of the common man was remarkable above all for how few rich men were in fact descended of common folk.

When it is compared with earlier periods in American history, the age of egalitarianism appears to have been an age of increasing social rigidity. According to a recent study of seventeenth-century Salem, while "some members of the rapidly emerging elite began their careers prop-ertyless and benefited from the opportunities for investment . . . more often they emigrated with considerable wealth which was further aug-mented by fortuitous investment." Jackson Main has concluded that there was "remarkable opportunity for the man of modest property to become rich" in the late eighteenth century. Main's admittedly imperfect and partial data on the three greatest cities of the Northeast are of special interest. He finds that about one-third of the sixty wealthiest Bostonians of 1771 had started with little or nothing; in 1789 only one-half of a small number of the city's wealthiest merchants had been born into "wealthy or well-to-do families," with the rest scattered among middling or lower status occupations. Of a group of one hundred wealthy Phila-delphians, about "one third had made their own fortunes." He found that "between one third and two fifths of the merchants in pre-Revo-lutionary New York City [actually, members of the Chamber of Com-merce] were self-made men," while in the years immediately after the Revolution the high "mobility rate" actually went up: "probably sixty per cent at the least [of a number of merchants in 1786] were self-made men," and in 1791 fifty per cent of the wealthiest citizens of the east ward had risen from humble origins.

A recent study of post-Revolutionary New York City concludes, that for the period ending in 1815 "the evidence of upward social mo-bility is marked. Almost two thirds of the attorneys and merchants in public office had risen above the occupational level of their fathers who were mechanics or farmers." The evidence on the earlier period, scattered and partial though it may be, suggests that a substantial upward eco-nomic mobility that had characterized Northeastern urban life came to a halt during the so-called age of the common man. The self-made man, recently shown by William Miller and his students to have been more fantasy than fact in the post–Civil War decades, was evidently a creature of the imagination a generation earlier, at the very time that the great Henry Clay was asserting the phantom's corporeality and ubiquitousness.

A related belief holds that the second quarter of the nineteenth century was "a highly speculative age in which fortunes were made and lost overnight, in which men rose and fell . . . with dexterous agility." Tocqueville believed that fortunes here were both scanty and "insecure," wealth ostensibly circulating with "inconceivable rapidity." Contemporary American merchants insisted that theirs was the most precarious of callings, incapable of attaining the "secuirty which accompanied the more pedestrian occupations." True, the eminent Philip Hone had noted the resiliency of businessmen: "Throw down our merchants ever so flat [and] they roll over once and spring to their feet again"; but this optimistic judgment was confided to his private diary. The prevailing view was that the pre-industrial decades were characterized by great intragenerational economic mobility. It has recently been shown, however, that antebellum Philadelphia witnessed slight movement up and down the occupational ladder or to and from residential districts of clearly differentiated wealth and status. Another recent study examines the changing economic circumstances of thousands of Bostonians and New York City residents of different wealth levels over the course of a generation. Some generalizations, drawn from its detailed findings, follow.

The richest Bostonians of the early Jacksonian era were invariably among the very richest Bostonians late in the period. Very few persons of the upper-middle wealth level—only seven per cent of that group—moved upward into the wealthy category whose members were each assessed for $50,000 or more. The extent of an individual's early wealth was the major factor determining whether he would be among the rich later. Absolute increases in wealth of any sort followed the rule: the greater an individual's initial wealth, the greater the amount by which it was augmented. A companion rule was that the greater one's original riches, the more likely was he to enjoy an increase. Since the population by mid-century had increased substantially in two decades the ranks of the later rich necessarily had to be filled by many persons who earlier were not among the wealthy. More often than not these newly rich taxpayers were younger members of old families, since fewer than ten per cent of the later group of Boston's rich were new men. Not one member of the $100,000 group of mid-century who had paid taxes earlier had paid them on less than the $20,000 owned by the wealthiest two per cent of the population. Since many contemporaries claimed that the careers of successful merchants followed an erratic course in this kaleidoscopic economy, changes over short-run periods were also investigated to determine whether persons who started and ended the race strong may have lagged in between. They did not. In Boston "few new great families sprang up while fewer still fell away" during the era.

New York City's statistics for the period were not an exact replica of the Boston evidence. Since New York was richer all categories of wealth from the upper middle on up experienced greater gains in absolute wealth than did their counterparts in Boston. For the rest the general pattern was remarkably similar for the two great cities. Between the period of Andrew Jackson's first election to the presidency and his death not quite two decades later only one of New York City's fifty richest persons fell from the class of the rich, and even he barely failed to qualify. As in Boston the few New Yorkers who rose from the upper-middle wealth level to the rich during the course of the era "were more often than not from families of great wealth." The "newcomers" were younger members of the great Hendricks, Jones, Lenox, Lorillard, Barclay, Cruger, Grinnell, Bronson, Grosvenor, Hone, Lawrence, Post, Murray, Storm, Ward, Remsen, Schieffelin, and Van Rensselaer families or of "others of like distinction." About seventy-five per cent of the New York City families constituting the plutocracy of the so-called industrial era of the mid-1850s were families that comprised the elite of the merchant-capitalist era of a generation earlier.

Brooklyn assessment data exist for 1810 and 1841. If the earlier date falls before what even the most flexible classifications would consider the "Jacksonian era," that fact hardly detracts from its value. If anything the earlier starting point permits those so inclined to draw conclusions about economic fluidity between the "Jeffersonian" and "Jacksonian" periods. Brooklyn's wealthiest families of the early nineteenth century remained among the wealthiest families of the 1840s. Only one of the truly rich of 1810 fell by the wayside and not because of poverty but because of death. In Brooklyn, as in its mighty neighbor, riches achieved by early in the nineteenth century appeared to be the surest guarantee to the possession of wealth a generation later. The many wealthy persons of 1841 who were relative newcomers to the city had achieved their success almost without exception "as a result of a great boost given them at birth by wealthy or comfortably situated parents or relatives."

The pursuit of wealth in Jacksonian America was marked not by fluidity but by stability if not rigidity. Great fortunes earlier accumulated held their own through all manner of vicissitudes. The tax records indicate that the panic of 1837 appeared to have no effect on the minuscule rate by which the mighty fell or the puny rose during the years surrounding that economic convulsion. The Boston tax records disclose that of the owners of the modest property evaluated at between $5,000 and $7,000 prior to the panic of 1837, less than one per cent became significantly wealthier in its wake, while silghtly more than one-third were badly hurt by the cataclysm or compelled to leave the city. In contrast, only two of the nearly one hundred Bostonians worth $100,000 or more each suffered substantial losses, while about twenty-three per cent of them enjoyed gains of $20,000 or better in the immediate aftermath of the financial crisis.

That the rich typically were well born and held on to or increased their wealth does not prove that there was no social mobility during the era. The vast and swelling sociological literature on the related topics of "vertical mobility" and social stratification makes clear that the concept of social mobility is a most complex one, not least because it involves the intangible of status. As has recenlty been pointed out, "there are a host of different ways of measuring mobility. And mobility has many varied contours." No last word can ever be said concerning a subject so elusive and for which the data are so often imperfect.

If, as Ralf Dahrendorf has written, "the concept of social mobility is too general to be useful," there is much to be said for dealing with specific aspects of it rather than with the concept as a whole. All of which is to say that if no data can measure the immeasurable—social mobility in general—the evidence pointing to the upper-class backgrounds of the Jacksonian era's elite and the tenacity with which they held on to their wealth undermines two of the main supports of the long-popular belief in antebellum mobility.

The final question to be considered in this discussion concerns the distribution of wealth in the age of equality. Did the rich command an inordinate share and did it increase or dwindle during the period?

A keystone of the egalitarian intellectual structure is the belief that, in Tocqueville's words, a "general equality of condition" prevailed here. A perfect equality was of course out of the question. Pariah ethnic groups and hordes of unwashed new immigrants obviously were not in on the feast. But that the cornucopia was almost equally available to most others, like other elements in the egalitarian canon, remains a living belief. Even a modern scholar who dissents from the consensus, finding that in New York State "heavy immigration and industrialization" after 1830 widened the gulf between the classes, concedes that earlier "there did not appear to be any contradiction between the notion of equality of opportunity and a general equality of condition." By this version, the prefactory age, or what economic historians have called the age of merchant capitalism, was indeed an age of equality. The comprehensive evidence I have gathered on what almost every urbanite was worth early and late in the era makes possible an empirical test of this thesis. The fact that other scholars have performed similar quantitative studies of the distribution of wealth for earlier periods and that useful evidence exists for the Civil War years and later permits us to compare the degree of equality in the "age of egalitarianism" with that of other periods in American history.

During the colonial era wealth had become more unequally distributed with the passing years. This at least is the burden of the modern studies of scattered towns and villages. In Chester County, Pennsylvania, the richest ten per cent of the population owned slightly less than one-quarter of the wealth in 1693. Over the course of the next century their share increased to slightly under two-fifths, from 23.8 per cent to 38.3 per cent of the total, at the same time as the proportion owned by the poorest three-fifths of the population declined from 38.5 per cent to 17.6 per cent. Wealth was distributed less equally in commercial or seaport towns, and the tempo of increasing maldistribution was swifter in such communities. Where the wealthiest five per cent of property owners in Salem owned about one-fifth of its wealth during the quarter century before 1660, by 1681 their portion had risen to about one-half of the prospering Massachusetts town's total. In colonial Boston the wealthiest one per cent of the population owned about one-tenth, the richest five per cent about one-quarter, and the upper fifteen per cent about one-half of the city's real and personal estate in 1687. By 1771 the wealthiest three per cent of Boston's population held slightly over one-third of the city's wealth, while the upper ten per cent owned about fifty-five per cent of the property of a Boston community that had become "more stratified and unequal." Precisely the same share was owned by Philadelphia's upper tenth of "potential wealthholders" in 1774. On the eve of the Revolution, the richest ten per cent of Northerners owned about forty-five per cent of the wealth, a figure slightly greater than the amount of net worth controlled by the richest tenth of the middle colonies for 1774. A less detailed comparison of New York City between 1789 and 1815 notes that the wealthiest thirty per cent of the city's fourth ward increased slightly their share, from seventy-one to seventy-six per cent of the community's wealth during that quarter of a century.

Was the inegalitarian trend reversed in the nineteenth century? During the "age of equality" wealth in Boston became more unequally distributed than ever before. On the eve of the Revolution Boston's richest tenth had held slightly more than one-half of the city's wealth. Very little change evidently occurred over the course of the next half century, according to a local census report, whose table of Boston's tax payments for 1820 indicated that the upper one per cent controlled about one-sixth of the city's wealth, while the richest tenth continued to own the slightly more than one-half they had held in 1771. Significant changes occurred over the following decade, since by 1833 the pattern of distribution had been sharply altered. The inegalitarian trend accelerated during the next fifteen years. (See tables 1 and 2.)

Actually the richest Bostonians owned a larger share of their city's wealth than tables 1 and 2 indicate. In Boston as elsewhere a small number of rich men appeared to own most of the capital of their city's great financial institutions. A careful check reveals that Boston's wealthiest merchants and businessmen were the officers and directors, and therefore the major shareholders, of the city's fifty largest banks and insurance companies. The disparity between the actual proportion of Boston's entire wealth owned by the elite and the share indicated in the tables 1 and 2 (based on the assessments) is not as great, it will be

TABLE 1   Distribution of Wealth in Boston in 1833

Level of Wealth	Percentage of Population	Approximate Total Wealth Owned [a]	Percentage Non-corporate Wealth
$75,000 or more	1%	$19,439,000	33%
$30,000 to $75,000	3%	$15,000,000	26%
$ 5,000 to $30,000	10%	$16,047,400	27%
Under $5,000	86%	$ 8,331,000	14%

[a] In 1833 Boston wealth was listed at one-half its assessed value. In this table, therefore, the sums are doubled.

TABLE 2   Distribution of Wealth in Boston in 1848

Level of Wealth	Percentage of Population	Approximate Total Wealth Owned	Percentage Non-corporate Wealth
$90,000 or more	1%	$47,778,500	37%
$35,000 to $90,000	3%	$34,781,800	27%
$ 4,000 to $35,000	15%	$40,636,400	32%
Under $4,000	81%	$ 6,000,000	4%

shown, as were the disparities for New York City and Brooklyn. Boston banks and insurance companies were assessed only on their real estate, a relatively small component of the city's wealth. Private individuals who owned corporate wealth were evidently assessed for their holdings; in sharp contrast to New York City and Brooklyn, therefore, taxpayers in Boston were assessed for personal property almost equal in value to their real estate. The fact, however, that in Boston as elsewhere the undervaluation of all property favored the rich above all, since they had the most to hide, is the chief assurance that actual wealth was more unequally distributed than was assessed wealth.

A contemporary yeasayer wrote that in Jacksonian New York City, "wealth [was] universally diffused." Even the normally optimistic Philip Hone disagreed, noting disconsolately that his beloved New York City late in the era had "arrived at the [unhappy] state of society to be found in the large cities of Europe," in which "the two extremes of costly luxury in living, expensive establishments and improvident waste are presented in daily and hourly contrast with squalid misery and hopeless desitution." The evidence bears out Hone's gloomy assessment.

In the year of Andrew Jackson's election to the presidency the wealthiest four per cent of the population of New York City, in owning almost half the wealth, controlled a larger proportion of the city's wealth than the richest ten per cent had evidently owned in the urban Northeast as a whole a half century earlier. By 1845 the disparities had sharply increased.

To judge from the New York City evidence, the rate by which the rich got proportionately richer became much more rapid during the nineteenth century than it had been during the seventeenth or eighteenth. As for the city's inequality in 1828 and 1845, its full extent is not disclosed in the assessment figures for these years.

A committee of the Common Council had reported that it was persons of "very extensive capital" who paid taxes on personal porperty "far less in proportion than those in moderate and low circumstances." In view of the way in which the underassessments of all wealth masked the true wealth of the rich above all, it is clear that the proportion of the city's wealth owned by a small upper crust was greater than the figures indicate. If, as contemporary municipal officials believed, the richest of the rich owned most of the hidden personal wealth, the proportion of the city's total wealth they controlled goes up by a figure dependent on the percentage of the undiscolsed wealth that is attributed to them. On the basis that the personal property of the rich equaled the worth of their real estate, and that the wealthiest four per cent owned about nine-tenths of New York City's unassessed personal property, the upper one per cent would have owned about thirty-five per cent and the next wealthiest three per cent about twenty-two per cent of all noncorporate wealth in 1828. In 1845, by this reckoning, the richest one per cent would have owned about forty-seven per cent, while the next

TABLE 3   Distribution of Wealth in New York City in 1828

Level of Wealth	Percentage of Population	Approximate Non-corporate Wealth Owned	Percentage Non-corporate Wealth
$35,000 or more	1%	$25,517,000	29%
$ 7,500 to $35,000	3%	$17,520,000	20%

TABLE 4   Distribution of Wealth in New York City in 1845

Level of Wealth	Percentage of Population	Approximate Non-corporate Wealth Owned	Percentage Non-corporate Wealth
$55,000 or more	1%	$85,804,000	40%
$20,000 to $55,000	3%	$55,000,000	26%

wealthiest three per cent would have held an additional thirty-two per cent of the city's noncorporate wealth. Nor do these estimates take into account the likelihood that the actual worth of the real propery owned by the largest wealth holders was also undervalued. Perhaps the latter distortion can be compensated for or canceled out by an adjustment that attempts to take into account the ownership of corporate wealth.

In 1828 corporations, mainly banks and insurance companies, were assessed for $23,984,660 or twenty-one per cent of the city's total estate of $112,019,533 (exclusive of partnerships). It is probably impossible to track down the owners of all corporate wealth; records, inadequate to begin with, have been lost. Yet for all the imprecision attending the attribution of corporate capital, certain conclusions can be drawn that affect significantly the distribution of wealth.

Poor men and for that matter the great bulk of the city's population owned either nothing or merely minuscule portions of such capital. The minimum cost of a share, typically fifty dollars to one hundred dollars, priced out such people. As Cadwallader C. Colden and Peter A. Jay pointed out in behalf of the Bank for Savings in 1823, "a depositor is not a stockholder." The directors of the corporations regularly listed in the annual New York City directories were overwhelmingly the merchant elite, many of the same individuals forming a kind of interlocking directorate over the great city's banks and insurance companies. These directors were required to own stock in their corporations. According to an insider, himself an officer in several New York City banks during the era, directors usually "own[ed] in the aggregate a considerable portion of the stock" in their companies. They had been chosen in the first place "for their wealth, commercial experience and influence in attracting to the institution a good class of dealers." Precise information available for a number of contemporary banks and insurance companies discloses that a small number of directors owned almost all the capital in their corporations. When allowance is made for the inordinate share of corporate wealth owned by the elite it is likely that in New York City the richest one per cent actually owned as much as forty-one per cent and the next wealthiest three per cent owned twenty-two per cent of all wealth in 1828. By 1845 the wealthiest one per cent would have owned one-half of all wealth, while the upper four per cent owned eighty-one per cent of the city's total wealth.

The evidence for Brooklyn is unusually interesting because it permits a comparison of the degree of equality that obtained in the village of 1810, populated by fewer than 5,000 persons, with the bustling city of 1841, whose population of about 41,000 placed Brooklyn seventh among the nation's cities. The richest wealth holders of the early nineteenth-century village held a slightly larger portion of Brooklyn's wealth than had typically been controlled by the upper tenth in the urban Northeast late in the "Revolutionary era." Although the poorer half of the population owned only a tiny fraction of Brooklyn's wealth in 1810, the fact that seven out of eight families paid taxes on some property, even if slight, suggests that few residents of the community could be classified as propertyless proletarians. By 1841 important changes had occurred.

The distribution of wealth in the commercial Brooklyn of 1841 was strikingly similar to the division that obtained in its great neighbor across the East River. By 1841 the poorest two-thirds of Brooklyn's population

TABLE 5   Distribution of Wealth in Brooklyn in 1810

Level of Wealth	Percentage of Population	Approximate Non-corporate Wealth Owned	Percentage Non-corporate Wealth
$15,000 or more	1%	$262,400	22%
$ 4,000 to $15,000	7%	$383,122	33%
$ 2,500 to $ 4,000	6%	$137,944	11%
$ 1,000 to $ 2,500	20%	$290,000	25%
$ 500 to $ 1,000	12%	$ 67,500	6%
Under $500	54%	$ 30,000	3%

owned less than one per cent of its wealth, with only about one out of five families (exclusive of nonresident taxpayers) taxed on any property at all. Corporate wealth had come to be a factor of some significance, accounting for seven per cent of the total. As in New York City, this type of wealth was evidently monopolized by the elite. Data on the holdings and ownership of the Fulton Ferry, the Brooklyn White Lead Company, the Long Island Bank, and the Brooklyn Fire Insurance Company—firms assessed for about seventy-five per cent of the city's corporate wealth—indicate that the percentage of assessed wealth owned by the richest one per cent was closer to forty-five than forty-two per cent. In addition, Brooklyn's wealthiest taxpayers for the most part admitted to no personal wealth whatever. If the personal wealth of the richest one per cent is treated as though it equaled in value their real property, and when the underassessment of the latter form of property is accounted for by working into our estimate an adjustment that presumes ownership of three-quarters of corporate capital by Brooklyn's elite (outsiders owned close to one-quarter), Brooklyn's richest one per cent emerge with one-half of their city's wealth.

The trend toward increasingly unequal distribution of wealth in the antebellum era was not confined to the great cities of the Northeast. While

TABLE 6   Distribution of Wealth in Brooklyn in 1841

Level of Wealth	Percentage of Population	Approximate Non-corporate Wealth Owned	Percentage Non-corporate Wealth
$50,000 or more	1%	$10,087,000	42%
$15,000 to $50,000	2%	$ 4,000,000	17%
$ 4,500 to $15,000	9%	$ 5,730,000	24%
$ 1,000 to $ 4,500	15%	$ 2,804,000	12%
$ 100 to $ 1,000	7%	$ 1,000,000	4%
Under $100	66%	—	—

the pattern of distribution in rural communities and small towns was not as skewed as it was in large urban centers, inequality in the former milieus was dramatic and worsening. In Hamilton, Ontario, "a small commercial lakeport almost entirely lacking in factory industry, with a population just over 14,000" shortly after mid-century, the poorest four-fifths of the population owned less than four per cent of the town's property, in contrast to the richest tenth, who owned almost ninety per cent. As small Massachusetts communities, such as Worcester, became increasingly urbanized, the rich became relatively richer, the numbers of propertyless citizens increased drastically, and "patterns of ownership" became "sharply skewed."

Recent research indicates that on the eve of the Civil War the pattern of maldistribution in Philadelphia and in a number of Southern and Western cities was quite similar to the inequality that prevailed in New York City, Brooklyn, and Boston in the 1840s. By 1860 the wealthiest one per cent of Philadelphia's population evidently owned one-half, while the lower eighty per cent held only three per cent of the city's wealth. In Baltimore, New Orleans, and St. Louis the richest one per cent of the population owned about two-fifths, the richest five per cent better than two-thirds, and the upper ten per cent more than four-fifths of the wealth. An impressionistic recent account of Galveston at mid-century finds that the affluent social and economic elite were one hundred times wealthier than their fellow citizens, the wealth of the former group contrasting "strikingly with that of their nearest neighbors." The division of property was not as unequal in rural counties, Southern or Western, although even in such areas the distribution has been found to have been skewed to a surprising extent. In cotton counties the wealthiest five per cent of landholders held more than two-fifths of the wealth, while the upper ten per cent owned almost three-fifths. (According to Gavin Wright, a close student of rural wealth distribution, the actual degree of inequality was greater than the census data indicate.) While wealth was more equally distributed on the northeastern frontier, even there the upper tenth by 1860 held close to two-fifths of taxable wealth. In the words of two modern students, property holding on the Michigan frontier became "more concentrated" with the passage of time, while the distribution of wealth "scarcely supports the typical American image of the frontier as the land of promise for the poor, ambitious young man."

During the age of egalitarianism wealth became more unequally distributed with each passing season. Shared less equally, even at the era's beginnings, than it had been a generation or two earlier, in the aftermath of the Revolution, wealth became concentrated in the hands of an ever smaller percentage of the population. The trend persisted through the 1850s, resulting in wider disparities than ever by the time of the Civil War. Far from being an age of equality, the antebellum decades were featured by an inequality that surpasses anything experienced by the United States in the twentieth century.

15

Beauty, the Beast and the Militant Woman: A Case Study in Sex Roles and Social Stress in Jacksonian America

CARROLL SMITH-ROSENBERG

The universally accepted occasion for the beginning of the women's rights movement is the 1848 Seneca Falls, New York, convention. Carroll Smith-Rosenberg discusses a considerably earlier and, in some respects, more fundamental movement for women's rights. By recording the anger and frustration, the anxiety and discontent felt by many women playing roles not of their own choosing, she suggests why thousands of women joined reform movements in the Jacksonian era.

On a spring evening in May 1834, a small group of women met at the revivalistic Third Presbyterian Church in New York City to found the New York Female Moral Reform Society. The Society's goals were ambitious indeed; it hoped to convert New York's prostitutes to evangelical Protestantism and close forever the city's numerous brothels. This bold attack on prostitution was only one part of the Society's program. These

From *American Quarterly* 23 (1971):562–84. Reprinted with omissions by permission of the author and *American Quarterly*. © 1971, Trustees of the University of Pennsylvania.

self-assertive women hoped as well to confront that larger and more
fundamental abuse, the double standard, and the male sexual license
it condoned. Too many men, the Society defiantly asserted in its statement of goals, were aggressive destroyers of female innocence and happiness. No man was above suspicion. Women's only safety lay in a militant
effort to reform American sexual mores—and, as we shall see, to reform
sexual mores meant in practice to control man's sexual values and autonomy. The rhetoric of the Society's spokesmen consistently betrayed an unmistakable and deeply felt resentment toward a male-dominated society.

Few if any members of the Society were reformed prostitutes or
the victims of rape or seduction. Most came from middle-class native
American backgrounds and lived quietly respectable lives as pious wives
and mothers. What needs explaining is the emotional logic which under-
lay the Society's militant and controversial program of sexual reform.
I would like to suggest that both its reform program and the anti-male
sentiments it served to express reflect a neglected area of stress in mid-
19th century America—that is, the nature of the role to be assumed by
the middle-class American woman.

American society from the 1830s to the 1860s was marked by advances in political democracy, by a rapid increase in economic, social
and geographic mobility, and by uncompromising and morally relent-
less reform movements. Though many aspects of Jacksonianism have
been subjected to historical investigation, the possibly stressful effects of
such structural change upon family and sex roles have not. The following pages constitute an attempt to glean some understanding of women
and women's role in antebellum America through an analysis of a self-
consciously female voluntary association dedicated to the eradication of
sexual immorality.

Women in Jacksonian America had few rights and little power.
Their role in society was passive and sharply limited. Women were,
in general, denied formal education above the minimum required by
a literate early industrial society. The female brain and nervous system,
male physicians and educators agreed, were inadequate to sustained intellectual effort. They were denied the vote in a society which placed a
high value upon political participation; political activity might corrupt
their pure feminine nature. All professional roles (with the exception of
primary school education) were closed to women. Even so traditional
a female role as midwife was undermined as male physicians began to
establish professional control over obstetrics. Most economic alternatives
to marriage (except such burdensome and menial tasks as those of seam-
stress or domestic) were closed to women. Their property rights were
still restricted and females were generally considered to be the legal

wards either of the state or of their nearest male relative. In the event of divorce, the mother lost custody of her children—even when the husband was conceded to be the erring party. Women's universe was bounded by their homes and the career of father or husband; within the home it was woman's duty to be submissive and patient.

Yet this was a period when change was considered a self-evident good, and when nothing was believed impossible to .a determined free will, be it the conquest of a continent, the reform of society or the eternal salvation of all mankind. The contrast between these generally accepted ideals and expectations and the real possibilities available to American women could not have been more sharply drawn. It is not implausible to assume that at least a minority of American women would find ways to manifest a discontent with their comparatively passive and constricted social role.

Only a few women in antebellum America were able, however, to openly criticize their socially defined sexual identity. A handful, like Fanny Wright, devoted themselves to overtly subversive criticism of the social order. A scarcely more numerous group became pioneers in women's education. Others such as Elizabeth Cady Stanton, Lucretia Mott and Susan B. Anthony founded the women's rights movement. But most respectable women—even those with a sense of ill-defined grievance—were unable to explicitly defy traditional sex-role prescriptions.

I would like to suggest that many such women channeled frustration, anger and a compensatory sense of superior righteousness into the reform movements of the first half of the 19th century; and in the controversial moral reform crusade such motivations seem particularly apparent. While unassailable within the absolute categories of a pervasive evangelical world-view, the Female Moral Reform Society's crusade against illicit sexuality permitted an expression of anti-male sentiments. And the Society's "final solution"—the right to control the mores of men —provided a logical emotional redress for those feelings of passivity which we have suggested. It should not be surprising that between 1830 and 1860 a significant number of militant women joined a crusade to establish their right to define—and limit—man's sexual behavior.

Yet adultery and prostitution were unaccustomed objects of reform even in the enthusiastic and millennial America of the 1830s. The mere discussion of these taboo subjects shocked most Americans; to undertake such a crusade implied no ordinary degree of commitment. The founders of the Female Moral Reform Society, however, were able to find both legitimization for the expression of grievance normally unspoken and an impulse to activism in the moral categories of evangelical piety. Both pious activism and sex-role anxieties shaped the early years of the Female Moral Reform Society. This conjunction of motives was hardly accidental.

The lady founders of the Moral Reform Society and their new organization represented an extreme wing of that movement within American Protestantism known as the Second Great Awakening. These women were intensely pious Christians, convinced that an era of millennial perfection awaited human effort. In this fervent generation, such deeply felt millennial possibilities made social action a moral imperative. Like many of the abolitionists, Jacksonian crusaders against sexual transgression were dedicated activists, compelled to attack sin wherever it existed and in whatever form it assumed—even the unmentionable sin of illicit sexuality.

New Yorkers' first awareness of the moral reform crusade came in the spring of 1832 when the New York Magdalen Society (an organization which sought to reform prostitutes) issued its first annual report. Written by John McDowall, their missionary and agent, the report stated unhesitatingly that 10,000 prostitutes lived and worked in New York City. Not only sailors and other transients, but men from the city's most respected families, were regular brothel patrons. Lewdness and impurity tainted all sectors of New York society. True Christians, the report concluded, must wage a thoroughgoing crusade against violators of the Seventh Commandment.

The report shocked and irritated respectable New Yorkers—not only by its tone of righteous indignation and implied criticism of the city's old and established families. The report, it seemed clear to many New Yorkers, was obscene, its author a mere seeker after notoriety. Hostility quickly spread from McDowall to the Society itself; its members were verbally abused and threatened with ostracism. The society disbanded.

A few of the women, however, would not retreat. Working quietly, they began to found church-affiliated female moral reform societies. Within a year, they had created a number of such groups, connected for the most part with the city's more evangelical congregations. These pious women hoped to reform prostitutes, but more immediately to warn other God-fearing Christians of the pervasiveness of sexual sin and the need to oppose it. Prostitution was after all only one of many offenses against the Seventh Commandment; adultery, lewd thoughts and language, and bawdy literature were equally sinful in the eyes of God. These women at the same time continued unofficially to support their former missionary, John McDowall, using his newly established moral reform newspaper to advance their cause not only in the city, but throughout New York State.

After more than a year of such discreet crusading, the women active in the moral reform cause felt sufficiently numerous and confident to organize a second city-wide moral reform society, and renew their efforts to reform the city's prostitutes. On the evening of May 12, 1834, they met at the Third Presbyterian Church to found the New York Female Moral Reform Society.

Nearly four years of opposition and controversy had hardened the women's ardor into a militant determination. They proposed through their organization to extirpate sexual license and the double standard from American society. A forthright list of resolves announced their organization:

> Resolved, That immediate and vigorous efforts should be made to create a public sentiment in respect to this sin; and also in respect to the duty of parents, church members and ministers on the subject, which shall be in stricter accordance with . . . the word of God.
>
> .   .   .   .
>
> Resolved, That the licentious man is no less guilty than his victim, and ought, therefore, to be excluded from all virtuous female society.
>
> Resolved, That it is the imperious duty of ladies everywhere, and of every religious denomination, to co-operate in the great work of moral reform.

A sense of urgency and spiritual absolutism marked this organizational meeting, and indeed all of the Society's official statements for years to come. "It is the duty of the virtuous to use every consistent moral means to save our country from utter destruction," the women warned. "The sin of licentiousness has made fearful havoc . . . drowning souls in perdition and exposing us to the vengeance of a holy God." Americans hopeful of witnessing the promised millennium could delay no longer.

The motivating zeal which allowed the rejection of age-old proprieties and defied the criticism of pulpit and press was no casual and fashionable enthusiasm. Only an extraordinary set of legitimating values could have justified such commitment. And this was indeed the case. The women moral reformers acted in the conscious conviction that God imperiously commanded their work. As they explained soon after organizing their society: "As Christians we must view it in the light of God's word—we must enter into His feelings on the subject—engage in its overthrow just in the manner He would have us. . . . We must look away from all worldly opinions or influences, for they are perverted and wrong; and individually act only as in the presence of God." Though the Society's pious activism had deep roots in the evangelicalism of the Second Great Awakening, the immediate impetus for the founding of the Moral Reform Society came from the revivals Charles G. Finney conducted in New York City between the summer of 1829 and the spring of 1834.

Charles Finney, reformer, revivalist and perfectionist theologian from western New York State, remains a pivotal figure in the history of American Protestantism. The four years Finney spent in New York had a profound influence on the city's churches and reform movements, and upon the consciences generally of the thousands of New Yorkers who crowded his revival meetings and flocked to his churches. Finney insisted that his disciples end any compromise with sin or human injustice. Souls were lost and sin prevailed, Finney urged, because men chose to sin—because they chose not to work in God's vineyard converting souls and reforming sinners. Inspired by Finney's sermons, thousands of New Yorkers turned to missionary work; they distributed Bibles and tracts to the irreligious, established Sunday schools and sent ministers to the frontier. A smaller, more zealous number espoused abolition as well, determined, like Garrison, never to be silent and to be heard. An even smaller number of the most zealous and determined turned—as we have seen—to moral reform.

The program adopted by the Female Moral Reform Society in the spring of 1834 embraced two quite different, though to the Society's founders quite consistent, modes of attack. One was absolutist and millennial, an attempt to convert all of America to perfect moral purity. Concretely the New York women hoped to create a militant nationwide women's organization to fight the double standard and indeed any form of licentiousness—beginning of course in their own homes and neighborhoods. Only an organization of women, they contended, could be trusted with so sensitive and yet monumental a task. At the same time, the Society sponsored a parallel and somewhat more pragmatic attempt to convert and reform New York City's prostitutes. Though strikingly dissimilar in method and geographic scope, both efforts were unified by an uncompromising millennial zeal and by a strident hostility to the licentious and predatory male.

The Society began its renewed drive against prostitution in the fall of 1834 when the executive committee appointed John McDowall their missionary to New York's prostitutes and hired two young men to assist him. The Society's three missionaries visited the female wards of the almshouse, the city hospital and jails, leading prayer meetings, distributing Bibles and tracts. A greater proportion of their time, however, was spent in a more controversial manner, systematically visiting—or, to be more accurate, descending upon—brothels, praying with and exhorting both the inmates and their patrons. The missionaries were especially fond of arriving early Sunday morning—catching women and customers as they awoke on the traditionally sacred day. The missionaries would announce their arrival by a vigorous reading of Bible passages, followed by prayer and hymns. At other times they would station themselves across the street from known brothels to observe and note the identity of customers. They soon found their simple presence had an important deterring effect, many men, with doggedly innocent expressions, pausing momentarily and then hastily walking past. Closed coaches, they also reported, were observed to circle suspiciously for upwards of an hour until, the missionary remaining, they drove away.

The Female Moral Reform Society did not depend completely on paid missionaries for the success of such pious harrassment. The Society's executive committee, accompanied by like-thinking male volunteers, regularly visited the city's hapless brothels. (The executive committee minutes for January 1835, for example, contain a lengthy discussion of the properly discreet makeup of groups for such "active visiting.") The members went primarily to pray and to exert moral influence. They were not unaware, however, of the financially disruptive effect that frequent visits of large groups of praying Christians would have. The executive committee also aided the concerned parents (usually rural) of runaway daughters who, they feared, might have drifted to the city and been forced into prostitution. Members visited brothels asking for information about such girls; one pious volunteer even pretended to be delivering laundry in order to gain admittance to a brothel suspected of hiding such a runaway.

In conjunction with their visiting, the Moral Reform Society opened a House of Reception, a would-be refuge for prostitutes seeking to reform. The Society's managers and missionaries felt that if the prostitute could be convinced of her sin, and then offered both a place of retreat and an economic alternative to prostitution, reform would surely follow. Thus they envisioned their home as a "house of industry" where the errant ones would be taught new trades and prepared for useful jobs— while being instructed in morality and religion. When the managers felt their repentant charges prepared to return to society, they attempted to find them jobs with Christian families—and, so far as possible, away from the city's temptations.

Despite their efforts, however, few prostitutes reformed; fewer still appeared, to their benefactresses, to have experienced the saving grace of conversion. Indeed, the number of inmates at the Society's House of Reception was always small. In March 1835, for instance, the executive committee reported only fourteen women at the House. A year later, total admissions had reached but thirty—only four of whom were considered saved. The final debacle came that summer when the regular manager of the House left the city because of poor health. In his absence, the executive committee reported unhappily, the inmates seized control, and discipline and morality deteriorated precipitously. The managers reassembled in the fall to find their home in chaos. Bitterly discouraged, they dismissed the few remaining unruly inmates and closed the building.

The moral rehabilitation of New York's streetwalkers was but one aspect of the Society's attack upon immorality. The founders of the Female Moral Reform Society saw as their principal objective the creation of a woman's crusade to combat sexual license generally and the double standard particularly. American women would no longer willingly tolerate that traditional—and role-defining—masculine ethos which allotted respect to the hearty drinker and the sexual athlete. This age-old code of masculinity was as obviously related to man's social preeminence as it was contrary to society's explicitly avowed norms of purity and domesticity. The subterranean mores of the American male must be confronted, exposed and rooted out.

The principal weapon of the Society in this crusade was its weekly, *The Advocate of Moral Reform*. In the fall of 1834, when the Society hired John McDowall as its agent, it voted as well to purchase his journal and transform it into a national women's paper with an exclusively female staff. Within three years, the *Advocate* grew into one of the nation's most widely read evangelical papers, boasting 16,500 subscribers. By the late 1830s the Society's managers pointed to this publication as their most important activity.

Two themes dominated virtually every issue of the *Advocate* from its founding in January 1835, until the early 1850s. The first was an angry and emphatic insistence upon the lascivious and predatory nature of the American male. Men were the initiators in virtually every case of adultery or fornication—and the source, therefore, of that widespread immorality which endangered America's spiritual life and delayed the promised millennium. A second major theme in the *Advocate's* editorials and letters was a call for the creation of a national union of women. Through their collective action such a united group of women might ultimately control the behavior of adult males and of the members' own children, particularly their sons.

The founders and supporters of the Female Moral Reform Society entertained several primary assumptions concerning the nature of human sexuality. Perhaps most central was the conviction that women felt little sexual desire; they were in almost every instance induced to violate the Seventh Commandment by lascivious men who craftily manipulated not their sensuality, but rather the female's trusting and affectionate nature. A woman acted out of romantic love, not carnal desire; she was innocent and defenseless, gentle and passive. "The worst crime alleged against [the fallen woman] in the outset," the *Advocate's* editors explained, "is . . . 'She is without discretion.' She is open-hearted, sincere, and affectionate. . . . She trusts the vows of the faithless. She commits her all into the hands of the deceiver."

The male lecher, on the other hand, was a creature controlled by base sexual drives which he neither could nor would control. He was, the *Advocate's* editors bitterly complained, powerful and decisive; unwilling (possibly unable) to curb his own willfulness, he callously used it to coerce the more passive and submissive female. This was an age of rhetorical expansiveness, and the *Advocate's* editors and correspondents felt little constraint in their delineation of the dominant and aggressive male. "Reckless," "bold," "mad," "drenched in sin" were terms used commonly to describe erring males; they "robbed," "ruined" and "rioted." But one term above all others seemed most fit to describe the lecher— "The Destroyer."

A deep sense of anger and frustration characterized the *Advocate's* discussion of such all-conquering males, a theme reiterated again and again in the letters sent to the paper by rural sympathizers. Women saw themselves with few defenses againt the determined male; his will was far stronger than that of woman. Such letters often expressed a bitterness which seems directed not only against the specific seducer, but toward all American men. One representative rural subscriber complained, for example: "Honorable men; they would not plunder; . . . an imputation on their honour might cost a man his life's blood. And yet they are so passingly mean, so utterly contemptible, as basely and treacherously to contrive . . . the destruction of happiness, peace, morality, and all that is endearing in social life; they plunge into degradation, misery, and ruin, those whom they profess to love. O let them not be trusted. Their 'tender mercies are cruel.' "

The double standard seemed thus particularly unjust; it came to symbolize and embody for the Society and its rural sympathizers the callous indifference—indeed at times almost sadistic pleasure—a male-dominated society took in the misfortune of a passive and defenseless woman. The respectable harshly denied her their friendship; even parents might reject her. Often only the brothel offered food and shelter. But what of her seducer? Conventional wisdom found it easy to condone his greater sin: men will be men and right-thinking women must not inquire into such questionable matters.

But it was just such matters, the Society contended, to which women must address themselves. They must enforce God's commandments despite hostility and censure. "Public opinion must be operated upon," the executive committee decided in the winter of 1835, "by endeavoring to bring the virtuous to treat the guilty of both sexes alike, and exercise toward them the same feeling." "Why should a female be trodden under foot," the executive committee's minutes questioned plaintively, "and spurned from society and driven from a parent's roof, if she but fall into sin—while common consent allows the male to habituate himself to this vice, and treats him as not guilty. Has God made a distinction in regard to the two sexes in this respect? The guilty woman too should be condemned, the Moral Reform Society's quarterly meeting resolved in 1838: "But let not the most guilty of the two—the deliberate destroyer of female innocence—be afforded even an 'apron of fig leaves' to conceal the blackness of his crimes."

Women must unite in a holy crusade against such sinners. The Society called upon pious women throughout the country to shun all social contact with men suspected of improper behavior—even if that behavior consisted only of reading improper books or singing indelicate songs. Church-going women of every village and town must organize local campaigns to outlaw such men from society and hold them up to public judgment. "Admit him not to your house," the executive committee urged, "hold no converse with him, warn others of him, permit not your friends to have fellowship with him, mark him as an evildoer, stamp him as a villain and exclaim, 'Behold the Seducer.'" The power of ostracism could become an effective weapon in the defense of morality.

A key tactic in this campaign of public exposure was the Society's willingness to publish the names of men suspected of sexual immorality. The *Advocate's* editors announced in their first issue that they intended to pursue this policy, first begun by John McDowall in his *Journal.* "We think it proper," they stated defiantly, "even to expose names, for the same reason that the names of thieves and robbers are published, that the public may know them and govern themselves accordingly. We mean to let the licentious know, that if they are not ashamed of their debasing vice, we will not be ashamed to expose them. . . . It is a justice which we owe each other." Their readers responded enthusiastically to this invitation. Letters from rural subscribers poured into the *Advocate,* recounting specific instances of seduction in their towns and warning readers to avoid the men described. The editors dutifully set them in type and printed them.

Within New York City itself the executive committee of the Society actively investigated charges of seduction and immorality. A particular target of their watchfulness was the city's employment agencies—or information offices as they were then called; these were frequently fronts for the white-slave trade. The *Advocate* printed the names and addresses of suspicious agencies, warning women seeking employment to avoid them at all costs. Prostitutes whom the Society's missionaries visited in brothels, in prison or in the city hospital were urged to report the names of men who had first seduced them and also of their later customers; they could then be published in the *Advocate*. The executive committee undertook as well a lobbying campaign in Albany to secure the passage of a statute making seduction a crime for the male participant. While awaiting the passage of this measure, the executive committee encouraged and aided victims of seduction (or where appropriate their parents or employers) to sue their seducers on the grounds of loss of services.

Ostracism, exposure and statutory enactment offered immediate, if unfortunately partial, solutions to the problem of male licentiousness. But for the seduced and ruined victim such vengeance came too late. The tactic of preference, women moral reformers agreed, was to educate children, especially young male children, to a literal adherence to the Seventh Commandment. This was a mother's task. American mothers, the *Advocate's* editors repeated endlessly, must educate their sons to reject the double standard. No child was too young, no efforts too diligent in this crucial aspect of socialization. The true foundations of such a successful effort lay in an early and highly pietistic religious education and in the inculcation of a related imperative—the son's absolute and unquestioned obedience to his mother's will. "Obedience, entire and unquestioned, must be secured, or all is lost." The mother must devote herself whole-heartedly to this task for self-will in a child was an ever-recurring evil. "Let us watch over them continually. . . . Let us . . . teach them when they go out and when they come in—when they lie down, and when they rise up. . . ." A son must learn to confide in his mother instinctively; no thought should be hidden from her.

Explicit education in the Seventh Commandment itself should begin quite early for bitter experience had shown that no child was too young for such sensual temptation. As her son grew older, his mother was urged to instill in him a love for the quiet of domesticity, a repugnance for the unnatural excitements of the theater and tavern. He should be taught to prefer home and the companionship of pious women to the temptations of bachelor life. The final step in a young man's moral education would come one evening shortly before he was to leave home for the first time. That night, the *Advocate* advised its readers, the mother must spend a long earnest time at his bedside (ordinarily in the dark to hide her natural blushes) discussing the importance of maintaining his sexual purity and the temptations he would inevitably face in attempting to remain true to his mother's religious principles.

Mothers, not fathers, were urged to supervise the sexual education of sons. Mothers, the Society argued, spent most time with their children; fathers were usually occupied with business concerns and found little time for their children. Sons were naturally close to their mothers and devoted maternal supervision would cement these natural ties. A mother devoted to the moral reform cause could be trusted to teach her son to reject the traditional ethos of masculinity and accept the higher—more feminine—code of Christianity. A son thus educated would be inevitably a recruit in the women's crusade against sexual license.

The Society's general program of exposure and ostracism, lobbying and education depended for effectiveness upon the creation of a national association of militant and pious women. In the fall of 1834, but a few months after they had organized their Society, its New York officers began to create such a woman's organization. At first they worked through the *Advocate* and the small network of sympathizers John Mc-Dowall's efforts had created. By the spring of 1835, however, they were able to hire a minister to travel through western New York State "in behalf of Moral Reform causes." The following year the committee sent two female missionaries, the editor of the Society's newspaper and a paid female agent, on a thousand-mile tour of the New England states. Visiting women's groups and churches in Brattleboro, Deerfield, Northampton, Pittsfield, the Stockbridges and many other towns, the ladies rallied their sisters to the moral reform cause and helped organize some forty-one new auxiliaries. Each succeeding summer saw similar trips by paid agents and managers of the Society throughout New York State and New England. By 1839, the New York Female Moral Reform Society boasted some 445 female auxiliaries, principally in greater New England. So successful were these efforts that within a few years the bulk of the Society's membership and financial support came from its auxiliaries. In February 1838, the executive committee voted to invite representatives of these auxiliaries to attend the Society's annual meeting. The following year the New York Society voted at its annual convention to reorganize as a national society —the American Female Moral Reform Society; the New York group would be simply one of its many constituent societies.

This rural support was an indispensable part of the moral reform movement. The local auxiliaries held regular meetings in churches, persuaded hesitant ministers to preach on the Seventh Commandment, urged Sunday school teachers to confront this embarrassing but vital question. They raised money for the executive committee's ambitious projects, convinced at least some men to form male moral reform societies, and did their utmost to ostracize suspected lechers. When the American Female Moral Reform Society decided to mount a campaign to induce the New York State legislature to pass a law making seduction a criminal offense, the Society's hundreds of rural auxiliaries wrote regularly to their legislators, circulated petitions and joined their New York City sisters in Albany to lobby for the bill (which was finally passed in 1848).

In addition to such financial and practical aid, members of the moral reform society's rural branches contributed another crucial, if less tangible, element to the reform movement. This was their commitment to the creation of a feeling of sisterhood among all morally dedicated women. Letters from individuals to the *Advocate* and reports from auxiliaries make clear, sometimes even in the most explicit terms, that many American women experienced a depressing sense of isolation. In part, this feeling merely reflected a physical reality for women living in rural communities. But since city- and town-dwelling women voiced similar complaints, I would like to suggest that this consciousness of isolation also reflected a sense of status inferiority. Confined by their non-maleness, antebellum American women lived within the concentric structure of a family organized around the needs and status of husbands or fathers. And such social isolation within the family—or perhaps more accurately a lack of autonomy both embodied in and symbolized by such isolation—not only dramatized, but partially constituted, a differentiation in status. The fact that social values and attitudes were established by men and oriented to male experiences only exacerbated women's feelings of inferiority and irrelevance. Again and again the Society's members were to express their desire for a feminine-sororial community which might help break down this isolation, lighten the monotony and harshness of life, and establish a counter-system of female values and priorities.

The New York Female Moral Reform Society quite consciously sought to inspire in its members a sense of solidarity in a cause peculiar to their sex, and demanding total commitment, to give them a sense of worthiness and autonomy outside woman's traditionally confining role. Its members, their officers forcefully declared, formed a united phalanx twenty thousand strong, "A UNION OF SENTIMENT AND EFFORT AMONG . . . VIRTUOUS FEMALES FROM MAINE TO ALABAMA." The officers of the New York Society were particularly conscious of the emotional importance of female solidarity within their movement—and the significant role that they as leaders played in the lives of their rural supporters. "Thousands are looking to us," the executive committee recorded in their minutes with mingled pride and responsibility, "with the expectation that the principles we have adopted, and the example we have set before the world will continue to be held up & they reasonably expect to witness our *united onward* movements till the conflict shall end in Victory."

For many of the Society's scattered members, the moral reform cause was their only contact with the world outside farm or village— the *Advocate* perhaps the only newspaper received by the family. A sense of solidarity and of emotional affiliation permeated the correspondence between rural members and the executive committee. Letters and even official reports inevitably began with the salutation, "Sisters,"

"Dear Sisters" or "Beloved Sisters." Almost every letter and report expressed the deep affection Society members felt for their like-thinking sisters in the cause of moral reform—even if their contact came only through letters and the *Advocate*. "I now pray and will not cease to pray," a woman in Syracuse, New York, wrote, "that your hearts may be encouraged and your hands strengthened." Letters to the Society's executive committee often promised unfailing loyalty and friendship; members and leaders pledged themselves ever ready to aid either local societies or an individual sister in need. Many letters from geographically isolated women reported that the Society made it possible for them for the first time to communicate with like-minded women. A few, in agitated terms, wrote about painful experiences with the double standard which only their correspondence with the *Advocate* allowed them to express and share.

Most significantly, the letters expressed a new consciousness of power. The moral reform society was based on the assertion of female moral superiority and the right and ability of women to reshape male behavior. No longer did women have to remain passive and isolated within the structuring presence of husband or father. The moral reform movement was, perhaps for the first time, a movement within which women could forge a sense of their own identity.

And its founders had no intention of relinquishing their new-found feeling of solidarity and autonomy. A few years after the Society was founded, for example, a group of male evangelicals established a Seventh Commandment Society. They promptly wrote to the Female Moral Reform Society suggesting helpfully that since men had organized, the ladies could now disband; moral reform was clearly an area of questionable propriety. The New York executive committee responded quickly, firmly—and negatively. Women throughout America, they wrote, had placed their trust in a female moral reform society and in female officers. Women, they informed the men, believed in both their own right and ability to combat the problem; it was decidedly a woman's, not a man's issue. "The paper is now in the right hands," one rural subscriber wrote: "This is the appropriate work for *women*. . . . Go on Ladies, go on, in the strength of the Lord."

In some ways, indeed, the New York Female Moral Reform Society could be considered a militant woman's organization. Although it was not overtly part of the woman's rights movement, it did concern itself with a number of feminist issues, especially those relating to woman's economic role. Society, the *Advocate's* editors argued, had unjustly confined women to domestic tasks. There were many jobs in society that women could and should be trained to fill. They could perform any light indoor work as well as men. In such positions—as clerks and artisans—

they would receive decent wages and consequent self-respect. And this economic emphasis was no arbitrary or inappropriate one, the Society contended. Thousands of women simply had to work; widows, orphaned young women, wives and mothers whose husbands could not work because of illness or intemperance had to support themselves and their children. Unfortunately, they had now to exercise these responsibilities on the pathetically inadequate salaries they received as domestics, washerwomen or seamstresses—crowded, underpaid and physically unpleasant occupations. By the end of the 1840s, the Society had adopted the cause of the working woman and made it one of their principal concerns—in the 1850s even urging women to join unions and, when mechanization came to the garment industry, helping underpaid seamstresses rent sewing machines at low rates.

The Society sought consciously, moreover, to demonstrate woman's ability to perform successfully in fields traditionally reserved for men. Quite early in their history they adopted the policy of hiring only women employees. From the first, of course, only women had been officers and managers of the Society. And after a few years, these officers began to hire women in preference to men as agents and to urge other charitable societies and government agencies to do likewise. (They did this although the only salaried charitable positions held by women in this period tended to be those of teachers in girls' schools or supervisors of women's wings in hospitals and homes for juvenile delinquents.) In February 1835, for instance, the executive committee hired a woman agent to solicit subscriptions to the *Advocate*. That summer they hired another woman to travel through New England and New York State organizing auxiliaries and giving speeches to women on moral reform. In October of 1836, the executive officers appointed two women as editors of their journal—undoubtedly among the first of their sex in this country to hold such positions. In 1841, the executive committee decided to replace their male financial agent with a woman bookkeeper. By 1843 women even set type and did the folding for the Society's journal. All these jobs, the ladies proudly, indeed aggressively stressed, were appropriate tasks for women.

The broad feminist implications of such statements and actions must have been apparent to the officers of the New York Society. And indeed the Society's executive committee maintained discreet but active ties with the broader woman's rights movement of the 1830s, 40's and 50s; at one point at least, they flirted with official endorsement of a bold woman's rights position. Evidence of this flirtation can be seen in the minutes of the executive committee and occasionally came to light in articles and editorials appearing in the *Advocate*. As early as the mid-1830s, for instance, the executive committee began to correspond with a number of women who were then or were later to become active in the woman's rights movement. Lucretia Mott, abolitionist and pioneer feminist, was a founder and secretary of the Philadelphia Female Moral Reform Society; as such she was in frequent communication with the New York executive committee. Emma Willard, a militant advocate of women's education and founder of the Troy Female Seminary, was another of the executive committee's regular correspondents. Significantly, when Elizabeth Blackwell, the first woman doctor in either the United States or Great Britain, received her medical degree, Emma Willard wrote to the New York executive committee asking its members to use their influence to find her a job. The Society did more than that. The *Advocate* featured a story dramatizing Dr. Blackwell's struggles. The door was now open for other women, the editors urged; medicine was a peculiarly appropriate profession for sensitive and sympathetic womankind. The Society offered to help interested women in securing admission to medical school.

One of the most controversial aspects of the early woman's rights movement was its criticism of the subservient role of women within the American family, and of the American man's imperious and domineering behavior toward women. Much of the Society's rhetorical onslaught upon the male's lack of sexual accountability served as a screen for a more general—and less socially acceptable—resentment of masculine social preeminence. Occasionally, however, the *Advocate* expressed such resentment overtly. An editorial in 1838, for example, revealed a deeply felt antagonism toward the power asserted by husbands over their wives and children. "A portion of the inhabitants of this favored land," the Society admonished, "are groaning under a despotism, which seems to be modeled precisely after that of the Autocrat of Russia. . . . We allude to the tyranny exercised in the HOME department, where lordly man, 'clothed with a little brief authority,' rules his trembling subjects with a rod of iron, conscious of entire impunity, and exalting in his fancied superiority." The Society's editorialist continued, perhaps even more bitterly: "Instead of regarding his wife as a help-mate for him, an equal sharer in his joys and sorrows, he looks upon her as a useful article of furniture, which is valuable only for the benefit derived from it, but which may be thrown aside at pleasure." Such behavior, the editorial carefully emphasized, was not only commonplace, experienced by many of the Society's own members—even the wives of "Christians" and of ministers—but was accepted and even justified by society; was it not sanctioned by the Bible?

At about the same time, indeed, the editors of the *Advocate* went so far as to print an attack upon "masculine" translations and interpretations of the Bible, and especially of Paul's epistles. This appeared in a lengthy article written by Sarah Grimké, a "notorious" feminist and abolitionist. The executive committee clearly sought to associate their organization more closely with the nascent woman's rights movement. Calling upon American women to read and interpret the Bible for themselves, Sarah Grimké asserted that God had created woman the absolute equal of man. But throughout history, man, being stronger, had usurped woman's natural rights. He had subjected wives and daughters to his physical control and had evolved religious and scientific rationalizations to justify this domination. "Men have endeavored to entice, or to drive women from almost every sphere of moral action." Miss Grimké charged: "'Go home and spin' is the . . . advice of the domestic tyrant. . . . The first duty, I believe, which devolves on our sex now is to think for themselves. . . . Until we take our stand side by side with our brother; until we read all the precepts of the Bible as addressed to woman as well as to man, and lose . . . the consciousness of sex, we shall never fulfil the end of our existence." "Those who do undertake to labor," Miss Grimké wrote from her own and her sister's bitter experiences, "are the scorn and ridicule of their own and the other sex." "We are so little accustomed *to think for ourselves,*" she continued,

> that we submit to the dictum of prejudice, and of usurped authority, almost without an effort to redeem ourselves from the unhallowed shackles which have so long bound us; almost without a desire to rise from that degradation and bondage to which we have been consigned by man, and by which the faculties of our minds, and the powers of our spiritual nature, have been prevented from expanding to their full growth, and are sometimes wholly crushed.

Each woman must re-evaluate her role in society; no longer could she depend on husband or father to assume her responsibilities as a free individual. No longer, Sarah Grimké argued, could she be satisfied with simply caring for her family or setting a handsome table. The officers of the Society, in an editorial comment following this article, admitted that she had written a radical critique of woman's traditional role. But they urged their members, "It is of immense importance to our sex to possess clear and *correct* ideas of our rights and duties."

Sarah Grimké's overt criticism of woman's traditional role, containing as it did an attack upon the Protestant ministry and orthodox interpretations of the Bible, went far beyond the consensus of the *Advocate's* rural subscribers. The following issue contained several letters sharply critical of her and of the managers, for printing her editorial. And indeed the *Advocate* never again published the work of an overt feminist. Their membership, the officers concluded, would not tolerate explicit attacks upon traditional family structure and orthodox Christianity. Anti-male resentment and anger had to be expressed covertly. It was perhaps too threatening or—realistically—too dangerous for respectable matrons in relatively close-knit semi-rural communities in New York, New England, Ohio or Wisconsin so openly to question the traditional relations of the sexes and demand a new and ominously forceful role for women.

The compromise the membership and the officers of the Society seemed to find most comfortable was one that kept the American woman within the home—but which greatly expanded her powers as pious wife and mother. In rejecting Sarah Grimké's feminist manifesto, the Society's members implicitly agreed to accept the role traditionally assigned woman: the self-sacrificing, supportive, determinedly chaste wife and mother who limited her "sphere" to domesticity and religion. But in these areas her power should be paramount. The mother, not the father, should have final control of the home and family—especially of the religious and moral education of her children. If the world of economics and public affairs was his, the home must be hers.

And even outside the home, woman's peculiar moral endowment and responsibilities justified her in playing an increasingly expansive role, one which might well ultimately impair aspects of man's traditional autonomy. When man transgressed God's commandments, through licentiousness, religious apathy, the defense of slavery, or the sin of intemperance—woman had both the right and duty of leaving the confines of the home and working to purify the male world.

The membership of the New York Female Moral Reform Society chose not to openly espouse the woman's rights movement. Yet many interesting emotional parallels remain to link the moral reform crusade and the suffrage movement of Elizabeth Cady Stanton, the Grimké sisters and Susan B. Anthony. In its own way, indeed, the war for purification of sexual mores was far more fundamental in its implications for woman's traditional role than the demand for woman's education—or even the vote.

Many of the needs and attitudes, moreover, expressed by suffragette leaders at the Seneca Falls Convention and in their efforts in the generation following are found decades earlier in the letters of rural women in the *Advocate of Moral Reform*. Both groups found woman's traditionally passive role intolerable. Both wished to assert female worth and values in a heretofore entirely male world. Both welcomed the creation of a sense of feminine loyalty and sisterhood that could give emotional strength and comfort to women isolated within their homes —whether in a remote farmstead or a Gramercy Park mansion. And it can hardly be assumed that the demand for votes for women was appreciably more radical than a moral absolutism which encouraged women to invade bordellos, befriend harlots and publicly discuss rape, seduction and prostitution.

It is important as well to re-emphasize a more general historical perspective. When the pious women founders of the Moral Reform Society gathered at the Third Free Presbyterian Church, it was fourteen years before the Seneca Falls Convention—which has traditionally been accepted as the beginning of the woman's rights movement in the United States. There simply was no woman's movement in the 1830s. The future leaders were either still adolescents or just becoming dissatisfied with aspects of their role. Women advocates of moral reform were among the very first American women to challenge their completely passive, home-oriented image. They were among the first to travel throughout the country without male chaperones. They published, financed, even set type for their own paper and defied a bitter and long-standing male opposition to their cause. They began, in short, to create a broader, less constricted sense of female identity. Naturally enough, they were dependent upon the activist impulse and legitimating imperatives of evangelical religion. This was indeed a complex symbiosis, the energies of pietism and the grievances of role discontent creating the new and activist female consciousness which characterized the history of the American Female Moral Reform Society in antebellum America. Their experience, moreover, was probably shared, though less overtly, by the thousands of women who devoted time and money to the great number of reform causes which multiplied in Jacksonian America. Women in the abolition and the temperance movements (and to a less extent in more narrowly evangelical and religious causes) also developed a sense of their ability to judge for themselves and of their right to publicly criticize the values of the larger society. The lives and self-image of all these women had changed—if only so little—because of their new reforming interests.

The Economy 1815–1860

DOUGLASS C. NORTH

Historians associate the enormous growth of the American economy—particularly of
industry—with the post-Civil War decades. Douglass C. North, a leading econometrician
(one who applies statistical and mathematical models to economic history), has compiled massive data pointing to a much earlier critical period in American economic
development. The spread of the market economy was the "strategic influence" on
economic growth, and its first surge (based on export trade) occurred during the
prosperous years 1793 to 1808. Subsequent early nineteenth-century surges are discussed
in this reading.

1815 ushered in more than an era of peace for the United States; it
marked a transitional period in the American economy. Some features of
the new era were not apparent until 1819 and the depression that followed three years after the end of the war, but even in 1815 it was clear
that the Atlantic economy and its components were very different from
the western world of 1790. Only war-induced distortion in the economies
of the countries of the Atlantic community delayed some of the consequences.

The re-export and carrying trades, main sources of expansion in the
economy during the boom years prior to the Embargo, never again
played so important a role. The re-export trade revived partially after

From Douglass C. North, *The Economic Growth of the United States, 1790–1860*,
pp. 61–74. © 1961 by Prentice-Hall, Inc., Englewood Cliffs, New Jersey. Reprinted
with omissions by permission of the publisher.

the war and into the 1820's, but declined absolutely thereafter until almost 1850, and was unimportant in our foreign trade relative to domestic exports. The carrying trade remained significant in our international economic accounts, but the radical decline in freight rates after 1818, revival of navigation laws, and vigorous competition of other ocean carriers prevented earnings from equalling the years of the neutral trade. While it remained an important credit in our balance of payments, it was no longer an expansive force in the economy.

The rapid development of manufacturing after 1807, which partially substituted for re-exports and shipping, likewise suffered a serious setback. English manufactured goods, denied the lucrative American market during the war, made up for lost time in the years 1815–1818. Industrialization had proceeded apace in Britain even during the war years, and English supremacy in manufacturing was immediately felt by higher cost competitiors throughout the world after 1815. A combination of technological leadership, the ability of English manufacturers to dump upon the American market during the years 1815–1818, and the auction system of distribution proved disastrous to a good deal of American manufacturing. The textile industry in particular found that it could not compete in quality goods.

As a result of these circumstances, the decade 1810–1820 was the only one in our history in which urbanization did not increase. Indeed, there was a slight decline: from 7.3 per cent of the population to 7.2 per cent. The major seaports of New York, Philadelphia and Boston barely held their own in population growth. Secondary ports such as Salem and Providence, which had grown rapidly as shipbuilding and re-export centers, showed little increase. Only Baltimore among the seaports and inland Cincinnati exhibited rapid growth. In the South, New Orleans alone grew rapidly, particularly after the beginning of upriver steamboat traffic in 1816. Charleston grew scarcely at all, despite the cotton boom after the war.

While neither the re-export nor the carrying trade were ever again as important relatively, or absolutely, for the economy, the cotton trade in 1815 showed every sign of vigorous if not wildly speculative prosperity. Cotton prices began to rise in 1812; by 1815 they were in excess of twenty cents a pound in New York. The growing demand of the English cotton textile industry was not matched by an equal expansion in supply, and the downward trend in cotton prices which had commenced in 1801 was reversed. Prices reached a peak of twenty-nine cents a pound in 1816 and remained high until 1818. The boom in land sales and cotton expansion was under way well before the end of the war. By 1815 the South was committed to cotton, and an era had began which was to continue until the Civil War.

Whatever the problems of readjustment to a world at peace, the American economy in 1815 exhibited a marked contrast to the conditions of 1790. . . . The population was approximately 8,400,000, more than twice the figure for 1790. Since immigration had been negligible, this reflected a high rate of domestic increase. A striking feature was the regional differentiation which characterized the Northeast, the South, and the West. Climate, topography, and resources, together with the level of technology (particularly in transport), had conspired to produce three sharply different areas. Border states like Maryland, Delaware, and Kentucky did not fit as neatly into the separate regional patterns, but they were minor exceptions to the increasingly distinct patterns of economic life that developed.

Almost one-half of the total population resided in the Northeast, and it was in this region—the New England and Middle Atlantic States —that urbanization and the resulting commercial market were most highly developed. Both New York and Philadelphia had populations in excess of 100,000. Boston and Baltimore were in excess of 35,000; Salem, Albany and Providence were all in excess of 10,000. The heritage of rapid growth in international commerce and shipping prior to 1807 was evidenced by the Northeast's preeminence in the development of a capital market, marketing and transport facilities, insurance companies, and other social overhead facilities connected with shipping and external trade. With the decline of the re-export trade, merchants in the Northeast had become closely tied to cotton. New York in particular became both the center of the import trade and the financial center for the cotton trade.

Slightly more than one-third of the people in the United States lived in the South. Virginia, once the most populous state in the Union, increased only slightly. South Carolina, Georgia, Alabama, and Louisiana all showed rapid population growth, although they did not show a corresponding increase in urbanization. Cotton plantations extended up navigable waterways, and as the land closest to water transport was taken up, plantations developed farther from these transport arteries. The extensive waterways of the South permitted a vast expansion of improved acreage not far removed from the only cheap method of shipping cotton. The towns that did develop were collection points for cotton and for the reshipment of imports to the upriver plantations. New Orleans, an important entrepôt since the days of French and Spanish possession, was the one city in the South exhibiting all the signs of commercial expansion which characterized Northeastern ports. As the shipping port for the vast hinterland of the Mississippi, Ohio, and Missouri river systems, its expansion had just begun with the application of steam to water transport and its successful initiation on the Mississippi in 1816.

By 1815, population growth west of the mountains had become substantial. In 1810 the census listed 1,337,946 people living in the Mississippi Valley; by 1820 there were 2,419,369. As of 1815, however, the West still had little influence upon the American economy. The bulk of the populace was still either outside the market or peripheral to it. . . . Approximately two million people were scattered over a vast area effectively separated from eastern markets by the intervening mountains. The one-way trade down the Mississippi, the driving of livestock over the mountains, or wagon shipment of high value goods which could take the overland freight rates were supplements to a self-sufficient way of life geared to local exchange in the small trading centers which sprang up throughout the area. The most characteristic feature of the emerging pattern of urbanization was the small town providing a wide variety of local trade and manufactures. Ties with the national economy were still tenuous, and such a pattern supported few large urban areas. Cincinnati was the outstanding center, and Pittsburgh also developed rapidly. As Callender has pointed out, nothing better illustrates the frontier, self-sufficient character of the area than the fact that a population of two million people supported almost no urbanization. In 1815 the integration of the West into the American economy awaited the development of cheap means of transportation and markets.

Between the end of the second war with England and the firing on Fort Sumter were nearly fifty years of peace, interrupted only briefly by the Mexican War on this continent and the Crimean War abroad. Neither was a major disturbing force, although the latter had repercussions upon economic stability in the 1850's. It was an era of tremendous expansion for the Atlantic economy as a whole and for the United States in particular.

The contrast between the sources of expansion in periods just before and after the War of 1812 is striking. In the former period the Western World was at war, and the rapid development of the American economy for fourteen years reflected our ability to take advantage of this war. The exigencies of war relaxed the mercantilist restrictions of European powers, and war created the demand for shipping and re-exports and the very favorable terms of trade that produced unequalled American prosperity up to 1808.

The period following 1815 was not only one of peace, but one in which artificial national barriers to the free movement of goods, services, productive factors, and ideas were being relaxed. An international economy was emerging in which the parts were interrelated by the forces of comparative prices of goods, services, and productive factors. An analysis of the United States economic development must necessarily be put into the context of the expansion of the Atlantic economy. Institutions and national policies which both impeded and fostered the international exchange of goods, services, productive factors and ideas must be continually brought into view. It was the "anonymous," impersonal forces of the evolving international economy which were the basic influence on the developing Atlantic economy and its constituent parts. National policies and institutional influences modified rather than generated the economic growth that ensued. The very forces of the Atlantic economy which were inducing expansion in the United States were thereby making this country increasingly independent of the international economic context, so that during these years there was a fundamental shift away from dependence upon the Atlantic economy toward dependence on our own internal economy as the mainspring of expansion.

In 1815 the international context was still critical. The expanding industrialization of England and Europe in the years after the Napoleonic wars was accompanied not only by the gradual relaxation of restrictions on trade and factor mobility, but the resultant structural changes accelerated the movement of productive factors in response to differential rates of return. While the immigration of people and particularly capital into the United States played an important part in our growth in the thirty years after 1815, it was the growth of the cotton textile industry and the demand for cotton which was decisive. In 1815 the previous sources of expansion, the re-export and carrying trade and manufactures, were declining as a result of peacetime competition. The West was still largely unintegrated into the national economy. The United States was left with only cotton as the major expansive force. The vicissitudes of the cotton trade—the speculative expansion of 1818, the radical decline in prices in the 1820's and the boom in the 1830's—were the most important influence upon the varying rates of growth of the economy during the period. Cotton was strategic because it was the major independent variable in the interdependent structure of internal and international trade. The demands for western foodstuffs and northeastern services and manufactures were basically dependent upon the income received from the cotton trade. This dependence resulted not only from the developing regional specialization, but from the characteristics of the South itself.

A marked characteristic of the South was that income received from the export of cotton (and sugar, rice and tobacco) flowed directly out of the regional economy again in the purchase of goods and services. The South provided neither the services to market its own exports nor the consumer goods and services to supply its own needs, and had a very high propensity to import. It was the West which provided food for the South and, since the South was the West's major market until the problems of cross-mountain transport had been solved, the growth of the market for western foodstuffs was geared to the expansion of the southern cotton economy.

The Northeast provided not only the services to finance, transport, insure, and market the South's cotton, but also supplied the South with manufactured goods, either from its own industry or imported and re-shipped to the South. Major markets for the Northeast were the South and the West. Both depended, directly in the first case and indirectly in the second, on the income from the cotton trade.

It was cotton which was the most important influence in the growth in the market size and the consequent expansion of the economy: the slow development of the 1820's, the accelerated growth in the 1830's. In this period of rapid growth, it was cotton that initiated the concomitant expansion in income, in the size of domestic markets, and creation of the social overhead investment (in the course of its role in the marketing of cotton) in the Northeast which were to facilitate the subsequent rapid growth of manufactures. Cotton also accounted for the accelerated pace of westward migration as well as for the movement of people out of self-sufficiency into the market economy.

Cotton was not the only expansive influence in the economy during this period. Clearly there were others, and they will be considered. Had there been no cotton gin, it is certain that the resources directly and indirectly devoted to the cotton trade would have been at least partially absorbed in other types of economic activity. Given the social structure, attitudes and motivation of American society, and the rich quantity and quality of resources which made even the self-sufficient farmer well off as compared with his European counterpart, the United States economy would not have stagnated. But cotton was the commodity for which foreign demand was significantly increasing, it accounted for over half the value of exports, and the income directly or indirectly from cotton was the major independent influence on the evolving pattern of inter-regional trade. Without cotton the development in the size of the market would have been a much more lengthy process, since there was no alternative way to expand the domestic market rapidly without recourse to external demand. In short, cotton was the most important proximate cause of expansion, and by tracing out the resulting interrelationships light may be shed on the pace and character of the economy's development, particularly in the years up to 1843.

The argument advanced . . . with respect to the strategic role of certain industries is pertinent here. A great deal of economic activity is a passive rather than an active source of economic expansion. It grows up either dependent upon an "active" industry or in response to the growth of income initially generated by the carriers of economic change.

In the examination of economic change it is important to distinguish between an independent variable initiating the change and the expansion of dependent economic activity which is induced by the "carrier" industry. This distinction is undoubtedly more difficult to make today than it was before 1860, when transport barriers and distinct patterns of regional specialization and internal trade all pointed to the strategic role of cotton. Direct income from the cotton trade was probably no more than 6 per cent of any plausible estimate of national income which we might employ, but when income from cotton exports, including shipments to textile mills in our own Northeast, grew from $25 million in 1831 to $70 million in 1836, it set in motion the whole process of accelerated expansion which culminated in 1839. Certainly the views of contemporaries, northern observers as well as southerners, support the position that in this period cotton was indeed king.

The cotton trade remained an important influence upon the economy until 1860, but its role declined in relative importance after the boom and depression that followed 1839. It is not that income from cotton did not grow. On the contrary, the 1850's represented another prosperous era, though not as wildly speculative as former ones, in which the value of the cotton trade exceeded any former period. However, a major consequence of the expansive period of the 1830's was the creation of conditions that made possible industrialization in the Northeast. Transport facilities developed to connect the East and West more efficiently; a new market for western staples developed in the rapidly urbanizing East and, sporadically, in Europe. The dependence of both the Northeast and the West on the South waned.* The discovery of gold in California in 1848 created a third source of expansion outside the South. The Far West was not only a major market for the goods and services of the Northeast, but its one export, gold, played a vital role in the whole expansion of the 1850's.

It should not be forgotton that the United States expansion was taking place within the larger context of the Atlantic economy. While the demand for cotton in England and to a lesser extent in France played perhaps the most prominent part, the terms of trade, relative price levels here and abroad, the movement of productive factors, and the flow of ideas, particularly technological information, were all a part of the interrelated pattern of development.

Throughout the whole period the secular movement of the terms of

---

* The most striking evidence of the changing role of cotton is provided by its role in cyclical turning points. While cotton set the pace in the booms and depressions of 1815–1823 and 1823–1843, it lagged a full two years behind the recovery that began in 1843 and was clearly not a major influence in the cyclical downturn of 1857. In fact, the South was relatively unaffected by that depression.

trade became increasingly favorable. In the expansive surges of 1815–1818 and 1832–1839 they became very favorable, reflecting a rapid rise in the price of American exports. In these two periods, it was cotton that accounted for the rise and appeared to initiate the subsequent flow of capital in response to the increased profitability of opening up and developing new sources of supply of the export staple and western foodstuffs. The consequent divergence of domestic and foreign price levels, and the increase in imports and specie movements, determined the timing of cyclical movements. Attractive employment opportunities during these surges of expansion were the pull which brought immigrants to American shores in increasing numbers.

Expansion in the 1850's, unlike that of the two previous booms, was not preceded by favorable movements of the terms of trade—instead it was the domestic price level which began to rise before the export price index. Cotton played a part in the boom, but it was industrialization in the Northeast and the opening up of the West and Far West which were primarily responsible for the growth of the 1840's and 1850's. The influence of the international economy was felt less in the flow of capital than in the flow of people, with the first big wave of immigration coming in this period.

The foregoing summary has emphasized surges in growth followed by periods of depression, then gradual expansion preceding still another boom. The explanation of these long swings is that these movements are initiated by the movement of prices in the key "carrier" industries. Shifts in supply and demand result in a shift of resources into these areas in periods of rising prices. There is concomitant expansion in the wide variety of subsidiary, complementary, and residentiary activities whose fortunes are tied to the growth of the "carrier" industries and to the rise in income that is initiated by these surges of expansion. The process is a lengthy and cumulative one, ultimately overlayed with speculative excesses; the tremendous expansion in supply results in a painful period of declining prices and readjustment. In the first two expansive periods analyzed here, 1815 to 1818 and 1832 to 1839, cotton was the key industry in both the boom and the subsequent collapse and readjustment. In the last period the sources of expansion are more diffuse, but grain in the West played the most important role.

Underlying the uneven pattern of development were the shape of the supply curve of cotton (or grain) and the way in which the supply curve shifted. During each period of expansion, millions of acres of new land were purchased from the government for cotton production. Once this land had been cleared and a crop or two of corn planted to prepare the soil, the amount of cotton available could be substantially increased, and the supply curve of cotton shifted very sharply to the right. With the depressed cotton prices that followed such expansion, a good deal of this land was devoted to alternative uses. For the most part, it was put to crop and livestock use to feed slaves and reduce the costs of purchasing foodstuffs. In effect, it represented unused capacity with respect to cotton, and any slight increase in cotton prices could and did lead to shifting some of this land into cotton. In the old South, where slaves as such were an important intermediate goods, this was clearly a rational redirection of resources during periods of depressed prices. The result is that the supply curve of cotton approximated the shape indicated in Chart I–VII. It was highly elastic over a range of output which included

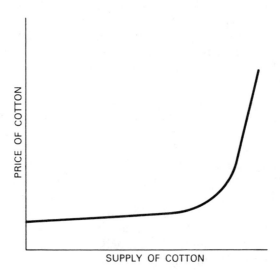

CHART I-VII   *Shape of Supply Curve of Cotton*

all the available land that had been cleared and readied for crop production and was suitable for cotton. Even with the rapid growth in demand that characterized the cotton textile industry in the first half of the nineteenth century, it took a decade for demand to shift to the right sufficiently to absorb this potential supply. During this decade very little new land was sold in the cotton states, and the expansion of potential capacity was at a much slower rate than during the previous boom. When the growth of demand for cotton finally brought all this potential capacity into production, a further increase in demand resulted in substantial price increases as the supply curve became increasingly inelastic. With the readily available cotton land already in production, higher prices brought forth little additional production in the short run.

   While there had been little incentive to buy and clear new land for cotton during the period of low prices, rising prices triggered a land boom in the new South. Millions of acres of virgin land were sold; planters and their slaves migrated in large numbers to open up and exploit the rich land in the Southwest—Alabama, Louisiana, Mississippi, and Arkansas were the major states. A lengthy period intervened between the initial impetus from rising prices and substantial output increases for putting this land into production. While imperfections in the capital market and land speculation partially explain this delay, the more important reasons were the time it took to obtain slaves from the old South, clear the land, and plant a crop or two of corn to prepare the soil. The results of this delay are clearly evident in Chart II–VII. Note

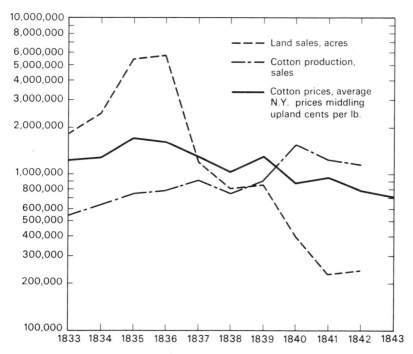

CHART II-VII *Land Sales, Cotton Production and Prices: 1833–1843 (Ala., Ark., Miss., Fla., La.)*

the output of cotton in the five cotton states. There was a lag of approximately four years between the peak in land sales and a large increase in cotton production. The consequence was a vast shift to the right in the supply curve of cotton and the beginning of a new period of depressed prices. Cotton output actually fell as some of this land was diverted into corn with the low cotton prices that prevailed after 1839.

In the West, the same general pattern prevailed with respect to wheat and corn. Land sales in the western states paralleled the prices of those staples, with one important difference. Little transportation or other social overhead investment was necessary to increase the supply of cotton in the South. In the West, transportation was the major limiting factor in increasing supply. The accessible lands close to water transportation were taken up first. Initially, the rise in prices brought into cultivation land further and further from cheap transportation. As a result, the supply curve of wheat and corn land was probably less inelastic than cotton as it began to slope upward. However, it also encouraged a boom in land sales and at the same time a growing agitation for large-scale investment in new transportation facilities. Canal and railroad building was a lengthy process, but a completed canal or railroad opened up large amounts of new land. The canal construction era of the 1830's and the railroad construction period of the 1850's each served to make possible, along with the land sales and influx of settlers that accompanied them, a large shift to the right in wheat and corn supplies, with much the same results as cotton.

17

Slave Songs and Slave Consciousness: An Exploration in Neglected Sources

LAWRENCE W. LEVINE

Stanley M. Elkins's *Slavery* (1959) was the most original and exciting book to appear on that subject in a generation. Elkins compared American slavery with slavery elsewhere as well as with the Jewish experience in concentration camps, applied psychoanalytic theory to his findings, and concluded that slavery emasculated the slave's personality by forcing him to play a childlike role. Drawing upon oral tradition, music, and folklore, Lawrence W. Levine shows that slaves had some effective means to defend the integrity of their personalities from the onslaught of the slave system.

Negroes in the United States, both during and after slavery, were anything but inarticulate. They sang songs, told stories, played verbal games, listened and responded to sermons, and expressed their aspirations, fears, and values through the medium of an oral tradition that had characterized the West African cultures from which their ancestors had come. By largely ignoring this tradition, much of which has been preserved, historians have

From *Anonymous Americans: Explorations in Nineteenth-Century Social History*, Tamara K. Hareven, ed., pp. 99–126. © 1971 by Prentice-Hall, Inc., Englewood Cliffs, N.J. Reprinted by permission of the publisher.

rendered an articulate people historically inarticulate, and have allowed the record of their consciousness to go unexplored.

Having worked my way carefully through thousands of Negro songs, folktales, jokes, and games, I am painfully aware of the problems inherent in the use of such materials. They are difficult, often impossible, to date with any precision. Their geographical distribution is usually unclear. They were collected belatedly, most frequently by men and women who had little understanding of the culture from which they sprang, and little scruple about altering or suppressing them. Such major collectors as John Lomax, Howard Odum, and Newman White all admitted openly that many of the songs they collected were "unprintable" by the moral standards which guided them and presumably their readers. But historians have overcome imperfect records before. They have learned how to deal with altered documents, with consciously or unconsciously biased first-hand accounts, with manuscript collections that were deposited in archives only after being filtered through the overprotective hands of fearful relatives, and with the comparative lack of contemporary sources and the need to use their materials retrospectively. The challenge presented by the materials of folk and popular culture is neither totally unique nor insurmountable.

In this essay I want to illustrate the possible use of materials of this kind by discussing the contribution that an understanding of Negro songs can make to the recent debate over slave personality. In the process I will discuss several aspects of the literature and problems related to the use of slave songs.

The subject of Negro music in slavery has produced a large and varied literature, little of which has been devoted to questions of meaning and function. The one major exception is Miles Mark Fisher's 1953 study, *Negro Slave Songs in the United States,* which attempts to get at the essence of slave life through an analysis of slave songs. Unfortunately, Fisher's rich insights are too often marred by his rather loose scholarly standards, and despite its continuing value his study is in many respects an example of how *not* to use Negro songs. Asserting, correctly, that the words of slave songs "show both accidental and intentional errors of transmission," Fisher changes the words almost at will to fit his own image of their pristine form. Arguing persuasively that "transplanted Negroes continued to promote their own culture by music," Fisher makes their songs part of an "African cult" which he simply wills into existence. Maintaining (again, I think, correctly), that "slave songs preserved in joyful strains the adjustment which Negroes made to their living conditions within the United States," Fisher traces the major patterns of that adjustment by arbitrarily dating these songs, apparently unperturbed by the almost total lack of evidence pertaining to the origin and introduction of individual slave songs.

Fisher aside, most other major studies of slave music have focused almost entirely upon musical structure and origin. This latter question especially has given rise to a long and heated debate. The earliest collectors and students of slave music were impressed by how different that music was from anything familiar to them. Following a visit to the Sea Islands in 1862, Lucy McKim despaired of being able "to express the entire character of these negro ballads by mere musical notes and signs. The odd turns made in the throat; and that curious rhythmic effect produced by single voices chiming in at different irregular intervals, seem almost as impossible to place on score, as the singing of birds, or the tones of an Aeolian Harp." Although some of these early collectors maintained, as did W. F. Allen in 1865, that much of the slave's music "might no doubt be traced to tunes which they have heard from the whites, and transformed to their own use, . . . their music . . . is rather European than African in its character," they more often stressed the distinctiveness of the Negro's music and attributed it to racial characteristics, African origins, and indigenous developments resulting from the slave's unique experience in the New World.

This tradition, which has had many influential twentieth-century adherents, was increasingly challenged in the early decades of this century. Such scholars as Newman White, Guy Johnson, and George Pullen Jackson argued that the earlier school lacked a comparative grounding in Anglo-American folk song. Comparing Negro spirituals with Methodist and Baptist evangelical religious music of the late eighteenth and early nineteenth centuries, White, Johnson, and Jackson found similarities in words, subject matter, tunes, and musical structure. Although they tended to exaggerate both qualitatively and quantitatively the degrees of similarity, their comparisons were often a persuasive and important corrective to the work of their predecessors. But their studies were inevitably weakened by their ethnocentric assumption that similarities alone settled the argument over origins. Never could they contemplate the possibility that the direction of cultural diffusion might have been from black to white as well as the other way. In fact, insofar as white evangelical music departed from traditional Protestant hymnology and embodied or approached the complex rhythmic structure, the percussive qualities, the polymeter, the syncopation, the emphasis on overlapping call and response patterns that characterized Negro music both in West Africa and the New World, the possibility that it was influenced by slaves who attended and joined in the singing at religious meetings is quite high.

These scholars tended to use the similarities between black and white religious music to deny the significance of slave songs in still another way. Newman White, for example, argued that since white evangelical hymns also used such expressions as "freedom," the "Promised Land," and the "Egyptian Bondage," "without thought of other than spiritual meaning," these images when they occurred in Negro spirituals could not have been symbolic "of the Negro's longing for physical freedom." The familiar process by which different cultural groups can derive varied meanings from identical images is enough to cast doubt on the logic of White's argument. In the case of white and black religious music, however, the problem may be much less complex, since it is quite possible that the similar images in the songs of both groups in fact served similar purposes. Many of those whites who flocked to the camp meetings of the Methodists and Baptists were themselves on the social and economic margins of their society, and had psychic and emotional needs which, qualitatively, may not have been vastly different from those of black slaves. Interestingly, George Pullen Jackson, in his attempt to prove the white origin of Negro spirituals, makes exactly this point: "I may mention in closing the chief remaining argument of the die-hards for the Negro source of the Negro spirituals. . . . How could any, the argument runs, but a natively musical and sorely oppressed race create such beautiful things as 'Swing Low,' 'Steal Away,' and 'Deep River'? . . . But were not the whites of the mountains and the hard-scrabble hill country also 'musical and oppressed'? . . . Yes, these whites were musical, and oppressed too. If their condition was any more tolerable than that of the Negroes, one certainly does not get that impression from any of their songs of release and escape." If this is true, the presence of similar images in white music would merely heighten rather than detract from the significance of these images in Negro songs. Clearly, the function and meaning of white religious music during the late eighteenth and early nineteenth centuries demands far more attention than it has received. In the interim, we must be wary of allowing the mere fact of similarities to deter us from attempting to comprehend the cultural dynamics of slave music.

Contemporary scholars, tending to transcend the more simplistic lines of the old debate, have focused upon the process of syncretism to explain the development of Negro music in the United States. The rich West African musical tradition common to almost all of the specific cultures from which Negro slaves came, the comparative cultural isolation in which large numbers of slaves lived, the tolerance and even encouragement which their white masters accorded to their musical activities, and the fact that, for all its differences, nothing in the European musical tradition with which they came into contact in America was totally alien to their own traditions—all these were conducive to a situation which allowed the slaves to retain a good deal of the integrity of their own musical heritage while fusing to it compatible elements of Anglo-American music. Slaves often took over entire white hymns and folk songs, as White and Jackson maintained, but altered them significantly in terms of words, musical structure, and especially performance before making them their own. The result was a hybrid with a strong African base.

One of the more interesting aspects of this debate over origins is that no one engaged in it, not even advocates of the white derivation theory, denied that the slaves possessed their own distinctive music. Newman White took particular pains to point out again and again that the notion that Negro song is purely an imitation of the white man's music "is fully as unjust and inaccurate, in the final analysis, as the Negro's assumption that his folk-song is entirely original." He observed that in the slaves' separate religious meetings they were free to do as they would with the music they first learned from the whites, with the result that their spirituals became "the greatest single outlet for the expression of the Negro folk-mind." Similarly, George Pullen Jackson, after admitting that he could find no white parallels for over two-thirds of the existing Negro spirituals, reasoned that these were produced by Negro singers in true folk fashion "by endless singing of heard tunes and by endless, inevitable, and concomitant singing differentiation." Going even further, Jackson asserted that the lack of deep roots in Anglo-American culture left the black man "even freer than the white man to make songs over unconsciously as he sang . . . the free play has resulted in the very large number of songs which, though formed primarily in the white man's moulds, have lost all recognizable relationship to known individual white-sung melodic entities." This debate over origins indicates clearly that a belief in the direct continuity of African musical traditions or in the process of syncretism is not a necessary prerequisite to the conclusion that the Negro slaves' music was their own, regardless of where they received the components out of which it was fashioned; a conclusion which is crucial to any attempt to utilize these songs as an aid in reconstructing the slaves' consciousness.

Equally important is the process by which slave songs were created and transmitted. When James McKim asked a freedman on the Sea Islands during the Civil War where the slaves got their songs, the answer was eloquently simple: "Dey make em, sah." Precisely *how* they made them worried and fascinated Thomas Wentworth Higginson, who became familiar with slave music through the singing of the black Union soldiers in his Civil War regiment. Were their songs, he wondered, a "conscious and definite" product of "some leading mind," or did they grow "by gradual accretion, in an almost unconscious way"? A freedman rowing

Higginson and some of his troops between the Sea Islands helped to resolve the problem when he described a spiritual which he had a hand
in creating:

> Once we boys went for some rice and de nigger-driver he keep a-callin'
> on us; and I say, "O de ole nigger-driver!" Den anudder said, "Fust ting
> my mammy tole me was, notin' so bad as nigger-driver." Den I made a
> sing, just puttin' a word, and den anudder word.

He then began to sing his song:

> *O, de ole nigger-driver!*
> *O, gwine away!*
> *Fust ting my mammy tell me,*
> *O, gwine away!*
>
> *Tell me 'bout de nigger-driver,*
> *O, gwine away!*
> *Nigger-driver second devil,*
> *O, gwine away!*

Higginson's black soldiers, after a moment's hesitation, joined in the
singing of a song they had never heard before as if they had long been
familiar with it. "I saw," Higginson concluded, "how easily a new 'sing'
took root among them."

This spontaneity, this sense of almost instantaneous community
which so impressed Higginson, constitutes a central element in every
account of slave singing. The English musician Henry Russell, who lived
in the United States in the 1830's, was forcibly struck by the ease with
which a slave congregation in Vicksburg, Mississippi, took a "fine old
psalm tune" and, by suddenly and spontaneously accelerating the tempo,
transformed it "into a kind of negro melody." "Us old heads," an ex-slave
told Jeanette Robinson Murphy, "use ter make 'em up on de spurn of de
moment. Notes is good enough for you people, but us likes a mixtery."
Her account of the creation of a spiritual is typical and important:

> We'd all be at the "prayer house" de Lord's day, and de white preacher
> he'd splain de word and read whar Esekial done say—
>
> *Dry bones gwine ter lib ergin.*
>
> And, honey, de Lord would come a-shinin' thoo dem pages and revive dis
> ole nigger's heart, and I'd jump up dar and den and holler and shout
> and sing and pat, and dey would all cotch de words and I'd sing it to
> some ole shout song I'd heard 'em sing from Africa, and dey'd all take it
> up and keep at it, and keep a-addin' to it, and den it would be a spiritual.

. . .

Clifton Furness has given us an even more graphic description. During a visit to an isolated South Carolina plantation in 1926, he attended a prayer meeting held in the old slave cabins. The preacher began his reading of the Scriptures slowly, then increased his tempo and emotional fervor, assuring his flock that "Gawd's lightnin' gwine strike! Gawd's thunder swaller de ert!"

> Gradually moaning became audible in the shadowy corners where the women sat. Some patted their bundled babies in time to the flow of the words, and began swaying backward and forward. Several men moved their feet alternately, in strange syncopation. A rhythm was born, almost without reference to the words that were being spoken by the preacher. It seemed to take shape almost visibly, and grow. I was gripped with the feeling of a mass-intelligence, a self-conscious entity, gradually informing the crowd and taking possession of every mind there, including my own.

In the midst of this increasing intensity, a black man sitting directly in front of Furness, his head bowed, his body swaying, his feet patting up and down, suddenly cried out: "Git right—sodger! Git right—sodger! Git right—wit Gawd!"

> Instantly the crowd took it up, moulding a melody out of half-formed familiar phrases based upon a spiritual tune, hummed here and there among the crowd. A distinct melodic outline became more and more prominent, shaping itself around the central theme of the words, "Git right, sodger!"
>
> Scraps of other words and tunes were flung into the medley of sound by individual singers from time to time, but the general trend was carried on by a deep undercurrent, which appeared to be stronger than the mind of any individual present, for it bore the mass of improvised harmony and rhythms into the most effective climax of incremental repetition that I have ever heard. I felt as if some conscious plan or purpose were carrying us along, call it mob-mind, communal composition, or what you will.

Shortly after the Civil War, Elizabeth Kilham witnessed a similar scene among the freedmen, and described it in terms almost identical to those used by observers many years later. "A fog seemed to fill the church," she wrote, ". . . an invisible power seemed to hold us in its iron grasp; . . . A few moments more, and I think we should have shrieked in unison with the crowd."

These accounts and others like them make it clear that spirituals both during and after slavery were the product of an improvisational communal consciousness. They were not, as some observers thought, totally new creations, but were forged out of many preexisting bits of old songs mixed together with snatches of new tunes and lyrics and fit into a fairly traditional but never wholly static metrical pattern. They were, to answer Higginson's question, *simultaneously* the result of individual and mass creativity. They were products of that folk process which has been called "communal re-creation," through which older songs are constantly recreated into essentially new entities. Anyone who has read through large numbers of Negro songs is familiar with this process. Identical or slightly varied stanzas appear in song after song; identical tunes are made to accommodate completely different sets of lyrics; the same song appears in different collections in widely varied forms. In 1845 a traveler observed that the only permanent elements in Negro song were the music and the chorus. "The blacks themselves leave out old stanzas, and introduce new ones at pleasure. Travelling through the South, you may, in passing from Virginia to Louisiana, hear the same tune a hundred times, but seldom the same words accompanying it." Another observer noted in 1870 that during a single religious meeting the freedmen would often sing the words of one spiritual to several different tunes, and then take a tune that particularly pleased them and fit the words of several different songs to it. Slave songs, then, were never static; at no time did Negroes create a "final" version of any spiritual. Always the community felt free to alter and recreate them.

The two facts that I have attempted to establish thus far—that slave music, regardless of its origins, was a distinctive cultural form, and that it was created or constantly recreated through a communal process—are essential if one is to justify the use of these songs as keys to slave consciousness. But these facts in themselves say a good deal about the nature and quality of slave life and personality. That black slaves could create and continually recreate songs marked by the poetic beauty, the emotional intensity, the rich imagery which characterized the spirituals—songs which even one of the most devout proponents of the white man's origins school admits are "the most impressive religious folk songs in our language"—should be enough to make us seriously question recent theories which conceive of slavery as a closed system which destroyed the vitality of the Negro and left him a dependent child. For all of its horrors, slavery was never so complete a system of psychic assault that it prevented the slaves from carving out independent cultural forms. It never pervaded all of the interstices of their minds and their culture, and in those gaps they were able to create an independent art form and a distinctive voice. If North American slavery eroded the African's linguistic and institutional life, if it prevented him from preserving and developing his rich heritage of graphic and plastic art, it nevertheless allowed him to continue and to develop the patterns of verbal art which were so central to his past culture. Historians have not yet come to terms with what the continuance of the oral tradition meant to blacks in slavery.

In Africa, songs, tales, proverbs, and verbal games served the dual function of not only preserving communal values and solidarity, but also of providing occasions for the individual to transcend, at least symbolically, the inevitable restrictions of his environment and his society by permitting him to express deeply held feelings which he ordinarily was not allowed to verbalize. Among the Ashanti and the Dahomeans, for example, periods were set aside when the inhabitants were encouraged to gather together and, through the medium of song, dance, and tales, to openly express their feelings about each other. The psychological release this afforded seems to have been well understood. "You know that everyone has a *sunsum* (soul) that may get hurt or knocked about or become sick, and so make the body ill," an Ashanti high priest explained to the English anthropologist R. S. Rattray:

> Very often . . . ill health is caused by the evil and the hate that another has in his head against you. Again, you too may have hatred in your head against another, because of something that person has done to you, and that, too, causes your *sunsum* to fret and become sick. Our forbears knew this to be the case, and so they ordained a time, once every year, when every man and woman, free man and slave, should have freedom to speak out just what was in their head, to tell their neighbours just what they thought of them, and of their actions, and not only their neighbours, but also the king or chief. When a man has spoken freely thus, he will feel his *sunsum* cool and quieted, and the *sunsum* of the other person against whom he has now openly spoken will be quieted also.

Utilization of verbal art for this purpose was widespread throughout Africa, and was not confined to those ceremonial occasions when one could directly state one's feelings. Through innuendo, metaphor, and circumlocution, Africans could utilize their songs as outlets for individual release without disturbing communal solidarity.

There is abundant internal evidence that the verbal art of the slaves in the United States served many of these traditional functions. Just as the process by which the spirituals were created allowed for simultaneous individual and communal creativity, so their very structure provided simultaneous outlets for individual and communal expression. The overriding antiphonal structure of the spirituals—the call and response pattern which Negroes brought with them from Africa and which was reinforced by the relatively similar white practice of "lining out" hymns—placed the individual in continual dialogue with his community, allowing him at one and the same time to preserve his voice as a distinct entity and to blend it with those of his fellows. Here again slave music confronts us with evidence which indicates that however seriously the slave system may have diminished the strong sense of community that had bound Africans together, it never totally destroyed it or left the individual atomized and emotionally and psychically defenseless before his white masters. In fact, the form and structure of slave music presented the slave with a potential outlet for his individual feelings even while it continually drew him back into the communal presence and permitted him the comfort of basking in the warmth of the shared assumptions of those around him.

Those "shared assumptions" can be further examined by an analysis of the content of slave songs. Our preoccupation in recent years with the degree to which the slaves actually resembled the "Sambo" image held by their white masters has obscured the fact that the slaves developed images of their own which must be consulted and studied before any discussion of slave personality can be meaningful. The image of the trickster, who through cunning and unscrupulousness prevails over his more powerful antagonists, pervades slave tales. The trickster figure is rarely encountered in the slave's religious songs, though its presence is sometimes felt in the slave's many allusions to his narrow escapes from the devil.

> The Devil's mad and I'm glad,
> He lost the soul he thought he had.

> Ole Satan toss a ball at me.
> O me no weary yet . . .

> Him tink de ball would hit my soul.
> O me no weary yet . . .

> De ball for hell and I for heaven.
> O me no weary yet . . .

> Ole Satan thought he had a mighty aim;
> He missed my soul and caught my sins.
> Cry Amen, cry Amen, cry Amen to God!

> He took my sins upon his back;
> Went muttering and grumbling down to hell.
> Cry Amen, cry Amen, cry Amen to God!

The single most persistent image the slave songs contain, however, is that of the chosen people. The vast majority of the spirituals identify the singers as "de people dat is born of God," "We are the people of God," "we are de people of de Lord," "I really do believe I'm a child of God,"

"I'm a child ob God, wid my soul sot free," "I'm born of God, I know I am." Nor is there ever any doubt that "To the promised land I'm bound to go," "I walk de heavenly road," "Heav'n shall-a be my home," "I gwine to meet my Saviour," "I seek my Lord and I find Him," "I'll hear the trumpet sound/In that morning."

The force of this image cannot be diminished by the observation that similar images were present in the religious singing of white evangelical churches during the first half of the nineteenth century. White Americans could be expected to sing of triumph and salvation, given their long-standing heritage of the idea of a chosen people which was reinforced in this era by the belief in inevitable progress and manifest destiny, the spread-eagle oratory, the bombastic folklore, and, paradoxically, the deep insecurities concomitant with the tasks of taming a continent and developing an identity. But for this same message to be expressed by Negro slaves who were told endlessly that they were members of the lowliest of races *is* significant. It offers an insight into the kinds of barriers the slaves had available to them against the internalization of the stereotyped images their masters held and attempted consciously and unconsciously to foist upon them.

The question of the chosen people image leads directly into the larger problem of what role religion played in the songs of the slave. Writing in 1862, James McKim noted that the songs of the Sea Island freedmen "are all religious, barcaroles and all. I speak without exception. So far as I heard or was told of their singing, it was all religious." Others who worked with recently emancipated slaves recorded the same experience, and Colonel Higginson reported that he rarely heard his troops sing a profane or vulgar song. With a few exceptions, "all had a religious motive." In spite of this testimony, there can be little doubt that the slaves sang nonreligious songs. In 1774, an English visitor to the United States, after his first encounter with slave music, wrote in his journal: "In their songs they generally relate the usage they have received from their Masters or Mistresses in a very satirical stile and manner." Songs fitting this description can be found in the nineteenth-century narratives of fugitive slaves. Harriet Jacobs recorded that during the Christmas season the slaves would ridicule stingy whites by singing:

> *Poor Massa, so dey say;*
> *Down in de heel, so dey say;*
> *Got no money, so dey say;*
> *God A'mighty bress you, so dey say.*

"Once in a while among a mass of nonsense and wild frolic," Frederick Douglass noted, "a sharp hit was given to the meanness of slaveholders."

We raise de wheat,
Dey gib us de corn;
We bake de bread,
Dey gib us de crust;
We sif de meal,
Dey gib us de huss;
We peal de meat,
Dey gib us de skin;
And dat's de way
Dey take us in;
We skim de pot,
Dey gib us de liquor,
And say dat's good enough for nigger.

Both of these songs are in the African tradition of utilizing song to bypass both internal and external censors and give vent to feelings which could be expressed in no other form. Nonreligious songs were not limited to the slave's relations with his masters, however, as these rowing songs, collected by contemporary white observers, indicate:

We are going down to Georgia, boys,
Aye, aye.
To see the pretty girls, boys,
Yoe, yoe.
We'll give 'em a pint of brandy, boys,
Aye, aye.
And a hearty kiss, besides, boys,
Yoe, yoe.

Jenny shake her toe at me,
Jenny gone away;
Jenny shake her toe at me,
Jenny gone away;
Hurrah! Miss Susy, oh!
Jenny gone away;
Hurrah! Miss Susy, oh!
Jenny gone away;

The variety of nonreligious songs in the slave's repertory was wide. There were songs of in-group and out-group satire, songs of nostalgia, nonsense songs, songs of play and work and love. Nevertheless, our total stock of these songs is very small. It is possible to add to these by incorporating such post-bellum secular songs which have an authentic slavery ring to them as "De Blue-Tail Fly," with its ill-concealed satisfaction at the death of a master, or the ubiquitous

My ole Mistiss promise me,
W'en she died, she'd set me free,
She lived so long dat 'er head got bal',
An' she give out'n de notion a dyin' at all.

The number can be further expanded by following Constance Rourke's suggestion that we attempt to disentangle elements of Negro origin from those of white creation in the "Ethiopian melodies" of the white minstrel shows, many of which were similar to the songs I have just quoted. Either of these possibilities, however, forces the historian to work with sources far more potentially spurious than those with which he normally is comfortable.

Spirituals, on the other hand, for all the problems associated with their being filtered through white hands before they were published, and despite the many errors in transcription that inevitably occurred, constitute a much more satisfactory source. They were collected by the hundreds directly from slaves and freedmen during the Civil War and the decades immediately following, and although they came from widely different geographical areas they share a common structure and content, which seems to have been characteristic of Negro music wherever slavery existed in the United States. It is possible that we have a greater number of religious than nonreligious songs because slaves were more willing to sing these ostensibly innocent songs to white collectors who in turn were more anxious to record them, since they fit easily with their positive and negative images of the Negro. But I would argue that the vast preponderance of spirituals over any other sort of slave music, rather than being merely the result of accident or error, is instead an accurate reflection of slave culture during the ante-bellum period. Whatever songs the slaves may have sung before their wholesale conversion to Christianity in the late eighteenth and early nineteenth centuries, by the latter century spirituals were quantitatively and qualitatively their most significant musical creation. In this form of expression slaves found a medium which resembled in many important ways the world view they had brought with them from Africa, and afforded them the possibility of both adapting to and transcending their situation.

It is significant that the most common form of slave music we know of is sacred song. I use the term "sacred" not in its present usage as something antithetical to the secular world; neither the slaves nor their African forebears ever drew modernity's clear line between the sacred and the secular. The uses to which spirituals were put are an unmistakable indication of this. They were not sung solely or even primarily in churches or praise houses, but were used as rowing songs, field songs, work songs, and social songs. On the Sea Islands during the Civil War, Lucy McKim heard the spiritual "Poor Rosy" sung in a wide variety of contexts and tempos.

> On the water, the oars dip "Poor Rosy" to an even andante; a stout boy and girl at the hominy-mill will make the same "Poor Rosy" fly, to keep up with the whirling stone; and in the evening, after the day's work is done, "Heab'n shall-a be my home" [the final line of each stanza] peals up slowly and mournfully from the distant quarters.

For the slaves, then, songs of God and the mythic heroes of their religion were not confined to any specific time or place, but were appropriate to almost every situation. It is in this sense that I use the concept sacred—not to signify a rejection of the present world but to describe the process of incorporating within this world all the elements of the divine. The religious historian Mircea Eliade, whose definition of sacred has shaped my own, has maintained that for men in traditional societies religion is a means of extending the world spatially upward so that communication with the other world becomes ritually possible, and extending it temporally backward so that the paradigmatic acts of the gods and mythical ancestors can be continually reenacted and indefinitely recoverable. By creating sacred time and space, man can perpetually live in the presence of his gods, can hold on to the certainty that within one's own lifetime "rebirth" is continually possible, and can impose order on the chaos of the universe. "Life," as Eliade puts it, "is lived on a twofold plane; it takes its course as human existence and, at the same time, shares in a transhuman life, that of the cosmos or the gods."

This notion of sacredness gets at the essence of the spirituals, and through them at the essence of the slave's world view. Denied the possibility of achieving an adjustment to the external world of the ante-bellum South which involved meaningful forms of personal integration, attainment of status, and feelings of individual worth that all human beings crave and need, the slaves created a new world by transcending the narrow confines of the one in which they were forced to live. They extended the boundaries of their restrictive universe backward until it fused with the world of the Old Testament, and upward until it became one with the world beyond. The spirituals are the record of a people who found the status, the harmony, the values, the order they needed to survive by internally creating an expanded universe, by literally willing themselves reborn. In this respect I agree with the anthropologist Paul Radin that

> The ante-bellum Negro was not converted to God. He converted God to himself. In the Christian God he found a fixed point and he needed a fixed point, for both within and outside of himself, he could see only

vacillation and endless shifting. . . . There was no other safety for people faced on all sides by doubt and the threat of personal disintegration, by the thwarting of instincts and the annihilation of values.

The confinement of much of the slave's new world to dreams and fantasies does not free us from the historical obligation of examining its contours, weighing its implications for the development of the slave's psychic and emotional structure, and eschewing the kind of facile reasoning that leads Professor Elkins to imply that, since the slaves had no alternatives open to them, their fantasy life was "limited to catfish and watermelons." Their spirituals indicate clearly that there *were* alternatives open to them—alternatives which they themselves fashioned out of the fusion of their African heritage and their new religion—and that their fantasy life was so rich and so important to them that it demands understanding if we are even to begin to comprehend their inner world.

The God the slaves sang of was neither remote nor abstract, but as intimate, personal, and immediate as the gods of Africa had been. "O when I talk I talk wid God," "Mass Jesus is my bosom friend," "I'm goin' to walk with [talk with, live with, see] King Jesus by myself, by myself," were refrains that echoed through the spirituals.

> *In de mornin' when I rise,*
> *Tell my Jesus huddy [howdy] oh,*
> *I wash my hands in de mornin' glory,*
> *Tell my Jesus huddy oh.*
>
> *Gwine to argue wid de Father and chatter wid de son,*
> *The last trumpet shall sound, I'll be there.*
> *Gwine talk 'bout de bright world dey des' come from.*
> *The last trumpet shall sound, I'll be there.*
>
> *Gwine to write to Massa Jesus,*
> *To send some Valiant soldier*
> *To turn back Pharaoh's army, Hallelu!*

The heroes of the Scriptures—"Sister Mary," "Brudder Jonah," "Brudder Moses," "Brudder Daniel"—were greeted with similar intimacy and immediacy. In the world of the spirituals, it was not the masters and mistresses but God and Jesus and the entire pantheon of Old Testament figures who set the standards, established the precedents, and defined the values; who, in short, constituted the "significant others." The world described by the slave songs was a black world in which no reference was ever made to any white contemporaries. The slave's positive reference group was composed entirely of his own peers: his mother, father, sister, brother, uncles, aunts, preacher, fellow "sinners" and "mourners" of whom he sang endlessly, to whom he sent messages via the dying, and with whom he was reunited joyfully in the next world.

The same sense of sacred time and space which shaped the slave's portraits of his gods and heroes also made his visions of the past and future immediate and compelling. Descriptions of the Crucifixion communicate a sense of the actual presence of the singers: "Dey pierced Him in the side . . . Dey nail Him to de cross : . . Dey rivet His feet . . . Dey hanged him high . . . Dey stretch Him wide. . . ."

> *Oh sometimes it causes me to tremble,–tremble,–tremble,*
> *Were you there when they crucified my Lord?*

The Slave's "shout"—that counterclockwise, shuffling dance which frequently occurred after the religious service and lasted long into the night —often became a medium through which the ecstatic dancers were transformed into actual participants in historic actions: Joshua's army marching around the walls of Jericho, the children of Israel following Moses out of Egypt.

The thin line between time dimensions is nowhere better illustrated than in the slave's visions of the future, which were, of course, a direct negation of his present. Among the most striking spirituals are those which pile detail upon detail in describing the Day of Judgment: "You'll see de world on fire . . . see de element a meltin', . . . see the stars a fallin' . . . see the moon a bleedin' . . . see the forked lightning, . . . Hear the rumblin' thunder . . . see the righteous marching, . . . see my Jesus coming . . . ," and the world to come where "Dere's no sun to burn you . . . no hard trials . . . no whips a crackin' . . . no stormy weather . . . no tribulation . . . no evil-doers . . . All is gladness in de Kingdom." This vividness was matched by the slave's certainty that he would partake of the triumph of judgment and the joys of the new world:

> *Dere's room enough, room enough, room enough in de heaven,*
>   *my Lord*
> *Room enough, room enough, I can't stay behind.*

Continually, the slaves sang of reaching out beyond the world that confined them, of seeing Jesus "in de wilderness," of praying "in de lonesome valley," of breathing in the freedom of the mountain peaks:

> *Did yo' ever*
> *Stan' on mountun,*
> *Wash yo' han's*
> *In a cloud?*

Continually, they held out the possibility of imminent rebirth; "I look at de worl' an' de worl' look new, . . . I look at my hands an' they look so too . . . I looked at my feet, my feet was too."

These possibilities, these certainties were not surprising. The religious revivals which swept large numbers of slaves into the Christian fold in the late eighteenth and early nineteenth centuries were based upon a *practical* (not necessarily theological) Armianism: God would save all who believed in Him; Salvation was there for all to take hold of if they would. The effects of this message upon the slaves who were exposed to and converted by it have been passed over too easily by historians. Those effects are illustrated graphically in the spirituals which were the products of these revivals and which continued to spread the evangelical word long after the revivals had passed into history.

The religious music of the slaves is almost devoid of feelings of depravity or unworthiness, but is rather, as I have tried to show, pervaded by a sense of change, transcendence, ultimate justice, and personal worth. The spirituals have been referred to as "sorrow songs," and in some respects they were. The slaves sang of "rollin' thro' an unfriendly world," of being "a-trouble in de mind," of living in a world which was a "howling wilderness," "a hell to me," of feeling like a "motherless child," "a po' little orphan chile in de worl'," a "home-e-less child," of fearing that "Trouble will bury me down.'"

But these feelings were rarely pervasive or permanent; almost always they were overshadowed by a triumphant note of affirmation. Even so despairing a wail as "Nobody Knows the Trouble I've Had" could suddenly have its mood transformed by lines like: "One morning I was a-walking down, . . . Saw some berries a-hanging down, . . . I pick de berry and I suck de juice, . . . Just as sweet as de honey in de comb." Similarly, amid the deep sorrow of "Sometimes I feel like a Motherless chile," sudden release could come with the lines: "Sometimes I feel like/A eagle in de air. . . . Spread my wings an'/Fly, fly, fly." Slaves spent little time singing of the horrors of hell or damnation. Their songs of the Devil, quoted earlier, pictured a harsh but almost semicomic figure (often, one suspects, a surrogate for the white man), over whom they triumphed with reassuring regularity. For all their inevitable sadness, slave songs were characterized more by a feeling of confidence than of despair. There was confidence that contemporary power relationships were not immutable: "Did not old Pharaoh get lost, get lost, get lost, . . . get lost in de Red Sea?"; confidence in the possibilities of instantaneous change: "Jesus make de dumb to speak. . . . Jesus make de cripple walk. . . . Jesus give de blind his sight. . . . Jesus do most anything"; confidence in the rewards of persistence: "Keep a' inching along like a poor inch-worm,/Jesus will come by'nd bye"; confidence that nothing could stand in the way of the justice they would receive: "You kin hender me here, but you can't do it dah," "O no man, no man can hinder me"; confidence in the prospects of the future: "We'll walk de golden streets/Of de New Jerusalem." Religion, the slaves sang, "is good for anything, . . . Religion make you happy, . . . Religion gib me patience . . . O member, get Religion . . . Religion is so sweet."

The slaves often pursued the "sweetness" of their religion in the face of many obstacles. Becky Ilsey, who was 16 when she was emancipated, recalled many years later:

> 'Fo' de war when we'd have a meetin' at night, wuz mos' always 'way in de woods or de bushes some whar so de white folks couldn't hear, an' when dey'd sing a spiritual an' de spirit 'gin to shout some de elders would go 'mongst de folks an' put dey han' over dey mouf an' some times put a clof in dey mouf an' say: "Spirit don talk so loud or de patterol break us up." You know dey had white patterols what went 'roun' at night to see de niggers didn't cut up no devilment, an' den de meetin' would break up an' some would go to one house an' some to er nudder an' dey would groan er w'ile, den go home.

Elizabeth Ross Hite testified that although she and her fellow slaves on a Louisiana plantation were Catholics, "lots didn't like that 'ligion."

> We used to hide behind some bricks and hold church ourselves. You see, the Catholic preachers from France wouldn't let us shout, and the Lawd done said you gotta shout if you want to be saved. That's in the Bible.
>
> Sometimes we held church all night long, 'til way in the mornin'. We burned some grease in a can for the preacher to see the Bible by. . . .
>
> See, our master didn't like us to have much 'ligion, said it made us lag in our work. He jest wanted us to be Catholicses on Sundays and go to mass and not study 'bout nothin' like that on week days. He didn't want us shoutin' and moanin' all day'-long, but you gotta shout and you gotta moan if you wants to be saved.

The slaves clearly craved the affirmation and promise of their religion. It would be a mistake, however, to see this urge as exclusively otherworldly. When Thomas Wentworth Higginson observed that the spirituals exhibited "nothing but patience for this life,—nothing but triumph in the next," he, and later observers who elaborated upon this judgment, were indulging in hyperbole. Although Jesus was ubiquitous in the spirituals, it was not invariably the Jesus of the New Testament of whom the slaves sang, but frequently a Jesus transformed into an Old Testament warrior: "Mass' Jesus" who engaged in personal combat with the Devil; "King Jesus" seated on a milk-white horse with sword and shield in hand. "Ride on, King Jesus," "Ride on, conquering King," "The God I serve is a man of war," the slaves sang. This transformation of Jesus is symptomatic of the slaves' selectivity in choosing those parts of the Bible which were to serve as the basis of their religious consciousness. Howard Thurman, a Negro minister who as a boy had the duty of reading the Bible to his grandmother, was perplexed by her refusal to allow him to read from the Epistles of Paul.

> When at length I asked the reason, she told me that during the days of slavery, the minister (white) on the plantation was always preaching from the Pauline letters—"Slaves, be obedient to your masters," etc. "I vowed to myself," she said, "that if freedom ever came and I learned to read, I would never read that part of the Bible!"

Nor, apparently, did this part of the Scriptures ever constitute a vital element in slave songs or sermons. The emphasis of the spirituals, as Higginson himself noted, was upon the Old Testament and the exploits of the Hebrew children. It is important that Daniel and David and Joshua and Jonah and Moses and Noah, all of whom fill the lines of the spirituals, were delivered in *this* world and delivered in ways which struck the imagination of the slaves. Over and over their songs dwelt upon the spectacle of the Red Sea opening to allow the Hebrew slaves past before inundating the mighty armies of the Pharaoh. They lingered delightedly upon the image of little David humbling the great Goliath with a stone—a pretechnological victory which post-bellum Negroes were to expand upon in their songs of John Henry. They retold in endless variation the stories of the blind and humbled Samson bringing down the mansions of his conquerors; of the ridiculed Noah patiently building the ark which would deliver him from the doom of a mocking world; of the timid Jonah attaining freedom from his confinement through faith. The similarity of these tales to the situation of the slave was too clear for him not to see it; too clear for us to believe that the songs had no worldly content for the black man in bondage. "O my Lord delivered Daniel," the slaves observed, and responded logically: "O why not deliver me, too?"

> *He delivered Daniel from de lion's den,*
> *Jonah from de belly ob de whale,*
> *And de Hebrew children from de fiery furnace,*
> *And why not every man?*

These lines state as clearly as anything can the manner in which the sacred world of the slaves was able to fuse the precedents of the past, the conditions of the present, and the promise of the future into one connected reality. In this respect there was always a latent and symbolic element of protest in the slave's religious songs which frequently became overt and explicit. Frederick Douglass asserted that for him and many of his fellow slaves the song, "O Canaan, sweet Canaan,/I am bound for the land of Canaan," symbolized "something more than a hope of reaching heaven. We meant to reach the *North*, and the North was our Canaan," and he wrote that the lines of another spiritual, "Run to Jesus, shun the danger,/I don't expect to stay much longer here," had a double meaning which first suggested to him the thought of escaping from slavery. Similarly, when the black troops in Higginson's regiment sang:

> *We'll soon be free, [three times]*
> *When de Lord will call us home.*

a young drummer boy explained to him, "Dey think *de Lord* mean for say *de Yankees*." Nor is there any reason to doubt that slaves could have used their songs as a means of secret communication. An ex-slave told Lydia Parrish that when he and his fellow slaves "suspicioned" that one of their number was telling tales to the driver, they would sing lines like the following while working in the field:

> *O Judyas he wuz a 'ceitful man*
> *He went an' betray a mos' innocen' man.*
> *Fo' thirty pieces a silver dat it wuz done*
> *He went in de woods an' e' self he hung.*

And it is possible, as many writers have argued, that such spirituals as the commonly heard "Steal away, steal away, steal away to Jesus!" were used as explicit calls to secret meetings.

But it is not necessary to invest the spirituals with a secular function only at the price of divesting them of their religious content, as Miles Mark Fisher has done. While we may make such clear-cut distinctions, I have tried to show that the slaves did not. For them religion never constituted a simple escape from this world, because their conception of the world was more expansive than modern man's. Nowhere is this better illustrated than during the Civil War itself. While the war gave rise to such new spirituals as "Before I'd be a slave/I'd be buried in my grave,/And go home to my Lord and be saved!" or the popular "Many thousand Go," with its jubilant rejection of all the facets of slave life—"No more peck o' corn for me, . . . No more driver's lash for me, . . . No more pint o' salt for me, . . . No more hundred lash for me, . . . No more mistress' call for me"—the important thing was not that large numbers of slaves now could create new songs which openly expressed their views of slavery; that was to be expected. More significant was the ease with which their old songs fit their new situation.

With so much of their inspiration drawn from the events of the Old Testament and the Book of Revelation, the slaves had long sung of wars, of battles, of the Army of the Lord, of Soldiers of the Cross, of trumpets summoning the faithful, of vanquishing the hosts of evil. These songs especially were, as Higginson put it, "available for camp purposes with very little strain upon their symbolism." "We'll cross de mighty river," his troops sang while marching or rowing,

> *We'll cross de danger water, . . .*
> *O Pharaoh's army drownded!*
> *My army cross over.*

"O blow your trumpet, Gabriel," they sang,

> *Blow your trumpet louder;*
> *And I want dat trumpet to blow me home*
> *To my new Jerusalem.*

But they also found their less overtly militant songs quite as appropriate to warfare. Their most popular and effective marching song was:

> *Jesus call you, Go in de wilderness,*
> *Go in de wilderness, go in de wilderness,*
> *Jesus call you. Go in de wilderness*
> *To wait upon de Lord.*

Black Union soldiers found it no more incongruous to accompany their fight for freedom with the sacred songs of their bondage than they had found it inappropriate as slaves to sing their spirituals while picking cotton or shucking corn. Their religious songs, like their religion itself, was of this world as well as the next.

Slave songs by themselves, of course, do not present us with a definitive key to the life and mind of the slave. They have to be seen within the context of the slave's situation and examined alongside such other cultural materials as folk tales. But slave songs do indicate the need to rethink a number of assumptions that have shaped recent interpretations of slavery, such as the assumption that because slavery eroded the linguistic and institutional side of African life it wiped out almost all the more fundamental aspects of African culture. Culture, certainly, is more than merely the sum total of institutions and language. It is also expressed by something less tangible, which the anthropologist Robert Redfield has called "style of life." People as different as the Lapp and the Bedouin, Redfield has argued, with diverse languages, religions, customs, and institutions, may still share an emphasis on certain virtues and ideals, certain manners of independence and hospitality, general ways of looking upon the world, which give them a similar life style. This argument applies to the West African cultures from which the slaves came. Though they varied widely in language, institutions, gods, and familial patterns, they shared a fundamental outlook toward the past, present, and future and common means of cultural expression which could well have constituted the basis of a sense of community and identity capable of surviving the impact of slavery.

Slave songs present us with abundant evidence that in the structure of their music and dance, in the uses to which music was put, in the survival of the oral tradition, in the retention of such practices as spirit possession which often accompanied the creation of spirituals, and in the ways in which the slaves expressed their new religion, important elements of their shared African heritage remained alive not just as quaint cultural vestiges but as vitally creative elements of slave culture. This could never have happened if slavery was, as Professor Elkins maintains, a system which so completely closed in around the slave, so totally penetrated his personality structure as to infantalize him and reduce him to a kind of *tabula rasa* upon which the white man could write what he chose.

Slave songs provide us with the beginnings of a very different kind of hypothesis: that the preliterate, premodern Africans, with their sacred world view, were so imperfectly acculturated into the secular American society into which they were thrust, were so completely denied access to the ideology and dreams which formed the core of the consciousness of other Americans, that they were forced to fall back upon the only cultural frames of reference that made any sense to them and gave them any feeling of security. I use the word "forced" advisedly. Even if the slaves had had the opportunity to enter fully into the life of the larger society, they might still have chosen to retain and perpetuate certain elements of their African heritage. But the point is that they really had no choice. True acculturation was denied to most slaves. The alternatives were either to remain in a state of cultural limbo, divested of the old cultural patterns but not allowed to adopt those of their new homeland—which in the long run is no alternative at all—or to cling to as many as possible of the old ways of thinking and acting. The slaves' oral tradition, their music, and their religious outlook served this latter function and constituted a cultural refuge at least potentially capable of protecting their personalities from some of the worst ravages of the slave system.

The argument of Professors Tannenbaum and Elkins that the Protestant churches in the United States did not act as a buffer between the slave and his master is persuasive enough, but it betrays a modern preoccupation with purely institutional arrangements. Religion is more than an institution, and because Protestant churches failed to protect the slave's inner being from the incursions of the slave system, it does not follow that the spiritual message of Protestantism failed as well. Slave songs are a testament to the ways in which Christianity provided slaves with the precedents, heroes, and future promise that allowed them to transcend the purely temporal bonds of the Peculiar Institution.

Historians have frequently failed to perceive the full importance of this because they have not taken the slave's religiosity seriously enough. A people cannot create a music as forceful and striking as slave music out of a mere uninternalized anodyne. Those who have argued that Negroes did not oppose slavery in any meaningful way are writing from a modern, political context. What they really mean is that the slaves found no *political* means to oppose slavery. But slaves, to borrow Professor Hobsbawm's term, were prepolitical beings in a pre-political situation. Within their frame of reference there were other—and from the point of view of personality development, not necessarily less effective—means of escape and opposition. If mid-twentieth-century historians have difficulty perceiving the sacred universe created by slaves as a serious alternative to the societal system created by southern slave-holders, the problem may be the historians' and not the slaves'.

Above all, the study of slave songs forces the historian to move out of his own culture, in which music plays a peripheral role, and offers him the opportunity to understand the ways in which black slaves were able to perpetuate much of the centrality and functional impor-tance that music had for their African ancestors. In the concluding lines of his perceptive study of primitive song, C. M. Bowra has written:

> Primitive song is indispensable to those who practice it. . . . they can-not do without song, which both formulates and answers their nagging questions, enables them to pursue action with zest and confidence, brings them into touch with gods and spirits, and makes them feel less strange in the natural world. . . . it gives to them a solid centre in what other-wise would be almost chaos, and a continuity in their being, which would too easily dissolve before the calls of the implacable present . . . through its words men, who might otherwise give in to the malice of circumstances, find their old powers revived or new powers stirring in them, and through these life itself is sustained and renewed and fulfilled.

This, I think, sums up concisely the function of song for the slave. Without a general understanding of that function, without a specific understanding of the content and meaning of slave song, there can be no full comprehension of the effects of slavery upon the slave or the meaning of the society from which slaves emerged at emancipation.

18

The Economics of Slavery
in the Ante Bellum South

ALFRED H. CONRAD AND JOHN R. MEYER

Those historians—particularly U. B. Phillips—who have regarded the Civil War as a "needless conflict" have long held that slavery was an unprofitable institution which if left alone would have disappeared. Other historians—notably Lewis C. Gray and Kenneth Stampp—have disagreed. The most impressive dissent, however, comes from econometricians Alfred H. Conrad and John R. Meyer whose conclusions have stood up well for a decade and a half. These conclusions have been closely examined and basically confirmed by a spate of other econometricians. Utilizing economic theory and statistical concepts, Conrad and Meyer show clearly that slavery below the Mason-Dixon line was alive and well.

. . .

II. THE ECONOMIC RETURNS ON SLAVEHOLDING

From the standpoint of the entrepreneur making an investment in slaves, the basic problems involved in determining profitability are analytically the same as those met in determining the returns from any other kind of capital investment. The acquisition of a slave represented the tying-up

From the *Journal of Political Economy* 66 (1958):98–122. Copyright by the Aldine Publishing Co. Reprinted with omissions by permission of Aldine-Atherton, Inc.

of capital in what has appropriately been called a roundabout method of production. Like the purchase of any capital, a slave purchase was made in the anticipation of gaining higher returns than are available

TABLE 1   Expectation of Life at Birth in Years for White and Colored Males, United States, 1850

State	White	Colored
Massachusetts	38.3	39.75
Maryland	41.8	38.47
Louisiana	—	28.89

from less time-consuming or capital-using methods. This model is particularly applicable in the present case, because slave investments, like the forests or wine cellars of classic capital theory, produced a natural increase with the passage of time.

Investment returns are properly computed by using the capital-value formula, $y = x_t / (1 + r)^t$, where y is the cost of the investment, x_t is realized return t years hence, and r is the internal rate of return or what Keynes called the marginal efficiency of capital. When returns are realized over a number of years, the total earnings of the capital can be found by simple summation in this formula. The criterion for a profitable investment is that the marginal efficiency exceeds the interest rate (in the Keynesian terminology). From this statement of the problem, it is obvious that the following information is needed to determine the profitability of slaveholding from the slaveholder's point of view: (a) the longevity of slaves; (b) the costs of slaves and any necessary accompanying capital investments; (c) the interest rate; and (d) the annual returns from slave productive activities, defined to include both field labor and procreation. We shall consider each of these in turn and then put the pieces together to determine the approximate profitability of slave investments.

A. The Longevity of Slaves

Slave longevity corresponds, of course, to the period for which a slave investment was made. We shall limit attention here to the purchase of twenty-year-old Negroes in the immediate pre–Civil War era, and we shall deal only with the typical or median life-expectancy for this group. These limits greatly simplify the problem and still include the vast majority of relevant cases.

There is a scarcity of good longevity data for the period, but it is known that in 1850 Negroes lived just about as long as whites in the two states for which acceptable data are available. The available figures are given in Table 1. There is doubt about the quality of these estimates because they show Negroes in New England expecting a longer life than whites. This is not the case today, nor was it the case in 1900, when the first good data became available. Also, Negroes would appear in this table to have had a longer life-expectancy in 1850 than they had fifty years later. Although surprising, this may be prefectly correct. Negroes could have received better care under slavery, because plantation owners had an economic interest in keeping Negroes alive. Furthermore, the Negro in the period after emancipation generally lacked the means to participate equally in the new medical advances, in contrast to his position of roughly equal medical care in the period before 1860. . . . Looking back at the data in Table 1, there is no reason to expect twenty-year-old Massachusetts Negroes to have a lower life-expectancy than Massachusetts whites, though both clearly lived longer than southern Negroes of the period. Taking all these factors into account, an estimate of thirty to thirty-five years of life-expectancy seems most plausible for twenty-year-old Negroes working as prime cotton hands on southern plantations in the period 1830–50, and a thirty-year life-expectancy will generally be used in the succeeding calculations.

B. The Cost of the Capital Investment

The capital investment in plantation operations included investment both in slaves and in the land and equipment on which the slaves worked. The price of slaves fluctuated widely, being subject to the waves of speculation in cotton. Furthermore, the price depended, among other things, upon the age, sex, disposition, degree of training, and condition of the slave. In order to hold these variables roughly constant, we shall confine our present analysis to eighteen–twenty-year-old prime field hands and wenches. Some summary data on slave prices were compiled by U. B. Phillips on the basis of available market quotations, bills of transactions, and reports of sales in most of the important slave markets of Georgia. His estimates of the best averages for several years between 1828 and 1860 are presented in Table 2. On the basis of these data it would appear that both the median and the mean price for prime field hands were in the range of from $900 to $950 in the period 1830–50. Because of the substantial price increases in the last ante bellum decade, these averages would run substantially higher for the entire slave period after 1830; specifically, about $1,100–$1,200. Since the prices of field wenches usually averaged about $100–$150 less than those of hands,

TABLE 2   Estimated Average Slave Prices in Georgia, Selected Years, 1828–60

Year	Average Price of Prime Field Hands
1828	$ 700
1835	900
1837	1,300
1839	1,000
1840	700
1844	600
1848	900
1851	1,050
1853	1,200
1859	1,650
1860	1,800

they were probably in the range of from $800 to $850 in the years 1830–50 and between $900 and $1,100 for the entire period 1830–60. . . .

As for the non-slave capital, by far the most important was the investment in land. Since the land values varied widely, depending on the quality of the soil and the type of agriculture pursued, experimental control on our calculations requires that attention be confined to cotton culture. The range in cotton-land prices in the period 1830–50 is fairly well bracketed by the $6 per acre paid for poor upland pine land in Alabama and the $35–$40 per acre paid for cleared Mississippi alluvium. . . . There was also variation in the number of acres needed per hand. Counting garden land and woodlots, as well as productive fields, the usual number of acres per field hand was between 15 and 35, the exact figure depending primarily on the quality of the land. This meant an original land investment per hand of somewhere between $90 and $1,400, with $180–$600 encompassing the vast majority of instances.

The price per acre was, of course, related to the durability of the land, which immediately introduces a further dimension into the capital cost problem. Cotton lands lasted between ten and forty years, depending upon original quality and fertilization. In the land-rich, labor-scarce economy of the nineteenth-century United States, fertilization was a rare practice. Furthermore, planters clearly had the choice between operating less capital intensively on low-durability land or more capital intensively on high-durability land. For example, poor Alabama pine land might be expected to last ten years and require 30–35 acres per hand; this meant that $180–$210 had to be reinvested every ten years to utilize the slave force properly. Assuming thirty-year slave longevity and an 8 per cent interest rate, the present value of the land investment for one slave's lifetime was $302–$350 for an upland-pine operation. On the alluvium, by contrast, the land would typically outlast the slave in usefulness; assuming, though, that both lasted the same number of years and that 16 acres of cleared and 10 of uncleared land (at $10 per acre) were used per hand, a total land investment of $660 per hand is indicated. This difference in value of the land investment was presumably a function of different yields. At any rate, the typical case was probably halfway between these two, involving a land investment of about $450 per hand.

Similar problems arise in estimating the investment in plows, gins, wagons, cabins, and miscellaneous implements. Such investments ran about $25 per hand in original outlay and had to be renewed every fifteen years. This gives a total present value in such items (again on the assumption of thirty-year slave longevity and 8 per cent interest) of about $33. A small investment was required in work horses and oxen, but in this case the stock was likely to be self-replenishing, reducing the costs to interest on the investment at most. Putting all these capital costs together indicates that $1,400–$1,450 was a fair approximation of the typical or average total investment per male slave in terms of present values. The range ran from $1,250 to $1,650.

C. The Interest Rate

Determining the relevant rate of interest—the rate with which the cotton-slave returns must be compared—is perhaps empirically the easiest and conceptually the most difficult of the tasks in computing the economic returns on slave investments. While there is a relative abundance of data on interest rates in this period, none corresponds exactly to the desired rate. In a strict conceptual sense, the relevant rate of interest is that which plantation owners or other investors in southern agriculture could have earned on their money in other pursuits if slavery had gone out of existence. This is difficult to arrive at on the basis of historical evidence, since it assumes circumstances contrary to the facts. The closest substitute would be earnings on other investments that were *least* dependent upon cotton and southern agriculture. Given the importance of cotton in the American economy prior to the Civil War and the general interdependence of economic systems, even in so primitive an economy as that of the United States in the first half of the nineteenth century, it is difficult to find any conceptually correct figures. The figures that follow are offered in complete recognition of their fallibility on this count, yet they are probably as good as are available.

In the contemporary chronicles it is obvious that southerners and northerners alike considered 6–8 per cent a reasonable rate of return and a reasonable asking price for loans. Figures in this range are repeated over and over again and must be given some significance. This is all the more true because these figures are consistent with reported rates charged on prime commercial paper and other debt instruments in the principal money markets before 1860. The prime commercial rates charged in New York and Boston in the period 1830–65, shown in Table 3, illustrate this point. Similarly, the rates on New York Stock Exchange call loans, New England municipal issues, and rail debentures, shown in Table 4, fall for the most part within, or below, this same 6–8 per cent range. While the average annual rates fluctuated widely in the years between 1830 and 1850 and the distribution of rates is skewed, the central tendency was clearly close to the 6–8 per cent range. Specifically, the New York average was 9.2 per cent, the median was 8.0, and the mode was between 6.0 and 7.0 per cent. Because of the skew, the median rate of 8 per cent is probably the best measure of central tendency for the present analysis.

The interest rates for the Civil War years, although they lie somewhat outside the time period of this investigation, may be conceptually the most pertinent figures in Tables 3 and 4. The Civil War represents as good an approximation as is achievable of a controlled experiment to determine investment returns in the North under complete divorce from the plantation economy. . . .

The realization on short-term, high-quality commercial paper might normally be expected to be below the realization on longer-term investments of the type represented by ownership of a cotton plantation. However, in the period 1840–60 banking practices were rather lax and potentially or actually inflationary, as indicated by the recurrent financial panics of the time. Such unstable financial conditions may have given equity a premium that it might otherwise not have enjoyed. Furthermore, the existence of well-established slave and real estate markets made most plantation investments highly negotiable, thereby reducing the time commitment in such investments. There are some reports available on the realizable returns on longer-term investments; for example, Table 4 presents the rates at which some municipal and railroad development bonds were floated in the prewar period. In addition, [Lance E.] Davis reports returns of 16.76 per cent on total capital stock in the 1844–48 period and 5.75 per cent in the 1848–53 period for nine of the larger and more prosperous Massachusetts textile firms.

From these many disparate sources it seems safe to estimate that a wholesale withdrawal of capital from slave operations in southern agriculture would not have depressed marginal investment returns in the

TABLE 3   Average Annual Interest Rates on Prime Commercial Paper from 1831 to 1860

	New York *	Boston †		New York *	Boston †
1831	5.1	6.5	1849	10.0	12.0
1832	5.3	6.5	1850	8.0	7.5
1833	6.9	6.0	1851	9.7	7.0
1834	14.6	14.5	1852	6.6	6.0
1835	7.0	5.0	1853	10.2	10.7
1836	18.4	20.3	1854	10.4	12.0
1837	14.1	6.0	1855	8.9	7.0
1838	9.0	7.0	1856	8.9	10.0
1839	13.2	9.0	1857	12.9	9.0
1840	7.8	6.0	1858	5.0	4.5
1841	6.9	6.0	1859	6.8	7.0
1842	8.1	7.8	1860	7.0	6.0
1843	4.5	3.0	1861	6.5	—
1844	4.9	5.0	1862	5.8	—
1845	6.0	6.0	1863	5.0	—
1846	8.3	8.0	1864	6.0	—
1847	9.6	6.0	1865	7.6	—
1848	15.1	15.0			

* Two-name sixty–ninety-day paper.
† "First class three to six months, bankable paper." The rate reported is either one sustained for a major portion of the year or an arithmetic average.

TABLE 4   Yields on Various Economic Activities, 1857–65

Year	New England Municipal Bond Yields (January Index Numbers)	Call Money Rates at the New York Stock Exchange (Arithmetic Average of Months)	Railroad Bond Yields (January Average for All Railroads)
1857	5.2	9.3	8.1
1858	5.3	4.2	8.7
1859	4.8	5.4	7.4
1860	4.8	6.0	7.5
1861	4.9	5.8	7.4
1862	5.2	5.2	7.5
1863	4.4	6.2	5.6
1864	4.7	6.6	6.0
1865	5.2	6.2	6.2

prewar United States economy much below 4.5–5 per cent. Similarly, it seems safe to conclude that the withdrawn capital could not have expected to earn returns much in excess of 8 per cent. Between these high and low estimates, a return of 6 per cent seems the most probable and, therefore, appropriate for comparison in our model.

D. Annual Returns

The appropriate return figure to enter in the capital equation is the net return on current account, or the difference between gross sales and all out-of-pocket expenses. The expense deduction is limited to out-of-pocket expenses, because all the book charges that complicate the usual accounting procedures are taken into account in the process of constructing the capital cost estimate.

Estimates of plantation expenses have been taken primarily from three excellent, exhaustive records of the available material: J. L. Watkins' *The Cost of Cotton Production*, Lewis C. Gray's *History of Agriculture in the Southern United States to 1860*, and Kenneth Stampp's *The Peculiar Institution*. A reasonably thorough check of these secondary sources against some primary sources and against one another for consistency indicates that these surveys have been reliably and accurately made. A digest of the estimates is presented in Table 5. The total

TABLE 5   Typical Annual Out-of-Pocket Costs of Maintaining and Working Prime Field Hands on Southern Plantations in the Period 1840–60

A. Food and Clothing

(1) Out-of-pocket costs where most food was produced on plantation and most clothing was hand-sewn	$ 2.50–$ 3.46
(2) Cash costs if purchased	$25.00–$40.00
(3) Out-of-pocket costs where some ready-made clothing and meat, fish, and other food "delicacies" were purchased	$ 7.00–$10.00
B. Medical care	$ 1.50–$ 2.00
C. Taxes	$ 0.39–$ 1.20
D. Supervision	$ 5.00–$15.00
Total, based on means of the estimates above and option (3) under A	$20.00–$21.00

figure of $20–$21 annual out-of-pocket slave maintenance costs will be used in subsequent calculations. These costs are to be subtracted from the annual gross return figures on slave activities.

For a male field hand the returns considered will be limited to the sales of products realized from his field labor; in the case of a female hand, an addition must be made for the returns realized on the labor and sale of her children. Because of these basic differences in the production function for the two sexes, they will be treated separately.

For the male field hand, limited to the returns on his field labor, the gross proceeds will depend on the price of cotton and the quantity of his annual output. The output, in turn, will be crucially dependent on the quality of the land on which the slave was employed and, to a much lesser degree, upon the quality and amount of capital goods with which he was equipped. The figures in Table 6 illustrate the possible variation

TABLE 6   Reported Yields per Prime Field Hand

Location	Year	Bales per Hand
South Carolina coastal	1849	4⅓
Mississippi (De Soto County)	1849	4
Unidentified	1844	7
Alabama (Cherokee County)	1855	4
Mississippi (Vicksburg area)	1855	8
New Southwest land	1850's	5
South Carolina upland	1852	3
Texas	1859	10
Arkansas River	1859	7

in productivity per hand. These estimates agree with frequent statements in contemporary journals that in the typical case a prime field hand could be expected to raise from 3.5 to 4 bales per year. The maximum seems to have been 7–8 bales on the best lands, and 2–3 bales was the minimum on the poorest land.

The relevant price of cotton for valuing these yields is the net price realized at the farm (in order that price and cost data be comparable). This means that export prices at the major ports must be adjusted downward by the amount of freight, insurance, storage, drayage, and factor's commission charges that were properly chargeable to the planter. Gray estimates that these costs generally ran between $2.50 and $4 per bale. Somewhat more detailed information is presented by Watkins, whose findings are summarized in Table 7. The Gray and Watkins findings are fully compatible, and a marketing cost of from 0.7 to 0.8 cent per pound appears to be properly deductible from the export price in determining the price f.o.b. farm.

TABLE 7   Cotton Marketing Costs per Bale Chargeable to Planters in 1840

	At Mobile	At Charleston
Freight in	$1.50 *	$1.25 †
Drayage	0.125	0.13
Weighing	0.125	0.06
Storage (1 month)	0.20	0.24
Insurance (1 month)	‡	0.25
Factor's commission (2–2.5 per cent)	0.80	0.60–1.61
Total per bale	$2.75	$3.03 §
Total cents per pound ‖	0.69	0.76 §

* By river.
† From Columbia.
‡ Not reported. Note that the higher (Charleston) figures have been used in the profit computations to follow.
§ Assuming $1.10 factor's commission.
‖ Four hundred pounds to a bale.

The export price itself fluctuated widely over the period. As can be seen from Table 8, New Orleans cotton prices averaged almost 50 per cent higher in the thirties and fifties than they did in the depressed forties. Even in the forties, however, the export price level was sufficient to insure an average net farm price of not much less than 6.5 cents. Since prices at any given port were usually equal to the Liverpool price

TABLE 8   Weighted Yearly Average Prices of Short-Staple Cotton (Usually Louisiana or Mississippi Middling or Second Grade) at New Orleans for the Crop Years 1830–60

Year	Price	Year	Price	Year	Price
1830	8.4	1840	9.1	1850	11.7
1831	9.0	1841	7.8	1851	7.4
1832	10.0	1842	5.7	1852	9.1
1833	11.2	1843	7.5	1853	8.8
1834	15.5	1844	5.5	1854	8.4
1835	15.2	1845	6.8	1855	9.1
1836	13.3	1846	9.9	1856	12.4
1837	9.0	1847	7.0	1857	11.2
1838	12.4	1848	5.8	1858	11.5
1839	7.9	1849	10.8	1859	10.8
				1860	11.1
Decade average price	11.2		7.6		11.2

minus ocean shipping rates, the New York and Mobile prices were generally somewhat higher. Taking all this into consideration, 7–8 cents seems a realistic and conservative estimate of the average realized farm price for the whole period.

Finally, the price, productivity, and capital cost estimates must be combined in order to compute the actual profitability of investments in male slave labor for cotton production. Capital costs must be included in the computations, since the present value of the capital outlay will depend, as was previously shown, upon the rate of return. In lieu of a single computation, several cases involving different capital outlays, yields per hand, and realized farm prices have been constructed; the results are given in Table 9. Cases 1, 2, and 3 are the most typical; cases 4, 5, and 6 represent the situation on somewhat better land. These first six cases, with returns ranging between 4½ and 8 per cent, encompass the majority of ante bellum cotton plantation operations. Cases 7, 8, and 9 represent the minimum of profitability or what might be expected on poor upland pine country or the worked-out lands of the eastern seaboard. By contrast, cases 10, 11, and 12 show the upper range of profitability which was realized on the best lands of the new Southwest, the Mississippi alluvium, and the better South Carolina and Alabama plantations.

The calculations in Table 9 represent an estimate of potential returns for the relatively simple production function of prime field hands. With the female hand or prime field wench the situation becomes much more complex: in addition to her productivity, the productivity of her

TABLE 9   Realized Returns on Prime Field Hands under Various Hypothesized Conditions

Case	Present Value of Capital Outlay per Hand	Yield per Hand (Bales)	Average Net Farm Price (Cents)	Approximate Return (Per Cent)
1	$1,350–$1,400	3¾	7	4.5
2	$1,350–$1,400	3¾	8	5.2
3	$1,350–$1,400	3¾	9	6.5
4	$1,600	4½	7	5.0
5	$1,600	4½	8	7.0
6	$1,600	4½	9	8.0
7	$1,250–$1,300	3	7	2.2
8	$1,250–$1,300	3	8	3.9
9	$1,250–$1,300	3	9	5.4
10	$1,700	7	7	10.0
11	$1,700	7	8	12.0
12	$1,700	7	9	13.0

children and the returns realized on their sale must be considered. Similarly, the extra cost of maintaining the children and the maternity and nursery costs associated with their birth must also be counted.

To make the calculations in this rather complex situation manageable, the following assumptions will be made.

1. Each prime field wench produced five to ten marketable children during her lifetime. . . .

2. The prime field wench was one-half to two-thirds as productive as a prime field hand when she was actually at work in the field. . . .

3. The wench's children began to be productive in field labor at age six, with the males becoming self-sustaining by age nine (that is, they then earned the adult maintenance charge of $20 per year), while females became self-sustaining by age thirteen. . . . After reaching a self-sustaining status at these ages, it is further assumed that their productivity continued to rise linearly until the children reached their full adult productivity at age eighteen. . . .

4. The typical wench had as many male as female children. . . .

5. Nursery costs were about $50 per successful pregnancy.

Using these assumptions, hypothetical annual returns for a typical prime field wench can be determined; such calculations are shown in Tables 10 and 11. In constructing these tables, it was assumed that the prime field wench and her children worked on land that returned 3.75 bales of cotton per year for every prime male hand employed; that is, the land is of approximately average fertility. Also, a 7.5 cent net farm price for cotton has been used. The first successful pregnancy has been assumed to occur in the second year after the prime field wench is purchased; further successful pregnancies occur at regular two-year intervals. The children were sold at age eighteen, and the annual maintenance cost per child was assessed at the rate of $10 per year for one–six-year-old, $15 per year for seven–twelve-year-olds and $20 per year, the full adult maintenance cost, for those age thirteen and over. The maternity costs have been included in the annual charge for the children's upkeep; similarly, the $16 decline every other year for the first few years in the wench's own field returns represents the allowance for time lost because of pregnancy. Rates of return were computed on the streams of net returns shown in the far right-hand columns of the tables on the assumption that the total investment in the prime field wench, land, and equipment amounts to $1,200–$1,300, figures which would appear to be very good averages. A rate of return of 8.1 per cent was thus obtained for the mother bearing ten children and a return of 7.1 per cent for the mother with five children. . . .

TABLE 10   Annual Returns on a Prime Field Wench Investment (Working on Land Which Yielded 3.75 Bales per Prime Male Field Hand, Assuming a 7.5-Cent Net Farm Price for Cotton and Ten "Salable" Children Born to Every Wench)

Year from Purchase Date	Personal Field Returns	Child Field Returns	Child Sale Returns	Personal Upkeep	Child Upkeep	Net Returns
1	$56	......	....	$20	....	$ 36
2	40	......	....	20	$ 50	−30
3	56	......	....	20	10	26
4	40	......	....	20	60	−40
5	56	......	....	20	20	16
6	40	......	....	20	70	−50
7	56	......	....	20	30	6
8	40	$ 3.75	....	20	80	−56.25
9	56	7.50	....	20	45	−1.50
10	40	15.00	....	20	95	−50.00
11	56	22.50	....	20	60	−1.50
12	40	37.50	....	20	110	−52.50
13	56	52.50	....	20	75	13.50
14	40	75.00	....	20	130	−35.00
15	56	97.50	....	20	95	47.50
16	40	127.50	....	20	150	−2.50
17	56	157.50	....	20	115	78.50
18	40	195.00	....	20	165	55.00
19	56	232.50	....	20	130	134.30
20	40	195.00	$875	20	170	920.00
21	56	232.50	....	20	130	138.50
22	56	195.00	875	20	120	986.00
23	56	232.50	....	20	120	148.50
24	56	195.00	875	20	110	996.00
25	56	232.50	....	20	110	158.00
26	56	195.00	875	20	100	1,006.00
27	56	232.50	....	20	100	168.00
28	56	187.50	875	20	90	1,008.50
29	56	225.00	...	20	90	171.00
30	56	180.00	875	20	80	1,011.00
31	...	210.00	....	...	80	130.00
32	...	157.50	875	...	60	972.50
33	...	180.00	....	...	60	120.00
34	...	120.00	875	...	40	955.00
35	...	135.00	....	...	40	95.00
36	...	67.50	875	...	20	922.50
37	...	75.00	....	...	20	55.00
38	...	......	875	...	....	875.00

TABLE 11   Annual Returns on a Prime Field Wench Investment (Working on Land Which Yielded 3.75 Bales per Prime Male Field Hand, Assuming a 7.5-Cent Net Farm Price for Cotton and Five "Salable" Children Born to Every Wench)

Year from Purchase Date	Personal Field Returns	Child Field Returns	Child Sale Returns	Personal Upkeep	Child Upkeep	Net Returns
1	$56			$20		$ 36
2	40			20	$50	−30
3	56			20	10	26
4	40			20	60	−40
5	56			20	20	16
6	40			20	70	−50
7	56			20	30	6
8	40	$ 3.75		20	80	−56.25
9	56	7.50		20	45	−1.50
10	40	15.00		20	95	−50.00
11	56	22.50		20	60	−1.50
12	56	37.50		20	60	13.50
13	56	52.50		20	65	23.50
14	56	75.00		20	65	46.00
15	56	97.50		20	75	58.50
16	56	127.50		20	75	88.50
17	56	157.50		20	85	108.50
18	56	191.25		20	85	142.25
19	56	225.00		20	90	171.00
20	56	180.00	$875	20	75	1,016.00
21	56	210.00		20	75	171.00
22	56	157.50	875	20	60	1,008.50
23	56	180.00		20	60	156.00
24	56	120.00	875	20	40	991.00
25	56	135.00		20	40	131.00
26	56	67.50	875	20	20	958.50
27	56	75.00		20	20	91.00
28	56		875	20		911.00
29	56			20		36.00
30	56			20		36.00

. . . Slavery was apparently about as remunerative as alternative employments to which slave capital might have been put. Large or excessive returns were clearly limited to a few fortunate planters, but apparently none suffered excessively either. This general sharing in the prosperity was more or less guaranteed, moreover, if proper market mechanisms existed so that slaves could be bred and reared on the poorest of land and then be sold to those owning the best. Slavery in the immediate ante bellum years was, therefore, an economically viable institution in virtually all areas of the South as long as slaves could be expeditiously and economically transferred from one sector to another.

III. REPRODUCTION, ALLOCATION, AND SLAVE MARKETS

It thus remains to be determined whether an efficient supply mechanism —efficient in both its generative and its allocative functions—existed in the ante bellum South. That the slave force might reproduce itself was not sufficient; there must also have been a capital market capable of getting the labor to the areas where production was expanding if slavery was to be profitable. It will be useful to introduce the secondary propositions by stating several arguments which together form the orthodox opposition to the present hypothesis. The arguments follow . . .: (i) slaves are notoriously inefficient and unwilling workers; (ii) slave property, unlike wage labor, must be supported in the years before and after the slave is economically productive; (iii) slaveholding absorbed plantation earnings; (iv) slave economies are constantly threatened by decline because they cannot in general maintain the number of slaves; and (v) capitalization of the labor force inhibits the efficient allocation of labor.

The first and second of these arguments are implicitly tested in the computation of the rate of return on slave capital. We are not concerned with efficiency per se, however, that might be measured, or with the efficiency of slaves as opposed to free white laborers. The more sophisticated version of this efficiency argument—that slave ineptness forced the planters to use a particularly wasteful form of agriculture—is probably untestable because of the difficulties of identification where impetus or motives are being considered. It might be suggested as a partial answer, however, that extensive farming was not peculiarly a characteristic of slave agriculture or even of plantation cotton culture. It was common to all North American colonial agriculture and, as late as the end of the nineteenth century, was reputed to be characteristic of farming in the Northwest wheat lands. It is, generally, a salient feature of agriculture where labor is scarce relative to land. But, insofar as slaves were inefficient, the inefficiency must be reflected in the returns computed in our model. Similarly, the costs of maintaining slaves in infancy and dotage are accounted for in our cost of production.

The third argument—that the South lost from the payment of interest and the constant enhancement of prices (and, therefore, overcapitalization of the labor force)—rests in part upon two misapprehensions, attributable to U. B. Phillips: (1) that capitalization involves a net loss through the payment of interest and (2) that slaves were, somehow, a fictitious form of wealth. We have already shown that slave capital earned returns at least equal to those earned by other contemporary forms of capital. For the overcapitalization part of the argument, it remains to be shown that slave prices did not run away from cotton values.

The last two of the assertions state the negative of our principal secondary hypothesis, which is that an efficient market system existed for the supply of slaves to the rapidly growing cotton industry of the Southwest from the exhausted land of the Old South. It will be shown below that the slave population, in all but the Louisiana sugar area, more than reproduced itself. It will be further shown that the border states were not being depleted to provide for western needs but that only the natural increase was being exported. Finally, avoiding the emotion-wracked testimony of the time, we will attempt to demonstrate the existence of regional specialization and an efficient market by comparing the demographic composition of the cotton and border states and by examining the price behavior in the market for Negro slaves.

A. The Reproduction of the Slave Labor Force

. . . The ante bellum cotton-slave economy of the southern states managed to maintain and allocate its labor supply by a system of regional specialization which produced slaves on the worn-out land of the Old South and the border states for export to the high-yield cotton land of the Mississippi and Red River valleys. For the whole nation the Negro rate of increase in the six decades before the Civil War was only slightly below the rate for the white population; for most of the period, the slave rate was very much above that for free Negroes. In the South the disparity between Negro and white rates of increase is in favor of the Negro rate; considering the relative rates of immigration of whites and Negroes after the first decade of the nineteenth century, the discrepancy in natural increase is even more striking. The evidence in Table 12 does not admit of any doubt that the slave population was capable of producing a steady supply of labor for the plantation economy.

B. Slave Markets and Allocation

The more important issue, however, is whether or not the slave force could be allocated efficiently. The natural rate of increase was more than sufficient in the Old South to meet the needs of agriculture in the region, but in the West it was less than sufficient to meet the demands for increased cotton production. By direct export and by the

TABLE 12   Percentage Decennial Increase in White and Negro Population, 1790–1860

Increase During Preceding Ten Years

Census Year	Total	White	Negro Total	Slave	Free
1800	35.1	35.8	32.3	28.1	82.2
1810	36.4	36.1	37.5	33.1	71.9
1820	33.1	34.2	28.6	29.1	25.3
1830	33.5	33.9	31.4	30.6	36.8
1840	32.7	34.7	23.4	23.8	20.9
1850	35.9	37.7	26.6	28.8	12.5
1860	35.6	37.7	22.1	23.4	12.3

The sharp declines in the rate of increase for slaves in the decades ending in 1840 and 1860 probably reflect the generation cycle following the increase in importations, mostly of mature Negroes, in the years just prior to 1808.

migration of planters with their work forces, the eastern areas supplied the needs of the Southwest. In every decade before the Civil War, the increase of slaves in the cotton states was much above and in the Atlantic and border states much below the rate of increase for the whole slave population. Indeed, in the decades ending in 1840 and 1860, the net rate of population increase in the Old South was only slightly above the level sufficient to maintain the population at a constant level, 4.5 per cent and 7.1 per cent (see Table 13). From 1790 to 1850 the increase of slaves in

TABLE 13   Percentage Rate of Population Increase, by Race, in the Cotton and Border States, 1790–1860

Decade Ending	Cotton States * White	Negro	Border States † White	Negro
1800	42.9	47.4	27.9	24.4
1810	37.5	61.3	23.5	23.4
1820	38.8	48.0	19.5	15.5
1830	40.0	46.8	19.0	14.0
1840	31.3	37.6	21.1	4.5
1850	34.1	35.6	34.5	11.0
1860	27.6	29.0	39.2	7.1

* North Carolina, South Carolina, Georgia, Florida, Alabama, Mississippi, Louisiana, Texas, Arkansas, and Tennessee.
† Delaware, Maryland, District of Columbia, Virginia, West Virginia, Kentucky, and Missouri.

the Atlantic states was just 2 per cent per annum, while in the Gulf states (including Florida), Arkansas, and Tennessee the rate was 18 per cent per annum. . . . The slaveowners of the border states, consciously or unconsciously, were engaged in a specialized breeding operation, producing chattel labor for the growing Southwest. . . . It is clear that sales of slaves provided an important capital gain for the exporting states. . . .

The existence of such specialization is evident in the demographic composition of the cotton and breeding areas and in the price behavior in the markets for slaves. Table 14 demonstrates that the selling states

TABLE 14   Slave Population by Age (Per Cent)

| Age (Years) | Total | 1860 | | Total | 1850 | |
		Selling States *	Buying States †		Selling States *	Buying States †
Under 15	44.8	45.6	43.8	44.9	45.6	44.3
15–19	11.4	11.5	11.4	11.1	11.3	11.0
20–29	17.6	16.5	18.9	18.0	17.0	18.9
30–39	11.7	10.7	11.8	11.3	10.5	12.1
40–49	36.4	34.4	38.1	36.4	34.6	38.1
50 and over	7.5	8.5	6.7	7.5	8.5	6.6

* Virginia, Maryland, Delaware, South Carolina, Missouri, Kentucky, District of Columbia.
† Georgia, Alabama, Mississippi, Florida, Texas, Louisiana.

contained, in 1850 and 1860, a greater proportion of children under fifteen years and a substantially greater proportion of slaves above the age of fifty than did the buying states. While the proportions are not great enough to characterize the selling states as a great nursery, the age composition is in the direction which our hypothesis would lead one to expect. The relationship between the prices of men and women in the slave market, when compared with the ratio of hiring rates for male and female field hands, gives an even stronger indication that the superior usefulness of females of breeding age was economically recognized. The relative hiring rates for men and women in 1860, shown in Table 15, can be taken as a measure of their relative values in the field.

To compare to these rates, we have purchase prices of male and female slaves, in the same markets, in 1859 and 1860. The purchase prices should reflect the relative usefulness of the sexes for field work. More than this, however, if there is any additional value to slave women

TABLE 15   Annual Hiring Rates for Male and Female Slaves (Including Rations and Clothing), by States, 1860

State	Men	Women	Ratio (Men: Women)
Virginia	$105	$ 46	2.28
North Carolina	110	49	2.25
South Carolina	103	55	1.87
Georgia	124	75	1.65
Florida	139	80	1.74
Alabama	138	89	1.55
Mississippi	166	100	1.66
Louisiana	171	120	1.43
Texas	166	109	1.52
Arkansas	170	108	1.57
Tennessee	121	63	1.92

—for breeding purposes, presumably—there should be a premium in the form of a narrower price differential than is found in the hiring rates. . . . Table 16 includes age designations and, when available, a description of the grade or class represented in the average price. This evidence is a striking confirmation of the validity of the model. In every case but

TABLE 16   Selected Prices of Male and Female Slaves, 1859 and 1860

State (Year)	Age	Condition	Male Price	Female Price	Ratio
Virginia (1859)	17–20	Best	$1,350–$1,425	$1,275–$1,325	1.07
South Carolina		Prime	$1,325		1.03
		Wench		$1,283	
South Carolina (1859)		Field hand	$1,555		.91
		Girl		$1,705	
Georgia	21	Best field hand	$1,990		.88
	17	(9 mo. inf.)		$2,150	
Georgia (1859)		Prime, young	$1,300		1.04
		Cotton hand, houseservant		$1,250	
Alabama (1859)	19		$1,635		1.37
	18, 18, 8			$1,193	
Mississippi		No. 1 field hand	$1,625	$1,450	1.12
Texas	21, 15		$2,015	$1,635	1.23
Texas (1859)	17, 14		$1,527	$1,403	1.09

one, the purchase-price differential is narrower than the hiring-rate differential. The price structure clearly reflects the added value of females due to their ability to generate capital gains. It is especially interesting in this regard to note that the price ratios in Virginia and South Carolina, the two breeding states represented in the list, show practically no differential. This evidence clearly shows that the Old South recognized in the market the value of its function as the slave-breeding area for the cotton-raising West.

C. The "Overcapitalization" of the Labor Force

The aspect of slave economics that causes the most confusion and outright error is that which relates to the capitalization, and, in the ante bellum southern case, the presumed overcapitalization, of slave labor. Phillips speaks of an "irresistible tendency to overvalue and overcapitalize" and argues that slave-holding had an unlimited capacity for absorbing the planters' earnings through the continual payment of interest and the enhancement of prices. For the Cotton Belt this was presumably aggregated into a continuous public drain of wealth, first, to England and New England and, later, to the upper South. . . .

Table 17 and Chart 1 demonstrate the relationship among slave prices, cotton prices, and the value of cotton output per slave (of field work age, ten to fifty-four). Several things become clear in this comparison. To begin, the relationship between slave and cotton prices is significant for Phillips' purposes only if there is no increase in productivity. While he is struck by the fact that slave prices rise more rapidly than cotton prices in the long upswing starting the early 1840's, it is equally striking to observe that (New Orleans) slave prices rose about one and one-half times between the low point in 1843–45 to 1860, while values of cotton production per hand rose more than three times from the low in 1842. . . . Furthermore, it would appear that slave prices fluctuate less than do cotton prices. This and the less clear-cut lag of the slave prices make it difficult to accept the image of unwary planters helplessly exposing themselves in a market dominated by speculators. It would make more sense to argue simply that the rising trend of slave prices coupled with a growing slave population is in and of itself strong evidence of the profitability of slavery.

D. The Efficiency of Allocation

The second point relates to geographic allocation and, to a lesser extent, to the mobility of the slave labor force among crops. The slave

TABLE 17   Value of Cotton Production and Slave Population, 1802–60, New Orleans
Prices

Year	Crop (Thousands of Pounds)	Average Price (Cents per Pound)	Value (Thousands)	No. of Slaves, Aged 10–54 Years	Crop Value per Slave	Price of Prime Field Hand	Crop Value per Hand per Dollar Slave Price
1802 ...	55,000	0.147	$ 8,085	550,708	$ 14.68	$ 600	.02
1803 ...	60,000	.150	9,000	568,932	15.82	600	.03
1804 ...	65,000	.196	12,740	587,157	21.70	600	.04
1805 ...	70,000	.233	16,310	605,381	26.94	600	.05
1806 ...	80,000	.218	17,440	623,606	27.97	600	.05
1807 ...	80,000	.164	13,120	641,831	20.44	600	.03
1808 ...	75,000	.136	10,200	660,055	15.45	640	.02
1809 ...	82,000	.136	11,152	678,280	16.44	780	.02
1810 ...	85,000	.147	12,495	696,505	17.94	900	.02
1811 ...	80,000	.089	7,120	717,376	9.93	860	.01
1813 ...	75,000	.155	11,625	759,118	15.31	600	.03
1814 ...	70,000	.169	11,830	779,989	15.17	650	.02
1815 ...	100,000	.273	27,300	800,860	34.09	765	.05
1816 ...	124,000	.254	31,496	821,731	38.33	880	.04
1817 ...	130,000	.298	38,740	842,602	45.98	1,000	.05
1818 ...	125,000	.215	26,875	863,473	31.12	1,050	.03
1819 ...	167,000	.143	23,881	884,344	27.00	1,100	.03
1820 ...	160,000	.152	24,320	905,215	26.88	970	.03
1821 ...	180,000	.174	31,320	933,517	33.55	810	.04
1822 ...	210,000	.115	24,150	961,818	25.11	700	.04
1823 ...	185,000	.145	26,825	990,120	27.04	670	.04
1824 ...	215,000	.179	38,485	1,018,421	37.99	700	.05
1825 ...	255,000	.119	30,345	1,046,723	28.99	800	.04
1826 ...	350,000	.093	32,550	1,075,024	30.28	840	.04
1827 ...	316,900	.097	30,739	1,103,326	27.86	770	.04
1828 ...	241,399	.098	23,657	1,131,627	20.91	770	.03
1829 ...	296,812	.089	26,416	1,159,929	22.77	770	.03
1830 ...	331,150	.084	27,817	1,208,034	23.03	810	.03
1831 ...	354,247	.090	31,882	1,247,489	25.56	860	.03
1832 ...	355,492	.100	35,549	1,275,061	27.88	900	.03
1833 ...	374,653	.112	41,961	1,302,633	32.21	960	.03
1834 ...	437,558	.155	67,821	1,330,206	50.99	1,000	.05
1835 ...	460,338	.152	69,971	1,357,778	51.53	1,150	.05
1836 ...	507,550	.133	67,504	1,385,350	46.79	1,250	.04
1837 ...	539,669	.090	48,510	1,412,923	34.38	1,300	.03
1838 ...	682,767	.124	84,663	1,440,495	58.77	1,220	.05
1839 ...	501,708	.079	39,635	1,468,067	27.00	1,240	.02

Year	Crop (Thousands of Pounds)	Average Price (Cents per Pound)	Value (Thousands)	No. of Slaves, Aged 10–54 Years	Crop Value per Slave	Price of Prime Field Hand	Crop Value per Hand per Dollar Slave Price
1840	834,111	.091	75,904	1,507,779	50.34	1,020	.05
1841	644,172	.078	50,245	1,568,022	32.04	870	.04
1842	668,379	.057	38,098	1,611,269	23.65	750	.03
1843	972,960	.075	72,972	1,654,516	44.11	700	.06
1844	836,529	.055	46,009	1,697,762	27.10	700	.04
1845	993,719	.068	67,573	1,741,009	38.81	700	.06
1846	863,321	.099	85,469	1,784,256	47.90	750	.06
1847	766,599	.070	53,662	1,827,503	29.36	850	.04
1848	1,017,391	.058	59,009	1,870,750	31.54	950	.03
1849	1,249,985	.108	134,998	1,913,996	70.53	1,030	.07
1850	1,001,165	.117	117,136	1,979,059	59.19	1,100	.05
1851	1,021,048	.074	75,558	2,034,482	37.14	1,150	.03
1852	1,338,061	.091	121,764	2,080,554	58.53	1,200	.05
1853	1,496,302	.088	131,675	2,126,626	61.92	1,250	.05
1854	1,322,241	.084	111,068	2,172,698	51.12	1,310	.04
1855	1,294,463	.091	117,796	2,218,770	53.09	1,350	.04
1856	1,535,334	.124	190,381	2,264,843	84.06	1,420	.06
1857	1,373,619	.112	153,845	2,310,915	66.57	1,490	.05
1858	1,439,744	.115	165,571	2,356,988	70.25	1,580	.04
1859	1,796,455	.108	194,017	2,403,060	80.74	1,690	.05
1860	2,241,056	0.111	$248,757	2,460,648	$101.09	$1,800	.06

prices in all regions move very closely with cotton prices and products per hand. It is clear, too, that the eastern prices move directly with the cotton-area slave prices, although in the last two decades the rate of increase of prices fell behind in the breeding area. If the market were extremely imperfect and the transfer between the breeding and consuming states inefficient, in contradiction to our hypothesis, then there should be much less evidence of regional arbitrage than is found here. In response to the western demand, Virginia and the other eastern states shipped their natural increase to the cotton areas. . . . It is not clear that slavery was able to continue only by skinning the topsoil and moving on, leaving exhausted land and low slave and land value in its wake. Quite the contrary, the evidence can plausibly be interpreted as indicating a unified, specialized economy in which the settlers on the naturally superior western lands (superior even before the deterioration of the older regions by single-crop cultivation of tobacco and cotton)

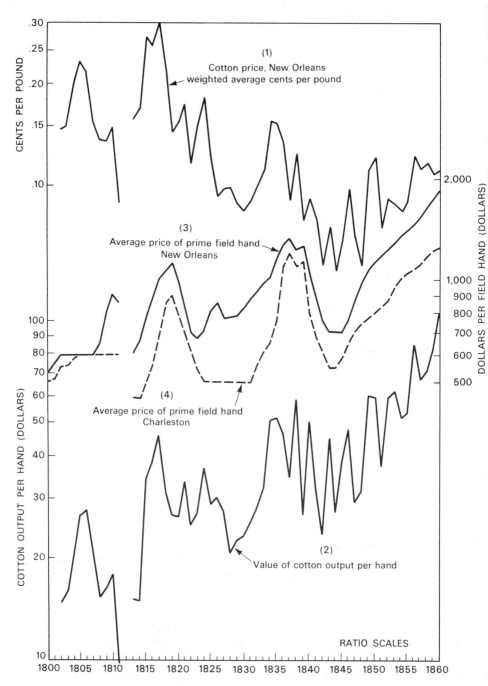

CHART I *Slave Population and Prices and the Value of Cotton Production, 1802–60*

were able to bid slave labor away from general farming and to make wholesale removal unnecessary, if indeed there had ever been such a necessity.

E. Slavery and Southern Economic Growth

Finally, there are two economic arguments about slavery and potential southern growth to be considered. The assertion that slavery per se was inimical to economic growth rests in part upon the alleged inefficiency of slave labor in industrial pursuits and in part upon the loss of capital that might otherwise have gone into industrialization and diversification.

The inefficiency argument is not supported very securely. There were slaves employed in cotton factories throughout the South. Slaves were used in the coal mines and in the North Carolina lumbering operations. In the ironworks at Richmond and on the Cumberland River, slaves comprised a majority of the labor force. Southern railroads were largely built by southern slaves. Crop diversification, or the failure to achieve diversification, appears to have been a problem of entrepreneurship rather than of the difficulties of training slaves. In the face of the demand for cotton and the profits to be had from specializing in this single crop, it is hardly difficult to explain the single-minded concentration of the planter.

In what ways was slavery allegedly responsible for the drain of capital from the South? The lack of diversification, to the extent of a failure even to provide basic supplies, made necessary the import of much food and virtually all manufactured articles from the North. But half of this assertion, the argument that laid the responsibility for the single-crop culture upon slavery, has been found questionable already.

The major avenues by which wealth is said to have been drained from the cotton states were the excessive use of credit (through dependence upon factors' services) and the "absorption" of capital in slaves. The dependence upon advances was, in effect, a dependence upon the New York or London money market and was, therefore, an impediment to the accumulation of capital in the South. Good crop years bring the temptation to expand production; bad years do not bring any release from the factors. But resort to factoring is characteristic of speculative, commercial agriculture, whether or not the labor force is organized in slavery. . . .

There remains only the absorption of capital in slaves to set the responsibility for lack of growth in the South upon the peculiar institution. Earnings that might have gone out of the South to bring in investment goods were fixed in the form of chattel labor. For the early years, during the external slave trade, there is some plausibility to this argument, though it is difficult to see how the capitalization of an income stream, excellent by contemporary standards, can be said to count as a loss of wealth. In the later years there was, except to the extent that northern or English bankers drew off the interest, a redistribution of wealth only within the slave states: from the cotton lands back to the less profitable field agriculture of the older section. . . . We are left with the conclusion that, except insofar as it made speculation in cotton possible on a grander scale than would otherwise have been the case and thereby weakened whatever pressure there might have been for diversification, capitalization of the labor force did not of itself operate against southern development.

IV. CONCLUSION

In sum, it seems doubtful that the South was forced by bad statesmanship into an unnecessary war to protect a system which must soon have disappeared because it was economically unsound. This is a romantic hypothesis which will not stand against the facts.

On the basis of the computation of the returns to capital in our model of the ante bellum southern economy and the demonstration of the efficiency of the regional specialization, the following conclusions are offered:

1. Slavery was profitable to the whole South, the continuing demand for labor in the Cotton Belt insuring returns to the breeding operation on the less productive land in the seaboard and border states. The breeding returns were necessary, however, to make the plantation operations on the poorer lands as profitable as alternative contemporary economic activities in the United States. The failure of southern agriculture on these poorer lands in the post bellum period is probably attributable, in the main, to the loss of these capital gains on breeding and not, as is so often suggested, to either the relative inefficiency of the tenant system that replaced the plantations or the soil damage resulting from war operations. These factors were unquestionably contributing elements to the difficulties of post bellum southern agriculture, but they were of relatively small quantitative importance compared with the elimination of slave-breeding returns.

2. There was nothing necessarily self-destructive about the profits of the slave economy. Neither the overcapitalization argument nor the assertion that slavery must have collapsed because the slaves would not

reproduce themselves is tenable. Slave prices did not outpace productivity, and the regional slave price structure would imply a workable transfer mechanism rather than the contrary.

3. Continued expansion of slave territory was both possible and, to some extent, necessary. The maintenance of profits in the Old South depended upon the expansion, extensive or intensive, of slave agriculture into the Southwest. This is sufficient to explain the interest of the Old South in secession and does away with the necessity to fall back upon arguments of statesmanship or quixotism to explain the willingness to fight for the peculiar institution.

4. The available productive surplus from slavery might have been used for economic development or, as in totalitarian regimes in this century, for militarism. In spite of this good omen for development, southern investment and industrialization lagged. It is hard to explain this except on the social ground that entrepreneurship could not take root in the South or on the economic ground that the South did not really own the system but merely operated it. Furthermore, the American experience clearly suggests that slavery is not, from the strict economic standpoint, a deterrent to industrial development and that its elimination may take more than the workings of "inexorable economic forces." Athough profitability cannot be offered as a sufficient guaranty of the continuity of southern slavery, the converse argument that slavery. must have destroyed itself can no longer rest upon allegations of unprofitability or upon assumptions about the impossibility of maintaining and allocating a slave labor force. To the extent, moreover, that profitability is a necessary condition for the continuation of a private business institution in a free-enterprise society, slavery was not untenable in the ante bellum American South. Indeed, economic forces often may work toward the continuation of a slave system, so that the elimination of slavery may depend upon the adoption of harsh political measures. Certainly that was the American experience.

19

An Approach to the Historical Study of National Character

MURRAY G. MURPHEY

Much that has been written on national character is impressionistic, unscientific, prejudiced, and at worst racist. Rejecting racial determinism and embracing scientific methodology, social psychologists and anthropologists agree that national characteristics do differ and are the product of culture and personality. Borrowing theory and methodology from both psychology and anthropology, Murray G. Murphey suggests that the nursery, not the frontier, made the American male aggressive.

Ever since Thucydides first called us to the scientific study of the past, historians have been struggling to find reasons for the varying fates of human societies. That Athens, or Rome, or England should wax powerful and carry all before it, and then, for some occult cause, should decline and fall, posed for the historian more, and more subtle, problems of human behavior than he could well deal with. Faced with such unsearchable mysteries, the historian retreated to all too simple answers. The fate of nations was declared subject to climate, or topography, or race, or destiny, or any one of a number of similar factors, scrutable or inscrutable.

From *Context and Meaning in Cultural Anthropology*, Melford E. Spiro, ed., pp. 144–63. Notes omitted. Reprinted with permission of The Macmillan Company. © 1965 by The Free Press, a division of The Macmillan Company.

Often these determinants were regarded as inducing in the members of the society certain common psychological characteristics which were thought to be relatively stable from generation to generation, due either to constant environment or to transmission through heredity. So, in an era before modern genetic theory, one often finds race and nationality combined, and historians speak of the English race or the German race, meaning really no more than that Englishmen seem to have certain traits in common and that this community outlasts a generation. Similarly, the interpretation of our own history has long labored under the curse of [F. J.] Turner's frontier, to whose ubiquitous presence all characteristics of Americans have been attributed. Thus historians have long been wedded to concepts of national character, meaning by this that character, or set of characteristics, common to a given national group. Yet these concepts, however useful, have remained always at an intuitive and poetic level, and so have never been refined into instruments serviceable for a scientific theory of human behavior.

Meanwhile the social sciences have come of age. The comparative study of cultures soon led anthropologists to the recognition that there are characteristic psychological differences between societies; consequently in the 1930's [R.] Benedict (1934); [R.] Linton and [A.] Kardiner (1939), and others turned their attention to the study of group personality. It may be admitted that in its early years this field of study was not characterized by precision, but this defect has been substantially remedied. The definition of group personality as the modal personality of the group substituted a statistically exact notion for an intuitively vague one, and by so doing redefined the entire area of study. The concept of basic personality structure as expressed by Kardiner (1939), and the demonstration of the relation of child-rearing techniques to adult personality structure, hypothesized by Freud and confirmed and extended in modern studies such as that of [J. M.] Whiting and [I. L.] Child (1958), have clarified the problem of intergenerational transmission by substituting the laws of learning for ill-defined and false conjectures regarding heredity or simple environmental determinism. [A. I.] Hallowell (1955), [G.] Spindler (1955), and others have used the Rorschach to identify distinctive psychological constellations characteristic of particular groups, and have examined the fate of such personality constellations under acculturation. Moreover, Hallowell has succeeded in integrating modal personality with world view by pointing out the psychological significance of the basic orientations which the world view affords to the individual. Thus the last thirty years have witnessed a rapid development in the study of the relations betweeen personality, culture, and society, and the general principle that there are personality characteristics common to the members of groups is no longer seriously challenged.

The characteristic concern of anthropologists with preliterate societies has directed their attention away from problems of historical reconstruction, since obviously such societies have left no written records on
the basis of which such a reconstruction might be undertaken. Some
anthropologists however have been concerned with historical problems.
Hallowell, for example, used the accounts of the early Woodland Indians
contained in the *Jesuit Relations* to attempt a· reconstruction of the
aboriginal Woodland Indian personality—a reconstruction ingeniously confirmed by comparison with contemporary Woodland Indians under varying degrees of acculturation, and now widely accepted by both historians
and anthropologists. Other social scientists have also turned their attention
to historical problems. The psychologist David McClelland (1961) has
attempted to investigate levels of need achievement in historical populations and the relation between such need strengths and other aspects of
the sociocultural system. Similarly, David Riesman (1950) has written
a highly controversial book which attempts to utilize a triadic personality
typology in the interpretation of American history. It is notable that all
these attempts to apply modern culture and personality theory to historical
material have been made by social scientists—not by historians. The historians themselves have been loath to enter upon this uncharted sea, and
there are reasons why this is so.

Modal personality is a statistical concept, and if one is to apply this
concept to a particular society, then, as [A.] Inkeles and [D.] Levinson
have so clearly pointed out, statements about modal personality must be
supported by reference to a sample of individuals drawn from the society
in question. Where one is dealing with the history of a preliterate society
this is *a priori* impossible: those who cannot write leave no written records. But even in the case of a highly literate historical society, such as
the United States in 1800, there are very serious problems involved in
obtaining samples from which any generalization can be made. Furthermore, one cannot give Thomas Jefferson a psychiatric interview. If we are
to investigate questions of group personality in America in 1800, the
investigation must be made through such evidence as now survives. And
so far as documents which give intimate personal information are concerned, we are really limited to letters, diaries, and autobiographies.
Whether, and to what degree, the relevant information can be obtained
from such documents, is a question which requires careful consideration.

We may conceive of a given historical population as a set N of n
individuals, and we may conceive of the set of all those members of N
for whom the data relevant to our questions now exists as a subset K of
N. It is obvious that we can draw random samples from K, but whether
such random samples of K are random samples of N depends upon

whether or not K itself is a random sample of N. Unfortunately our knowledge of the processes of record formation and preservation is quite sufficient to assure us that K is not a random selection out of N. The probability that a record was ever made depends upon many variables such as literacy, educational level, occupation, class, degree of prominence or notoriety in the society, and a number of ill-understood psychological variables controlling the proclivity to commit the record of one's affairs to paper. And the probability that a record once made will survive for any given period depends upon further variables such as the material on which the record was made, the number of copies made, the interest which family or friends or enemies may have felt in preserving such records, and the physical dangers to which the records were exposed (fire, flood, loving daughters, bombing raids, mold, rot, riot, revolution, and invading hoards, to mention only the most obvious, have all taken their toll). Such factors do not select at random, and the result of their selection is a sample which must be regarded as grossly biased. Moreover, the selective processes involved are so complex that no reasonably exact quantitative estimate of the bias is possible. We therefore confront a situation which makes the application of statistical concepts such as model personality to historical data extremely difficult.

A similar situation was confronted by Inkeles and [R.] Bauer in their study *The Soviet Citizen* (1959). Since they did not have access to the Soviet citizens themselves, they were forced to work with refugees who either had fled from the Soviet Union or had been forced by the Nazis to leave it and had subsequently chosen not to return. This situation is precisely analogous to that confronted by the historian: an inaccessible population concerning which information is desired, and a biased subset concerning which information can be obtained. Yet by adroit use of their data Inkeles and Bauer did obtain considerable information about the citizenry of the Soviet Union. To do this, they used their knowledge of the direction of the bias to interpret the significance of their findings. Thus they found their sample to be strongly in favor of state ownership of heavy industry. Since the sample is biased against the Soviet regime, yet favors this particular Soviet policy, it is reasonable to assume that people within Russia also favor it. Again, they found in the sample that degree of hostility to the Soviet regime increased as one descends the class scale. They therefore held that

> It is reasonable to assume that whatever selective factors account for the anti-Soviet bias of our sample operate relatively uniformly on all the subgroups in our sample, and that comparable groups in the Soviet population will stand in the same *relationship* to each other as do the members of our sample.

This approach is equally applicable to historical problems. The chief difference is that the historian will rarely, if ever, confront so simple and clear-cut a problem of bias as that which Inkeles and Bauer had, and he will therefore have to take more and subtler biases into account.

The failure to achieve randomness in historical sampling calls into question the applicability of the statistical techniques of hypothesis testing and estimation. These techniques do require randomness, and accordingly Inkeles and Bauer carefully avoided their use. But there is an important sense in which such techniques are fully applicable even in this case. If, for example, the historical population under study is the American people in 1860, there may remain to us data concerning several thousand individuals from that population. It is unlikely that all of this data can be utilized, but it can be sampled, and if this is done intelligently estimation and hypothesis testing can be used to generalize from the sample to the set of all those for whom the data now remains. And this generalization, while it does not take us to the original historical population, is nevertheless important and should be made, for it is clearly worth knowing whether our findings hold for fifty or five thousand people. But when we wish to generalize from the 5000 to the original historical population classic statistical inference fails us and we must now include intuitive estimates of the bias. Thus one may summarize a major difference between history and the social sciences as follows: For the social scientist in the general case sample bias can be eliminated by the use of an adequate methodology, while for the historian sample bias is inescapable and must therefore be taken into account in the formation and testing of his generalizations.

But sampling is not the only problem facing the historian; he must also face certain inevitable limitations imposed by the nature of his data. It seems reasonable to assume that information concerning personality is most likely to be available in those documents in which the author speaks with greatest freedom about his own actions, thoughts, and feelings —what we may call "personal documents." The chief classes of such documents concerning historical individuals are private letters, diaries, and autobiographies; since the latter category is the only one utilized in this paper we may limit the discussion to it. An autobiography may be defined as a document in which an individual writes a history of his own life from birth. Such documents are therefore not life histories in the sense of [H. A.] Murray (1962) or [J.] Dollard (1949); rather, what one finds in an autobiography is an account of those events and experiences which the author remembers or has been told about, considered significant, and is willing to let the village gossips know. Thus an autobiography rarely gives data concerning the author's weaning or toilet training, because the author cannot remember those experiences, usually has never been told about them, and would generally consider them too private for discussion if he did know about them. Similarly, in the autobiographies used in this paper there are no accounts of sexual experience, presumably because the authors did not regard such matters as proper for public revelation. Consequently the information available from these sources is highly selective, and the criteria of selection are not those we should have chosen.

With such data, what kinds of questions about personality can we hope to answer? Specifically, can we investigate problems of the relation of child-rearing practices to adult personality? Clearly, the autobiographies will give us no data on infant rearing, but they do give considerable information concerning childhood, early upbringing, and discipline (i.e., after age five or six), parental roles, and the author's attitude toward his parents. Is this enough, or must we also have precise data on infancy? The answer, of course, is that the more data the better, but some information is better than none. After all, the great importance of such infantile experiences as weaning and toilet training lies in the fact that they are the child's first experience with the discipline of impulse and that the patterns of behavior and the attitudes learned in these experiences are enduring and are subsequently generalized into characteristic modes of response to similar needs. But what has been learned can be unlearned. If we conceive personality as a dynamic structure developing continuously through time, it is clear that the persistence and generalization of these infant patterns depend upon the existence of continuity and consistency in the whole child-rearing pattern from cradle to adulthood. There is no time at which the personality can be said to be "fixed," although it does seem likely that infantile experience is disproportionately influential. We should therefore expect to find that disciplines imposed at any time will have an effect upon subsequent patterns of behavior and attitude.

There is a further way in which the autobiographies can be used to investigate the problem of the relation of child rearing to adult personality. Although we cannot obtain information regarding the infantile experiences of the specific persons whose autobiographies we have, we can generally obtain information about the child-rearing practices prevailing in the society into which these people were born. We may therefore pose to ourselves the following types of problems: Supposing such and such a child-rearing pattern prevailed in this society, what attitudes would we expect the people so reared to have toward their parents and toward their parents' discipline; what kind of account of their childhood would we expect these people to leave; are attitudes toward parents generalized to others of the same sex or age, and so forth? We may then regard the autobiographies as a sample of individuals drawn from the society, and test our expectations against the data they afford.

Two sets of hypotheses are under examination in this paper: The first set concerns the child-rearing practices prevailing in the Middle Atlantic region during the early nineteenth century; the second set concerns the relation of those practices to certain adult personality characteristics in the population so reared. The generalizations about child rearing which compose the first set must be regarded as hypotheses because our knowledge of those practices is not sufficient to permit positive assertion. Nevertheless, these hypotheses are supported by considerable qualitative data, and to explain both their origin and their plausibility it will be necessary to review briefly what is known about child rearing in this period.

Few studies have been done on early American child rearing, and the results to date are far from conclusive. What is known is derived from two kinds of data: accounts of foreign travelers, and manuals on how to rear children addressed to the parents of the time. Such data are of course biased. Foreign travelers chiefly saw the urban upper classes and saw them at best fleetingly. The manuals are also addressed chiefly to the urban upper classes and represent, not descriptions of actual practice, but prescriptions as to what practice ought to be. Nevertheless, the picture of child rearing which emerges from these disparate sources is fairly consistent, and needs to be briefly stated.

Virtually all European travelers in the early nineteenth century comment on American children, and it is clear that they found them very puzzling. There are four characteristics of the children which they particularly stress. First, they were startled by the familiar and affectionate relation existing between parents and children. Second, they all remark upon what they call the lack of discipline of American children. Under this heading they include the rarity of corporal punishment, the extreme permissiveness of the parents, the absence of attitudes of deference and submissiveness in the children, and the corresponding lack of authority of the parents. Third, they were astonished by the independence of American children. This is not to be equated with lack of parental restraint; rather, it means that the children were capable of taking care of themselves, of doing things for themselves, and of thinking and talking for themselves. Fourth, they remark on the precocity and early maturity of the children. To the traveler, these children appeared to acquire the attitudes and behavior of adults so early that one writer claimed they were born middle-aged.

The Europeans were clearly puzzled by these children, and one suspects that the root of their puzzlement was the fact that this seemingly indulgent and permissive method of child rearing produced, not the spoiled, dependent, pampered, child they expected, but rather a highly self-reliant, self-sufficient, precociously mature child. Yet that such was in fact the case they all agree.

The description of child-rearing practices given in the manuals is generally consistent with that given by the travelers but differs from it in some particulars. The manuals point out, as the travelers do not, the differences in parental roles. Early child rearing, until perhaps the age of six, seems to have been almost exclusively the mother's function. She was responsible, not only for the child's physical care and training, but also for his early moral and religious training. Although family religious services were conducted by the father, individual moral and religious training was the mother's task, and the conscience is even described as the internalization of the mother's voice. In the phrase of the day, "The mother sways the dominion of the heart, the father that of the intellect." The father's role receives little discussion in these manuals, since they are chiefly concerned with the child's early years. The father's primary task appears to have been providing for the family as a whole. He was, however, expected to administer corporal punishment to the child when the need for it arose and, as the child grew older, to assume responsibility for his education and for preparing him to make his way in the world.

The manuals do not give a very precise picture of the specific rearing practices used in infancy. Breast feeding was evidently the rule. There was apparently little attempt to impose feeding schedules and the child was fed whenever it was hungry. Weaning occurred sometime between the eighth and the twelfth month and was probably gradual. The manuals complain of children being overfed both before and after weaning; consequently, the general picture of oral training appears to be one of indulgence. The facts respecting anal and sexual training are not so clear. Toilet training was undoubtedly early, but just how early we do not know. Since the manuals express disgust with the child's soilage and stress cleanliness, anal discipline may well have been severe. Similarly, although detailed information on sexual discipline is not available, the vigor with which masturbation is condemned and sexual purity is praised suggests that training in this area may also have been strict. Independence training was evidently inaugurated early and given considerable emphasis, both in practical and in moral and religious respects. The objective was to make the child "at an early age a self-maintaining moral being." But the stress on independence did not involve any inhibition of maternal affection. The importance of mothering is uniformly emphasized: direct physical contact between mother and child was regarded as desirable and the mother was enjoined to care for all the child's needs herself and to give freely of love and affection.

In his study of the child-rearing literature of this period, Sunley found three distinct theories of child rearing expressed. The first and apparently most prevalent was the Calvinist theory which regarded the child as innately depraved and therefore emphasized severe discipline, obedience, and "breaking the child's will." A second and less prevalent theory, stemming from Locke, viewed the child as an innocent creature born into a corrupt society and emphasized severe child-rearing practices which would "harden" the child against the demoralizing influences around it. The third theory, which was apparently widespread, emphasized gentle treatment.

> The child was to be led, not driven; persuaded to the right, not commanded. Consistency and firmness were counseled, but with understanding and justice to the child. Encouragements and rewards should be offered; beatings, reproaches, slaps, dark closets, and shaming were to be avoided. Punishment and reward were to be administered not according to the consequences of the child's act but according to the motives. . . . Corporal punishment was undesirable, partly because it did not bring about the desired results, partly because the child was felt to be too tender for such treatment. . . . The child was ignorant of right rather than bent to wrong. Consequently, the fear of indulging the child and of being dominated by it was not marked, nor was it imperative to "break the will." A firm stand by the parents eliminated obedience problems.

These three theories are not wholly exclusive: It is notable that a group among the Calvinist writers advocated a modified view which had much in common with the gentle treatment theory.

How accurate is the picture presented by the manuals? We must accept the fact that these books contain an urban upper-class bias. Nevertheless, the picture of the parental roles is undoubtedly accurate for both farm and city. Owing to the division of labor which prevailed on the farm, the child was in the mother's care until he was old enough to go to work in the fields—usually at seven or eight years of age. Thereupon his childhood freedom was ended, and he worked under his father's direction as a regular member of the labor force. In the city more or less the same pattern existed, and although there was no such abrupt transition as that involved in going into the fields, the father's direction of the child certainly increased as the child matured. With respect to specific infant-rearing practices we have no independent data upon which to assess the accuracy of the manuals, but since the severity of these practices should be a function of the general child-rearing theory held, we can inquire which of these general theories was dominant. In view of the large number of adherents that the various Calvinist denominations had in America—particularly in New England—there can be no doubt that the Calvinist theory was widespread and was probably practiced with rigor by the devout. On the other hand, it is clear that a strong group within the Calvinist clergy itself was propounding a modified theory not unlike the gentle treatment theory, although we do not know how many adherents this liberal version had. Outside the

Calvinist denominations there is no reason to believe that such severity was enjoined or practiced. Indeed, if we admit the accounts of the foreign travelers as evidence, we can hardly avoid the conclusion that the gentle treatment theory was all but universal. Although the travelers had biases of their own and are hardly to be regarded as trained observers, nevertheless the unanimity of their reports is impressive. Accordingly, it seems quite likely that outside the hard-core Calvinist ranks, and possibly outside New England, the prevailing theory and practice approximated the gentle treatment theory.

On the basis of these reflections, one may hazard the following hypotheses concerning child rearing in early nineteenth century America, at least for the Middle Atlantic region.

1. Early child rearing was conducted chiefly by the mother and was affectionate, used mild discipline, and attempted to lead the child by love rather than to drive it by fear or force.
2. Corporal punishment was usually administered by the father.
3. Early moral and religious training was effected chiefly by the mother.
4. The child was trained for early independence.
5. After six or seven the father's direction of the child increased and was usually more severe and exacting than the mother's, particularly in the areas of work and practical knowledge.

If these hypotheses concerning child rearing are true, what effects would we expect these practices to have upon the people so reared? Specifically, what would we expect to find in autobiographies written by people raised in this fashion? It seems clear that the following hypotheses ought also to be true.

1. The mother should be idealized and described in terms of such qualities as lovingness, tenderness, kindness, solicitude, etc.
2. Attitudes toward the mother should be more favorable than those toward the father.
3. Religion and morality should be particularly associated with the mother.
4. Father's discipline should be perceived as more severe than mother's discipline, and should be more resented.
5. Resentment of father's discipline in childhood should be correlated with adult aggressiveness toward other males in situations of threat.
6. Aggression toward women should rarely occur.
7. There should be no relation between resentment toward mother's discipline and adult aggressiveness toward males in situations of threat.

The first four hypotheses essentially translate the five hypotheses concerning child-rearing practices into a form in which they can be tested against the autobiographical data. If the child's perception of the parents corresponds at all to the actual behavior of the parents toward the child, it is very difficult to see how the child-rearing hypotheses can be true and the first four hypotheses above be false.

The reasoning underlying the fifth hypothesis is somewhat more complex and is based upon the following argument. First, it seems clear that to the degree that the father's discipline is more severe than the mother's discipline, it should be perceived as frustrating, and that when this difference is very large, the father's discipline should be perceived as aggressive. It is well known that anger, hostility, and aggression are likely to be aroused by frustration, and are even more likely to be aroused by aggressive acts. These three responses are not equivalent: anger is an emotional response having the properties of a drive state which may serve as the drive for aggression; hostility is an enduring attitude which arises as a conditioned anger response and which does not possess drive properties; aggression is a behavioral response which "delivers noxious stimuli to another organism." These responses can occur separately, but in the case here considered it is clear that they should occur together. Accordingly, one would expect that the greater the difference in severity between father's and mother's discipline, the more likely it is that anger, hostility, and aggression against the father will be aroused in the child.

Second, the more intense these responses are, the more likely it is that they will be elicited by other comparable stimuli. The usual explanation for this is afforded by the classic stimulus generalization model, according to which if a stimulus S evokes a response R, other stimuli similar to S will also evoke R, in direct proportion to their similarity to S. Hence if the threatening and frustrating father evokes anger, or hostility, or aggression, other males in similar situations may be expected to provoke a similar reaction. The generalization of aggression, however, may be given an alternative explanation in terms of the effects of anger on the thresholds for aggressive responses. On this model, the existence of an anger state has the effect of lowering the threshold for aggressive responses, so that noxious or annoying characteristics of stimulus objects, which under ordinary circumstances would not be sufficient to elicit aggression, now do so. Thus a child who is angry at its father kicks its dog for a trivial reason which under ordinary circumstances would elicit no such response. The two models may be combined: we may explain the generalization of anger by stimulus generalization and the occurrence of aggression in the substitute situation by lowered thresholds. But whichever of these models one adopts, the result should be that the child who is intensely angry, hostile, or aggressive toward the father should display anger, hostility, or aggression more frequently and against a wider class of stimulus objects than the child who is not.

While the father may not be aware of the child's anger and hostility, he will certainly be aware of its direct aggression and will punish the child for such acts. Such punishment, or the expectation of it, will produce aggression anxiety in the child which will inhibit direct aggression. In his classic paper on stimulus generalization and displacement, [N.] Miller showed how the approach-avoidance model can be applied to this situation to explain the displacement of aggression to other stimulus objects. If the generalization gradient of avoidance is steeper than that for approach, but such that the two gradients intersect, direct aggression will be inhibited over the domain of stimulus objects for which the avoidance gradient lies above the approach gradient, but not for those objects for which the avoidance gradient lies below the approach gradient. Under these circumstances, Miller showed that aggression will be "displaced" to the point where the avoidance gradient cuts the abscissa, since the net approach strength is maximum at that point. Miller's construction is wholly in terms of the stimulus generalization theory, but it is easy to see that a similar result will follow in terms of the threshold model. The lowering of thresholds will be offset within the domain of stimulus objects for which the inhibitions exist, and so will lead to increased aggression only outside that domain. In either case, one has the displacement of aggression from one class of stimulus object to another, the difference being that in Miller's model the substitution depends upon similarity to the original while for the threshold model it depends upon increased sensitivity to noxious or annoying characteristics of the substitute. On either model, therefore, one would expect the child to displace his aggression against the father to substitute objects against whom it can be expressed with less danger. Whether in this case anger or hostility is also displaced depends upon the particular situation: the displacement of aggression does not require the displacement of anger or hostility but merely their generalization. Nevertheless, for convenience in the present discussion and to avoid cumbersome locution, we may speak of "anger and aggression being displaced from S to S'," meaning that anger is either generalized or displaced from S to S' and that aggression is displaced from S to S'.

The choice of model is not irrelevant to the question of what objects can serve as substitutes, but both models agree that displacement of anger and aggression should occur against other males who are to some degree threatening or frustrating to the child. On either model, therefore, we may expect anger and aggression against a male in threat situations to occur more frequently for displacing subjects than for non-displacing subjects. This is so not only because the drive strength—the amount of anger—should be greater for displacers, but also because the strength of the habit of making aggressive responses in threat situations should be greater for displacers. There are several grounds for the latter expectation. The simple occurrence of aggressive responses in threat situations will not lead to the formation of a habit of so responding unless there is reinforcement, and such reinforcement must inevitably be partial, but for a constant ratio of reinforced to nonreinforced trials, the greater the number of trials the greater the habit strength should be. Furthermore, there is some reason to believe that the reinforcement for displacing subjects may be greater than that for nondisplacing subjects. To see this, consider two subjects confronting a stimulus sufficiently noxious to elicit anger and an aggressive response, and suppose one subject is also displacing anger and aggression from another source against this stimulus. Then we should expect the level of anger of the displacing subject to be higher than that of the nondisplacing subject, i.e., that the anger components summate. If both subjects now make the same aggressive response, both will experience catharsis, i.e., a drop in the anger level, and this catharsis serves as the internal reinforcement for the response. Now is the catharsis equal for the two subjects? It would seem reasonable to suppose that the catharsis for the displacing subject should involve both diminution of the anger aroused by the present stimulus and diminution of the displaced anger, and if that is so the total reinforcement of the aggressive act should be greater for the displacing subject than for the nondisplacing subject. If this supposition is correct, it follows that the strength of the habit of making aggressive responses to such stimuli should be greater for the displacing subject, and this effect should hold whether the stimulus generalization model or the threshold model is used. Accordingly, we may conclude that for displacing subjects the probability of responding to threat situations by aggressive acts will be greater, by an amount proportional to the amount of the anger displaced, than for nondisplacing subjects.

If such a difference in the behavior of displacing and nondisplacing subjects were once created, it ought to be enduring. The hostility toward threatening males should be stronger in displacers than in nondisplacers, and so one would expect that even after the parent's death the amount of anger aroused by the threat stimuli should remain greater for the displacers than for the nondisplacers. Similarly, the habit strength of the displacers should remain higher than that of the nondisplacers. It thus appears that if such differences were established in childhood, they should continue into adult life, and this yields the fifth hypothesis.

The expectation that there will be few acts of aggression against women stems from several factors, among which the cultural prohibitions against such behavior and the relative mildness of the maternal discipline are the chief. Indeed, the cultural factor alone is here so powerful that one would be astonished if many such acts were recorded. On the other hand, the mother does exercise discipline over the child, and the child must inevitably develop a certain amount of frustration and anger against her. If this frustration and anger were sufficiently strong, it might be expected that resentment to maternal discipline would be significantly related to aggression in threat situations by a construction similar to that outlined above. It is our expectation here that the relative mildness of maternal discipline is sufficient to prevent this from occurring, and this yields the final hypothesis.

The sample used in this study consisted of twenty-three autobiographies written by men born between 1794 and 1830 in the states of New York, Pennsylvania, New Jersey, and Delaware. New England was excluded because it could be assumed that the Calvinist views of child rearing were more prevalent there, and the South was excluded because the known differences between northern and southern society in this period are sufficient to require that they be treated separately. The occupational distribution of the sample was as follows: 5 businessmen, 2 editors, 3 teachers, 3 political figures, 2 doctors, 2 lawyers, 2 ministers, 2 farmers, 2 writers. The upper-class urban bias of the sample compared with the total population is obvious. On the other hand, the sample is probably representative of the total population of writers of autobiographies. Men who write the story of their lives have generally not been failures and they are apt to be better educated than the average. The occupational distribution of the fathers of the sample members is as follows: 15 farmers, 2 doctors, 1 mechanic, 1 cartman, 2 ministers, 1 politician, 1 surveyor. The father's distribution, while still skewed, is much closer to that of the general population for this period than is the distribution of the sample itself, and this fact indicates that although most members of the sample were successful in attaining high status they did not begin with it. Six of the parents were members of Calvinist denominations; the others were non-Calvinist.

Not all of the twenty-three cases were equally usable, since several did not give the information necessary to answer some of the questions asked. There are, for example, two cases of men who give no information concerning either parent. Unfortunately, little can be inferred from such silence: it may reflect hostility to the parents but it may also reflect merely a strong sense of privacy. Such cases had therefore to be excluded from the sample used for that particular question.

The analysis of such data to obtain expression of value and attitude requires the use of some form of content analysis. The obvious choice for this case appeared to be the method of value analysis developed by Ralph K. White (1951). This technique is designed to reveal the goals of the writer of the document and the standards of judgment used by the writer in evaluating other people. Moreover, White himself applied this method to the analysis of autobiographical data, and his results indicated that the needed information could be so obtained. Unfortunately, experience in working with the method has revealed certain difficulties. Although White's scheme is partly derived from Murray's needs, he includes no distinction between press and response, and without this distinction it was found impossible to make a meaningful analysis. Accordingly, the analytic scheme was readapted by classifying situations in terms of the press which they exhibited, and then classifying the responses to those press in terms of White's categories.

If the first hypothesis is true we ought to find that in the descriptions of the mother the most frequently occurring categories in White's scheme are G and Lo (givingness and family love). This is in fact the case.

Number of Mothers for Whom the Most Frequently Occurring Categories Are

G and Lo	Other than G and Lo
14	2

This difference is significant at the .002 level by the binomial test.

To test the second hypothesis, a rating was made for each autobiography which gave the necessary information as to which parent was most favorably described. The results were: mother more favored than father, 8; father more favored than mother, 3; parents equally favored, 5. The difference in favor of the mothers is significant at the .11 level using the sign test.

The third hypothesis was tested by determining which parents are described as giving the religious instruction. The results are:

Parent(s) Giving Religious Instruction

Mother	Father	Both
9	3	4

It is not clear how to interpret the cases in which both parents are said to have given religious instruction. Since the father normally did take some part in religious instruction, e.g., he conducted the family religious services, it is impossible to tell whether this response is consistent with the hypothesis or not, and accordingly these cases should probably be ignored. If this is done the difference is significant at the .07 level by the binomial test.

The fourth hypothesis asserts that resentment to the father's discipline should occur more frequently than resentment to the mother's. The results are:

		Mother's Discipline	
		Resented	*Not Resented*
Father's Discipline	Not Resented	1	14
	Resented	0	6

The sign test permits the rejection of the null hypothesis at the .06 level of significance.

To test the fifth hypothesis we require a measure of aggressiveness, which was obtained as follows. We examined all situations in the autobiographies where the press was a threat. For each book, the responses to such press were categorized on White's plan and the results tabulated to determine the frequency with which each class of responses occurred. Then, for each book, the responses were ranked in order of frequncy of occurrence. An individual was judged high aggressive if aggression was above the median for his list of responses, and low aggressive if aggression was at or below the median for his list of responses. Using this definition, the test result is:

		Aggressiveness	
		High	*Low*
Father's Discipline	Not Resented	0	13
	Resented	4	2

This difference is significant at .004 by [R. A.] Fisher's exact test.

The sixth hypothesis is confirmed by the fact that no instances of aggression against a woman were recorded. Finally, the last hypothesis is confirmed by the result

		Aggressiveness	
		High	Low
	Not Resented	3	13
Mother's Discipline			
	Resented	0	1

This difference is significant at the .82 level by Fisher's exact test.

There are several points about these results which require particular comment. First, the sample is obviously too small to permit these results to be regarded as more than suggestive. Nevertheless, some of the relations are strong, particularly that between resentment to father's discipline and aggression, and all the results are in the expected direction. Second, the sample is clearly biased toward the urban upper classes. But the distribution of fathers' occupations is only slightly so biased, and it is the fathers' occupations which are relevant in determining the relation between class and the child rearing of members of the sample. Since two thirds of the fathers were farmers, and most were at best middle class, it is unlikely that there is any appreciable class or urban bias involved. What does represent a biasing factor is of course the fact that these children succeeded, but it is not clear that this bias should vitiate the generality of any of these results.

Third, the sample yields a very low percentage of high aggressives and of resenters of father's discipline. This is, I believe, the result of errors of measurement. The criterion used to separate high and low aggressives turned out to be far stronger than was anticipated. Our high aggressives therefore represent, not the most aggressive half of the sample, but the extreme aggressives in the sample. Unfortunately, the fact that absolute numbers of responses could not be compared from book to book made it necessary to stay with this criterion. Similarly to qualify as a resenter of the father's discipline, one had to specifically and overtly express resentment in unambiguous terms. Had more indirect measures been employed, the number of resenters would certainly have been increased. What the figures give us is the relation of very extreme aggressives to very strong resentment. There is no reason to expect a reversal of the relation as the intensity is decreased.

Fourth, the bare descriptive categories of the content analysis do not convey the variations in intensity of the data. This is particularly true of the descriptions of the mother. For example, the most aggressive man in the sample writes of his mother as follows:

> Beautiful in person, cultivated in mind, gentle in heart, sober and sure in judgment, she was to me an incarnation of the qualities which the

mothers of the all-absorbing Anglo-Teutonic race have almost unconsciously developed and transmitted to the best and noblest of its sons.
She was companion and friend, joy, solace, and delight to every member
of her family, and when in 1878, after a long life devoted to their happiness, at the ripe age of seventy-four, she died surrounded by her children, calm, fearless and triumphant, something was taken from their lives
which changed the tenor of their thoughts forever.

Such rhapsodic descriptions indicate a degree of idealization of the mother
which is strikingly different from even the most favorable descriptions of
the father.

Finally, it may be asked whether the data supporting the first, second, and fourth hypotheses are not more simply explained by the Freudian
oedipal theory. The data are certainly consistent with that theory, but
that fact does not vitiate the approach used here. Even if the oedipal
theory is a correct description of certain universal features of the psychological development of male children, there are still variations in that
development from culture to culture which remain to be explained. It
seems clear that these variations must be related to specific child-
rearing practices obtaining in those cultures, so that some theory of the
relation between these specific practices and psychological development
is necessary in any case. Whether such a theory is sufficient is perhaps
another question.

To the student of nineteenth-century American social history it
would seem utterly banal to remark that American men of that time
worshiped God, home, and mother—not necessarily in that order—and
were highly aggressive. But as historians we have been prone to accept
these traits simply as given, or, if we have sought explanations for them
at all, to explain them by vague reference to "the requirements of the
frontier" or to some similar irrelevancy. That this extraordinary idealization of the mother might be connected to the high levels of intermale
aggression through structural relationships within the family and child-
rearing practices has not even been suggested. Yet if these traits were
as general as most historians believe they were, it seems reasonable to
conclude on the basis of current theories of personality formation that
they must be rooted in child-rearing practices. And it is therefore a non-
trivial problem for the historian to determine whether or not such practices and processes can be investigated with the data and methods at his
command. The purpose of this exploratory paper is to suggest that such
investigations are possible.

20

Sectional Stress
and Party Strength

THOMAS B. ALEXANDER

The decades before the Civil War are renowned for their growing sectionalism and for their lack of party cohesion. By feeding into a computer House of Representatives roll call votes on important issues from 1836 to 1860 and by utilizing agreement scores and scalogram analyses, Thomas B. Alexander was able to assess the relationship of party, section, and issue in determining votes. His findings delineate precisely the degrees of party cohesion and of sectional antagonism, particularly when economic and slavery-related issues arose.

The roll-call responses analyzed in this study point toward a remarkable continuity and consistency in political behavior over the years between 1836 and 1860. The effectiveness of the two-party system in ordering the work of the national legislature is evident. Although Democrats and Whigs differed with regard to certain aspects of this structuring role, the similarities outweigh the differences. Both major parties maintained a high level of cohesion and intersectional comity as long as a varied fare of public business could be served to the representatives. Only when sectional matters overwhelmed a session, as in 1850, was party discipline

From Thomas B. Alexander, *Sectional Stress and Party Strength: A Computer Analysis of Roll-Call Voting Patterns in the United States House of Representatives, 1836–1860,* pp. 110–13. © 1967 by Vanderbilt University Press, Nashville, Tenn. Reprinted with omissions by permission of the publisher.

impotent. As the Republicans supplanted the Whigs, some confusion was an attendant circumstance; but as soon as the new party organization was firm, the function it performed in the House came to resemble very closely that discharged by the Whigs before it.

Forces greater than party discipline or loyalty, nonetheless, were evidently at work continuously, relentlessly forcing party to yield to section on a definable array of issues. This can better be summarized by focusing attention separately on economic factors and on the slavery involvements.

ECONOMIC CONSIDERATIONS

A wide range of economic issues were firmly incorporated in party-oriented divisions in the House of Representatives throughout almost all of the period from 1836 to 1860. A coherent economic philosophy was encompassed in the dominant Whig party positions, and a consistent Democratic response to economic issues could usually be expected. The most characteristic pattern for scalograms relating to economic questions produced a polarization according to party alignment, with only modest amounts of overlapping between the two party contingents in the House.

From not later than the Twenty-fourth Congress [1836] onward, however, an element of North-South sectionalism lurked within each major party. When one party was on the defensive it generally managed to compress its stands into such a narrow range that sectional distinctions were obscured. But when either party was strong and aggressively seeking to implement a positive program, sectionalism appeared distinctly. There is no doubt that northern and southern congressmen, whether Whigs or Democrats, had to struggle against sectional pull to achieve any very high level of cohesion on economic questions. The spectacular abandonment of party for sectional or local interests, such as was exemplified by the behavior of Pennsylvania Democrats on tariff votes, was but the exposed and minor part of a very massive iceberg. Only strong party discipline reinforced by favorable election prospects could keep this element of sectionalism from getting beyond partisan control.

Both major parties were remarkably successful in maintaining substantial cohesion on economic matters, keeping the party lines clearly distinct in this area of federal policy until after the crisis of 1850. A period of evident confusion followed, affecting the Whigs more severely than the Democrats, before the familiar pattern re-emerged in the late 1850s. This re-emergence, however, was achieved by a fateful kind of clarification of the issues; for what had happened was more a fusion of partisan and sectional attitudes than the triumph of party over section as during the 1840s.

The dominant Democratic party position on matters economic more closely conformed to the southern sectional attitudes. By the mid-1850s the consequence of this fusion of southern and Democratic position on economic matters, reinforcing a comparable blending on slavery concerns, had cost the northern Democrats so dearly in political appeal that the demise of the party in New England and its virtual elimination throughout the upper North was immediately to follow. In a similar but inverted pattern, dominant Whig party positions on economic issues long suited the majority in the Northeast and came in the 1850s to suit that in the Northwest. Here, too, a comparable blending of northern and Whig attitudes on slavery reinforced the trend that led to the demise of the Whig party in the deep South and its critical weakening even in the Border South. If therefore, a renewed clarity of party alignment on economic issues was achieved after the emergence of the Republican party, it meant no more than that sectionalism had so triumphed over party as to coerce party lines into sectional ones.

It is difficult to avoid the conclusion that fundamental economic differences, cast by the contemporary leaders in the form of antagonism, were too much for party loyalty to resist. Each party apparently tried to resist, persistently and in the face of great difficulties, only to have an arm lopped off in the section not satisfied with the party stands. The time sequence of patterns emerging from this study of roll-call voting in the House powerfully suggests the efficacy of real problems and antagonistic interests of substance, stubbornly refusing to be shaped by party interests only bending under party pressure and always exerting force in the direction of sectional antagonisms, ever more effectively as party strength waned.

SLAVERY INVOLVEMENTS

The extensive range of slavery-related topics confronted by the United States House of Representatives between 1836 and 1860 produced a party and sectional pattern of roll-call voting distinguished for its persistence and consistency. Little evidence exists in the sequence of scalograms or in the profiles of agreement scores that the people of any section of the country, or their representatives in Congress, substantially altered their views on slavery during these years. Rather, the onslaught of events, some in the manifest destiny category and others as a product of careful and determined organization and agitation, forced upon congressional attention recurrent tides of issues associated with the subject until eventually slavery-related problems became the all-encompassing object of attention and drowned the cohesive and nationalizing elements in the nation's central legislative body.

From the earliest stages of nationwide two-party structure in the House, the congressional Democrats had shown considerable capacity to manage the slavery questions, principally because northern Democrats were persuaded to stand with their southern colleagues in the interest of harmony. From almost the beginning of the period, however, a distinction between southern and northern Democrats can be observed, sometimes greater, sometimes muted, but tending toward more distinct cleavage within a limited range of attitudes. Never did the main body of northern Democrats take a sectional stand on slavery issues directly, although in 1850 the issues were sufficiently wide in range and the tension sufficiently high that a momentary North-South polarization did occur. Harmony was quickly restored in the Democratic ranks in Congress, however, and northern Democrats generally continued to avoid taking a seriously sectionalized stand on slavery-related issues. The consequence was simply the virtual elimination of Democrats of the upper North from the House. This "national" stand by northern Democrats, successfully branded as "doughface" by northern opponents, proved to be political suicide.

Whigs, on the other hand, never achieved any degree of unity on matters directly associated with slavery. At the time of the expansionist crisis a façade of party unity obscured some of the intraparty sectionalism on slavery, but the sectionalism was neither obliterated nor muted thereby. From beginning to end, the Whig party in the House was substantially polarized every time a significant block of slavery-related roll calls had to be confronted. It was never a matter of changing attitudes nor of abrupt parting of the ways on the subject. It was always a North-South antagonism when the issues arose. The only significant question was how much of the work of a session was conducted in the slavery-related arena, for internal division in the Whig ranks was substantially predictable and in rough ratio to the proportion of slavery business to be transacted.

Hence, in 1850 a stunning polarization of Whigs in North-South antagonism existed in the House roll calls. Slavery issues were kept partly under wraps for a short time after 1850, but when they again erupted into prominence, an entirely predictable similar polarization reappeared. This time, furthermore, the degree of such antagonism was too great for the party structure to contain; and Whigs of the North could see little to gain and much to lose by continuing to carry along the ever-diminishing southern Whig contingent at the price of watering down a sectional appeal on slavery matters. Northern Whigs, after all, had every reason to claim credit for a generally hostile view of slavery as a long-standing tradition of their wing of the party. The Republican party after 1854 was many things in appeal and in maneuver, but in a meaningful sense it was the unencumbered continuity of northern Whiggery insofar as slavery was concerned.

Seeking to hold middle ground and draw at least moderately close to party colleagues across the slavery line had substantially the same effect on northern Democrats and southern Whigs. The effort eliminated the Democrats from the upper North and the Whigs from the lower South. If this does not point to the presence of powerful forces at work moulding the national legislature in the image of a nation in imminent danger of dividing, the thrust of this analysis of congressional roll-call voting is hard to explain. The "blunderers" of the "blundering generation" triumphed; those who by such interpretation did not blunder were quietly retired to obscurity, North and South. Is this the story of dominant leadership, making mistakes or willfully subordinating national interest to personal or party success? Or is it the selective survival of those who swam with the currents of the generation? And for those who would be gravely concerned with the last crisis and the footwork at the Charleston Democratic Convention, or in the Senate as it confronted Crittenden's proposals, or at the Old Gentlemen's Convention in Washington, what of the quarter-century continuity of responses to the slavery-related issues? One could take the pattern of the first two or three Congresses after the emergence of the Whigs as a national party and, given the rising ratio of slavery business, calculate reasonably well the consequences in House voting of a decade or two decades later.

As an exercise in hypothetical analysis and interpretation of the coming of the Civil War, one might profitably address himself to the proposition that each of five factors was indispensable to that coming: (1) Negro slavery; (2) moot questions in the Constitution relating to secession and ultimate authority to interpret the Constitution; (3) territorial expansion of the United States; (4) geographic differences reflected in economic distinctions and antagonisms among the sections; and (5) political decisions of the generation of leaders sometimes called blundering. The first four were, by 1836, almost foreordained in the sense that they either existed or were to be avoided only by an unthinkable consensus requiring superhuman self-sacrifice. After 1836, only through the fifth factor could the nation's agony of 1861–1865 have been averted.

The indications of this analysis of House voting over the crucial quarter century is that sectional attitudes regarding slavery were almost as immutable as the geography of the continent. An unflagging abolition crusade was not indispensable to the maintenance of these attitudes; they were revealed in the earliest congressional divisions on the subject after 1836. What was needed to produce strife and perhaps war was a sequence of events thrusting the slavery subject to the forefront. Antislavery agitation could contribute to that objective, but its contribution was probably modest compared with the onset of hurricane winds blowing from the west as the nation spread inexorably into the vacuum that was supposed to separate it from the Pacific shores.

Statesmen of the quarter century under review could not have been unaware of the currents of congressional voting on slavery-related subjects, nor of the scarcely submerged shoals directing and agitating that current with every rise of the winds of slavery business. Could northern statesmen have said, with conviction, to their people: this nation is destined to be for the foreseeable future a slave nation and we must adjust our thinking and policies to arrive safely at that predetermined haven? To state the question is all that is required to show its absurdity. Could southern statesmen have begun to tell their people that all the Western world was abandoning slavery and in the normal course of human events such abandonment would have to be accommodated in the southern United States? Could they have charted a course from their contemporary circumstance to an inevitable future condition and led their people to accept both the port of distination and some better manner of arriving there than being driven aground by irresistible currents? Perhaps not. But to conclude that they could not is to conclude that as early as 1836 the "logjam" had piled up and Americans were no longer master of their destiny but hapless playthings of sadistic gods.

The signs were in the patterns of roll-call responses in the national legislature. Those who placed national unity and continuous co-operation above all else knew well that the slavery issues could not be allowed to overwhelm the attention of Congress; but southerners were unwilling to co-operate in placing slavery in a condition in which all could rest assured of its ultimate extinction, and northerners were unwilling to sacrifice manifest destiny to the cause of excluding an unmanageable issue from the halls of Congress. And always there were those who, like John Quincy Adams, had no intention of allowing the issue to be kept out of those halls because they knew that its continuing entry there would make less probable a prolonged existence for slavery.

The House of Representatives provided a continuing promise or threat, as one chose to view it, that the nation would not continue to exist "half slave and half free" if only the question could be framed in a manner to confront the nation's legislators with an unavoidable decision. From the origin of the "gag rule," through the abortive efforts at finality in 1850, to the belated attempts of 1861 to exclude the whole subject from Congress once more, those who viewed the dyke as the permanent answer to rising tides were often the very ones with uncontrollable urges to cut through the dyke to sail a wider sea. Their blunder of statesmanship was not the failure to control their urges but rather in the initial strategy, which required defense of such a netherland as chattel slavery by a nation essentially expansive and aggressive in territorial acquisition, ideological influence, and economic relations with the outside world. A closed society bent on such outgoing missions is an internal contradiction by definition.

Both the slavery-oriented issues and the economic ones produced patterns in the roll-call voting of the House of Representatives between 1836 and 1860 which underscored the significance of real issues and problems of substance, which would not be wished away by any approach. The two major parties differed in response on the slavery topics: Democrats clung together on the essentially southern side; Whigs divided sectionally from the beginning. Neither approach obviated the problem nor worked out the salvation of the party. Northern Democrats were politically disinherited for their "doughface" decisions; southern Whigs were first strangled almost to extinction and then excommunicated by their northern fellow Whigs in the interest of purification of the creed.

The two parties tried much the same approach on the economic topics: establishment of a creed and calling all followers to accept and practice, within the limits of human frailties. The end result was no different. The party whose creed conformed to northern interests became the party of the North, although not without some fancy footwork and name manipulation; the opposition found itself equally triumphant in the South, having captured the losing side in the contest for power in the central government. This elaborate game of musical chairs was played on what appears to have been solid ground—real and persistent sectional differentials in interests and attitudes.

The Secession Conventions
of the South

RALPH A. WOOSTER

Whether southern states should secede from the Union was decided by the 1,859 members of conventions and legislatures of the fifteen slave states. Utilizing the information found in the 1860 manuscript census returns, Ralph A. Wooster has assembled a state-by-state collective biography of these men. Noting their age, occupation, real and personal wealth, and the number of slaves each owned, Wooster delineates the precise relationship of men favoring or opposing secession with slavery, wealth, and political affiliation.

The secession conventions and legislatures of the South were in many respects similar to one another. All were largely composed of middle-aged men; all were dominated by lawyers, planters, and farmers; and all were comprised of leading public figures of the state. In other ways, however, the conventions and legislatures varied appreciably from state to state. For example, delegates of the South Carolina and Louisiana

From Ralph A. Wooster, *The Secession Conventions of the South*, pp. 256–66. © 1962 by Princeton University Press. Reprinted with omissions by permission of the publisher.

conventions were wealthier and presumably more aristocratic than the delegates of the Arkansas convention or the Delaware legislature. To complete a study of the composition of the secession conventions and legislatures it is therefore necessary both to analyze the delegates in the aggregate and to compare with one another the memberships of the several bodies.

The proportion of native sons (i.e., delegates born *in* the state) in the conventions and legislatures varied widely. The conventions in the Atlantic coast states, representing the oldest communities, had much the highest proportion of native-born delegates—90.2 per cent of the Virginia convention, 88.5 per cent in North Carolina, 86.6 per cent in Delaware, 80.5 per cent in South Carolina, 78.4 per cent in Maryland, and 68.5 per cent in Georgia. On the other extreme, no member of the Texas convention was born in that state. Arkansas, like Texas a relatively new state, had 5.2 per cent natives in her convention and Florida, another new state, had 9.9 per cent natives in her convention. Following in ascending order were Missouri with 13.1 per cent natives, Mississippi with 16.0 per cent, Alabama with 17.0 per cent, Louisiana with 36.2 per cent, Tennessee with 56.0 per cent, and Kentucky with 76.8 per cent.

Slightly over half of the delegates in the conventions of the lower South were born in Georgia and South Carolina. This high percentage is due in the main to the size of the conventions in those two states, 301 and 169 members respectively, which were dominated by native sons. Both Georgians and South Carolinians were heavily in favor of secession, but this was true also of delegates born in every state, group of states, or foreign country and serving in conventions of the lower South. This majority was usually quite decisive, in most states more than two to one.

Over half of the delegates in conventions of the upper South were born in Virginia or North Carolina, again mainly due to the large conventions in those particular states. Here, however, a distinction is seen; the Virginians by nearly 2-1 opposed immediate secession, while the Carolinians were nearly this decisive in their support for immediate separation.* Tennesseans, the next largest group in the upper South, were strongly in favor of immediate secession, but Kentuckians, the fourth largest group, were evenly divided over the question of immediate separation.

Since there was no test vote in the Maryland and Delaware legislatures whereby members may be classified, it is impossible to give meaningful factional analysis to the four border states, but it may be

---

* It must be remembered, of course, that the North Carolina convention did not meet until after Lincoln's call for troops and therefore many of the post-Sumter secessionists may not have previously been secessionists.

noted that over a third (138) of the 360 members of the conventions or legislatures in this area were native-born Kentuckians. Seventy-four members were born in Maryland, thirty-seven in Virginia, and twenty-six in Delaware.

There appears to have been little relationship between occupations and attitude toward secession in the lower South. A majority of the members of all the leading occupations represented in the conventions of the lower South cast their votes for immediate separation, and the margin was usually in the neighborhood of two to one, or about the same as the ratio of strength in the conventions as a whole. For instance, 326 of the 473 farmers and planters, 207 of the 273 lawyers, and 48 of the 67 physicians supported separate state action. The only occupational groups in the conventions of the lower South rather equally divided over secession were the ministers, who voted ten for secession and eight for delay, and the lawyer-farmers, who voted seven for secession and five for delay.

In the conventions of the upper South, on the other hand, there was some relationship between occupations and attitude toward secession. Here the largest occupational group, farmers and planters, tended to be secessionists, as did most of the occupational groups; but the second largest group, lawyers, were opposed to secession by a sizeable margin, 87 to 62.

In the two border states in which there were factional divisions, Kentucky and Missouri, both the farmer and planter group and the lawyers supported the Union by 2–1, a ratio comparable to the factional division in the two states. All other occupational categories in the two states showed ratios in favor of the Union, some quite strong; for example, the merchants divided 15–3 for Union and the physicians divided 6–1 for Union.

The typical delegate to any one of the state conventions or legislatures was a substantial property-owner in 1860, but there were great differences in the median property holding of members of the various conventions and legislatures. In most cases the convention members of the states of the lower South were wealthier than those of the upper and border states, but there were exceptions; for instance, the median total property holding in both Virginia and North Carolina was higher than that in four states of the lower South. It may be noted in Table 64, which gives median property holdings for all the conventions and legislatures, that there is nearly a $60,000 difference between the state with the highest median property holding, South Carolina, and the state with the lowest holding, Kentucky.

A break-down of property-holding figures by factions shows that in all cases but one, Kentucky, the secessionist faction was wealthier

TABLE 64   Median Property Holdings of Delegates to Southern Conventions and
Legislatures

State	Real Property	Personal Property	Total
South Carolina	$18,875	$50,000	$68,875
Mississippi	15,712	32,000	47,712
Alabama	8,000	25,000	33,000
Florida	7,000	15,000	22,000
Georgia	7,000	17,000	24,000
Louisiana	30,000	20,000	50,000
Texas	6,000	10,000	16,000
Virginia	15,000	16,536	31,536
Arkansas	4,500	6,000	10,500
Tennessee	6,000	8,000	14,000
North Carolina	11,050	28,500	39,550
Kentucky	4,650	5,000	9,650
Missouri	10,000	6,500	16,500
Maryland	10,000	5,000	15,000
Delaware	9,000	2,500	11,500

than its opposition. In some instances, the difference between the factions
was substantial; for example, the median for the cooperationists in the
Alabama convention was $16,400, compared with the median of $57,765
for the secessionists, and the median for the unionists in the Arkansas
convention was $5,000, compared with $23,170 for the secessionists. In
Missouri and Tennessee the difference in property holding between secessionists and their opponents was also impressive. In other conventions
the difference was not so great, as reference to Tables 65 and 66 will
show, but in each state except Kentucky the secessionist median property holding was above that of their combined opposition. In Virginia
the moderate faction was actually wealthier than the secessionist, but

TABLE 65   Median Property Holdings of Factions in Conventions of Lower South

State	Conditional Unionists	Cooperationists	Immediate Secessionists
South Carolina	$	$	$68,875
Mississippi	47,000	48,409	57,765
Alabama		16,400	57,913
Florida		13,012	30,300
Georgia		23,840	25,000
Louisiana	19,500	59,900	60,250
Texas	13,000		16,000

TABLE 66   Median Property Holdings of Factions in Conventions and Legislatures of Upper and Border South [1]

State	Anti-Secessionists [2]	Secessionists [3]
Virginia [4]	$28,536	$33,700
Arkansas	5,000	23,170
Tennessee	9,175	15,300
North Carolina	26,700	33,185
Kentucky	9,250	7,725
Missouri	13,000	27,454

[1] There were no factional divisions in Maryland and Deleware legislatures; therefore, they are not shown.

[2] Anti-secessionist faction here includes Viriginia unionists; Arkansas, Tennessee, and Missouri unionists; North Carolina revolutionists; and Kentucky neutralists.

[3] Secessionist faction here includes Virginia, Arkansas, North Carolina, and Tennessee secessionists; Kentucky anti-neutralists; and Missouri southern-rights group.

[4] Median for Virginia moderates was $35,000.

if the moderates and unionists are combined their median is slightly less than that for the secessionists.

Slaveholding for delegates to the various conventions and legislatures varied considerably, ranging from the 37-slave median in South Carolina to less than one slave in Delaware. Delegates to conventions in the lower South were generally the larger holders of slaves, although the second highest of all medians belonged to North Carolina of the upper South. In six of the twelve states with factional divisions the median slaveholding for the secessionists was higher than the median for any faction opposed to them, and in three other states the secessionist median was higher than one of the two opposing factions but not as high as the other opposing faction. In two other states the medians were identical for the secessionists and their opponents.

TABLE 67   Median Number of Slaves Held by Delegates to Conventions in the Lower South

State	Conditional Unionists	Cooperationists	Immediate Secessionists	Entire Convention
South Carolina			37	37
Mississippi	12	21	16	15.5
Alabama		12	19	13
Florida		5	13	10
Georgia		14	14	14
Louisiana	9	17	12	12
Texas	4.5		5	5

This relationship between large slaveholding and secession was stronger in the upper South than in the lower South. In the conventions of the lower South the percentage of those who held 20 slaves or more was almost the same for the secessionists and their opponents, 41.8 per cent of secessionists and 41.0 per cent of the cooperationists and unionists held 20 or more slaves. In the upper South, however, there was considerable difference between the percentage of those in each faction who held 20 or more slaves; here 33.0 per cent of the secessionists held 20 or more slaves, whereas only 20.6 per cent of the anti-secessionists held this many slaves.

TABLE 68   Median Number of Slaves Held by Delegates to Conventions and Legislatures in the Upper and Border South

State	Anti-Secessionists [1]	Secessionists [2]	Entire Convention
Virginia [3]	4	9	9
Arkansas	†	10	1
Tennessee	2	6.5	6
North Carolina	12.5	25	21
Kentucky	3	2	2
Missouri	1	1	1
Maryland			1
Delaware			*

[1] Anti-secessionist faction here includes Virginia, Arkansas, Tennessee and Missouri unionists; North Carolina revolutionists; and Kentucky neutralists.

[2] Secessionist faction here includes Virginia, Arkansas, North Carolina, and Tennessee secessionists; Kentucky anti-neutralists; and Missouri southern-rights group.

[3] Median holding for Virginia moderates was 14 slaves.

† Median holding for Arkansas anti-secessionists was zero.

* Of the 30 members of the Delaware legislature only 6 held slaves; their total holdings were 16 slaves.

In the conventions of the lower South the delegates from old Whig counties tended more toward conditional union and cooperation than did those from the traditionally Democratic counties. The Whig party, which formed the bulwark against secession in the 1850 crisis, had virtually disintegrated by 1860, but the areas in which it had once held sway remained more conservative than the rest of the South. Particularly was this true in Georgia, Florida, Mississippi, and Louisiana— in these states delegates from a majority of the old Whig counties either opposed separate state action or were rather evenly divided over the issue. Only in Alabama in the lower South did Whig areas not conform to this rule; here they supported rather heavily the secessionist cause while the Democratic counties of the northern part of the state, where Jacksonianism had been particularly strong, were represented by co-operationists in the convention.

Whig counties in Virginia, Tennessee, North Carolina, and Kentucky tended more toward unionism than did the Democratic counties. In Missouri, however, the reverse was true; the Whig counties were fairly evenly divided on the question of unionism versus southern rights, while the Democratic counties were strongly pro-unionist. The Whig party had never been strong in Arkansas but those counties that had supported the Whig nominee in at least one of the four previous election were more prone to be secessionist than the rest of the state.

Comparison of the vote of the county delegation in the conventions of the upper and lower South with the vote of the county in the presidential elections of 1860 illustrates that the counties carried by John Bell—generally old Whig counties—were less susceptible to secession than those carried by John C. Breckinridge. Of the seventy-three Bell counties in the lower South, seven were represented in the conventions by conditional unionists, thirty-six by cooperationists, ten by divided delegations, and only twenty by secessionists. In the upper South ninety-two Bell counties were represented by anti-secessionists, nine by divided delegations, and fifty-eight by secessionists. A heavy majority of counties carried by Breckinridge, on the other hand, were represented by secessionists: in the lower South the division of Breckinridge counties was eleven conditional unionist, forty-nine cooperationist, twenty-two divided, and two hundred and seventy-one secessionist; in the upper South the division was seventy-nine antisecessionist, nine divided, and one hundred and ten secessionist. * The counties carried by Stephen A. Douglas tended to oppose secession in the 1861 crisis; in the lower South seven Douglas counties were represented by conditional unionists, seven by cooperationists, and four by secessionists, and in the upper South three Douglas counties were represented by antisecessionists, one by a divided delegation, and one by secessionists.

. . . The secessionist delegates came on an average from wealthier areas than did their opponents. This tendency was most pronounced in Alabama, Georgia, Tennessee, and Arkansas, states where the hilly, less

---

* In an analysis of political behavior in the presidential election and the secession movement, Seymour M. Lipset, *Political Man* (Garden City: Doubleday and Co., 1960), 349–51, notes that the Breckinridge counties which returned majorities against secession were mainly ones in which there was a comparatively small percentage of slaves in the total population; on the other hand, former Bell counties which were represented in the conventions by secessionists were mainly those with large percentages of slaves in the total population. In both instances economic factors evidently outweighed party loyalties.

fertile areas were the centers of opposition to immediate secession, while the fertile, cotton-producing areas supported separate state action. In several other states this tendency was true but to a slightly lesser degree; for example, per-capita wealth played a less important part in Mississippi and Louisiana. Although in these two states a majority of the wealthier areas supported immediate separation, instances were not uncommon in which rich sugar parishes in Louisiana and fertile Delta cotton counties in Mississippi elected cooperationists or conditional unionists to their state conventions.

A breakdown of votes by slave population shows that the secession movement in the lower South was particularly strong in counties where slaves constituted 62½ per cent or more of the total population. Among such counties the ratio for secession was greater than 4–1, whereas the overall ratio in the lower South was not quite 3–1. It may be noted in Table 69 that the ratio for secession was only 2–1 in the counties of the lower South with less than 25 per cent slave population.

TABLE 69   Comparison of Slave Population in Counties of the Lower South with Vote in Secession Conventions

Vote of County Delegation in Conventions *

Percentage of Slaves in Total Population of County	Conditional Unionists	Coopera-tionists	Immediate Seces-sionists	Divided	Total
Less than 12½%		16	34	5	55
12½% and less than 25%	3	20	36	4	63
25% and less than 37½%	5	19	54	7	85
37½% and less than 50%	1	18	64	4	87
50% and less than 62½%	5	14	52	5	76
62½% and less than 75%	4	8	37	9	58
75% and over	2	1	24		27
Total	20	96	301	34	451

* Counties not represented in vote are not included.

This tendency for secession to be stronger in counties with large slave population was even more pronounced in the upper South. Here, counties with less than 12½ per cent slave population were anti-secessionist by nearly 2–1, whereas the other counties showed a majority for secession. In counties of the upper South with slave population above 50 per cent this ratio for secession was better than 2–1. It may be surmised that the voters of these heavily slave-populated areas were con-

TABLE 70   Comparison of Slave Population in Counties of the Upper South with Vote in Convention or Legislature

Vote of County Delegation in Convention or Legislature *

Percentage of Slaves in Total Population	Anti-Secessionists [1]	Secessionists	Divided	Total
Less than 12½%	85	44	5	134
12½% and less than 25%	24	28	4	56
25% and less than 37½%	21	27	2	50
37½% and less than 50%	23	39	2	64
50% and less than 62½%	10	26	4	40
62½% and less than 75%	3	8		11
75% and over		1		1
Total	166	173	17	356

* Counties not represented in vote are not included.

[1] Includes Virginia unionists and moderates, Tennessee unionists, North Carolina revolutionists, and Arkansas unionists.

vinced that secession was necessary to protect their economic-social order from destruction, particularly after Fort Sumter indicated that war was inevitable. In any event this ratio for secession gave extremists a majority and carried these states out of the Union. The secession of the upper and lower South was now complete.

22

The Folklore Lincoln

DAVID DONALD

Along with Thomas Jefferson, Abraham Lincoln has become a symbol for the American people. Though the Lincoln of legend has little in common with the Lincoln of history, the image Americans have created in their minds is important and reveals much about their hopes and aspirations. David Donald has supplemented his Lincoln expertise with his insights into folklore to explore the rich and varied facets of the Lincoln legend and to help Americans better understand themselves.

.   .   .

III

Naturally the strongest growth of Lincoln legends has occurred in the North. There have been, in general, two opposing schools of tradition. One, essentially literary in character and often of New England or Eastern sponsorship, presented a prettified Lincoln, a combination of George Washington and Christ. Occasionally there were difficulties of reconciling the two ideas and the resulting portrait looks somewhat like a Gilbert Stuart painting with a halo dubbed in by later, less skillful hands. The problem was to reconcile the standards of democracy in the gilded age with the familiar pattern of the Christ story. Fortunately for authors, consistency is not an essential in folklore.

In eulogies, sermons, birthday speeches, Republican campaign

From David Donald, *Lincoln Reconsidered: Essays on the Civil War Era* (1956), pp. 148–66. © 1947 by David Donald. Reprinted by permission of Alfred A. Knopf, Inc.

addresses, orations before the G.A.R., and in poems too numerous to count and too tedious to read, one gets a glimpse of the pattern. This Lincoln has the outlines of a mythological hero; he is a demigod. Born in obscure circumstances, he rose over hardships, became President, was lawgiver to the Negro people, won a tremendous victory, and was killed at the height of his power. By his death he expiated the sins of his country. After one makes the obvious concessions required by mid-century morality and by the exigencies of a republican form of government, this Lincoln conforms very closely to the type of ideal hero in classical mythology.

The eulogists had some doubts as to how Lincoln's ancestry should be presented. A mythological hero should spring from unknown parentage (or at least it is concealed even from himself), sent by the gods to save his tribe. There are a number of Lincoln poets and biographers who ask: "Whence came this man?" and answer: "As if on the wings of the winds of God that blew!" On the other hand, it comported more with American notions of respectability that the hero should have at least some family connections. The Lincolns have, therefore, been traced in elaborate monographs back to the early Massachusetts settlers and even to the English family of that name. The Hankses have been "proved" to derive their name from an Egyptian dynasty, or, as an alternative explanation, they were relatives of the Lees of Virginia.

Regardless of origins, the biographers were sure of one thing. Lincoln loved his angel-mother. It is characteristic of the American attitude toward family life and of the extreme veneration for the maternal principle that the utterly unknown Nancy Hanks should be described as "a whole-hearted Christian," "a woman of marked natural abilities," of "strong mental powers and deep-toned piety," whose rigid observance of the Sabbath became a byword in frontier Kentucky—in short, "a remarkable woman." "A great man," asserted J. G. Holland in his widely circulated *Life of Abraham Lincoln*, "never drew his infant life from a purer or more womanly bosom than her own; and Mr. Lincoln always looked back to her with an unspeakable affection."

Lincoln's early life became, to this school of biography, an illustration of how determination and energy could triumph over circumstances; this Lincoln was the transcendent rail-splitter. It was a carefully manipulated symbolism that had begun at the Illinois state Republican convention of 1860 when rails that Lincoln might have split were introduced to elicit applause. The theme was drummed and piped and bugled all through the campaigns of 1860 and 1864, and the tale of Lincoln's "life of labor" that "brought forth his kingly qualities of soul" has become a part of the American tradition. Lincoln was never to escape; his Civil War administration would be appraised in terms of his early struggles:

Out yonder splitting rails his mind had fed
On Freedom—now he put her foes to rout.

From these origins he rose to become President of the United States, and, surprisingly enough, a successful President. There must have been, a great many people believed, some supernatural force, some divine guidance behind his rise. "Out of the unknown, and by ways that even he knew not," orated one centennial speaker, becoming more mystical with each phrase, "came to this place of power, Abraham Lincoln. He came mysteriously chosen . . . by the instinctive voice of a predestined people. Called because he was chosen; chosen, because he was already choice."

There were elements in Lincoln's personality and career which did not blend well in this portrait of a demigod. He was indubitably homely—not a major difficulty, to be sure, yet if a hero is not handsome he should at least be impressive. Rhymesters went to great length to explain the truth. Was Lincoln "ungainly, plain"? Not at all. "Grave was his visage," it was admitted, "but no cloud could dull the radiance from within that made it beautiful." A more serious obstacle was Lincoln's levity. He told jokes—a thing unprecedented in the record of mythology. Writers were more familiar with the idea of "one who knew not play, nor ever tasted rest." How could a man of sadness and tears laugh at Artemus Ward? One poet suggested that Lincoln's laughter was really a sort of anodyne "to cease his ceaseless dole." Thus Lincoln became the laughing man of sorrows.

Another difficulty was Lincoln's religion. It was embarrassing that this "soldier of his Captain Christ" belonged to no Christian church. Shortly after Lincoln's death there began to appear a veritable flood of affidavits and statements to prove, as Holland put it, that "Lincoln's power" had been the "power of a true-hearted Christian man." Reminiscences on this point probably include more nonsense than can be found anywhere else in the whole tiresome mass of spurious Lincoln recollections. To him are attributed the most improbable statements. Lincoln was supposed to have had a secret conference with Newton Bateman, Illinois superintendent of public instruction, during which he pulled a Testament from his bosom and pointed to it as *"this rock* on which I stand." "I know," he is alleged to have confided, "that liberty is right, for Christ teaches it and Christ is God."

Countless similar statements were given wide newspaper circulation. Lincoln reportedly ran upon one Benjamin B. Smith, a minister of Canton, Missouri, in a railway station, brought him into his office, and begged from the willing pastor a private, hour-long discourse upon "foreordination, election and predestination." During the darkest hours of the war Lincoln was supposed to have left his post in Washington in order to pray with Henry Ward Beecher in Brooklyn. So it went. There were those who could demonstrate that Lincoln was a Catholic, a Congregationalist, a Methodist, a Presbyterian, a Universalist, or a Spiritualist. Conflicting claims became so amusing that the editor of the Springfield *Illinois State Register* rejected them as "all wrong." "We are," he remarked whimsically, "prepared to prove by indisputable documentary evidence that he was a Mormon, and the boon companion of Joe Smith."

For these minor defects Lincoln amply compensated by the manner of his passing. His assassination at once brought to mind the tender, familiar outlines of the Christ story. Lincoln as "Savior of his country" was by his death expiating the sins of the nation. The idea had universal appeal. One has only to leaf through the pages of Lloyd Lewis's *Myths after Lincoln* to disover how frequently the idea of vicarious sacrifice recurred to Northern preachers on that dread Black Easter of 1865. Some pointed to the significance of Lincoln's martyrdom on Good Friday. "It is no blasphemy against the Son of God," asserted a Connecticut parson, "that we declare the fitness of the slaying of the second Father of our Republic on the anniversary of the day on which He was slain. Jesus Christ died for the world, Abraham Lincoln died for his country." Even so early the pattern of apotheosis was complete. America had a martyr hero, a perfect man, born to do great things, pure in heart, noble in action, and constant in principle. This was Lincoln, "President, savior of the republic, emancipator of a race, true Christian, true man."

IV

Lincoln was saved from this kind of deification by a different stream of tradition, frequently Western in origin and more truly folkloristic in quality. The grotesque hero—the Gargantua or the Till Eulenspiegel—is one of the oldest and most familiar patterns in folk literature. In America the type had been already exemplified by such favorites as Davy Crockett, Mike Fink, and Paul Bunyan. Of a like cut was the myth of Lincoln as frontier hero. This Lincoln of "folk say" was the practical joker, the teller of tall and lusty tales. Stupendously strong, he was also marvelously lazy. A true romantic, he pined over the grave of Ann Rutledge, but he also lampooned one woman who refused him and jilted another who accepted. He was Old Abe, a Westerner, and his long flapping arms were not the wings of an angel.

This folk pattern of Lincoln as frontier hero had been sketched in outline before his death. After his assassination the details were filled in. Many of the stories in the strong Western tradition can be traced back to Herndon, Lincoln's law partner, who has been called the "master myth-maker" of Lincoln folklore. Herndon did not invent the legends, but his singular personality made him peculiarly receptive to this type of Western mythology. Herndon was born in Kentucky, and, as an early German traveler put it, "the Kentuckian is a peculiar man." Moody, erratic, lo-quacious, addicted to high-flown "philosophical" language, but with a fondness for earthy stories, Herndon had shortly after his partner's death decided to write a biography of Lincoln. From the very outset he had in mind showing Lincoln as a Western character, shaped by the "power of mud, flowers, & mind" which he had encountered in the pioneer North-west. Deliberately he sought to emphasize those factors which would distinguish Lincoln as a Westerner from his Eastern contemporaries. He proposed to exhibit "the type" of the "original western and south-western pioneer— . . . at times . . . somewhat open, candid, sincere, energetic, spontaneous, trusting, tolerant, brave and generous."

Seeking information about Lincoln, Herndon interviewed older set-tlers in central Illinois and southern Indiana at just the time when the outlines of the folk portrait were becoming firmly established. From his notes emerged the essentially fictitious picture of a semilegendary frontier hero. The stories Herndon collected fall into patterns familiar to the stu-dent of American folklore. Some remembered Lincoln as a ring-tailed roarer of the Davy Crockett type, who would wave a whisky bottle over his head to drive back his foes, shouting that "he was the big buck at the lick." There were tales of the Paul Bunyan variety, describing how Lincoln would "frequently take a barrel of whiskey by the chimes and lift it up to his face as if to drink out of bung-hole," a feat that "he could accomplish with greatest ease."

This was the Lincoln who chastely wooed Ann Rutledge and, when she died, pined sadly over her grave. "My heart," he was supposed to have said, "lies buried there." More in the frontier tradition was his courtship of Mary Owens, a well-educated Kentucky lady who refused his hand. Afterward Lincoln described her as "weather-beaten," "over-size," and lacking teeth. Of a like pattern were the tales Herndon ac-cumulated of Lincoln's domestic unhappiness with Mary Todd, for the henpecked husband is one of the oldest comic types and was a favorite in the Western joke books of the day. Herndon also collected irreligious or, as he called them, "infidel" statements attributed to Lincoln; the folk hero is frequently anticlerical.

Many of these tales probably had a grain of historical truth, and their evolution exhibits the familiar developments of folk literature. "If a man has been well known for special powers," Robert Price has pointed out in his examination of the Johnny Appleseed traditions, "folk fancies soon seize upon particular instances of these powers, begin to enhance them into facts of remarkable quality, and then proceed, as the desire for greater color grows, to invent still others that will markedly emphasize the quality admired." As the historical personage becomes absorbed in the myth, "the whole cycle of his birth, youth, education, loves, mating, maturity, and death becomes significant and grows increasingly in color and particular detail." On a rather sophisticated plane, the Lincoln of Western legend represented a true folk-hero type.

The folkloristic quality of these stories is sometimes overlooked. When Herndon visited in Indiana, he was told of verses that Lincoln had written to celebrate the wedding of his sister:

> *When Adam was created*
> *He dwelt in Eden's shade,*
> *As Moses has recorded,*
> *And soon a bride was made.*

(The poem continues for seven additional stanzas.) Dr. Milo M. Quaife has traced this ballad back to early English folk verse and has shown that it was introduced into America before the Revolutionary War. In the process of being handed down, it somehow became identified in the minds of backwoods Hoosiers with Lincoln; it was related to Herndon as such; he published the verses in his Lincoln biography; and the poem is not infrequently cited as Lincoln's original composition. Of the making of myths there is no end.

The process of evolving Western legends about Lincoln neither began nor ended with Herndon. Gossip, imagination, delayed recollection, and hearsay have all continued to multiply "Lincoln" stories. Sometimes the results of this accumulation of "folk say" are amusing. One can take, for example, a less familiar episode in Lincoln's early career—his projected duel with James Shields. The actual facts of the affair are easily ascertained. In 1842 Mary Todd and Julia Jayne published anonymously in the *Sangamo Journal* some satirical verses about Shields, then Illinois state auditor. That hot-tempered Irishman demanded of the editor the names of the writers, and Lincoln, to protect the ladies, offered to take the blame. After some stilted correspondence and much dashing back and forth of seconds, a duel with broadswords was arranged. Ultimately, however, explanations and apologies were made, and actual combat was averted. The affair remained a sore memory to Lincoln, and he disliked hearing the episode referred to. The whole affair is summarized in any good Lincoln biography.

As this same tale comes down in folklore, the whole emphasis is altered. It becomes an illustration of Lincoln the humorist and the practical joker. The duel had an amusing origin, according to one old settler who had heard another old-timer tell the story:

> Lawyer Shields and Julia Jayne were seated together at the supper table. Across the table from them sat Abe and Mary Todd. By and by the lawyer squeezed Julia's hand. In those days, you know, a pin was a woman's weapon. Julia used it when Shields squeezed her hand. And that made him scream. . . . Lincoln, who was a laughing fellow, hawhawed right out loud, much to the embarrassment of Shields. Well to make a long story short, Shield[s] issued a duel challenge to Abe.

Another version gives a play-by-play account of the duel that never happened. "Shields fired and missed," says this "eyewitness," speaking of an encounter that was to have been fought with broadswords. "Lincoln then took steady aim and fired. A blotch of read [sic] appeared on the breast of Shields who fell to the ground thinking he was mortally wounded, but in fact was unhurt. Lincoln's gun was loaded with pokeberries."

To treat such statements simply as exaggerated reminiscences is to miss their significance. They are really folk stories. Seldom do they have an identifiable author, for the narrator is recounting what "they said." The very pattern of the statement is significant; "to make a long story short" is a frequent formula to conclude a folk tale. The Shields episode is only one less widely known incident about which a surprisingly large amount of folklore has accumulated. The body of tradition concerning Lincoln's courtship, his marriage, or his law practice is much more voluminous. And there is an extensive cycle of ribald and Rabelaisian stories attributed to Lincoln, for the most part unprintable and now almost forgotten.

V

Few Negroes have written books about their great emancipator, and the viciously anti-Lincoln publications are nearly forgotten, but the other two major currents of tradition have produced a mountainous pile of Lincoln literature. Writers who fitted Lincoln into the pattern of a mythological demigod had the early start at the printing presses. A series of widely read and often quoted biographies began to appear shortly after Lincoln's death, starting with the Arnold and the Holland lives and running without interruption through the work of Nicolay and Hay and that of Ida M. Tarbell. All were characterized by a highly laudatory tone and all presented Lincoln in an aura of great respectability.

Those who thought of Lincoln as the archetype of the frontiersman were outraged. Herndon was especially bitter at the "Finical fools," the "nice sweet smelling gentlemen" who tried to "handle things with silken gloves & 'a cammel [*sic*] hair pencil,'" but for personal reasons his own book about Lincoln was delayed for many years. The publication in 1872 of Ward Hill Lamon's biography, ghost-written from Herndonian sources, marked the first widespread circulation in print of the Western version of Lincoln's career. It was greeted as "a national misfortune." When *Herndon's Lincoln* appeared seventeen years later, it, too, met with shrill disapproval, and some shocked souls appealed to Anthony Comstock to suppress this indecent book. This food was too coarse for sensitive stomachs.

It is a mistake to consider these two opposing currents of Lincoln tradition as representing respectively the "ideal" and the "real" Lincoln. Each was legendary in character. The conflict in Lincoln biography between the Holland-Hay-Tarbell faction and the Herndon-Lamon-Weik contingent was not essentially a battle over factual differences; it was more like a religious war. One school portrayed a mythological patron saint; the other, an equally mythological frontier hero. Not all the Lincoln stories related by either school were false, but the facts were at most a secondary consideration. Acceptance or rejection of any Lincoln anecdote depended upon what was fundamentally a religious conviction. Even today this attitude is sometimes found. A recent writer has attacked certain legends that he asserts "libel" Lincoln on two grounds—first, because they "do not create a truer or finer image of him" and, second, because the myths are "unsupported by trustworthy evidence." The order of the reasons deserves notice.

It is widely recognized that the biographies of the Holland school are remote from reality. They present a conventionalized hero who is discussed from a "frankly eulogistic point of view." The temptation has naturally been to treat their opponents—such as Herndon, Lamon, and Weik—as realists, intent on giving a "true" picture of Lincoln. If there is any meaning left in the word "realism," which is rapidly becoming semantically obsolete, *Herndon's Lincoln* (a biography typical of this latter school) is realistic neither in literary style nor in biographical approach. Herndon's book was dedicated to proving a thesis—that Lincoln had his origin in a "stagnant, putrid pool" and rose through adversity to "the topmost round of the ladder." All of its contents Herndon deliberately arranged to support this contention and to enlist readers' sympathies in behalf of his protagonist. Rough and coarse elements were introduced into the biography, not primarily from conviction that these were vital aspects of human existence, but principally to serve the same function as the villain in the contemporary melodrama. Unlike the true realists,

Herndon was concerned with the unusual and the sensational. It is difficult to see how anyone can find in Herndon's emotionalized treatment
of the Ann Rutledge legend the work of a biographical or literary realist.
Actually the biographies of the Herndon school are stylized presentations
of Western folklore. Herndon's own book recounts the epic of the frontier
hero, transmogrified into the pattern of the sentimental novel.

Toward the end of the century the two conceptions of Lincoln—as
mythological demigod and as legendary frontier hero—began to blend,
sometimes with amusing results. John T. Morse's *Abraham Lincoln,* one
of the better early biographies, made no effort to reconcile the two concepts, but accepted both. For Lincoln's early years Morse followed Herndon, and for the period of the Presidency, Nicolay and Hay. The result,
he admitted, tended to show that Lincoln was "physically one creature,
morally and mentally two beings." In the huge file of newspaper reminiscences in the Lincoln National Life Foundation one can trace the process
by which demigod and hero become inextricably scrambled. By the centennial year of Lincoln's birth the frontier stories that had been considered
gamy and rough by an earlier generation had been accepted as typical
Lincolnisms; and on the other side, the harshness of the Herndonian
outlines was smoothed by the acceptance of many traits from the idealized Lincoln. The result was a "composite American ideal," whose "appeal
is stronger than that of other heroes because on him converge so many
dear traditions." The current popular conception of Lincoln is "a folk-
hero who to the common folk-virtues of shrewdness and kindness adds
essential wit and eloquence and loftiness of soul."

VI

One may question the value of studying these legendary accounts of
Lincoln. A more conventional procedure is to assault these air castles
of contemporary mythology, to use the sharp tools of historical criticism
to raze the imaginary structures, to purify the ground by a liberal sprin-
kling of holy water in the form of footnotes, and to erect a new and
"authentic" edifice. Such an approach has its merits. One cannot over-
estimate the importance of thoroughgoing historical investigation of
Lincoln's career; far too little of the huge bibliography of Lincolniana
is based upon scholarly, scientific research.

But there is also room for investigation of another sort. Referring
to the debunking of historical myths and legends, W. A. Dunning, in his
presidential address before the American Historical Association, reminded
his hearers that in many cases "influence on the sequence of human affairs

has been exercised, not by what really happened, but by what men erroneuosly believed to have happened." In turning to history for guidance, he observed, men have acted upon "the error that passes as history at the time, not from the truth that becomes known long after." He concluded by pointing out that "for very, very much history there is more importance in the ancient error than in the new-found truth."

His warning applies in the field of Lincoln·biography. As J. Frank Dobie has put it, "The history of any public character involves not only the facts about him but what the public has taken to be facts." It is important to examine the Lincoln legends as expressing a collective wish-fulfillment of the American people. This is no psychological jargon; it is simply a way of saying that "heroes embody the qualities that we most admire or desire in ourselves." Fully realizing their general inaccuracy and almost universal distortion, the student can use these myths for an understanding of what plain Americans have wished their leaders to be. "If the folk aspiration is worthy, its dreams of great men will be worthy too."

Unless one conceives of time as ending with 1865, the Lincoln of folklore is more significant than the Lincoln of actuality. The historian may prove that the Emancipation actually freed a negligible number of slaves, yet Lincoln continues to live in men's minds as the emancipator of the Negroes. It is this folklore Lincoln who has become the central symbol in American democratic thought; he embodies what ordinary, inarticulate Americans have cherished as ideals. As Ralph H. Gabriel says, he is "first among the folk heroes of the American people." From a study of the Lincoln legends the historian can gain a more balanced insight into the workings of the American mind. As it is now written, intellectual history is too often based on printed sources—sermons, speeches, commencement addresses, books, and newspapers. The result is inevitably a distortion. The men who write books or edit papers are not average citizens. It is much as though the Gallup poll were to interrogate only college presidents. To understand the thinking of ordinary men and women, the historian must delve into their beliefs, their superstitions, their gossip, and their folklore.

The Lincoln ideal offers an excellent starting-point for the investigation. As the pattern·has gradually become standardized, the folklore Lincoln is as American as the Mississippi River. Essentially national, the myth is not nationalistic. It reveals the people's faith in the democratic dogma that a poor boy can make good. It demonstrates the incurable romanticism of the American spirit. There is much in the legend which is unpleasant—Lincoln's preternatural cunning, his fondness for Rabelaisian anecdote, his difficulties with his wife—yet these traits seem to be attributed to every real folk hero. The fundamental qualities of the legendary Lincoln emphasize the essential dignity and humanity of our nation's everyday thinking. It speaks well for Americans that to the central hero in their history their folklore has attributed all the decent qualities of civilized man: patience, tolerance, humor, sympathy, kindliness, and sagacity.

23

A Medical Perspective
on the Civil War

RICHARD H. SHRYOCK

"War," General William T. Sherman concluded, "is all hell," and the more than one-half million men killed in the Civil War proved his point. Richard H. Shryock examines this grisly statistic from a medical point of view and increases understanding of both the suffering involved in that frightful toll and the state of American medical science from 1861 to 1865.

Among the various themes pertinent to Civil War history, medicine seems least apt to lend itself to centennial celebrations. Do we really wish to recall, a century later, the incredible suffering which occurred on battlefields and in hospitals during that conflict? One would judge, from much recent writing on the War itself, that there is no such desire. Yet, if medical aspects are omitted, the story is not only incomplete but is unrealistic as a total picture. It can provide analyses of military strategy or may portray the day to day life of troops in the field. But often it becomes a dramatic narrative which, though containing vivid accounts of

From the *American Quarterly* 14 (1962):161–73. Footnotes omitted. Reprinted by permission of the author's family and *American Quarterly*. © 1962, Trustees of the University of Pennsylvania.

battle scenes, fails to make real the tragedy inherent in the entire experience.

What actually happened was that a struggle which began almost lightheartedly at Bull Run, soon became one of the bloodiest wars of all time. A number of circumstances converged to make it so. First, this was a peoples' war and large numbers of troops were involved: perhaps three million all told. Second, although morale was not always high, armies sought out opponents with much determination. Third, in combat, most wounds were caused by musket or rifle fire, and the leaden bullets then employed did more damage than do modern, steel counterparts. Fourth, surgical practice was such that nearly all penetrating wounds were fatal except those of the extremities, and even the latter had a high mortality rate.

Most appalling, however, was the fact that many wounded who might have been saved were abandoned on battlefields. No adequate ambulance services and field hospitals were available as late as 1862. At Second Bull Run, for example, the Union army was supposed to have 170 ambulances but actually went into battle with 45—most of which broke down. Several days after the battle, in consequence, 3,000 wounded still lay where they had fallen. In this situation, many men bled to death or died from exposure and were then reported as "killed in action." Worse still, in certain instances—as at Chancellorsville in '63 and again at the Wilderness in '64—hundreds of the wounded actually burned to death when shells set the woods on fire!

After ambulance facilities were provided, field hospitals were sometimes overwhelmed by major-battle casualties. At Gettysburg, for example, the Union medical corps was well equipped with 1,000 ambulances, 650 officers, and about 3,000 drivers and stretchermen. But within three days, 21,000 wounded were brought in just when most of the medical officers were moving on with the army. Each remaining surgeon was thus left with an average of 900 cases on his hands. Haste and neglect were unavoidable under such circumstances.

Those among the wounded who *were* properly tended in field and base hospitals had still to run the risks of surgery. As is well known, anesthetics were usually available but there was no notion of aseptic procedures. Looking back in 1918, the Philadelphia surgeon W. W. Keen recalled that:

> We operated in old blood-stained and often pus-stained coats . . . with undisinfected hands. . . . We used undisinfected instruments . . . and marine sponges which had been used in prior pus cases and only washed in tap water.

No wonder that nearly all wounds became infected and that there was still some talk of "laudable pus" in the medieval manner. In the case of chest or abdominal wounds, surgeons probed with their fingers, pre-scribed morphine and tried to stop external bleeding. Otherwise, there was little they could do. The victims usually died within three days from hemorrhage and/or infection. The average Union mortality from gun-shot wounds of the chest was 62 per cent of cases; and from such wounds of the abdomen, no less than 87 per cent. By way of contrast, only about 3 per cent of all American wounded failed to survive in World War II.

Chances were better but not too good with injuries of the extremities, for joints could be removed or limbs amputated. It is difficult to find mortality rates for amputations but they were certainly high by modern standards. Here again, it was usually the ensuing infection which caused death—the so-called "surgical fevers" which included tetanus, erysipelas, hospital-gangrene and pyemia ("blood poisoning").

The infectious nature of wound gangrene was recognized and cases were isolated in hospitals when feasible. Efforts were also made to disin-fect wounds, as when bromine was used with some success against this same disease. Among the chemicals so employed was carbolic acid, the very agent which Lister used soon thereafter in the first demonstrations of antiseptic surgery. This being the case, why did not the Civil War surgeons anticipate Lister? Since they thought that carbolic would clean out infected wounds, why did they not use it to sterilize fresh wounds and instruments in the first place?

The difference on which the outcomes turned was largely a theoreti-cal one. Lister, impressed by Pasteur's view of bacterial origins of infec-tion, assumed that the surgeon's hand or instrument was introducing pathogenic organisms. Ergo, if wounds were sprayed at the start with carbolic acid, infection could be avoided. But American surgeons of the 1860s were either unfamiliar with bacteriology or did not take it seriously. They were "practical men" with more wound experience than was pos-sessed by any surgeons elsewhere, yet this did not prevent them from adhering to another old theory; namely, that infections were caused by "noxious miasms" arising from filth and carried through the air.

It followed that the way to prevent wound infection was to avoid these miasms. And this could be done by seeking ordinary cleanliness in hospitals—by carrying over into these institutions the sanitary controls already demanded in public hygiene. Surgeons, it was assumed, had nothing to do with introducing infectious poisons: the latter were just literally "in the air." But once infection appeared in a wound, the surgeon could then attempt to *dis*infect it by applying chemicals. All this was logical enough but we can now see that it was these practical men who were ultimately impractical. Their chemotherapy for already-infected wounds often came too late.

Cumulative experience enabled surgeons to improve certain tech-niques, as in handling the great arteries. Occasionally a new and useful procedure emerged, only to be forgotten after the War and perhaps re-introduced many years later. A striking illustration of this resulted from pure chance. Several Southern doctors, lacking supplies for keeping maggots out of wounds, found that these visitors actually cleaned out dead tissue and prevented infection. This fact had been stumbled upon during the Napoleonic Wars, was rediscovered in the '60s as noted, then was overlooked again and finally discovered for the third time—much to everyone's amazement—during World War I. Empirical findings of this sort, based simply on trial and error, were usually known only to those immediately involved and were then easily forgotten. In the case mentioned, most surgeons continued conscientiously to remove maggots and thus assured infection. In other words, incidental technical advances did little to check mortality resulting from wounds.

Statistical data on military losses vary widely, but it has been stated that as many as 110,000 Northern soldiers and 94,000 Southerners succumbed to battle injuries. One may roughly estimate from these data that from 6 to 10 per cent of Union troops and from 10 to 15 per cent of the Confederate died from wounds. The exact ratios depend on what estimates are accepted for the total number of troops involved.

High as were the casualties, it is well known that losses from disease were higher. While 110,000 Union soldiers perished from wounds, some 250,000 died from disease: the corresponding figures for Confederates were probably about 94,000 and 164,000. The average soldier, as a matter of fact, was ill between two and three times each year, and the annual mortality from sickness was more than 5 per cent. Compared with male civilians of military age, servicemen were five times as likely to become ill and experienced a mortality which was five times as high as that of those who remained at home.

Strangely enough, from the present viewpoint, army leaders thought their record very creditable—even when as many as 10 per cent of all troops were ill at one time. Actually, the record *was* creditable in comparison with preceding wars: it is only in contrast with later conflicts that the medical experience of 1861–65 seems so startling. Thus, while the annual disease mortality rate was then about 53 per thousand soldiers, this ratio fell to 16 per thousand during the Spanish War, and to about 12 per thousand during World War I. In other words, the disease death rate for troops during the Civil War was more than four times as great as that experienced in 1917–18.

The explanation of this relatively high mortality was not as simple as one might think. In the first place, the limitations of wound surgery were those of medicine in general. The War came just too soon to witness certain major advances in hygiene and surgery. If it could have been postponed for two decades, many deaths would have been avoided.

Even at that, the knowledge already available in 1861 would have made possible much lower mortality rates if it had only been applied effectively. The utter lack of preparation and subsequent inefficiency in the medical services must bear much of the blame for unnecessary illness. This inefficiency was not the fault of any one group. Sharing in responsibility were the original medical officers, indifferent generals and politicians, a mediocre profession, and rural regiments hitherto unexposed to infections and unfamiliar with the rudiments of hygiene. Over against such villains of the piece must be placed the many heroic figures. Among the latter were certain generals, such as McClellan, who supported reform in the medical services; a growing number of conscientious Army surgeons; and a host of civilian volunteers who called for better medical care and meantime ministered directly to those in need.

The chief diseases among troops were caused directly or indirectly by unhealthy environments and bad habits. In the early War years, sanitation in hastily constructed camps was crude at best. Both food and water supplies were infected, and typhoid, dysentery and diarrhea became the most common and most fatal of camp afflictions. White Union troops had an average annual rate of 711 cases and 15 deaths from these diseases for every thousand men. The gastro-enteritis problem was complicated by the standard ration of beans, salt beef and army biscuits, as well as by the men's habit of frying everything as long as they did their own cooking. Gastronomically, one can hardly imagine a worse regimen, and it is no wonder that there was some scurvy (13 cases annually per 1,000) as well as endless "dyspepsia."

The second most common type of illness was malaria, which involved an average annual rate of 522 cases per 1,000 Union troops but only 3 deaths. More fatal were the respiratory infections, resulting from exposure in the field and overcrowding in tents or barracks. Tuberculosis was serious, though its mortality was not recorded. What was termed "inflammation of the lungs" presumably included the pneumonias and was responsible among Union troops for an average of 6 deaths per 1,000 men each year. Rheumatism was common and there was an unknown amount of alcoholism and of mental illness. Measles and mumps were annoying but not fatal, and the same was thought to be true of venereal diseases.

Although a higher proportion of officers than of enlisted men were killed in battle, the latter suffered a disease mortality rate about twice as high as that for officers. Rural troops, until adjusted to crowded camp life, endured more illness than did urban soldiers; which may explain why Western volunteers had a sick rate in 1861 more than twice as high as that for Easterners. Illness was always more common and more fatal among Negro than with white troops: the lung infections which killed 6 white men per thousand annually, resulted in no less than 28 deaths among a corresponding number of Negroes. More significant was the relatively high mortality from disease among Confederate as compared with Union soldiers, especially from respiratory infections. During the first eighteen months of the War "half again as many Confederates died of diarrhea and dysentery, while more than *five times* as many died of pulmonary diseases."

It is hard to believe that there was so great a contrast between Union and Confederate mortality; but, if true, the excessive Southern losses may be hypothetically explained by unfamiliarity with northern winters and by the relative scarcity of food, clothing and drugs during the latter part of the War. On both sides, of course, resistance to infections was lowered by exposure or malnutrition. These and other adverse circumstances also lessened a man's chances in undergoing surgery.

In treating disease in the 1860s, medical men were at some disadvantage in comparison with both their predecessors of 1760 and their successors of 1960. They obviously lacked many present aids—the antibiotics, for example, or the resources of aseptic surgery. They did possess certain helpful drugs unknown during the Revolution, notably quinine against malaria and chloroform as an anesthetic. But, just because medical science had become more critical after 1820, Civil War surgeons had little of that confidence in traditional remedies which had heartened practitioners in earlier years.

Actually, there was more skepticism about the value of drugs during the later nineteenth century than in any other period before or since. Medical leaders had learned to distrust the old, therapeutic standbys of bleeding and purging but had as yet found few new remedies in their place. Bleeding was already frowned upon during the 1850s; and although some older doctors continued it into the '70s, it was little employed during the Civil War. If a man lost blood on the field, he was not subjected—as in Revolutionary days—to further bleeding in the hospital. And although emetics and laxatives, along with morphine and whiskey, were routine remedies, the chief medical officers shared a growing distrust of extreme vomiting and purging. This distrust found expression in an order issued by Union Surgeon General Hammond in 1863, banning the use of the mercurials tartar emetic and calomel. Some military surgeons resisted this order, which definitely reduced their "armamentarium." But the episode pointed in the direction which medical practice would follow thereafter.

A less fortunate aspect of medical thought at midcentury was its emphasis upon specific diseases rather than—as in earlier days—on the general state of the patient's "system." This emphasis upon specificity pointed toward the identification of particular illnesses, and how discover causes or cures until diseases themselves were first known? But, meantime, inquiring physicians became more interested in diseases or in injuries as such than in the patients who harbored them. Instead of being concerned about the total condition of John Smith in ward B, they were intrigued by the "strange case" of typhoid or by the "extraordinary wounds" found in this same location. Modern medicine, in contrast, has returned to older concern about complete physiologic reactions to disease or injury. Thus, reports on World War II wounds often relate to kidney involvement in resulting "shock," whereas those of the Civil War were limited to the immediate, structural damage involved.

The emphasis of the 1860s on specificity not only overlooked generalized pathology but also gave little heed to the patient's state of mind. Laymen sensed this situation at times, as when Louisa Alcott remarked of a surgeon in Washington that he:

> had acquired a somewhat trying habit of regarding a man and his wound [or illness] as separate institutions, and seemed rather annoyed that the former should express any opinion on the latter, or claim any right in it, while under his care.

Speaking elsewhere of the same surgeon, she added that:

> The more intricate the wound, the better he liked it. A poor private, with both legs off, and shot through the lungs, possessed more attractions for him than a dozen generals slightly scratched in some "masterly retreat. . . ."

The tendency to focus on diseases rather than on patients reflected the best hospital standards of the day. Back in the homes whence enlisted men had come, family doctors probably still viewed their patients as persons and not simply as "cases" of this or that; but in hospitals—including the military—such overall concern was often lost. It would have been lessened in any case, within army circles, by the tendency to give routine care to masses of sick or injured soldiers. One suspects that most medical officers, practicing a form of "State medicine," had neither time nor inclination to cultivate solicitude or even bedside manners.

Both scientific attitudes and military circumstances thus set limits to the effectiveness of the medical care provided. But, within these limits, what was the general quality of those who served on both sides as medical officers? At the start, most of these men had had little surgical experience, since specialization in surgery was still unknown in this country. It also must be remembered that the effort to train first-class practitioners (real physicians) had not yet had much success in America in 1860; indeed, would not fully succeed until the present century. Many medical schools were mediocre or worse, even by the standards of the time; and much the same thing can be said of most of their graduates. There had been frequent criticism of "regular" practitioners before 1860, as ignoramuses who killed their patients with the lancet and calomel; and such distrust, carrying over into the War years, apparently influenced attitudes in both the Army and in Congress.

On the other hand, a few first-rate physicians—some of them professors from the better schools—joined the medical departments or served as contract surgeons in base hospitals. Men of this stamp had taken postdoctoral work in Paris during the 1830s and '40s, and by the '50s were turning to Vienna for such training. A few of them had developed research interests while abroad. But the War temporarily checked migration to the Austrian center, and its demands on medical personnel left little time for investigations in pathology or physiology. The chief exceptions to this rule grew out of clinical studies based directly on hospital observations, as in the work done by W. W. Keen on nerve injuries.

Technical improvement in surgery also grew directly out of empirical experience. Although these achievements, as noted, had little effect on mortality rates, they did gain recognition abroad for American surgery. Even before 1860, Europeans had been impressed by American prowess in dental and in gynecologic operations. And since Civil War experience promoted military surgery in general, there was much foreign acclaim of "manipulative skills" in this country.

After the War, American surgical instruments were highly praised at an 1868 exposition in Paris. Even more impressive was the subsequent publication, by the U. S. Army Medical Department, of the ponderous *Medical and Surgical History of the War of the Rebellion* (1870–88), wherein masses of pathologic data were made available. The German pathologist, [Rudolph] Virchow, said of these collections that:

> Whoever . . . reads the extensive publications of the American medical staff will be constantly astonished at the wealth of experience therein found. The greatest exactness in detail, careful statistics, . . . and a scholarly statement . . . are here united, to preserve and transmit . . . the knowledge purchased at so vast an expense.

Probably the highest foreign praise accorded Civil War doctors was that expressed by the Swiss physician Edwin Klebs. Writing in the '80s, Klebs declared that:

> . . . the greatest and most admirable success has been attained by the North Americans in military medical work. The history of the war of the secession has to show a display of medical and scientific activities that leave anything that ever since has been achieved in Europe way in the background. . . .

Perhaps Klebs was a bit too appreciative. At any rate, granting that medical records were well preserved and granting also that surgeons acquired manipulative skill, it remains true that little that was basically new emerged from the War experience. This has usually been the case with war medicine. American physicians who had done little research before 1861 were still less inclined to pursue it under military pressures. As a matter of fact, they did not even keep up with new methods or instruments introduced in Europe from one to three decades earlier. Such simple, diagnostic procedures as the use of clinical thermometers and of stethoscopes were rarely employed in the military services.

If much of the medical story of the Civil War seems depressing to-day, it did at least have its brighter side. There is no better way of present-ing this than to forget the armed forces for the moment and to recall rather the civilian welfare organizations. The tradition of voluntary help in emergencies had already been established before 1861, as in the work of the so-called Howard associations during epidemics. But the Civil War called for such aid on a vastly increased scale. Women's relief agencies, in the form of local hospital societies or even of such state-wide bodies as the Georgia Relief and Hospital Association, were formed in the Con-federacy. But only in the Union, where states' rights were not taken so seriously, did such efforts result in the founding of regional or national organizations—notably of the Christian Commission, the Western Sani-tary Commission and the United States Sanitary Commission. Of these, the last-named was most significant.

Seeking at first to be helpful, women's relief societies were formed in Boston and in New York City in 1861. These and other groups coa-lesced into the U. S. Sanitary Commission, acquired able directors and officers and were officially recognized in Washington. But their repre-sentatives were appalled by the chaos they found there and particularly by the hopeless inefficiency of the Army medical corps. Protesting against resulting suffering among the troops, they were rebuffed by the Secretary of War as meddlers and termed by Lincoln a mere "fifth wheel" for the military agencies. That did it! From this time on, the Commission—directed by the able Frederick Law Olmsted—investigated, reported and successfully pressured the services into the reform of medical care both in the field and in hospitals. Their inspiration came from the sanitary ideal of the era; the conviction that pure water, good food, fresh air and general cleanliness would prevent nearly all human ills.

This is not the place to recall the endless negotiations of the Com-mission with cabinet members, field commanders, medical officers and congressmen. But out of its efforts and those of enlightened Army per-sonnel came improved camp sanitation, the use of ambulances, the com-bination of regimental into divisional field hospitals, the building of pavilion-plan base hospitals and the encouragement of nursing by women.

The greater part of so-called nursing in military hospitals was done by convalescent soldiers, who lacked training, aptitude and strength for the work. But Florence Nightingale's achievements in the Crimea had aroused interest in the possible services of women. Hence the Union War Department commissioned Dorothea Dix as the first Superintendent of Army Nurses; that is, of women in this program. Those who volunteered received little training but had to meet certain requirements, such as being strong, middle-aged and of plain appearance. (Miss Dix would have no nonsense in her outfit.) Most of these women made up in idealism what they lacked in other respects and so were able to do much for the morale of their patients. How important this could be, from a medical as well as from a humane viewpoint, was probably not as fully realized in the 1860s as it has been in recent decades.

The reminiscences of the volunteer nurses provide vivid pictures of suffering observed within base hospitals. (After all, such mortality statistics as have been noted here are abstractions: they provide basic data but are far removed from human experience.) Further lines from Alcott's *Sketches*, for example, will make the hospital picture more real than will all the figures in the world. Perhaps the following account of a boy's sudden death will serve our purpose.

Observing that a patient had not eaten his meal, Miss Alcott offered him coffee, whereupon he startled her by saying simply: "Thank you, ma'am; I don't think I'll ever eat again, for I'm shot in the stomach. But I'd like a drink of water, if you aint too busy:

> I rushed away [continues Miss Alcott] but the water pails were gone to be refilled, and it was some time before they reappeared. I did not forget my patient patient, meanwhile, and, with the first mugfull, hurried back to him. He seemed asleep; but something in the tired white face caused me to listen at his lips for a breath. None came . . . and then I knew that, while he waited, a better nurse than I had . . . healed him with a touch . . . half an hour later, the bed was empty. It seemed a poor requital for all he had . . . suffered—that hospital bed, lonely even in a crowd; for there was no familiar face . . . no friendly voice to say, Good-bye; no hand to lead him gently down into the Valley of the Shadow. . . . For a moment I felt bitterly indignant at this seeming carelessness of the value of life . . . then consoled myself with the thought that, when the great muster roll was called, these nameless men might be promoted above many whose tall monuments record the barren honors they have won.

Present readers may think this only Victorian sentimentality, and one must admit that modern writers might handle the same theme somewhat differently. Yet I sense in these lines, written by a New England girl almost one hundred years ago, a genuine and moving experience. By implication, moreover, the statement raises one of the eternal questions about war which may be posed here again in summing up the whole matter. Putting aside any thought of pacifism in principle, how can we balance suffering over against achievements in order to decide whether this particular conflict was really worth its cost? Did the aftermath fully compensate for the loss of some 600,000 young lives—to say nothing of further anguish among those who survived?

Obviously, such matters cannot be reduced to quantitative terms. There is no magic arithmetic which can multiply the value of one life by 600,000 and come up with a meaningful total. And if there were, who could determine for comparison the tangible merit of one Union or the real value of emancipation—even if we assume that these goals could have been attained only by combat? Although such questions cannot be answered with finality, they are not necessarily devoid of meaning. In the fullness of time, they may have some bearing on ultimate conclusions.

We do not often ponder the medical record of the Civil War. Other sources recall other evil consequences but it is this record which best suggests the full measure of human costs. One may emphasize the point by raising a simple question: What part of the country still recalls "the War" most persistently? Obviously, the South. Why? Because, we are told, that section lost more and suffered more. But did it? Well yes, in humiliation or bitterness, and—as Professor [Roy F.] Nichols has made clear—in power as well as in property. *But not in lives.* If the usual estimates may be depended on, almost 100,000 more Northern men than Southern died in this holocaust.

Yet for all our protestations about the sanctity of life, these vital losses present that aspect of war which is most soon forgotten. Such an outcome may be ascribed in part to the common habit of suppressing unhappy memories, but more than this has been involved. Consider, for example, Professor [C. Vann] Woodward's observation that Southerners, in recalling defeat and ruin in 1865, are the only Americans who have any memory of national frustration. It follows, by implication, that the death of thousands of fathers and sons in the North aroused no lasting feeling of this nature. Where victory was followed by prosperity, there was hardly even a surviving awareness of national tragedy.

These rather acrid thoughts are consistent with one's personal impressions. Over the years, I have known only one Northern family which recalled the Civil War with much feeling. And this was my own household, which lost no lives but did witness the destruction of its home town by Confederate troops—some time before Sherman marched through Georgia. It was probably after such experiences, direct or vicarious, that families passed on memories and resentments unto the third and fourth generations. Descendants living in ruined areas, moreover, were constantly reminded of "the War" by poverty or other adverse consequences long after an older generation's sacrifice in lives had ceased to have personal meaning.

If we could recall the actual suffering of 1861–65, we might not so readily view the Civil War in terms of epic grandeur. In fact, however, there is now a disinclination to admit that anything so vital could have been unfortunate in the long run. This disinclination may be based in some cases on thoughtful analyses. But more often, one suspects, a pessimistic view is almost instinctively avoided because it would disturb national optimism and therefore must not be incorporated into our philosophy of history. Such an attitude may be detected today in the South as well as in the North, and it presumably inspires current "celebrations" of the Centennial.

We shall never know the final truths here, since no one can discover what would have followed if things had happened otherwise in 1861. Yet those who believe that the War was an ultimate triumph, alike with those who view it as ultimate tragedy, must base their conclusions on some calculus of might-have-beens. The former must assume that alternatives to war would have been worse in the final reckoning; the latter, that they would have been better.

This much seems reasonably certain: we should guard against the assumption that all major outcomes in the American past must have been for the best. Time may heal all things but does not necessarily justify them. With this thought in mind and recalling the medical story, one may still cherish doubts about what was called in some circles the War between the States. This, of course, was just what it was not. It was not a conflict among abstract "states" but rather a struggle between real men—with all the consequences which this entailed.

24

The Economic Impact
of the Civil War

STANLEY L. ENGERMAN

Douglass C. North's essay on the crucial nature of early nineteenth-century American economic growth clearly deemphasized the traditional importance attached to the Civil War. In this move he followed a trend among economic historians begun in the 1960s by Thomas C. Cochran. This trend has been vigorously resisted by the followers of Charles A. Beard. Utilizing long-range statistics primarily, econometrician Stanley L. Engerman assesses in this selection the effect of the Civil War on the American economy.

During the past several years the controversy concerning the political and economic impact of the Civil War has been reopened. The traditional interpretation, which is customarily associated with the names of Charles Beard and Louis Hacker, has come under heavy attack. On the political side, Robert Sharkey and Irwin Unger have questioned the proposition that the war was a political revolution which vested power in a northern business class which had been previously denied it. On the economic side, Robert Gallman's estimates of commodity production and national income have raised many questions about the propositions that the Civil

From *Explorations in Entrepreneurial History*, 2d ser. 3 (1966):176–92. Footnotes omitted. Reprinted by permission of the author and *Explorations in Entrepreneurial History*. © Graduate Program in Economic History, University of Wisconsin.

War accelerated the course of economic growth and that the Civil War period itself was one of rapid economic expansion. Gallman's findings apparently helped to stimulate Thomas Cochran's notable essay, "Did the Civil War Retard Industrialization?" Despite these attacks, not all historians, political or economic, have modified their opinions. Quite the contrary, Cochran's critique of the Beard-Hacker thesis brought forth spirited counterattacks by Stephen Salisbury, Pershing Vartanian, and Harry Scheiber.

One of the major obstacles to the resolution of the debate is the extremely wide field over which the controversy has ranged. In this article I shall attempt to narrow the range of debate by defining the central issues in the controversy, analyzing some of the data used in the debate, and examining the conclusions drawn from these data. My emphasis will be on the economic rather than the political aspects of the problem. Political issues will be considered only to the extent that they bear upon the economic impact of the Civil War.

I. THE BEARD-HACKER THESIS

To Charles Beard and Louis Hacker, the Civil War was a great turning point in the political, social and economic life of the nation. It was, in the words of the Beards, a "second American revolution" which ended in "the unquestioned establishment of a new power in the government, making vast changes in the arrangement of classes, in the accumulation and distribution of wealth, in the course of industrial development, and in the Constitution inherited from the Fathers." Given this broad list of changes, it will be useful to mention specifically what are argued to be the key factors.

The main political shift stressed by Beard and Hacker is the presumed transfer of political power from the southern agrarians to the northern industrial capitalists. On attaining power these northerners were supposed to have passed legislation which provided a framework for, if it was not the direct means of, their economic aggrandizement. These wartime measures, as well as subsequent legislation, which presumably would not have become laws if the southerners were still in Congress, have been made the cause of the accelerated industrialization and growth in national income that was assumed to have occurred during the postwar era. In particular Hacker singles out the following wartime measures: the issuance of the greenbacks, the increase in tariffs, the institution of the National Banking System, the adoption of the Homestead Act, the grants of land and other subsidies to the transcontinental railroads, the passage of the Morrill Act, and the adoption of the contract labor laws. These enactments, it is argued, led not only to increased profits for northern industrialists, but also benefitted other groups who shared in the dividends of accelerated growth.

Perhaps the most important social change attributed to the war was the overthrow of southern slavery. This theme was well established before the writings of Beard and Hacker. Three decades before the publication of *The Rise of American Civilization,* Carroll D. Wright made the creation of a free labor force in the south the central issue of the Civil War. Wright's theme was repeated and elaborated upon by Beard and Hacker. They argued that the southern economy was stagnating in the ante-bellum era, and attributed this to the inefficiency of the slave system in the allocation of labor. Thus the war, and the end of slavery, provided the necessary conditions for subsequent industrialization and economic growth in the south.

Beyond this, Beard, Hacker, and their followers believed that the war had the "usual" stimulating effects of other wars. In analogy with the effects of World Wars I and II on the American economy, the years 1861–1865 are considered to have been a time of rapid economic expansion, with high levels of output and employment. Beard and Hacker, following [W. C.] Mitchell, argued that the inflation resulting from the issuance of greenbacks led to a fall in real wages and an increase in the share of income going to the rising class of industrialists. War contracts meant large profits in the "war industries," while the combination of increased aggregate demand and the labor shortage arising from military needs led to rapid mechanization in industry. Significant changes in the techniques of production presumably took place in many industries, with boots and shoes, woolens, and men's clothing being particularly affected. The sales volume of agricultural implements was said to have risen markedly. Hacker also placed great emphasis on the shift within manufacturing to heavy industry in the postwar years—a shift which he believed was initiated by wartime demands. The wartime profits, the improvements in technology, and the shift toward heavy industry are all taken to be major explanatory variables in the accelerated growth of the postwar era.

II. LONG-TERM TRENDS, 1840–1900

It must be remembered that neither Beard nor Hacker had reliable statistical data upon which to base the arguments about the effects of the Civil War upon the rate and pattern of American economic development. While the scattered items upon which they leaned were consistent with their interpretations, they were often incomplete for the strong conclusions drawn. Fortunately, more complete and relevant data have become available in recent years.

The estimates of commodity output and national income prepared by Robert Gallman gave a different view of economic growth before and after the Civil War than that conveyed by Beard and Hacker. Gallman's series indicate that the period between 1840 and 1860 was one of rapid expansion in total and per capita output, as well as one of pronounced change in the structure of economic activity. Total commodity output rose at an annual rate of 4.6 per cent between 1840 and 1860, and at an annual rate of 4.4 per cent between 1870 and 1900. Moreover, as measured by the absolute percentage point change in shares of output, the shift from agriculture to manufacturing was as rapid in the twenty years before the war as in the twenty years after it. Thus the relative increase in the share of manufacturing in output was larger in the prewar than in the postwar period.

Even if one were to interpret the Beard-Hacker thesis as focusing only upon growth in the manufacturing sector, the data point in a similar direction. Value-added in manufacturing, which grew at an annual average of 7.8 per cent from 1840 to 1860, grew only at 6 per cent from 1870 to 1900. It is true that the share (in current dollars) of value-added in durable goods within manufacturing did rise from 42.7 per cent in 1860 to 48.6 per cent in 1870. However, this share fell back to 42.5 per cent in 1880, so that any wartime change apparently was not irreversible.

Hence it is clear that post-Civil War trends with respect to the shift toward manufacturing in the rate of growth in total commodity output, and the rate of growth in manufacturing output were not above the trends established in the prewar years.

However, the growth of total commodity output from 1860 to 1870 averaged only 2.0 per cent, the lowest rate during any decade in the nineteenth century. Similarly, the annual growth rate of manufacturing value-added, 2.3 per cent, was also the lowest rate for any decade during the century. Moreover, the manufacturing share in total commodity output rose only from 32 per cent to 33 per cent in the decade. That was due to the decline of southern agriculture rather than to accelerated expansion in manufacturing (see Table 1). If we exclude the Confederacy, the relative share of agriculture in total commodity output actually rose. Finally, the sharp decline in value-added per worker in manufacturing from 1860 to 1870, 13 per cent, is a unique occurrence for the nineteenth century. Thus the new data show that while the Civil War decade marked a clear departure from the nineteenth-century trend, this departure is a direction opposite to that anticipated on the basis of the Beard-Hacker thesis.

While the postwar years saw some return to prewar growth patterns, we should note that there was a slight decline in the rate of growth of commodity output. For this reason, perhaps, the Civil War decade can be regarded as a period bringing about retardation in American economic development. Even if one were to claim that the differential in growth rates was too small to be regarded as significant, the war may be considered to have retarded the economy in another way. The uniquely low rates of growth of commodity output during the war decade meant that the level of 1870 output was beneath the level expected on the basis of extrapolating the prewar trend. It is estimated that it was not until almost five years later that output reached the predicted 1870 level, and, even if the rate of growth had not declined in the postwar period, this lag would have persisted. Thus the war decade saw a retardation in the growth of commodity output due both to a low rate of growth during the decade and to a decline in the rate of growth in the postwar era relative to that of the prewar years.

The growth in total commodity output can be separated into the growth in population and the growth in per capita output. When evaluating the aggregate behavior it is important to consider these components. The postwar rates of population growth were below those of the prewar period. Indeed, the Civil War decade marks the onset of a long period of decline in the rate of growth of population. Yet only a small part of this decline can be attributed to the direct and indirect effects of the war.

TABLE 1   Commodity Output, By Region and Industrial Sector, 1860–1880 (1879 prices; millions of dollars)

| | Non-South | | | South | | |
	Total	Agriculture	Manufacturing & Mining	Total	Agriculture	Manufacturing & Mining
1860	$1674	$ 853	$ 821	$710	$639	$ 71
1870	2337	1246	1091	534	477	57
1880	3876	1861	2015	838	738	100

Declines in the rate of growth of population have been associated with rising per capita income in most developed countries and follow from the fact that birth rates in these nations have fallen more rapidly than have death rates. In the U. S. the decline in the rate of growth continued almost uninterruptedly until the Second World War. Thus it appears that the impact of the war upon population growth was overwhelmed by influences seemingly independent of the war.

Per capita output did grow more rapidly between 1870 and 1900 than it had in the two prewar decades—at an annual rate of 2.1 per cent as contrasted with the earlier 1.45 per cent. Suggestive as these figures may be, they do not necessarily support the Beard-Hacker thesis. The higher postwar rate may merely reflect a "catching-up" process induced by the decline in per capita commodity output during the Civil War decade. This possibility is suggested both by the fact that the immediate postwar years show the highest growth rates and the fact that the growth rate of per capita commodity output is the same between 1860 and 1900 and between 1840 and 1860. Not until almost 20 years after the war did per capita commodity output reach the level estimated by extrapolating the prewar trend, and it is at this time that the rate of growth returns to this earlier level.

This "catching-up" notion can be examined in more detail by looking at the regional trends in commodity output per capita (see Table 2).

TABLE 2   Commodity Output per Capita by Region, 1860–1880

	Non-South	South
1860	$ 74.8	$ 77.7
1870	81.5	47.6
1880	105.8	61.5

TABLE 3   Manufacturing Value-added and Employment, Massachusetts and New York, 1855–1870 (Value-added in million dollars, 1879 prices; Employment in thousands)

	Massachusetts		New York	
	Value-Added	Employment	Value-Added	Employment
1855	$117	224	$142	215
1860	127	224	173	230
1865	98	244	72	171
1870	145	279	221	352

The victorious north underwent little internal devastation and presumably benefitted from wartime demands. However, the annual rate of growth per capita commodity output in the non-south from 1860 to 1870 was under 1 per cent, the lowest for any decade in the nineteenth century. While the annual growth rate between 1870 and 1880 was an unusually high 2.6 per cent, it was in part a "catching-up" phenomenon. The annual rate between 1860 and 1880, 1.75 per cent, was above the prewar level of 1.3 per cent. The non-southern growth rate from 1880 to 1900 was equal to the national average, 1.9 per cent. Thus the data indicate that there was an increase in the rate of growth of per capita income in the non-southern states after the war, although (as shall be pointed out in the next paragraph) after 1870 they grew no more rapidly than did the southern states. This increase, perhaps, is the key index favorable to the Beard-Hacker thesis.

It is in the south that the destructive effects of the war were most severely felt. Per capita commodity output declined by 39 per cent in the Civil war decade, and in 1880 was still 21 per cent below the 1860 level. Nevertheless, the growth rate of commodity output per capita in the 1870's, 2.6 per cent, was the same as that in the rest of the nation. From 1880 to 1900 southern per capita income also grew at the national average, so that the negative impact of the war on the southern growth rate appears to have been confined to the decade of the 1860's; but that impact was substantial. If southern per capita income had grown in that decade at the same rate as it had during the prewar period, 1.6 per cent, it would have been almost twice the actual 1870 level. If the Civil War is to be considered a precondition for southern economic growth, it was one which was exceedingly costly to the south as well as to the national economy.

One important indirect effect upon the subsequent economic growth attributed to the war was its effect upon the growth of capital stock, particularly industrial capital. It is argued that because of both warime measures and postwar legislation, the share of national income going to the investing classes rose. More will be said about this question, but we do have sufficient data to compare both the growth of capital stock before and after the war and the pre- and postwar shares of capital goods in commodity output. The annual rate of increase of the total stock of fixed capital was higher from 1840 to 1860 (8.1 per cent) than from 1870 to 1900 (5.1 per cent), with the Civil War decade and that of the 1870's being periods of low growth. The stock of fixed capital in manufacturing did grow more rapidly in postwar years, at an annual rate of 6.8 per cent as contrasted with the prewar rate of 6.3 per cent, but the declining growth rates for other components reduced that of the total capital stock. The share of capital goods in commodity output was higher in the postwar period, but we should note that Gallman's estimates show a rising trend in this ratio starting in 1840. Thus we need to account for the early upward movement, as well as the possible effects of the Civil War, in explaining the increased share of output invested in the postwar period.

III. ECONOMIC EXPANSION DURING THE WAR YEARS

Gallman's series on commodity output and income in the nineteenth century contain no estimates in the 1860's. The discussion of the Civil War decade was based upon comparisons made between census years

1860 and 1870. Thus we cannot make inferences about the behavior of output in the Civil War years themselves. While such data as we now have for the war years may be weaker than the comprehensive estimates for 1860 and 1870, they are suggestive as to movements in the economy during the war, as distinguished from postwar developments. If the postwar part of the decade was a period of more rapid expansion than were the war years, the use of Gallman's data would suggest a more favorable picture of economic change during the war than is warranted, understating wartime declines and overstating increases.

The most frequently used production indexes for these years are those prepared by Edwin Frickey. His index of manufacturing output shows a much sharper rate of increase between 1866 and 1870 than during the war years. This is true not only for the total, but for both its durable and non-durable components. The index of overall industrial and commercial production also indicates a sharper eye of expansion in the postwar than in the wartime years. Similarly almost all the measures relating to agriculture cited by [W. D.] Rasmussen increased more rapidly from 1866 to 1870 than from 1861 to 1865.

Other sources of data are New York and Massachusetts censuses for 1865. The Massachusetts census was for the year ending June 1, and the New York census was apparently for the same period. This means that wartime expansion will be included, since the National Bureau of Economic Research places the Civil War peak in April 1865 (the month the war ended). The behavior shown by manufacturing output in these censuses makes reliance upon them for anything but suggestions hazardous. They should not be ignored, however, since they do represent the only comprehensive censuses of manufacturing output available for a Civil War year. The measured declines in 1865 were widespread, not concentrated in any one industry or region, and no statements of exceptional difficulty in data collection were made.

Manufacturing value-added and employment in these states, at five-year intervals between 1855 and 1870, are shown in Table 3. (New York and Massachusetts together accounted for 33.3 per cent of manufacturing value-added in 1860 and 31.7 per cent in 1870.)

While the patterns of change are not entirely consistent, and the postwar boom would have had to have been unusually large, it is interesting that in both states declines in real output are shown not only between 1860 and 1865, but also between 1855 and 1865. While subject to more scrutiny, we can at least say that it appears that these two key manufacturing states did not have rapidly expanding manufacturing sectors during the war years.

As noted in the previous section, the Civil War decade did mark a rise in the share of capital goods in commodity output for the economy. In 1870 this ratio was at its nineteenth-century peak. However, the high share in this year may represent a "catching-up" to offset declines in the earlier part of the decade. This is suggested by the estimates of capital stock which Gallman and [E. S.] Howle have prepared on the basis of census data. The rate growth of fixed capital fell from 8.5 per cent in the 1850's to 4.1 per cent in the 1860's. Also suggestive in this regard is the residential building series prepared by Manuel Gottlieb. (Nonfarm residential buildings accounted for approximately 30 per cent of fixed capital in both terminal years of the decade.) Gottlieb's index shows a quantity of residential building in 1866–1870 about twice that of 1861–1865. Similarly, Earle Ross, in his study of Iowa agriculture, stated that "the records indicate the great increase in machinery for the decade came in the years after the war," a conclusion also pointed to by the sales pattern of the McCormick company. Thus it is also doubtful that the war years were a period of investment boom.

The "War Industries"

It is crucial to note that the industries most frequently cited as affected by the Civil War do not fit into the category of war-related industries as that term is customarily used. Rather, they are consumer goods industries, or industries whose demand was derived from that for consumer products. This suggests that the techniques of war were premodern and that any mechanization in heavy industries due to war demands was of minor importance, in contrast with twentieth-century wars.

Indeed Richard Wacht has shown that the consumption of iron attributable to small arms production during the war was only 1 per cent of total U. S. iron output between 1861 and 1865. The amount could have been used to lay about 650 miles of railroad track. The short-fall in mileage built during the war below the 1856–1860 level was 7 times that amount. Thus any expansion in iron output based upon arms production was more than offset by the effect of the war upon railroad construction.

Given the importance of consumer goods industries in war production, the relevant historical comparison becomes more difficult. If government demands merely replaced civilian demands for the same commodities, it is possible that no increase in demand over and above the probable non-war situation occurred. Thus arguments based upon the magnitude of demand for these products may attribute too much to the effects of the war.

Because of the absence of consistent data over the period, it is often difficult to discuss changes in rates of growth of output for specific consumer goods industries. However, some comparisons can be made on the basis of state and national census data. They suggest that the presumed effects of the war are often questionable, growth and technological change being rapid before the war in many industries.

The Massachusetts censuses for 1855 and 1865 provide some basis for discussing the changes in boots and shoes and textile production. Massachusetts accounted for about one-half of the national output of boots and shoes, one-third of the cotton textile output and one-fourth of the output of woolens in both 1860 and 1870.

Between 1855 and 1865 Massachusetts employment in the boot and shoe industry fell from 77,827 to 55,160, while output fell from 45 million pairs to 32 million. This decline has been attributed to the elimination of the southern market, in which a standard low quality shoe was demanded for slaves, which was only partially offset by rising military demands. The absence of capital figures for 1855 precludes comparison of the degree of mechanization, but output per worker remained relatively constant over the decade. This was in a period when the ratio of male to female employment in the industry was increasing, presumably indicative of an improvement in the quality of the labor force.

The woolen industry did expand rapidly in the war period, possibly hitting a peak level of output in 1865 before declining to 1870. In Massachusetts value-added per worker rose 12 per cent between 1855 and 1865. However this may not have been due to the introduction of new techniques. Yards worked per worker fell slightly, the increased dollar amount being attributable to a shift from the cheaper flannels to the more expensive cassimeres.

With the Massachusetts data we can examine another proposition about the effects of the war upon the textile industry. It is sometimes implied that the increased wartime output of woolens more than compensated for the decline in cottons and thus that total textile output increased. However, an index of value added for textiles (cottons, woolens, and worsteds) in Massachusetts declines 10 per cent from 1855 to 1865, with an employment decrease of 6 per cent. Moreover, based upon the changes in Massachusetts output, estimated U. S. textile output declined by about 30 per cent between 1860 and 1865. Thus the growth in woolen textiles did not offset the decline in the production of cotton textiles.

The effect of the war upon the agricultural implement industry is one requiring more detailed study, since there is some ambiguity in the data currently available. The traditional interpretation argues that not only did the war create a labor shortage, but it also led to a considerable expansion of agricultural demand. In the latter regard, however, it is important to note that wheat and corn output had been growing rapidly before the war, and that foreign markets became important in the early years of the war. Indeed, in 1866 the Department of Agriculture was quite concerned with the short-fall in wheat output below an extrapolation based on growth in earlier years. Non-southern wheat output declined in the last two years of the war, after peaking in 1863. While there was increased domestic consumption in the north, probably at least 50 per cent of the increase in non-southern production in this period is to be attributed to foreign markets. Average annual corn output in the non-south in the years 1863–1865 was equal to the 1859 level, and then only because of a large 1865 harvest. For these crops, then, the war apparently did not lead to an acceleration in the rate of growth of output.

There also are some questions about the changes in reaper and mower sales in this period. [W. T.] Hutchinson noted that McCormick sales in 1862, 1863, and 1864 fell below the 1861 level. He then made the point in regard to an 1864 survey of agricultural implement manufacturers that "it is significant that very few of them increased their annual output since 1861." Hutchinson also pointed out that the unsold stock of reapers held by McCormick after the 1864 harvest was equal to 40 per cent of sales, and that in 1865 the implement manufacturers were attempting to cartelize. Reaper sales had been growing rapidly before the war, and were higher after the war than during. Thus it is not clear that the war years were an abnormal boom period for the industry.

IV. PROFITS, INFLATION AND GROWTH

One of the central parts of the traditional thesis concerns the effects of the wartime inflation upon income distribution. The general argument, presented most forcibly by Earl Hamilton, is that in inflationary periods money wages lag behind prices, increasing the share of income going to profits. This shift to profits should lead to more rapid economic growth. In this section I shall review the data used to demonstrate this point for the Civil War period, and see what questions remain to be answered.

Real Wages and the Profit Share

There is little systematic evidence concerning income distribution for the war years. The main argument for the theory of an increase in the profit share is based upon what Mitchell called the residual claimant hypothesis. Since real wages apparently fell, and there was no marked rise in money interest rates or rents, the share going to the residual claimant—profits—must have risen. It is important to realize, however, that it is possible for real wages to fall without the profit share increasing. These are not mutually exclusive occurrences. Real wages can decline in proportion with total factor incomes, so that with unchanged employ-ment the relative shares remain unchanged. However, the analysis is really more complex since the relationship between changes in real wages and relative income shares would depend upon elasticities of substitu-tion between factors of production in each industry, as well as effects arising from the shifting composition of output among industries. To argue directly from falling real wages to a shift to profits is not valid.

The decline in real wages, which appears firmly based statistically, does provide a major puzzle. This is particularly true since the tradi-tional interpretation also argues that there was a labor shortage during the war, which encouraged mechanization. If this were true, the decline in real wages would be surprising (unless civilian output declined). In-deed, the Civil War pattern is markedly different from that of the two world wars of the twentieth century. In these wars, both periods of rapid inflation, real wages rose, as did the labor share in World War II.

There have been several attempts to explain the fall in real wages which do not imply an increase in the share of profits in income. David A. Wells, writing immediately after the war, argued that the quality of the labor force had deteriorated. Thus lower real wages could be based upon a decline in worker productivity. One possible source of deteriora-tion, emphasized by Wells, is a shift in the sex composition of the manu-facturing labor force. The extent of this shift can be determined for New York and Massachusetts. The results are ambiguous. The ratio of male to total manufacturing workers in New York rose from 76.9 per cent to 81.5 per cent between 1860 and 1865, while in Massachusetts this ratio fell from 67.3 per cent to 62.7 per cent. Moreover, changes in the age structure, as well as the importance of immigrants in the labor force, must also be determined in answering this question.

Another explanation is that of [R. A.] Kessel and [A. A.] Alchian. They emphasize the role of the depreciating foreign-exchange rate and the wartime tax structure in reducing the output available to civilians. With the loss of cotton as a source of foreign exchange earnings, the price of foreign exchange to the U. S. rose, making imported goods more expensive. (Their measures show that money wages actually rose as rapidly as did the prices of the non-internationally traded goods which were included in the consumer price index.) They attribute "at least half" of the fall in real wages in 1864 to the fall in the terms of trade. The use of custom duties and excise taxes reduced measured real wages since they raised all prices and imposed a wedge between total output and the amount of goods available to civilians. Kessel and Alchian attribute "most of the fall in 1865 relative to 1860" to the "tax policy used to finance the war." These explanations, as that of Wells, suggest that total factor incomes fell, so that the fall in real wages provides no basis for arguing that profits increased during the wartime inflation.

Estimates of income by factor shares, prepared by Edward Budd, have recently become available. Unfortunately, the series are for census years only, and therefore contain no direct evidence on the war period per se. However, the Beard-Hacker thesis can be interpreted as arguing for a long-run shift to profits, and the census-year data are relevant to this proposition. According to Budd, the share of wages in both total private income and in income originating in industry rose from 1860 to 1870—and indeed until 1890. While Budd does not give the distribution of property income among profits, rents, and interest, the main point is that the wage share rose relative to property income during and after the Civil War decade.

Growth Through Inflation

The preceding paragraphs argued that it is possible that no shift to profits occurred during the wartime inflation. There is another mechanism through which inflation can be argued to spur growth. Investor expectation of rising prices means that borrowing can occur at an effective real rate of interest lower than the nominal interest rate at the time of borrowing, thus encouraging investment.

Expectations about the future rate of price change should be reflected in the money rate of interest. If the money rate did not rise during inflation it would imply either that investors did not expect the price rise to continue or that the anticipated real rate of interest had fallen. The few measures we have do indicate that interest rates did not rise in the expected manner during the war inflation. Bond yield data collected by [F. R.] Macauley show falling yields through late 1864, followed by a rise to 1866. (Mitchell's price index peaked in January 1865, but the gold premium reached its maximum in mid-1864.) Also, at a time when short-term commercial paper rates were rising (mid-1863 to late 1864), long-term bond yields were still declining.

[M.] Friedman and [A. J.] Schwartz have argued that foreign expectations of a subsequent fall in the price of gold led to the U. S. being a net capital importer after 1863. Foreigners were speculating upon the expected future fall of the price of gold in the U. S. by purchasing U. S. securities, explaining, in part, the low level of interest rates in the period.

If these expectations were generally held by investors, this would tend to discourage investment during the war. This implication was clearly stated by Mitchell in another context. He noted the small number of business failures during the immediate postwar deflation, and explained this as due to the lack of desire on the part of businessmen to borrow during the war in anticipation of a postwar fall in prices.

V. QUESTIONS ABOUT ECONOMIC LEGISLATION

Even if we were to assume that the economic legislation of the Civil War years would not have been passed, or would have been passed only after a long wait, in the absence of the war, the question of its impact upon economic growth remains to be examined. We have seen that there was a slight decline in the rate of growth of total commodity output after the war. However, since it is possible to argue that without the legislation growth would have substantially retarded, it will be useful to see what can be said directly about the issue. Unfortunately, there are few economic analyses of the economic consequences of wartime laws. Such analysis is difficult, because one must consider not only the effects upon resource allocation and utilization, but also possible effects via changing income distribution and rates of capital formation.

Existing studies suggest that the effects of the contract labor laws and the transcontinental railroad grants upon subsequent economic growth are small. In her careful book, Charlotte Erickson concluded that "contract labor was rare in America during the years after the Civil War." She demonstrated that the legislation became controversial, not because it led to any major inflow of labor, but because it was periodically used to import skilled workers to break strikes. With respect to railroad grants, Robert Fogel has demonstrated that the Union Pacific yielded a social rate of return which made this investment justifiable. But this does not mean that it had a big effect upon the economy. The increase in national income made possible by the Union Pacific was only .01 of one per cent—much too small to bear the weight placed upon it by the Beard-Hacker thesis.

For other major pieces of economic legislation the effects upon growth remain to be determined. The impact of the tariff upon any one industry, let alone the entire economy, is still unknown. There is little to be found in the literature besides [F. W.] Taussig's agnosticism concerning possible benefits to either the specific industries or the economy. Some presumption exists in favor of the conclusion that tariffs shifted the income distribution in favor of capital, but there is as yet no indication of the possible quantitative importance of this effect.

Similarly little is known about the effects of the National Banking System and the Homestead Act provisions on economic growth. Not much has been agreed upon concerning efficient financial arrangements for economic growth, and it is not clear that the war-induced act provided an improvement over existing arrangements or provided a better set of financial arrangements than other bills possible at the time. The National Banking System certainly did not lead to a period free of financial difficulties. Perhaps even less can be said about the effects of the Homestead Act. Despite the voluminous literature, we still do not know who obtained farm land, how successful they were, nor even the extent of the incentive provided by "free land." It is possible that the social implications of this act greatly exceeded its effects upon the rate of economic growth.

VI. A NOTE ON POSTWAR INCOME REDISTRIBUTION

It has been argued that one of the mechanisms through which the rate of economic growth was spurred in the postwar period was income redistribution caused by the government debt. [H. E.] Krooss, for example, states:

> In the postwar years, the interest and principal on the debt was paid by levying regressive taxes. Thus, the federal fiscal policy transferred money from consumers to savers, augmenting the amount available for investment and encouraging the expansion of industry.

The magnitude of such effect can be estimated. We must know who held the bonds and the extent to which the tax system was regressive to establish redistribution of income. To determine the effects of income redistribution on growth we need information on the propensity to save at different income levels and the effect of increased capital formation upon the rate of economic growth.

The sum of interest payments and debt retirement over the period 1866–1890 was slightly in excess of $3.8 billion, at an annual average of $153.2 million. The annual current dollar value of net national product for the decade centered in 1879 was $8.36 billion. Thus the total sum to be redistributed due to the debt was about 1.8 per cent of annual NNP. If we assume that only the upper income groups received these funds, and that the entire tax was paid by lower income groups, this would be the maximum redistribution.

The effect of this redistribution of income upon the rate of capital formation will depend upon the savings-income ratio at different income levels. A plausible estimate of this difference, based upon [S.] Kuznets, is that the excess of the upper income group ratio over that of the lower income group was .40. Thus the redistribution would have increased the share of net capital formation in net national product by less than eight-tenths of a percentage point. The effect of this increased capital formation upon the rate of growth of output can be estimated by the use of a familiar proposition of neoclassical economic analysis. The growth contribution of capital is equal to the product of the share of income going to capital and the rate of growth of the capital stock. Using Budd's estimate of the non-service share as a measure of the share of capital in output, the increase in the growth rate resulting from the additional capital formation is about .09 of one percentage point—an amount less than one-fortieth of the observed growth rate in the period. I conclude that any income redistribution due to government debt had a small impact on the rate of growth in the twenty-five years after the war.

VII. CONCLUSION

This review of some evidence relevant to the debate concerning the economic impact of the Civil War has not exhausted the possibilities. The effects of the war upon invention, upon the size of the government budget, and upon the nature and location of financial markets, for example, have been ignored. However it should be noted that a 1964 conference of economic historians concluded that "aside from commercial banking, the Civil War appears not to have started or created any significant new patterns of economic institutional change."

While not always unambiguous in its implications, the evidence reviewed in this paper frequently runs counter to the Beard-Hacker thesis. Much work still remains on the analysis of the economic effects of the war but, at present, reservations regarding the traditional interpretation seem justified.